D1409436

Compliments of
COLUMBIA GAS OF OHIO

THE BUCKEYE EMPIRE

Photo Research by Jana C. Morford

"Partners in Progress" by Irene Chang, Peter D. Franklin, and Kathleen A. Taflinger

Produced in cooperation with the Ohio Chamber of Commerce

Windsor Publications, Inc.
Northridge, California

THE BUCKEYE EMPIRE

AN ILLUSTRATED HISTORY OF OHIO ENTERPRISE

BY EUGENE C. MURDOCK

Windsor Publications, Inc.—History Books Division
Vice President of Publishing: Hal Silverman
Editorial Director: Teri Davis Greenberg
Design Director: Alexander D'Anca
Corporate Biographies Director: Karen Story

Staff for *The Buckeye Empire*
Editor: Marilyn Horn
Photo Editor: Laura Cordova
Assistant Director, Corporate Biographies: Phyllis Fockler Gray
Editor, Corporate Biographies: Judith L. Hunter
Production Editor, Corporate Biographies: Una FitzSimons
Editorial Assistants: Didier Beauvoir, Brenda Berryhill, Thelma Fleischer, Alyson Gould, Kim Kievman, Kathy B. Peyser, Michael Nugwynne, Pat Pittman, Jeff Reeves, Theresa Solis
Proofreader: Susan J. Muhler
Layout Artist, Corporate Biographies: Mari Catherine Preimesberger
Sales Representatives: Ron George, Jack Hurt, Anne McCutcheon, Fred Smithco, Steve Snow

Designer: Christina L. Rosepapa

Library of Congress Cataloging-in-Publication Data
Murdock, Eugene Converse.
The Buckeye empire: an illustrated history of Ohio enterprise by Eugene C. Murdock: photo research by Jana C. Morford; Partners in progress, by Peter D. Franklin, Stephen G. Sawicki, and Kathleen A. Taflinger.
p. 9 cm.
Produced in cooperation with the Ohio Chamber of Commerce.
Bibliography: p. 316
Includes index.
ISBN 0-89781-250-6
1. Ohio—Industries—History. 2. Ohio—Industries—History—Pictorial works. 3. Ohio—Economic conditions. 4. Ohio—Economic conditions—Pictorial works. I. Title.
HC107.03M87 1988
338.09771—dc19 87-32183 CIP

Published 1988
Printed in the United States

Columbus, the capital of Ohio, lies in the center of the state. Founded in 1812, it is the largest city in the state to date and the only city in the northeast section of the U.S. that has continued to grow since 1970. Photo by David Lucas. Courtesy, the City of Columbus Development Department

Previous page:* Cincinnati from the Public Landing *was painted by John Caspar Wild in 1835. In the mid-1830s Cincinnati was growing rapidly, partly because of its ideal riverfront location. The city's nickname was "Queen City of the West." Courtesy, Cincinnati Historical Society

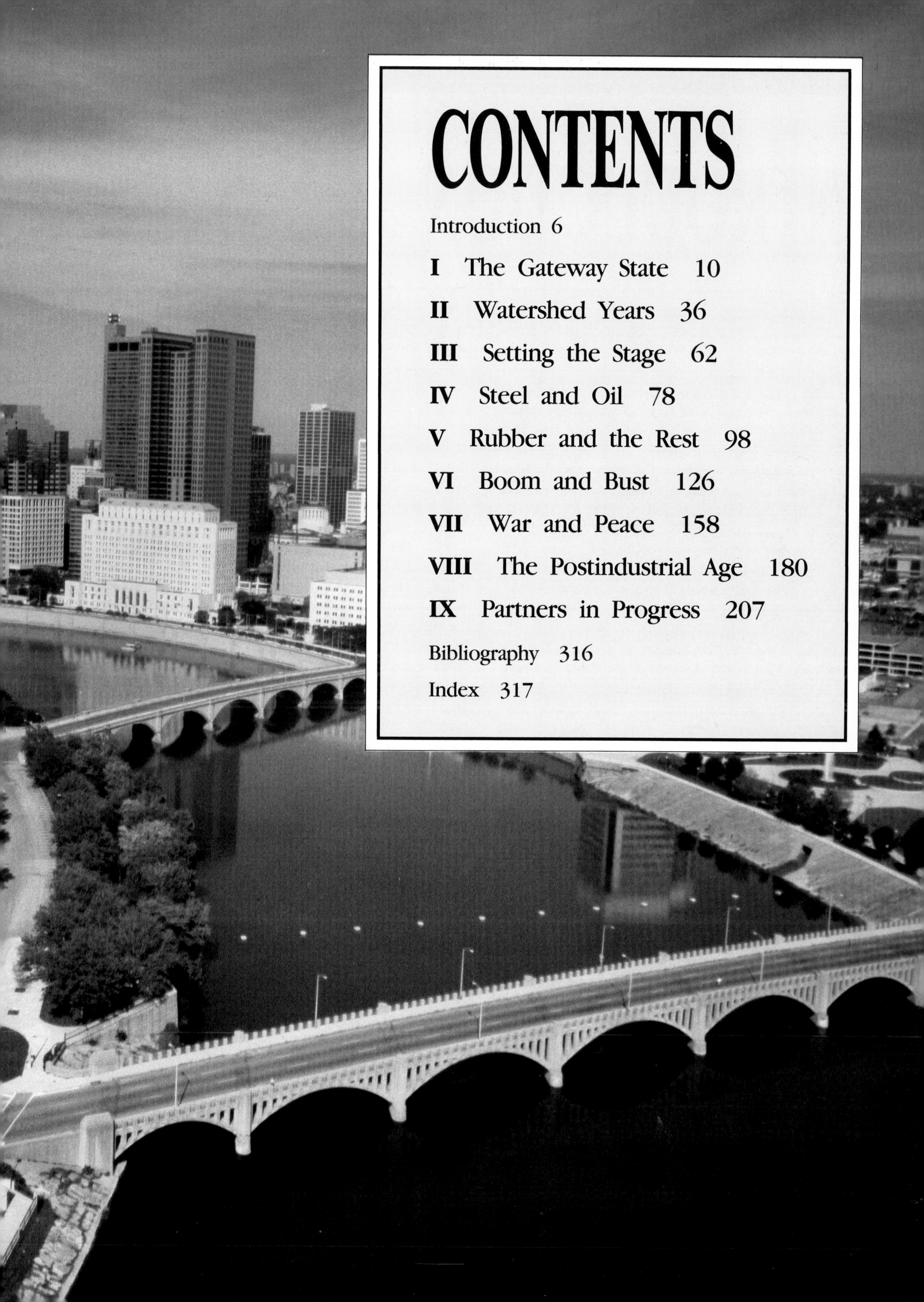

CONTENTS

Introduction 6

I The Gateway State 10

II Watershed Years 36

III Setting the Stage 62

IV Steel and Oil 78

V Rubber and the Rest 98

VI Boom and Bust 126

VII War and Peace 158

VIII The Postindustrial Age 180

IX Partners in Progress 207

Bibliography 316

Index 317

INTRODUCTION

A veteran scout, refreshed from a month's stay at the Wyandot village, set out on foot for Shawnee Town, 150 miles away. Later he confided to his journal,

> *. . . all the way is a fine, rich, level land, well timbered with large walnut, ash, sugar trees, cherry trees, etc.; it is well watered with a great number of little streams and rivulets, full of beautiful natural meadows covered with wild rye, bluegrass and clover, and abounds with turkey, deer, elk and all sorts of game, particularly buffaloes, thirty or forty of which are frequently seen feeding in one meadow; in short, it wants nothing but cultivation to make it a most delightful country.*

In these words Christopher Gist, agent for the Ohio Land Company, described the Ohio country in 1751. He wrote more accurately than he knew.

Ohio was fortunate in many respects. It possessed an ideal geographical location. Tens of thousands of migrants crossed the mountains to the future "Gateway State," traveling by foot, horse, or boat. By its proximity to the older settled regions, by its abundant waterways, and by its mostly smooth tabletop terrain, Ohio, indeed, was the gateway to the transmontane West. No natural barriers obstructed the first interstate highway—the National Road—or the network of canals, or railroad links with all sections of the country. As historian George Knepper has written, "with very few exceptions all the major East-West lines of travel, transport, and communication passed through the state."

Not only was Ohio blessed with excellent geography, it also fulfilled Christopher Gist's promise of an agrarian utopia. The land of the Interior Plains, smoothly sculptured and enriched by the ancient glacier bulldozer, would—once the forests were cleared—make Ohio a bountiful agricultural region. The receptive soil, wide temperature range, ample rainfall, and extensive growing season guaranteed a prosperous farming future.

But what was to give Ohio its claim to economic greatness was something which Christopher Gist could not have foreseen. The state was endowed with vast reserves of mineral wealth, which in time would transform Ohio into a major manufacturing center. Coal in the southeast, iron ore in the south and east, clay in the central east, and gas and oil in the northwest, formed the foundation of Ohio's industrial strength. True, Hanging Rock iron ore—found in the environs of Ironton in the south—would be superceded by the rich ore brought into Cleveland from the upper Great Lakes. But this new development only elevated the state to the first rank in steel production. So it came to pass that Ohio, by its location and natural wealth, rose to economic preeminence.

Yet the first arrivals in the Ohio country, not long after Gist's memorable pilgrimage, faced a formidable task: they had to carve homesteads for themselves—and provide the means for survival—in a friendless wilderness. Indians, perhaps hostile, perhaps not, were ever present. These hardy pioneers, however, did not shirk from the challenge. Log cabins were built, crops sprouted from the ground, villages emerged, and a rough-hewn civilization developed on the frontier.

In 1803 Ohio became a state, the "Seventeenth Star," as it was called; the first to be formed from the Northwest Territory. Its growth was rapid and by mid-century Ohio could boast a population of over 1,950,000, compared to 42,000 in 1800. Roads and canals crisscrossed the state and railroads had recently appeared. With Cincinnati leading the way, Ohio had moved to third place among all states in manufactured goods. But the Industrial Revolution was still several decades away and agriculture continued to play the dominant role in the economy.

While historians debate whether the Civil War was a stimulus or a deterrent to industrial growth, two developments unrelated to the war sparked Ohio's economic boom of the postwar years. In the mid-1850s the first shipload of iron ore—132 tons—arrived in Cleveland. Things were never quite the same again. The trade developed rapidly and by 1875 over half a million tons came to town each year. The marriage of iron ore to coal, now abundantly available in eastern Ohio and western Pennsylvania, was soon consummated and the world's greatest steel center—the Cleveland-Youngstown-Pittsburgh nexus—was born.

At almost the same time crude oil was discovered in western Pennsylvania, and under the astute, though ruthless organizing skill of John D. Rockefeller, Cleveland became the world's greatest oil refining center. The rise of the oil and steel industries in Cleveland shifted the balance of economic power in Ohio almost overnight. No longer was the Ohio River and Cincinnati the focus of industrial life. Not that the central and southern parts of the state slipped backward; rather, the northeastern section raced madly forward.

In addition to steel and oil, other booming industries dotted the business map of Ohio in the late nineteenth century. Akron became the hub of the rubber industry; Toledo was a major glass center; Dayton had the National Cash Register Company; machine tools and automobiles were being manufactured in several cities. By 1900 Ohio was no longer an agricultural state. The majority of the population now lived in cities. The value of manufactured goods far outdistanced that of farm produce.

The structure of Ohio's economy, which had taken shape by 1900, remained relatively stable through the first quarter of the twentieth century. But it was dealt a savage blow by the Great Depression. While no state remained immune to the ravages of the economic cancer, Ohio seemed to suffer more than others. Its unemployment and welfare rates were rivaled by only a few states. Although Ohio's industrial establishment was hurt by the Depression, World War II brought unprecedented prosperity to the state's factories, mills, and shops.

In the euphoria which followed the war it was hoped that American industrial growth would continue unabated, although major adjustments would have to be made to pick up the slack with the cancellation of war contracts. There was even concern that another major depression might occur; fortunately, that never happened. New plants were built and the economy prospered.

However, subtle changes were taking place which were eroding the bedrock upon which American industry was based. Markets were shifting as the population began to move into the South and West; new processes and materials were supplanting traditional ones; labor costs were beginning to escalate as unions became stronger. Still in the 1950s and 1960s Ohio's economy appeared relatively healthy.

The history of Ohio business is a tale of achievement. Following the conquest of the wilderness, the resourceful pioneers and their heirs proceeded to construct a mighty "inland empire," one of which Christopher Gist would have been proud. In the pages ahead the reader may follow the unfolding of this fascinating story.

Glass mosaic murals depicting Cincinnati workers were installed in the rotunda of Union Terminal in 1933. Created by Weinold Reiss, these murals were made from actual photographs. They are now on display at the Greater Cincinnati International Airport. Pictured are two of the fourteen murals, depicting work at Cincinnati Milling Machine. Courtesy, Cincinnati Milacron

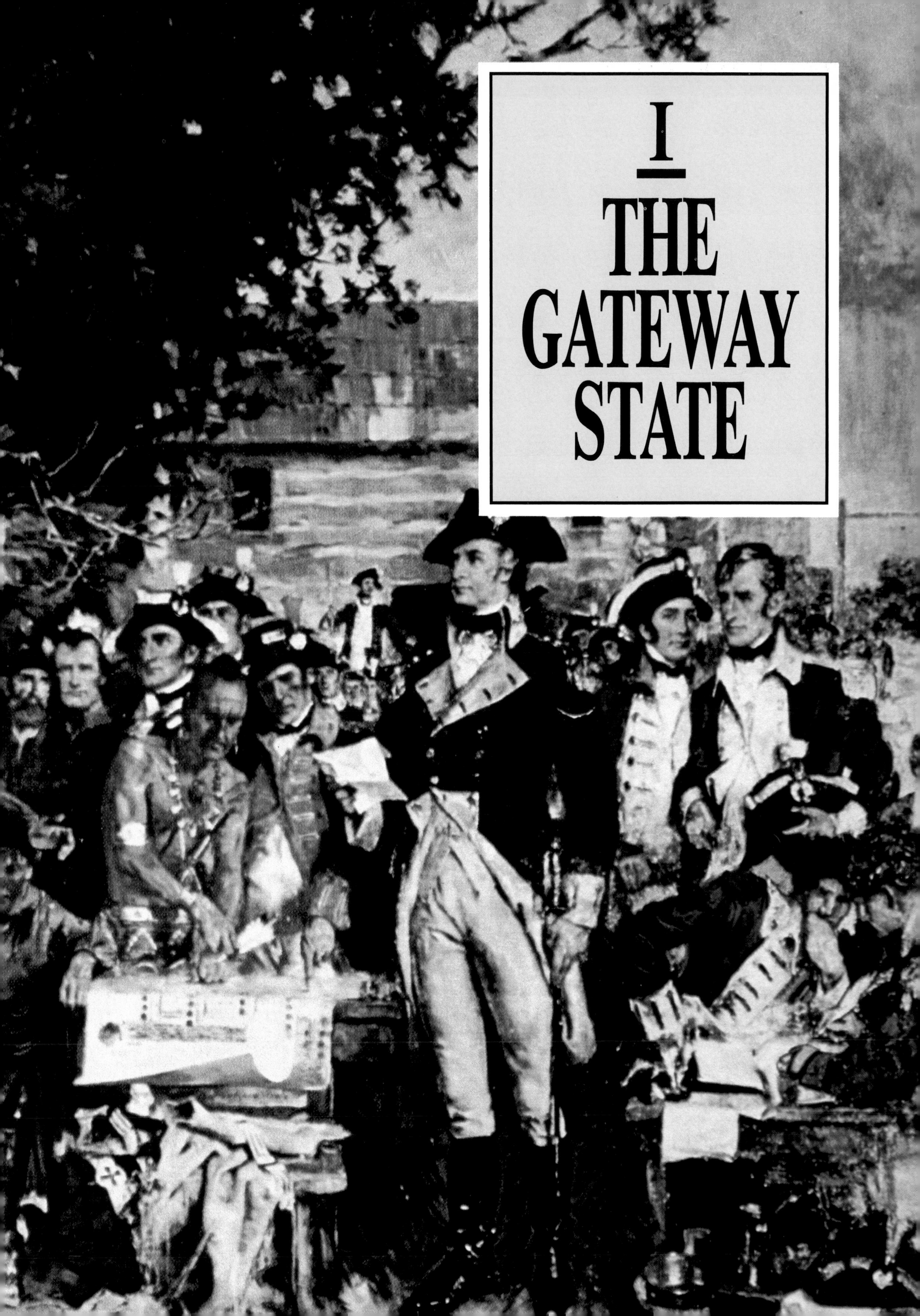

I
THE GATEWAY STATE

Howard Chandler Christie's famous painting, Treaty of Greene Ville, *shows Anthony Wayne, in 1795, standing at the right in uniform and the Indian chief, Little Turtle, offering him a symbol of peace. Surrounding the two men are famous historical figures such as William Henry Harrison, William Clark, Meriwether Lewis, Shawnee Chief Black Hoof, Blue Jacket, and Buckongahelas of the Delaware tribe. Courtesy, Ohio Historical Society*

Facing page: This map of the Ohio country shows boundaries and divisions, key forts, rivers, and villages in the new territory. Admitted to the Union on March 1, 1803, as the seventeenth state, Ohio was the first state to be formed from the Northwest Territory. Courtesy, Western Reserve Historical Society

That which would become Ohio was a land coveted by Indians, Englishmen, Frenchmen, and Americans. The passion for Ohio was not grounded in the area's wealth of mineral deposits, its fertile soil, or its virgin forests, but because of its convenient location. Ohio was a vast crossroads between East and West, a wilderness highway beyond the mountains. Whoever controlled Ohio controlled America. Well, almost.

Six Indian tribes roamed Ohio when the white man first arrived in the area. Most prestigious were the mighty Miami, a powerful tribe which dominated southwestern Ohio and much beyond. In the northwest were the Ottawa; in the northeast, the Wyandot and Mingo (mostly Seneca); in the south, the Shawnees; and in the Tuscarawas and Muskingum valleys were the reasonably friendly Delaware. But these tribes, strong as they were, had no future in Ohio once the white man arrived.

The British and French came into Ohio from different directions, but with the same determination to possess this valuable "heartland." The French arrived from the north through the Great Lakes, whereas the British migrated across the mountains and down inland streams. From 1689 to 1763 the British battled the French for control of what would be the United States. The British emerged triumphant at the conclusion of the French and Indian War in 1763, when the French were evicted from all of North America. Lands east of the Mississippi fell under the control of the British, while the Spanish dominated the lands west of that mighty river.

The British government was determined that the transmontane

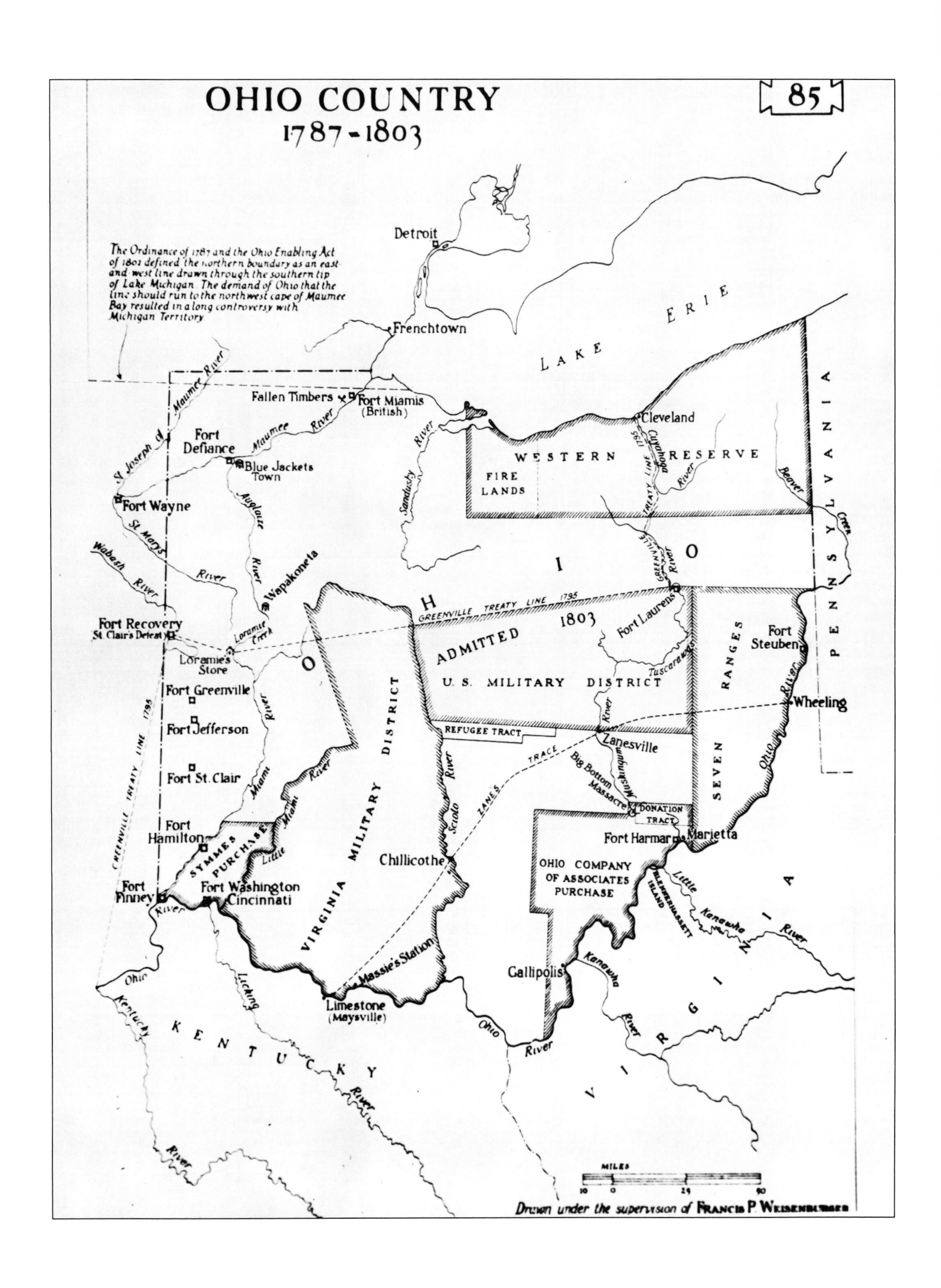

OHIO COUNTRY
1787-1803
85
The Ordinance of 1787 and the Ohio Enabling Act of 1802 defined the northern boundary as an east and west line drawn through the southern tip of Lake Michigan. The demand of Ohio that the line should run to the northwest cape of Maumee Bay resulted in a long controversy with Michigan Territory.
Detroit
Frenchtown
LAKE ERIE
Fallen Timbers
Fort Miamis (British)
Cleveland
Fort Defiance
Blue Jackets Town
WESTERN RESERVE
FIRE LANDS
Fort Wayne
Wapakoneta
OHIO
GREENVILLE TREATY LINE 1795
ADMITTED 1803
Fort Recovery
St Clair's Defeat
Loramie's Store
Fort Greenville
Fort Jefferson
Fort St. Clair
Fort Hamilton
Fort Finney
Fort Washington
Cincinnati
SYMMES PURCHASE
VIRGINIA MILITARY DISTRICT
U. S. MILITARY DISTRICT
REFUGEE TRACT
Fort Laurens
Fort Steuben
SEVEN RANGES
Wheeling
Zanesville
ZANE'S TRACE
Big Bottom Massacre
DONATION TRACT
Fort Harmar
Marietta
OHIO COMPANY OF ASSOCIATES PURCHASE
Chillicothe
Massie's Station
Limestone (Maysville)
Gallipolis
PENNSYLVANIA
VIRGINIA
KENTUCKY
MILES
Drawn under the supervision of Francis P. Weisenburger

region would be developed in a gradual, orderly manner. The Proclamation Line of 1763 prohibited British colonists from settling west of the Appalachian mountains and ordered squatters already there to vacate. When this proved unenforceable, Parliament enacted the Quebec Act in 1774 which annexed all of the Ohio country to the province of Quebec. The act further barred westward migration, denied claims of seaboard colonies to western lands, and reassured the Indians that their hunting grounds would remain inviolate—all of which aroused the colonists' anger.

The Quebec Act helped provoke the American Revolution. While no major battles were fought in Ohio, there was plenty of small-scale action between Indians (supplied by their British allies) and the Americans. The year 1777 marked the beginning of a series of Indian raids across Ohio directed at white settlements in Pennsylvania, Kentucky, and northwestern Virginia, and subsequent retaliatory raids by white frontiersmen. Hostilities lasted well beyond the battle at Yorktown in October 1781. One of the worst massacres in American history took place in March 1782 at Gnadenhutten where a band of frontier cutthroats murdered almost 100 peaceful Christian Indians—men, women, and children.

Such raids and killings had little bearing on the outcome of the Revolution. The peace treaty with Great Britain was ratified in 1783. By its terms the British surrendered all of the land between the mountains and the Mississippi River to the Americans. Though Indians caused trouble periodically—encouraged by the British in Detroit and Canada—they only temporarily delayed the development of Ohio.

Of those who initially coveted the land, only the Americans now remained. The pioneers came from

This painting by James A. Beard depicts weary travelers on their way to Ohio. At a fork in the road, the father leans on a post with signs pointing to North Carolina in one direction and Ohio in another. Courtesy, Cincinnati Historical Society

This bedroom scene is from the Golden Lamb in Lebanon and is Ohio's oldest hotel. Photo by Rick Dieringer

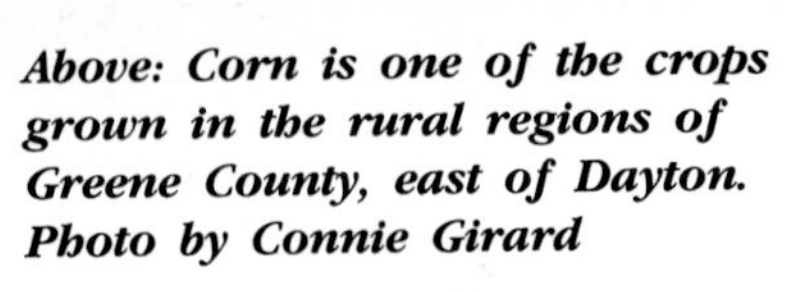

***Above:* Corn is one of the crops grown in the rural regions of Greene County, east of Dayton. Photo by Connie Girard**

***Right:* In Urbana, where this farm is located, vegetables and grains are the primary crops. Photo by Mark E. Gibson**

Left: In the fall the southwestern Ohio Valley takes on many colorful hues. In the distance is the Eagle Creek covered bridge, outside Decatur in Brown County. Photo by Jana C. Morford

Below: Some inquisitive cows attempt to get closer to the camera in this Greene County farm scene. Photo by Connie Girard

The Cleveland Industrial Exposition opened under the direction of the Cleveland Chamber of Commerce on June 7, 1909. This expo had a record attendance of 215,000, while thousands more were turned away from the twelve-day event. The purpose of the Industrial Exposition was "to teach Cleveland to know itself, and to teach the world to become better acquainted with Cleveland." Courtesy, Ohio Historical Society

The goal of the Industrial Exposition, held annually in the 1870s and 1880s, was to show the achievements of Cincinnati and the West. The 1879 exposition featured 1,000 exhibits and was attended by President Rutherford B. Hayes. The last Industrial Exposition was the elaborate 100-day Centennial Exposition of the Ohio Valley and Central States, held in 1888. Courtesy, Cincinnati Historical Society

many places. New Englanders settled in the lower Muskingum valley; New Jerseyites in the Miami valley; Virginians in the Military District between the Scioto and Little Miami rivers; and Moses Cleaveland and his fellows from Connecticut in the Western Reserve. Even from France came the unfortunate "500," who tried to establish homesteads in the unfriendly forests at Gallipolis. Ohio was the country's most impressive "melting pot." For this reason, perhaps, it has never been easy to label anything or any person as "typically Ohioan."

Not all the pioneers came to Ohio to settle. Some were merely passing through because Ohio's rivers and trails supplied the most direct route to lands further west. Whether one traveled from New England, New York, Pennsylvania, or Virginia, the most logical way west was through Ohio. Early in the nineteenth century the first important road to the west—the Cumberland or National Road—traversed the heart of Ohio. Once beyond the mountains, travelers passed through a gateway to the west, prompting some historians to call Ohio the "Gateway State."

What kind of land did the first pioneers gaze upon in Ohio? The terrain was relatively level, due to two glaciers which slid across most of the state during the last Ice Age. These huge masses of ice, inching their way down from Canada, leveled the land like monstrous bulldozers. Hilltops were sliced off and valleys were filled with rich, fertile soil. The only unglaciated part of the state is in the southeast, where the land is hilly, rugged, and less fertile.

When the settlers arrived, much of the state was heavily forested with stands of oak and maple, hickory and walnut, elm and—oh, yes—the buckeye. The grand Ohio forests, which extended throughout the glaciated as well as unglaciated regions, proved to be a hindrance to early arrivals. While the woods provided material for log huts and crude implements, for fences, furniture, and fuel, they also barred the cultivation of crops. Hence the trees came down so the crops could go in.

The first settlers were naturally unaware of the area's vast mineral resources. The unglaciated southeast had the richest store of subsurface wealth. Iron ore was found near Portsmouth and Ironton, and in the Mahoning valley; coal and clay deposits were extensive in the east central regions. Coal, still a major resource, was found in almost every county along the Ohio River from Columbiana to Lawrence, as well as in adjacent inland sections. Clay and clay products also were centered in the eastern sections, with Zanesville and East Liverpool as important centers. The southeast may not have been very good for farming, but it was excellent for industry.

The earliest people in the Ohio country, with no legal title to the land, were not bona fide settlers. They were "squatters." Historian Walter Havighurst has described them well:

> *Squatters were intruders on the public lands, ahead of legal survey and legal purchase. They had no maps or charts, no land warrants or certificates, and no specific destination. They simply made their way into wild country, looking for a southern hill-*

Although this man is under the homestead law, he can be likened to a squatter. Both groups of people came to the area, established themselves with homes, and began to farm. However, unlike the squatter who just moved into unoccupied territory and set up a claim, the homesteader held a grant of land from the U.S. government. Courtesy, Ohio Historical Society

***Below:** Manasseh Cutler, chaplain with the Massachusetts troops in the Revolutionary War, joined the Ohio Company in 1786 and helped to found Marietta in 1788. He served as a congressman from Ohio from 1801 to 1805. Courtesy, Ohio Historical Society*

***Bottom:** This map of the Northwest Territory, made by Samuel Lewis in 1796, shows land grant divisions, early settlements, and the Greenville Treaty line. Courtesy, Cincinnati Historical Society*

side with a trickling spring or a green opening where deer paths crossed. They came lightly laden—a rifle, ax, plow, and a bag of seed corn, a dog and a horse, and perhaps a few pigs and chickens.

Two different attitudes prevailed toward squatters. Some argued that those who settled first owned the land by right of occupation. Others believed such a policy led to disorder and chaos and said it was better to have an established plan: purchase the land from the Indians, survey it, and sell it at convenient land offices. In this fashion, titles would be unambiguous and revenue could accrue. In time, forced evictions, land sales by squatters to legitimate owners, and land purchases by the squatters themselves eventually cleared the land of these dubious claimants.

Squatters weren't the only ones to cause confusion over who owned land in Ohio. A number of eastern seaboard states, such as Virginia, New York, Connecticut, and Massachusetts, claimed ownership of western lands by their original charters. But

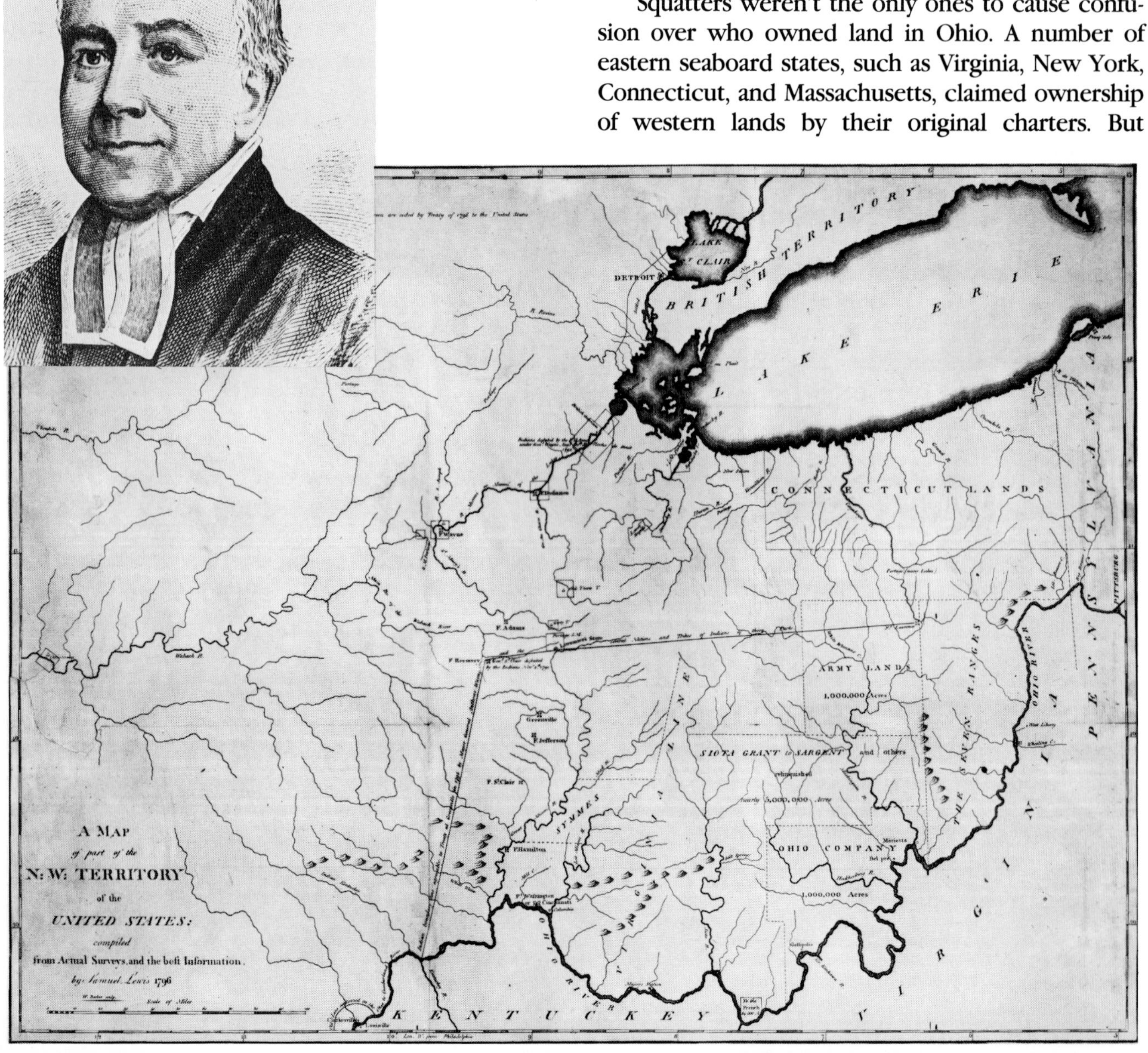

under pressure from the "have not" states, all western land claims were surrendered to the central government starting in 1784. Two exceptions to this influenced Ohio's future. A large section of land between the Scioto and Little Miami rivers, the so-called Virginia Military District, was reserved by Virginia as bounty land for its veterans of the Revolution. And in the northeast, a strip of land extending 120 miles west from the Pennsylvania boundary along the 41st parallel, the famous "Western Reserve," was reserved for Connecticut. By 1786 all land north and west of the Ohio River, reaching to the Mississippi River in the west and the Great Lakes in the north, the fabled "Northwest Territory," was property of the United States government.

In 1785 the Confederation Congress adopted an ordinance dealing with the newly acquired land. It provided for a system of rectilinear surveys to divide the territory into even, equal squares. These were called townships after the New England plan, measuring thirty-six square miles each. Townships were subdivided into thirty-six one-square-mile sections. Land was to be sold at auction for a minimum price of one dollar per acre, with a minimum purchase of 640 acres—not an inviting proposition when cash was in short supply. Section 16 of each township was reserved for public education and other sections were set aside for special purposes.

The 1785 ordinance eliminated the problem of disputed land claims which had plagued the older states, since now every inch of territory could be described specifically on property deeds. The first surveys in the Ohio country, the "Seven Ranges" along the Ohio River in the eastern part of the territory, were carried out in 1786 and 1787. However, so little land was sold to individuals because of the restrictive terms of the ordinance, a new approach was devised. Rather than trying to sell to cash-starved individuals, Congress decided to sell to companies interested in acquiring large units of land for either settlement or speculation.

In 1786 such a land company was formed in Massachusetts. The Ohio Company of Associates, organized in Boston, was composed principally of Revolutionary War officer veterans. But before negotiating for the land purchase, members of the Ohio Company wanted a civil government operating in the territory.

In July 1787 Manasseh Cutler, representing the Ohio Company, met with members of Congress. Within a week the Northwest Ordinance, which created the Northwest Territory and provided for an orderly evolutionary process from territory to statehood, had been drafted. Three stages of growth were defined: In stage one (where the population of free adult males was less than 5,000) there would be no self-government, the territory being administered by a governor, three judges, and a secretary, all appointed by Congress. In stage two (from 5,000 to 60,000 population) the governor stayed on with veto powers, but a territorial legislature, partly elected and partly appointed, provided a certain degree of self-government. In addition, the territory was permitted a non-voting delegate to represent it in Congress. In stage three (over 60,000 population) the territory was entitled to statehood with all the powers of self-government that were available to the older states. The form of the Northwest Ordinance and the timing of its adoption, July 13, 1787, was a direct result of the interest and energy of the Ohio Company.

In the fall of 1787 the Ohio Company purchased over one and a half million acres of land at the confluence of the Ohio and Muskingum rivers. The price was half a million dollars when the contract was signed and another half million when surveys of the grant were completed.

The Ohio Company settlers left Massachusetts in two groups, one in the fall of 1787 and the other in February 1788. They wintered at Sumrill's Ferry on the Youghiogheny River south of Pittsburgh, where they constructed flatboats for the trip down the Ohio in the spring. All was ready by the end of March 1788 and the momentous expedition commenced on April 1. Forty-eight hardy pioneers, no women or children, led by Rufus Putnam, made the trip. When the company arrived at the mouth of the Muskingum on April 7, overhanging branches obscured the river's entrance. Helpful soldiers at Fort Harmar on the west side of the Muskingum tossed ropes to the voyagers and pulled them ashore. Some friendly Delawares were also on hand to welcome the immigrants.

Putnam established his headquarters on the east side of the river opposite Fort Harmar. He erected a long shed-like structure covered with tenting, which became known as "The Picketed Point." Temporary shelters built from timber which had been brought along for the purpose were put up. The nearby land was quickly cleared and crops were planted. Broad thoroughfares were laid out for the town, which modern visitors to Marietta still marvel at. Early in July the next batch of settlers, including the official governing members of the territory and the families of the first "48," landed on the banks

Above: This building, the oldest one in Ohio, served as the land office of the Ohio Company at Marietta. Settlers from the Ohio Company, founded in 1786, arrived at the mouth of the Muskingum River on April 7, 1788, and founded the town of Marietta. Courtesy, Ohio Historical Society

Right: Early settlers traveled downriver on flatboats which carried all their belongings. Upon reaching their destination, the boats were sometimes broken up and the wood used to construct cabins. Courtesy, Ohio Historical Society

of the Muskingum. General Arthur St. Clair, of Revolutionary War distinction and a confidante of Washington, headed the party and served as the first governor of the territory. On July 15, 1788, amid elaborate and colorful ceremonies, he formally proclaimed the government open for business.

Within the next year many more settlers arrived in the Marietta area and a number of new communities sprang up. Belpre, farther down the Ohio, was one of these, while Waterford, Plainfield, and Big Bottom were founded along the Muskingum. Managers of the Ohio Company made it inviting for people to settle in their tract. Lots of 100 acres were granted to settlers free if within five years they would construct homes, plant orchards, cultivate their fields, and develop grazing land for cattle. Heavy traffic traveled the Ohio past Marietta in the latter 1780s and many of the immigrants accepted the "homestead" challenge.

The second grant in the Northwest Territory went to a New Jerseyite of note, John Cleves Symmes, who was attracted to land along the Ohio farther to the west, between the Great and Little Miami rivers. In October 1788 he negotiated for a one-million-acre tract in the Miami valley. Considerable confusion developed in the next few years because Symmes sold land to settlers which was not legally his. By the fall of 1789, however, Fort Washington was constructed at Losantiville and St. Clair transferred his territorial headquarters from Marietta to the new location. He renamed Losantiville "Cincinnati," in honor of the veterans' organi-

Above: Arthur St. Clair, 1736-1818, fought in the American Revolution and later served in the Continental Congress which appointed him as the first governor of the Northwest Territory. He assumed office in 1788. St. Clair, however, was not popular among the frontiersmen, and his opposition to Ohio's statehood led to his removal from office in 1802 by Thomas Jefferson. Courtesy, S. Durward Hoag Collection, Cincinnati Historical Society

Top: The first pioneers in Cincinnati landed at Yeatman's Cove in December 1788. The party of eleven families and twenty-four men arrived via flatboats and called the settlement Losantiville. One month earlier previous settlers had established the town of Columbia, a few miles upriver at the mouth of the Little Miami River. Courtesy, Cincinnati Historical Society

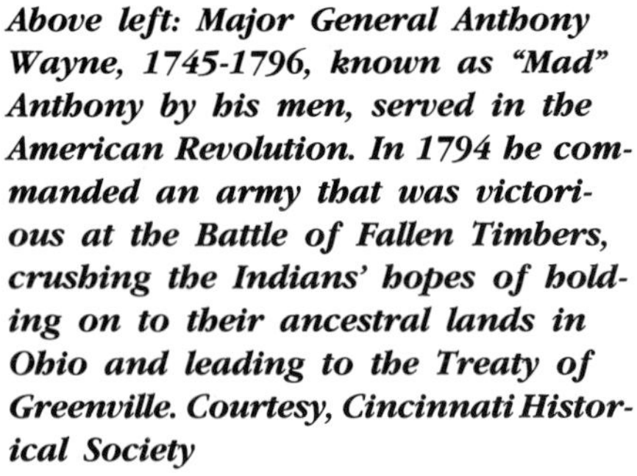

Above left: Major General Anthony Wayne, 1745-1796, known as "Mad" Anthony by his men, served in the American Revolution. In 1794 he commanded an army that was victorious at the Battle of Fallen Timbers, crushing the Indians' hopes of holding on to their ancestral lands in Ohio and leading to the Treaty of Greenville. Courtesy, Cincinnati Historical Society

Above right: John Cleves Symmes, 1742-1814, became associated with the Northwest Territory when he was appointed a judge for the territory in 1788. Congress granted him a charter to develop land lying between the Great and Little Miami rivers, referred to as the Miami Purchase. Because of his neglect in securing legal claim to all of the land he sold, he was the victim of several lawsuits and died penniless. Photo by Charles Willson Peale. Courtesy, Cincinnati Historical Society

zation to which he belonged.

Further settlement in Ohio was delayed by the outbreak of the Indian Wars. All the tribes resented the steady encroachment of white settlers into their lands, but divisions among them prevented the formation of a united front against the newcomers. The Delawares and Wyandots met with St. Clair to preserve peace; the Miamis and Shawnees, however, refused to compromise. In 1790 sporadic fighting broke out, beginning four years of conflict between frontiersmen and Indians. Three campaigns were launched by the Americans against Indian strongholds in the western part of Ohio before the region was pacified. British agents in Detroit—they had remained there in violation of the 1783 peace treaty because of the lucrative fur trade with the Indians—gave moral and material support to their allies.

The first campaign, composed of 1,500 poorly trained troops, was commanded by Colonel Josiah Harmar. This force worked its way north as far as present-day Fort Wayne, but besides burning a few Indian villages and suffering several setbacks, had nothing to show for its efforts. It returned to Cincinnati with its forces decimated and its mission unaccomplished. In 1791 St. Clair himself led a force of 3,000, but the undisciplined troops were no match for their wily adversaries. After a devastating defeat at Fort Recovery early in November, the Americans were forced to withdraw.

This picture illustrates important events in the life of William Henry Harrison, 1773-1841, hero of the Battle of Tippecanoe. Senator and congressman from Ohio, and later ninth president of the United States, Harrison used amusing ditties in his election campaign against Martin Van Buren such as, "Let Van from his coolers of silver drink wine/ And lounge on his cushioned settee./ Our man on his buckeye bench can recline./ Content with hard cider is he." Courtesy, Cincinnati Historical Society

With the news of St. Clair's humiliation, General Anthony Wayne, a hero of the Revolution, was charged to pacify the Ohio frontier once and for all. Borrowing an idea of St. Clair's, Wayne planned to erect a series of forts northward as he advanced toward the Indian strongholds in the Maumee valley. With a force of 2,500 Wayne arrived in Cincinnati in the spring of 1793 and began his advance in October. Eighty miles north of Cincinnati, Wayne established winter quarters at Fort Greenville. In the spring of 1794 he built Fort Defiance on the Maumee River. When peace talks with the Indians failed, the Americans pushed down the Maumee where they met the foe at Fallen Timbers. After a brief but momentous encounter on August 20, 1794, Wayne routed the approximately 2,000 Indians.

Humbled by this show of strength, the remaining Indians sought peace with Wayne. Most of the tribes were represented at Greenville a year later, in August 1795, when talks were held. The Treaty of Greenville, which resulted from these negotiations, provided for the surrender by the Indian tribes of all land claims east and south of a line drawn from modern Cleveland to the site of modern Bolivar on the Tuscarawas watershed, thence west to Loramie's post on the Great Miami, thence to Fort Recovery, and then southwest to the Ohio River. With Indian warfare over in Ohio, settlers began arriving quickly and steadily. The Western Reserve, the upper Ohio River, the Scioto valley, and the Miami valley all experienced a modest population explosion. Franklinton (Columbus), Chillicothe, Dayton, and Cleveland were among the new villages founded soon after the Indian fighting ceased.

But it was not only the cessation of warfare which stimulated settlement. A new law in 1796 slightly eased the financial strain for land-hungry pioneers. The measure provided that purchasers still had to buy 640-acre blocks at a minimum price of two dollars an acre, but the payments could now be made in installments over a twelve-month period.

Population growth was stimulated further when William Henry Harrison became Ohio's territorial delegate to Congress. Although he had no voting power, Harrison was influential in sponsoring liberal land legislation. The Harrison Land Law of 1800 reduced the minimum lot size for purchase to 320 acres. The price was still two dollars an acre, but buyers were now allowed four years to complete payment. Regional land offices were created at Steubenville, Marietta, Chillicothe, and Cincinnati.

Economic growth, stunted by the Indian Wars, also began to revive after the Treaty of Greenville. However, one important drawback to rapid development was the absence of good roads. Animal trails and Indian paths were the only routes available when white men first reached the area. While Indian paths crisscrossed the state in all directions, they were narrow and unsuitable for travel or transportation.

Most of the roads developed during the territorial period were crude refinements of these primitive trails. The only major road built in that time was subsidized by the federal government. In 1796 Ebenezer Zane was authorized to build a road from the Ohio border at Wheeling, Virginia, across the state in the direction of Chillicothe, and then southwest to Limestone (or Maysville), Kentucky. "Zane's Trace," as it was called, followed an old Indian trail most of the way. According to the plan, Zane was to establish ferries over the major rivers—the Muskingum, Hocking, and Scioto—which intersected the road and build hostelries at such crossing points. In exchange for all of this, Zane was granted sections of land at all of the river crossings. Zanesville grew out of one of these grants.

While Zane's Trace, completed in 1798, eventually became a major artery, at first it was not much more than a wide trail suited only for horse trains. The state of the road between Chillicothe and Cincinnati is revealed by the experience of a traveler in November 1801.

> *Set off very early, having 19 miles to ride before breakfast, and very soon I entered the White Oak Swamp,' which continued for 13 miles. The mire in the road was so deep that I found it impossible to pursue it without sticking fast, and had, therefore, to abandon it, and press through the dense and brushy forest on one side or the other. While in the midst of the swamp a violent storm of rain, with lightning and thunder, arose, which continued for two hours, the rain falling in torrents all the time. Of course, I was thoroughly wet, and even the feet of my boots were filled with water.*

> *Reached Williamsburg about noon and breakfasted, and dried my clothes as well as I could, and proceeded on my journey.*

This traveler, with incredible perseverance, reached his destination only two days later than planned. His experience was by no means unique.

Poor roads, distant markets, and the absence of a stable medium of exchange hindered Ohio's trade and commerce during its territorial stage. Yet the early settlers made up for what they didn't have with plenty of energy and ingenuity. And growth did occur, in spite of the handicaps which beset the pioneering Ohioans.

As trade began to emerge in the 1790s, Ohio merchants would make the arduous trip to Philadelphia or Baltimore for supplies. Following the arduous trip back to Ohio they would stock their shelves with the necessities so much desired by the frontiersmen. As agriculture and primitive industry became established in the territory and with ready cash in short supply, merchants began to accept local produce and products for exchange and export. Particularly after the Treaty of Greenville in 1795 and the Pinckney Treaty with Spain—which secured

Left: This sketch by Alfred R. Waud, included in the two-volume work entitled Picturesque America, 1872-74, *depicts Marietta's location where the Muskingum flows into the Ohio. Marietta, named in honor of Marie Antoinette, was settled by New Englanders who arrived on a flatboat called the* Mayflower. *Courtesy, Cincinnati Historical Society*

Below: This sketch is from an early history of Cincinnati by A.E. Jones. According to Jones, it was not uncommon to see women ride to town on horseback to trade farm products for store goods. Courtesy, Cincinnati Historical Society

America's right to navigate the lower Mississippi and deposit goods at New Orleans for transshipment abroad—the export trade on the Ohio-Mississippi route began to increase.

Cincinnati quickly emerged as the major commercial center in the West. Serving as the territorial capital for a few years and located on the Ohio near the mouths of two sizeable rivers, it attracted settlers more rapidly than any other early community. Farmers inland along the Great and Little Miami rivers began shipping their surplus to Cincinnati. On the opposite side of the Ohio, the Licking River provided a route into and out of central Kentucky. Merchants established wholesale and retail stores and commerce began to thrive. Beverley Bond, historian of the Old Northwest, describes the operations of Smith and Findlay and other commercial houses at this time:

> *Customers . . . rapidly increased as settlement expanded, coming from Cincinnati, and from the near-by settlements, Columbia, North Bend, White's Station, from "up Miami," from "up Licking," and from Fort Hamilton. Much of this trade was wholesale, and the different Cincinnati houses were soon making shipments to retailers in Bardstown, Frankfort, and other settlements in the interior of Kentucky, and occasionally even to such distant points as Vincennes. Of home products, Smith and Findlay by 1795 sold whiskey and brandy in large quantities, along with imported gin, Lisbon and Madeira wines, coffee, lump sugar, Bohea tea, and chocolate. In their stock of hardware they included cups and saucers, looking-glasses, china plates, "pains" of glass, spoons and tableware. In the list of "dry goods" were shawls, pocket handkerchiefs, combs, Nankeen linen, coating, and corduroy.*

Marietta was the next most important center of trade, servicing settlers on the Muskingum River and over on the Virginia side of the Ohio River, as well as supplying the ever-increasing number of travelers along the Ohio. Chillicothe, too, although founded slightly later, quickly grew as a center of trade for the mid-Scioto valley. Competing Chillicothe merchants advertised exotic beverages and comestibles, as well as the not-so-exotic "Overstreet's Chewing Tobacco, sold by the keg." Steubenville was another growing commercial district, as was Warren in the Western Reserve.

The shortage of specie and currency complicated the conduct of business. Without any medium of exchange, barter was the necessary alternative. Most area residents were farmers, so farm produce naturally made up the bulk of goods transferred to local merchants in exchange for other goods or credit. Dairy products, eggs, bacon, ham, and potatoes were high on the list of agricultural goods traded in, along with a few small manufactured items. Smith and Findlay disposed of some of these products locally, but shipped most to other markets down the river. Bond describes the nature of the barter trade as carried on by Smith and Findlay:

> *Occasionally, horses were offered in payment, and Griffin Yeatman, a well-known tavern keeper in Cincinnati, partially settled his account with a yoke of oxen. Another account was credited with 19 pounds, 12 shillings, and 6 pence, for "22 sheep and a bell," others with a keel boat, a Kentucky boat, or a "periogg," and there was a credit item of 700 pounds in 1796 for houses and lots in Hamilton. Smith and Findlay gave credit, too, for ordinary labor, listing such items as the repair of the firm's boat, labor in the garden, or work in making caps and "callicoe" shirts. Most unusual of all was the account of a Cincinnati clergyman for six pounds five shillings which included items of whisky that totaled four and a half gallons in less than three months. This account the firm settled by "our subscription for preaching."*

Other communities carried on in this way and as far as local trade was concerned barter seemed to meet the needs of the people. Merchants would advertise in the newspapers for the kinds of produce or livestock they would be happy to receive in exchange for their wares. A newspaper publisher even offered to cancel overdue subscription charges for a certain amount of "wheat, flour, corn, sugar, beef" and so forth. A Chillicothe dealer was willing to exchange everything he had for a herd of cattle. The list of exchangeable items covered just about everything produced in the territory.

Because of the scarcity of money throughout Ohio's territorial period, banknotes from eastern institutions (which were of uncertain value and could easily be counterfeited) began to circulate. The establishment of local banks which were fairly

THE
CENTINEL of the *North-Western* TERRITORY.

Open to all parties—but influenced by none.

(Vol. I.) SATURDAY, *November* 9, 1793. (Num. 1.)

The *Printer* of the CENTINEL of the *North-Western TERRITORY*, to the *Public*.

HAVING arrived at *Cincinnati*, he has applied himſelf to that which has been the principal object of his removal to this country, the Publication of a *News-Paper*.

This country is in its infancy, and the inhabitants are daily expoſed to an enemy who not content with taking away the lives of men in the field, have ſwept away whole families, and burnt their habitations. We are well aware that the want of a regular and certain trade down the Miſſiſſippi, deprives this country in a great meaſure, of money at the preſent time. Theſe are diſcouragements, nevertheleſs I am led to believe the people of this country are diſpoſed to promote ſcience, and have the fulleſt aſſurance that the *Preſs* from its known utility will receive proper encouragement. And on my part am content with ſmall gains, at the preſent, flattering myſelf that from attention to buſineſs, I ſhall preſerve the goodwiſhes of thoſe who have already countenanced me in this undertaking, and ſecure the friendſhip of ſubſequent population.

It is to be hoped that the CENTINEL will prove of great utility to the people of this Country, not only to inform them of what is going on on the eaſt of the Atlantic in arms, and in arts of peace—but what more particularly concerns us, the different tranſactions of the ſtates in the union, and eſpecially of our own Territory, at ſo great a diſtance from the ſeat of general government—it is a particular grievance, that the people have not been acquainted with the proceedings of the legiſlature of the union, in which they are as much intereſted, as any part of the United States.—It is expected the CENTINEL, will in a great meaſure remedy this miſfortune.

Theſe are ſubſtantial advantages, which will reſult from the publication of this *paper*; but it muſt be an agreeable amuſement to know a thouſand particulars which make up the intelligence, though not ſo immediately interesting to the property & perſons of men, whether they be of a philoſophical, political, hiſtorical or moral nature.

The EDITOR therefore reſts his ſucceſs on the merits of the publication, but as an inducement to the people of this country, to make exertions to ſupport the *Preſs*, he muſt obſerve that they will have an opportunity, by means of this *paper* to make themſelves and their ſituations known abroad; if they have valuable lands to diſpoſe of, it can be made known; if they have grievances to lay before the public, it can now be done. I hope therefore, all men of public ſpirit will conſider the undertaking as a proper object of attention, and not conſult merely their own perſonal intereſt, but the intereſt of the public and the coming time.

The MONK.

CALAIS.

A POOR monk of the order of St. Francis came into the room to beg ſomething for his convent. No man cares to have his virtues the ſport of contingencies—or one man may be generous, as another man is puiſſant—*ſed non, quo ad hanc*—or be as it may—for there is no regular reaſoning upon the ebbs and flows of our humours; they may depend upon the ſame cauſes, for ought I know, which influence the tides themſelves—'twould oft be no diſcredit to us ſuppoſe it was ſo; I'm ſure at leaſt for myſelf, that in many a caſe I ſhould be more highly ſatisfied, to have it ſaid by the world, "I had an affair with the moon, in which there was neither ſin nor ſhame," than have it paſs altogether as my own act and deed, wherein there was ſo much of both.

—But be this as it may. The moment I caſt my eyes upon him, I was predetermined not to give him a ſingle ſous, and accordingly I put my purſe into my pocket—buttoned it up—ſet myſelf a little more upon my center, and advanced up gravely to him: there was ſomething I fear forbidding in my look: I have his figure this moment before my eyes, and think there was that in it which deſerved better.

The monk, as I judged from the break in his tonſure, a few ſcatter'd white hairs upon his temples being all that remained of it, might be about ſeventy—but from his eyes, and that ſort of fire which was in them, which ſeemed more temper'd by courteſy than years, could be no more than ſixty—Truth might lie between—He was certainly ſixty-five; and the general air of his countenance, notwithſtanding ſomething ſeemed to have been planting wrinkles in it before their time, agreed to the account.

It was one of thoſe heads, which Guido has often painted—mild, pale—penetrating, free from all common-place ideas of fat-contented ignorance, looking downwards upon the earth—it look'd forwards; but look'd as if it look'd at ſomething beyond this world. How one of his order came by it, heaven above, who let it fall upon a monk's ſhoulders, beſt knows; but it would have ſuited a Bramin, and had I met it upon the plains of Indoſtan, I had reverenced it.

The reſt of his outline may be given in a few ſtrokes; one might put it into the hands of any one to deſign, for 'twas neither elegant nor otherwiſe, but as character and expreſſion made it ſo: it was a thin, ſpare form, ſomething above the common ſize, if it loſt not the diſtinction by a bend forwards in the figure—but it was the attitude of entreaty; and as it now ſtands preſented to my imagination, it gained more than it loſt by it.

When he had enter'd the room three paces, he ſtood ſtill; and laying his left hand upon his breaſt, (a ſlender white ſtaff with which he journey'd being in his right)—when I had got cloſe up to him, he introduced himſelf with the little ſtory of the wants of his convent, and the poverty of his order—and did it with ſo ſimple a grace—and ſuch an air of deprecation was there in the whole caſt of his look and figure—I was bewitched not to have been ſtruck with it——

—A better reaſon was, I had predetermined not to give him a ſingle ſous.

——'Tis very true, ſaid I, replying to a caſt upwards wi[illegible] his eyes, with which h[illegible] had [illegible] addreſs—'tis very true ——and hea[illegible] who have no other but [illegible] the ſtock of which, I fear, is no way [illegible] for the many *great claims* which are hourly made upon it.

As I pronounced the words *great claims*, he gave a ſlight glance with his eye downwards upon the ſleeve of his tunic—I felt the full force of the appeal—I acknowledge it, ſaid I—a coarſe habit, and that but once in three years, with meagre diet—are no great matters; and the true point of pity is, as they can be earn'd in the world with ſo little induſtry, that your order ſhould wiſh to procure them by preſſing upon a fund which is the property of the lame, the blind, the aged, and the infirm—the captive who lies down counting over and over again the days of his afflictions, languiſhes alſo for his ſhare of it; and had you been of the *order of Mercy*, inſtead of the order of St. Francis, poor as I am, continued I, pointing at my portmanteau, full cheerfully ſhould it have been open'd to you, for the ranſom of the unfortunate—The monk made me a bow—but of all others, reſumed I, the unfortunate of our own country, ſurely, have the firſt right; and I have left thouſands in diſtreſs upon our own ſhore.——The monk gave a cordial wave with his head—as much as to ſay, No doubt there is miſery enough in every corner of the world, as well as within our convent—But we diſtinguiſh, ſaid I, laying my hand upon the ſleeve of his tunic, in return for his appeal—we diſtinguiſh, my good father! betwixt thoſe who

Left: The **Centinel Of The North-Western Territory** *was the first newspaper published in Cincinnati; its purpose was to bring news to residents and acquaint them with happenings in the federal government. It also enabled Cincinnatians to "make themselves and their situations known abroad." Courtesy, Ohio Historical Society*

Below: Pictured is a banknote from the Miami Exporting Company, a company which was chartered by the State of Ohio in 1803 to build riverboats. Within four years the company, located in Cincinnati, left the shipping business and turned its interest to banking. Courtesy, Cincinnati Historical Society

well secured helped ease the money crisis. The first Ohio bank was the Miami Exporting Company. Formerly a Cincinnati mercantile house but recognized as a bank in 1803, it proved to be a successful venture and a boon to commerce. Other sound banks founded in the next few years were located in Marietta, Chillicothe, Steubenville, and Zanesville.

The immediate needs of the early settlers in Ohio as elsewhere were iron (necessary to forge tools and utensils), gristmills, sawmills, and salt. Gristmills were essential to grind wheat into flour and corn into meal. The Marietta settlers of 1788 got their corn and wheat in the ground the first year, but no mills were built until a year or so later. All grinding had to be done by hand. Several mills were built along the Muskingum River a short distance above Marietta in 1790 and 1791, but the outbreak of the Indian Wars made them difficult to use. An original "48-er," Jonathan Devol, built a floating gristmill in 1791 which was anchored between two boats in the Ohio River near Blennerhasset Island, a more secure location against Indian forays.

As settlement spread across southern Ohio and then along major rivers into the interior during the 1790s and early 1800s, the need for gristmills increased. Within two decades, hundreds of them had been built along creeks, streams, and rivers —wherever there was sufficient waterpower. In one case, a settlement's only access to water lay through a township on "congressional land." A petition was sent to Congress urging permission to build a mill on the reserved section, a petition which, happily, was granted. Usually a sawmill was built before or at the same time as a gristmill, in order to have lumber to construct the gristmill. The first sawmill in Ohio was erected on Wolf Creek, which flowed into the Muskingum River north of Marietta, at the present site of Waterford. This was also the location of the first gristmill built in 1790. Machinery for both mills had to be imported from the East. The millstones were so heavy that the flatboat carrying

When settlers first arrived in the Ohio area, they found the land covered with trees. This made the clearing of land in preparation for planting difficult, but the ample hardwood available facilitated building. Courtesy, Ohio Historical Society

them could not be anchored along the shore at Marietta. The stones were dropped into the water and hauled to land by a team of oxen.

Mills appeared somewhat later in the Western Reserve because of later settlement there. None existed prior to 1800, but by 1840 each county had about 14 mills. Prior to their appearance, the settlers, as in Marietta and other southern sections, had to grind their grain by hand. This laborious operation required two hours of manual grinding to secure a sufficient daily portion of flour for one person. An early Cleveland settler, John Doan, recalled the procedure:

> *In those days we ground corn in little handmills. There were two stones about two and one-half feet in diameter, one above the other, the upper being turned with a pole. The corn was poured through a hole in the upper stone.*

Salt was a necessity for the pioneers for food preservation and seasoning. Though there were numerous salt springs or "licks" in the eastern and southern parts of the territory, their exact location was not always known and it was necessary to import salt from across the mountains at steep prices—from six to ten dollars a bushel. It was important, therefore, to find and drill the local wells as soon as possible. A map from 1795 marked a few of the salt springs and creeks, but the pioneers knew nothing about the map or the springs.

The celebrated Moravian missionary David Zeisberger wrote in 1779 and 1780 about salt springs in the valley of the Muskingum. They were found along the banks of creeks or occasionally on a sandbar in the middle of a stream with pure water rushing past on both sides. The Indians of the Muskingum, however, did not use much salt. The arduous labor of boiling saline water apparently was not worth the effort. Rather than make it themselves, the Indians bartered for salt with white squatters who brought it with them.

Indians occasionally helped whites in locating salt licks. One man, a prisoner of the Indians who had been released after the Battle of Fallen Timbers, passed through Olive Green, west of present-day Caldwell, and informed the inhabitants of salt springs some miles away, which he had learned about from his captors. A group of men went off for a week and returned with a gallon of salt. Though it was not much, it was better than no salt at all. Two years later, in 1797, Indians assisted settlers at Waterford in finding salt springs at modern Chandlersville, forty miles up the Muskingum River.

Ephraim Cutler, son of Manasseh Cutler, frequently took part in salt searches. On one such trip the party camped in a log cabin. Two traveling Frenchmen happened by and were taken in for the night. The evening entertainment for the company included singing "The Marseillaise" and other well-known songs of the day. One of the guests, a well-dressed, well-mannered person, devoted most of his time quizzing Cutler about conditions in the Ohio Company's grant and also at the settlement of the "French 500" at Gallipolis. Only as the Frenchmen were ready to leave the next day did Cutler learn that he had been conversing with the Duke of Orleans. He could not know, of course, that the Duke would later become King Louis Philippe of France.

As a result of his experiences, Cutler described the problems locating and manufacturing salt.

> *The article of salt was extremely difficult to procure. Nearly all the salt consumed west of the Alleghenies was brought over the mountains on pack-horses. The price was seldom less than five, and was sometimes even eight dollars a bushel. People were sent to Marietta to purchase it by the quart or gallon. It was not only excessively dear, but scarce and hard to be obtained; and our means of realizing money were very limited. When the springs were discovered a public meeting was called, and a "Salt-Spring Company" was formed from the settlements of Olive Green, Wolf Creek Mills, Cat's Creek, and Waterford, for the purpose of making salt. They were divided into four classes, bearing the names of these places, and at stated times they relieved each other in the work. We took possession of the spring, cleaned it out, set the large iron kettles, which we had for making sugar, into arches, and began boiling the water for salt. It was a slow, tedious process. During a week of hard work four men could make about six bushels. We succeeded, however, in making a full supply for the several settlements represented in the company, and had some to spare. Afterwards when our conveniences were improved we could, by our best efforts, make five bushels a day; and it as a great relief to the whole country.*

While salt was obtainable in the Muskingum valley the biggest source for Ohio salt was in Jackson County, later the home of the Scioto Salt Works. These springs were of ancient origin, even predating the glacial era. Fossil remains inform us that animals made regular pilgrimages to the area. Jackson County was Shawnee territory before white settlement, and the Shawnees allowed tribes from near and far to visit their springs. Located on a well-traveled Indian trail which ran from the Kanawha River in Virginia to the Maumee, the Shawnees had plenty of visitors. One historian of Jackson County has written that

> *these gatherings resembled the Russian markets of the nineteenth century. Many of these visiting Indians bought their salt, giving in exchange flint implements, tobacco, beads, pipestone and other articles of aboriginal commerce. It is told that tribes at war with each other would observe a truce during these visits. The squaws performed all work, chopping the saplings for fuel, drawing the water and watching the fires day and night, while the men spent their time hunting, fishing, playing ball, gaming and telling yarns. In later years, they tortured white captives in the presence of the assembled tribes. Even after the whites had taken possession of the licks the Indians used to revisit them every summer until about 1815.*

Manufacturing salt was a long, laborious process which took a lot of salt water to recover even a small amount of salt. In Jackson County it took fifteen gallons of water to recover a pound of salt and 600 gallons to recover a bushel. The most common method of securing salt was to pour the water into huge kettles placed over or next to a stone furnace. In the early years kettles were almost as scarce as the salt itself. In good weather the water was poured into long wooden troughs and placed in the sun. But evaporation was an even slower process than boiling.

The first so-called "industry" in Jefferson County was salt manufacturing. Salt springs were discovered late in the 1790s near Irondale on Yellow Creek and soon furnaces went up all over the area. One furnace built in 1802 was able to produce three bushels a day. A visitor who came to the furnace from afar found that there was such a long line of people waiting their turn for the salt that he was

Left: The old saltworks belonging to Stephen A. Guthrie, located in Muskingum County, are pictured here. The large vats were used for boiling water to obtain salt—a long and involved process. Fifteen gallons of water might yield only one pound of salt. Courtesy, Ohio Historical Society

Below: The terrain surrounding this farm at Armstrong Mills in eastern Ohio demonstrates the division of land into areas for crops, cattle grazing, and orchards. Courtesy, Ohio Historical Society

forced to return home "saltless."

In spite of Ohio's salt springs the output never was sufficient to satisfy the needs of early settlers. At the time statehood was proclaimed in 1803 the federal government granted to the state all the licks on "congressional lands." The state government unsuccessfully tried to operate the springs and then leased them to private interests. This method did not work well either and much of the state's salt supply continued to be imported from outside, chiefly New York. It was shipped from Buffalo to Cleveland and transported by teams of packhorses and oxen overland to the central and southern sections of the state. Kentucky and Virginia also sent salt to Ohio. But domestic production continued to grow and by 1830 there was no longer a shortage.

But in spite of a few primitive industries, Ohio, like everywhere else, was overwhelmingly farm country. Since the Indians had scarcely cultivated the land, Ohio agriculture really commenced with the arrival of the pioneers. The oft-told tale of the pioneer's life—carving a clearing out of the wilderness, the drudgery, the isolation, the illness, the unfriendly animals—needs no retelling. It was a hard life. But in time, the farm was a going concern, new buildings had been added, the crops and the cattle provided sustenance and profit, and the isolation was broken down.

Ohio farmers in the early years engaged in self-sufficient, general farming. The land was usually divided into three sections, one devoted to grain crops, particularly corn and wheat, another to pastureland for grazing cattle, and a smaller portion for an orchard. While this provided ample produce for family needs, a sufficient surplus also permitted the sale elsewhere of grain, meat, livestock, and dairy products.

Several regions became distinguished by specialized forms of farming. The "cattle kingdom" was centered in the Scioto River valley. In the nineteenth century, annual cattle drives took thousands of surplus livestock to eastern markets, difficult as such drives were. The Connecticut Western Reserve stood out in the dairy cattle industry, although dairying was carried on throughout the state. Wheat, while grown in most counties, was especially suited to the "Backbone" Region south of the Western Reserve, where the soil was good.

In the southwest, the Miami River valley was known as "swine country." A surplus of corn production provided ample feed for hogs and production soared. Cincinnati acquired its famous "Porkopolis" sobriquet because of its proximity to "swine

Hearkening back to the city's German heritage, the names listed here are those of early Cincinnati citizens. The sketch portrays settlers crossing the Ohio River from the Kentucky shore on flatboats. Courtesy, Cincinnati Historical Society

country." The first hogs which accompanied settlers into the Miami valley were "razorbacks," described as being "long-legged, slim-bodied, fleet-footed." Efforts at producing fatter, heavier hogs succeeded, and the new breed was called the "Miami Valley Hog." "The standardization of this breed," writes historian William T. Utter, "is Ohio's greatest contribution fo American livestock." By the mid-1800s, farm output of grain, cattle, and dairy products had placed Ohio in the agricultural forefront of all states in the country.

Whiskey was also an important product in the country west of the Appalachians. Since shipping corn, rye, and barley, as well as fruit across the mountains to eastern markets was expensive, it was much more profitable to distill the product into whiskey and brandy which could be shipped at less cost. The newly formed United States Congress adopted a whiskey excise tax in 1791, in part to show the fiercely independent frontier farmers the power of the government. The farmers of western Pennsylvania ignored the whiskey tax and developed a prosperous commerce in the liquid merchandise. In the fall of 1794 a force of 15,000 militiamen from Virginia and Pennsylvania, accompanied by Secretary of the Treasury Alexander Hamilton, headed for Pittsburgh, the center of the "Whiskey Rebellion." Without bloodshed the frontiersmen were taught to behave and pay their taxes.

While agreeing that they must now pay the tax, farmers of the West still found it more profitable to distill the grain crops into liquor than to ship the crops themselves. Distilleries began to proliferate on the frontier, not only on the Pennsylvania-Virginia border, but in the Ohio country as well. A revenue officer was appointed for Ohio in 1795 to insure that distillers paid the whiskey tax. They did. One of the first Ohio distilleries was built in 1798 on the present site of Steubenville by a Mr. Snyder, a migrant from Uniontown, Pennsylvania, no doubt one of the "whiskey rebels." In addition to distilleries, breweries also made their appearance in the territorial period.

While the young economy was chugging along in low gear, the equally young territory was motoring toward statehood in high gear. Although Governor St. Clair opposed statehood, he may have hastened it along by his very perverseness. He had become increasingly autocratic as the years passed and had made important enemies in the process. The main reason for his opposition to statehood was his fear that Ohio would become another Republican state. A staunch Federalist, St. Clair was alarmed at Jefferson's election to the presidency in 1800 and was not about to strengthen the other party if he could avoid it.

By 1800 Ohio was sharply polarized along political lines. The Federalists with their strongholds in Cincinnati and Marietta stood against the Republicans centered in Chillicothe, the new territorial capital, in the Scioto valley. Despite Cincinnati's size and importance, the Republicans, led by such men as Thomas Worthington, held considerable power in the territory besides having close ties with Republicans in Congress. So bitter was St. Clair at the rising Republican tide that he proposed to divide the territory into three states with the Scioto River serving as the boundary line between the two easternmost states. In this way he hoped to dilute Republicanism on both sides of the river.

To overcome St. Clair's opposition, Republicans decided to ignore the governor and work through their friends in Washington. Worthington and Michael Baldwin were sent to the capital to plead their case for statehood. Resulting from this, Congress in April 1802 adopted an Enabling Act which permitted the people of Ohio to convoke a constitutional convention on their own initiative. In this fashion the obstructionist tactics of St. Clair were circumvented. Ohio Republicans planned carefully and propagandized thoroughly for statehood prior to the October election, called for by the Enabling Act. As a result, they easily carried the vote and when the convention met on November 1 in Chillicothe, twenty-six of the thirty-five delegates were Republicans. St. Clair was permitted to address the assemblage and delivered such an intemperate speech denouncing the whole proceedings, that when word of it reached Jefferson, the President dismissed him from office. The convention voted for statehood and completed drafting the constitution in less than a month. Worthington was requested to take the document to Washington for final acceptance. Early in the new year of 1803 Congress approved statehood for Ohio and Jefferson proclaimed March 1, the date on which the General Assembly was organized, as the formal date of Ohio's admission into the Union.

Ohio's first state capitol was in Chillicothe in the state's first stone public building. Chillicothe was the capital from 1803 to 1810 and then again from 1812 until 1816, when the capital was permanently located in Columbus. Zanesville served as an interim capital from 1810 to 1812. Courtesy, Cincinnati Historical Society

II
WATERSHED YEARS

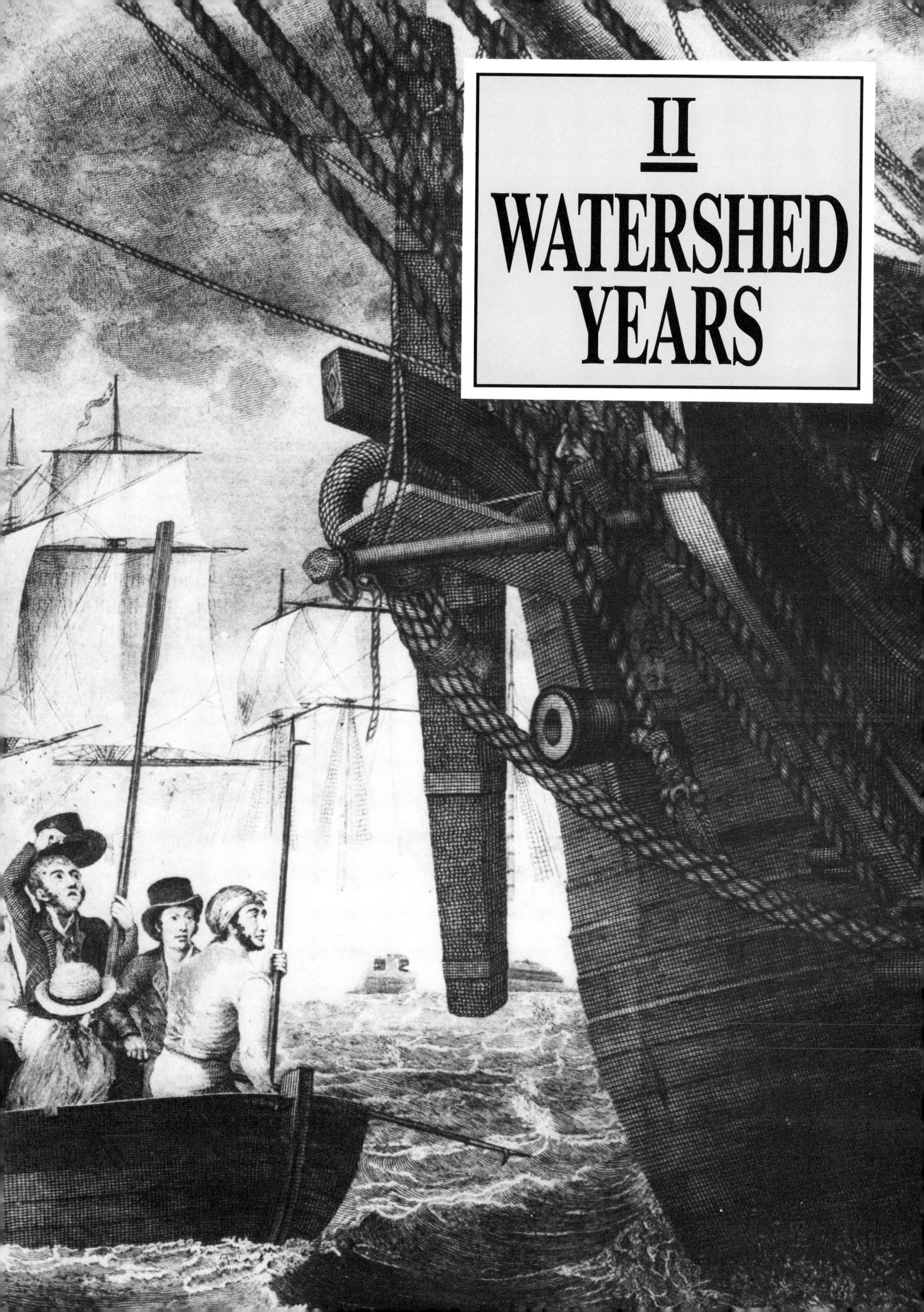

"Dear General—We have met the enemy, and they are ours, two ships, two brigs, one schooner, and one sloop." So read the message Oliver H. Perry sent to General William H. Harrison upon the American victory over the British in the Battle of Lake Erie in September 1812. This victory gave the Americans control of Lake Erie, as shown in this engraving of Perry transferring his flag to the Niagara. *Engraving by A. Lawson, after a painting by F. Birch. Courtesy, Western Reserve Historical Society*

Facing page: The Cincinnati, Hamilton and Dayton Railroad, built in 1851, was instrumental in the growth of suburban towns north of the city. Trains passing through and stopping in these outlying neighborhoods enabled people to commute to the city for work. Courtesy, Cincinnati Historical Society

Any attempt to divide Ohio's early economic history into two distinct periods—one before and one after statehood—is bound to fail. After Ohio became a state, economic development continued steadily and unspectacularly. Roads and turnpikes improved, new industries were founded, and trade and commerce expanded, much as in the territorial stage. The first major watershed came after the War of 1812, when a more advanced stage of development commenced.

Local industries developed in the territorial years—household manufactures, cotton and woolen mills, gristmills, and salt works—continued to flourish after statehood, while a number of new kinds of manufacturing establishments—tanneries, factories for making grindstones and paper, and iron furnaces—made their appearance. The list of manufacturing plants was a lengthy one at the time war broke out. Although the 1810 census estimates the annual value of Ohio products at $2.9 million, this figure is much too low, since it omitted several important industries.

Shipbuilding was established early in Ohio and continued to grow well into the nineteenth century. The industry was stimulated in 1803 by the purchase of the Louisiana Territory from Napoleon. This opened up the Ohio-Mississippi river route all the way to the Gulf of Mexico. Most of the ships constructed at Marietta, Cincinnati, and a few other river ports were designed for river trade and transport, although a few did travel to foreign places.

Marietta was the first important shipbuilding center in Ohio, and Jonathan Devol, who built the floating gristmill in the Ohio River near

BETWEEN

CINCINNATI

AND

DAYTON, TOLEDO,

DETROIT,

INDIANAPOLIS

RICHMOND, LOGANSPORT,

CHICAGO.

AND ALL WESTERN & NORTH WESTERN CITIES.

For Information Apply at the Principal Railroad Offices in the U.S. & Canada.

SAM'L. STEVENSON, Gen'l Ticket Agt D. McLAREN Prest.

In the mid-1800s, Cincinnati was one of the nation's largest boat builders, turning out approximately thirty boats a year. By 1880 nearly 1,000 steamboats had been built in the city. Pictured here is the construction of the steamboat* Sunrise, *designed for carrying cotton. Courtesy, Cincinnati Historical Society

Blennerhasset, was Marietta's first shipbuilder. A member of the Ohio Company and builder of the boats which brought the original contingent of settlers downstream in 1788, Devol continued his trade after he established his home in Marietta. In 1797 he built several mills and shipbuilding facilities on property he purchased on the Muskingum, a few miles north of Marietta.

Boats built by Devol and other early Ohio settlers were generally river barges and keelboats. A dispute has raged as to where the first oceangoing vessel was built on inland waters, but Marietta seems to have a good claim. The *St. Clair,* constructed there in 1800—not by Devol—traveled to Cuba with pork and flour under the command of Commodore Abraham Whipple, a Revolutionary War naval hero. The War of 1812 put a damper on boat construction along the Ohio, but between 1800 and 1812 twenty-six vessels, including brigs, schooners, ships, and gunboats, were built in Marietta alone.

One Marietta shipbuilder became innocently involved in the Aaron Burr "conspiracy," which excited the western frontier in 1805-1806. When Burr visited Harman Blennerhasset, who lived in his beautiful island mansion below Parkersburg, in August 1806, Blennerhasset was completely won over by the suave former Vice President. Whatever Burr's intentions were, and historians have never completely agreed about the matter, boats were needed for his expedition down the Ohio and Mississippi rivers. Blennerhasset contracted with Colonel Joseph Barker, who had built the Blennerhasset mansion, to construct fifteen boats. Barker had a shipyard at his farm on the Muskingum. Ten of the boats were to be forty feet long, the others fifty feet long. One of the latter was to have "partitions, a fireplace, and glass windows" for the comfort of the Blennerhassets. The total cost was $1,390. By the late fall of 1806, however, rumors of Burr's "treasonous" plot were abroad and local militia at

Marietta were ordered to arrest suspicious persons. Only one of Barker's boats was completed when on the night of December 6, 1806, Blennerhasset was forced to flee his home to avoid arrest by Virginia militiamen from Parkersburg.

More serious trouble for the frontier came with the revival of Indian hostilities. Quiescent since the Treaty of Greenville, Indian tribes were restless because of further white encroachment on their lands in Indiana and Illinois. The celebrated Shawnee war chief Tecumseh tried to form an alliance among different tribes to block this advance, but was not successful. Raids on frontier settlements increased and the demand rose that the Indians be crushed. General William Henry Harrison made his famous assault on the Indian base at Tippecanoe Creek on November 7, 1811, which delivered a sharp setback to the natives, but did not put the issue at rest.

The British in Canada were suspected of encouraging and supporting the Indian raids. Although the War of 1812 was supposedly caused by British depredations against American shipping on the high seas, the western cry of "Canada, Canada, Canada," was no doubt a more significant factor. A successful war against England and the acquisition of Canada would end once and for all the unholy alliance between the British and the Indians. While stirring

Above: Tecumseh, a Shawnee Indian war chief, organized a short-lived Indian confederacy against the encroachment of the white man on the Ohio territory and the lands beyond. He argued that all the land belonged to all tribes and therefore no single tribe could sell any part of it through a treaty. Tecumseh allied with the British during the War of 1812 and was killed at the Battle of the Thames in 1813. Courtesy, Ohio Historical Society

Left: Tenskwatawa, also known as the "Prophet," claimed to be a mystic and preached a return to ancient ways. He aided his brother Tecumseh in rallying tribes for an uprising against the white civilization. The Prophet's power was ended at the Battle of Tippecanoe when he made a premature and ill-advised attack on the forces of William Henry Harrison. Courtesy, Cincinnati Historical Society

naval battles were fought in the Atlantic early in the war, the most significant land fighting took place on the frontier.

The surrender of General William Hull and his force of 2,200 Americans, mostly from Ohio, at Detroit in August 1812 opened up the entire northwestern section of the state to invasion. Harrison, Hull's successor, held the line for the next year from his bases first at Upper Sandusky and later at Fort Meigs on the Maumee. On September 10 Oliver H. Perry won his great victory over the British Lake Erie flotilla at Put-in-Bay. This reopened the route to Canada and Harrison at once crossed the border. On October 5 he fought and won the Battle of the Thames and the war in the West was over. The Peace of Ghent, formally ending the war, was signed over a year later.

Some historians have asserted that whereas the American Revolution was a war for political independence, the War of 1812 was fought for economic independence. This is no doubt an oversimplification, but it does contain some truth. Overseas trade had been barred since Jefferson's "Embargo" policy was instituted in 1807, and this necessarily stimulated domestic manufacturing. The factory system emerged, industry expanded, and local trade and commerce increased. After the war, when overseas trade resumed, Ohio was the best example of heightened economic activity in the West.

The momentum for economic growth drove the state forward almost too rapidly after the war. With the restoration of peace, settlers flocked into the state thirsting for land. The population of Ohio increased from 230,000 in 1810 to 580,000 in 1820. Land sales were big business. Federal land offices had never been as busy. One million acres were sold in the West in 1815 and over five million in 1819. Settlers could purchase 160 acres at a minimum of two dollars an acre, one-quarter down and the balance in four years.

Since the settlers had little money, they borrowed from the state banks and paid the government with state banknotes. This was fine as long as the state banks were strongly structured and their notes backed by gold or silver. In January 1815, however, specie payment was suspended by Ohio banks as a result of similar action a few months before by eastern banks. State banknotes could now be issued with no specie backing at all, and they were issued—in great abundance. A number of new banks were chartered in the state over the next few years, and while most of them tried to observe sound banking practices, others were not so careful. Some "banks" formed were not even chartered. In any case, all of them began issueing large amounts of unbacked paper money. With land sales skyrocketing, the federal land offices and treasury were soon filled with unbacked banknotes.

The Second United States Bank was chartered

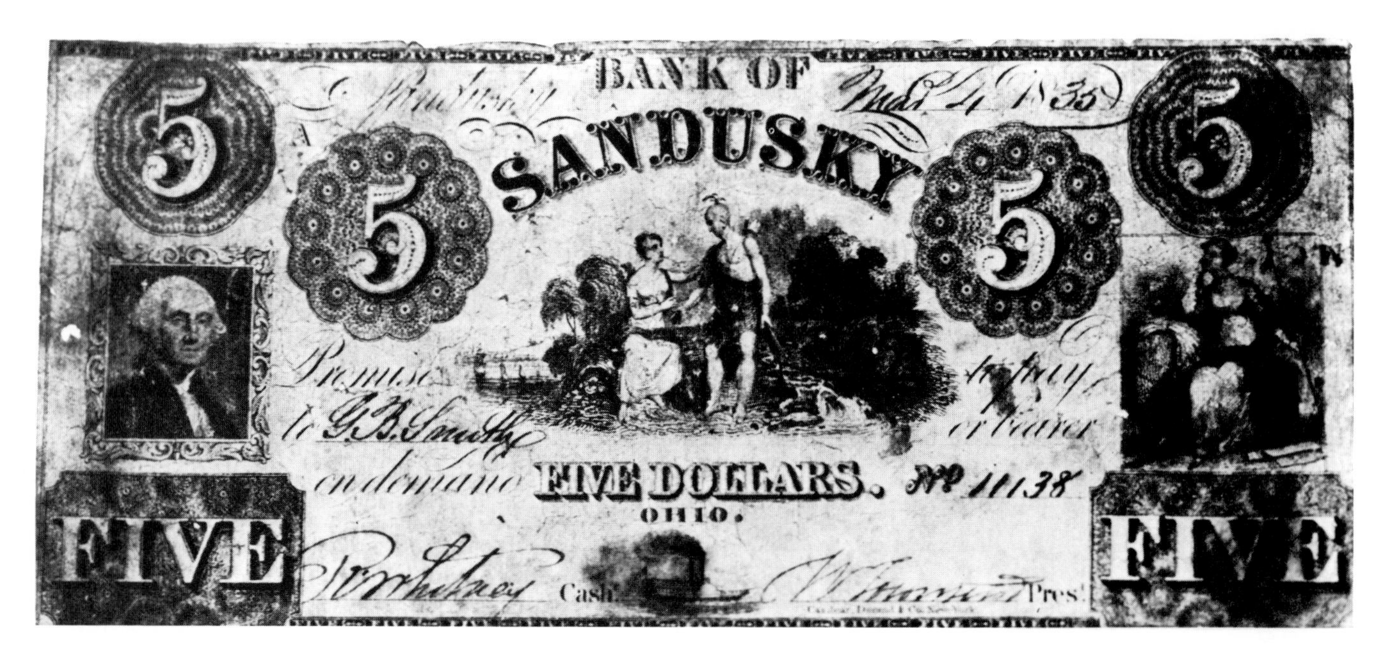

State banknotes were in great abundance in the early 1800s. This note from the Bank of Sandusky was issued in 1835 for five dollars, amid the rising number of counterfeit notes in the area. Courtesy, Ohio Historical Society

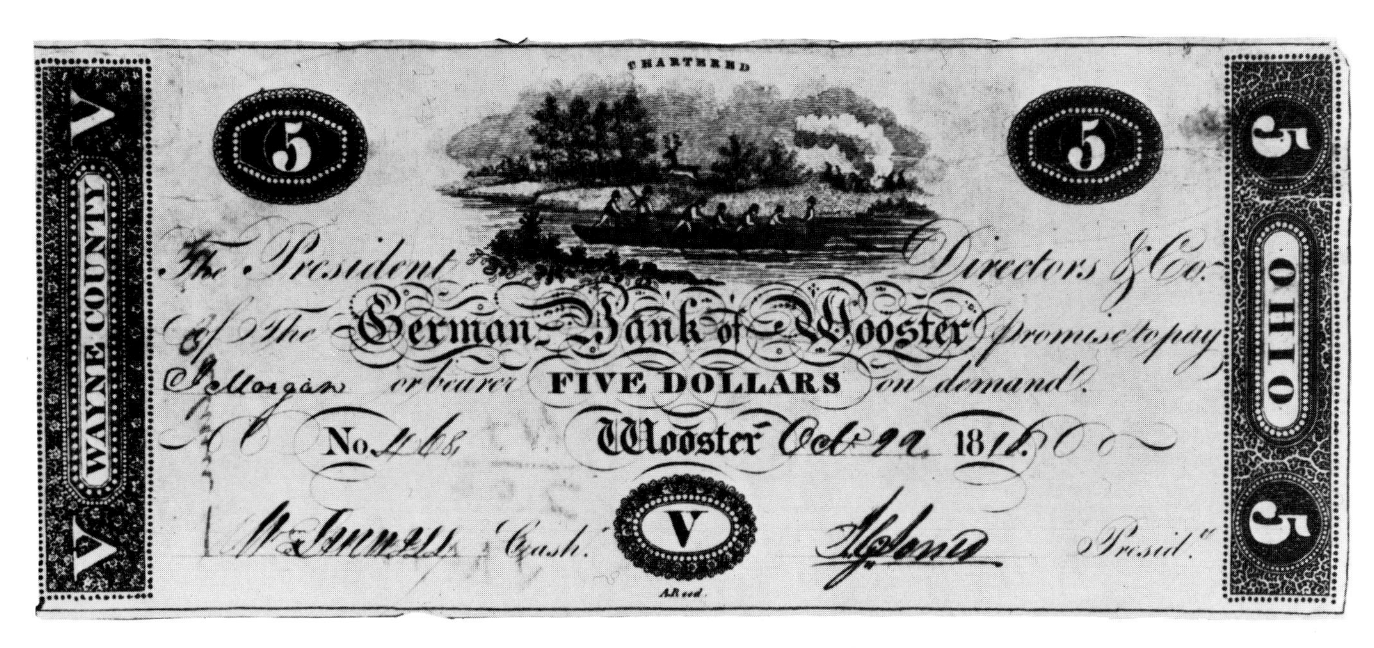

***Above:* The German Bank of Wooster in Wayne County issued this banknote early in the 1800s, when banknotes were quite popular. Courtesy, Ohio Historical Society**

***Left:* This banknote is from the Bank of Manhattan, which was incorporated in the mid-1830s in the newly established village of Toledo. At that time, the Locofoco, an antibank faction of the Ohio Democratic Party, objected to the profusion of banknotes of denominations lower than five dollars. Their concern resulted in a state tax of 20 percent on banks, an increase of 15 percent, unless the banks ceased issuing bills less than five dollars. Courtesy, Toledo-Lucas County Public Library**

in 1817 and two branches were created in Ohio at Cincinnati and Chillicothe. In July 1818 orders went out from the mother bank in Philadelphia to the western branches that only specie or its equivalent in United States notes would be accepted in the future. This precipitated a crisis. The branch banks, such as those in Cincinnati and Chillicothe, demanded specie from the state banks in exchange for their notes.

This sudden demand for specie payments was met with widespread protest. Requests for more time to shift to the new policy were rejected. Banks failed, mortgages were foreclosed, prices tumbled, and land speculators went to jail. Six years would pass before real prosperity would return, spurred then by canal construction. The "prosperity" of the post-War of 1812 years had been an artificial one, stimulated by a boom in public land sales based on cheaper paper money. "Probably half of the men living in Ohio," wrote historian William T. Utter, "were indebted to the Government for land purchases, and the fortunes of the other half were closely bound to theirs." But out of evil comes good. In 1820 a new land law reduced the minimum lot size to eighty acres at a dollar and a quarter an acre. Although no credit was allowed, for $100 a man could own his farm.

The rapid increase in population in the first years of the new century—from about 50,000 in 1800 to 230,000 in 1810—made it essential that more and better roads be built. When statehood was granted, the federal government allotted Ohio 3 percent of its annual income from all public land sales within the state to use for highway develop-

Above: The Cumberland or National Road became the main route of westward expansion in the first half of the nineteenth century. However, as this photo of Linnville, Ohio, reveals, the road could be a muddy mire in bad weather. Courtesy, Ohio Historical Society

Left: This tollgate, on the Lexington Pike outside Cincinnati, has seen many weary travelers as well as regular customers like this milkman. Courtesy, Cincinnati Historical Society

ment. The first fruits of this largesse in 1804 amounted to $17,000, with which the state legislature authorized the construction of several roads in and around Cincinnati. The legislature also required that all roads built with these monies meet certain width, strength, and grade standards. One specific clause required the removal of all stumps over one foot in height from the roadway.

The 3 percent fund provided the means for building a highway network over most of the state. By 1806 much of the south and central sections were linked and when war with England broke out in 1812 considerable construction had been completed in the Western Reserve. A traveler might now make his way from the Ohio River to Lake Erie over several different routes. Admittedly, this was not an easy nor comfortable trip, but it could be made. The legislature had expended by this time over $127,000 from the 3 percent fund and several hundreds of miles of roads had been built.

The state highway act of 1804 did not provide for the maintenance of the roads, leaving this responsibility in the hands of the county commissioners. The commissioners did very little to keep the roads in repair, judging from the complaints made about them. Because of this general dissatisfaction, two private turnpike companies were formed in 1809. One was authorized to construct a road in Trumbull County, the other a road from Zanesville to Columbus. These roads had to meet certain standards and be properly maintained. If this were done, tollgates could be built at eight-mile intervals and tolls charged for all users. But the real period of private turnpike construction came after the War of 1812.

The years following the war and before the depression of 1819 saw a sudden burst of turnpike construction, with twelve companies chartered in 1816 and 1817 alone. The new roads, which generally were improvements of the old, appeared in the more settled areas of the southeast and southwest, such as the links between Cambridge and Zanesville, Lancaster and Chillicothe, and Cincinnati and Hamilton.

Turnpike charters specified that the roads should be thirty-three feet wide, of which eighteen feet comprised the actual roadway. They were to be made of compacted stone, gravel, wood, or anything else which would provide a strong base, and graded gently from the crown to the sides for drainage. At every ten miles tollgates could be erected and rates charged for different forms of traffic. The charters also specified that the state could, at some future time, purchase these roads. Crude as these

Top: Thomas Worthington, governor of Ohio from 1814 to 1818, set the stage for future legislative approval of the construction of canals in the state. Courtesy, Ohio Historical Society

Above: Ethan Allen Brown, Ohio governor from 1818 to 1822, was known as the "Father of the Ohio Canals" and promoted internal improvements in the state. Upon his insistence, the legislature passed a law in February 1822 which provided for an engineer and a seven-member commission to determine the practicality and expense of various canal routes within the state. Courtesy, Ohio Historical Society

Above right: This map of Ohio counties shows the National Road, Zane's Trace, and the paths the canals followed. Major stopping points along each route are also depicted. Courtesy, Ohio Historical Society

early turnpikes were, they did provide an improved means of travel and transport for Ohio's burgeoning economy.

The completion of the National Road from Cumberland, Maryland, through the southwestern corner of Pennsylvania to Wheeling on the Ohio River in 1818 provided an important boost to trade. The demand that the road be continued across Ohio was made almost at once, but such expectations were stilled by the financial depression which broke out and lingered for almost six years. It was not until 1825 that federal appropriations permitted resumption of the construction of the road in Ohio. Tortuously working its way across the state, the National Road reached Zanesville in 1830, Columbus in 1833, Springfield in 1838, and the Indiana border in 1840.

While roads were improving, the construction of the Erie Canal in New York opened the eyes of Ohioans to the far more promising possibilities of a canal system. Governor Thomas Worthington (1814-1818), impressed by the importance of the Erie Canal to Ohio trade, called the legislature's attention to the matter. His successor Ethan Allen Brown (1818-1822) similarly understood the economic importance of the Erie Canal to Ohio and pressed hard for engineering surveys of possible canal routes. But local opposition—rising from Ohioans' fear that their communities might be bypassed by the canal—and economic problems stemming from the financial crisis of 1819 argued against appropriations for surveys.

In January 1822 the legislature overcame the obstacles and authorized surveys of several possible canal routes connecting Lake Erie with the Ohio River. A seven-member commission was created to supervise the surveys. The commissioners, men with broad experience in business and politics, understood the importance of a canal system to the state's economy. After extensive field studies, assisted by an engineer who had worked on the Erie Canal, the commission submitted its report to the legislature in January 1825.

The commission proposed two canals. The main one would begin at Portsmouth and follow the Scioto River to within twelve miles of Columbus, where it would veer eastward to the Muskingum River, and thence travel northward to Lake Erie at Cleveland. The estimated cost was roughly $2.8 million to $4 million. The second, or Miami Canal, would extend sixty-six miles from Cincinnati to Dayton and cost approximately $673,000. The report proposed that a new commission manage the canals and that a revision in property taxes be enacted to help fund construction of the two waterways. The commission argued strongly that not only would the canal system stimulate the economy, but would rapidly develop the northern part of the state.

Although opponents of the canals made themselves heard, the bill passed both houses easily on February 4, 1825. Plans were made to break ground on July 4, and the ceremonies at Newark, a halfway point, were witnessed by a huge crowd. The guest of honor was DeWitt Clinton himself, creative genius of the Erie Canal, who had expressed great interest in and support for an Ohio canal. Clinton turned the first spadeful of dirt and passed the shovel to Ohio Governor Jeremiah Morrow, who had worked long and hard for the canals and had been a member of the survey commission. Although the ground breaking had taken place at Newark, actual construction began much farther north because of the need to move Ohio products to New York. A couple of weeks after the event at Newark, Clinton

The Ohio and Erie Canal was one of the many canals that facilitated the movement of large quantities of freight. Shown here is the **George H. Watkins** *unloading its freight and taking on additional cargo. Courtesy, Ohio Historical Society and the* **Columbus Dispatch**

was back in the state again, this time at Middletown, to turn the first shovelful of dirt for the Miami Canal.

No serious difficulties arose in marketing the canal bonds—New York bankers bought most of them—nor in securing laborers. Hundreds of farmers and their families who lived along the canal routes were hired, while hundreds of Irishmen who had worked on the Erie Canal came over to join the ranks (Akron was born amid the shantytowns of these Irish canal diggers). By the close of 1825, nearly 2,000 diggers were at work on the northernmost section of the Ohio-Erie Canal, from Akron to Cleveland.

While recruiting laborers was not difficult, it was not easy to retain them. Workers, whether wallowing in several inches of mud or hacking their way through thick woods and underbrush, toiled long hours. While the pay was good—eight to ten dollars a month plus food and shelter—it was not good enough to keep them on the job for any length of time. Farmers, in particular, were likely to run off periodically to attend to their land. And not infrequently contractors ran off without paying their workers. Disease was a constant concern. Historians Raymond Boryczka and Lorin Lee Cary write:

> *Recurrent epidemics of typhoid, malaria, and cholera—popularly termed "canal fever"—not only compounded workers' woes but also depleted their numbers. So many were stricken or frightened off during an 1827 outbreak, for example, that the state legislature authorized the use of convict labor on the Columbus Feeder Canal; and in 1829 disease temporarily halted construction throughout the state. Unsanitary conditions in the jerry-built shanties commonly provided by employers*

Left: In the early days of river transportation, horses and mules were used to pull canal boats. The fare and proposed speed of travel on canal boats were a "cent and a half a mile and a mile and a half an hour." The best time made on the Ohio and Erie Canal was 307 miles in eighty hours between Cleveland and Portsmouth. Courtesy, Cincinnati Historical Society

Above: The Miami and Erie Canal went through Cincinnati in an area predominantly occupied by Germans. They called the canal the "Rhine," and when returning from downtown they would say they were going "over the Rhine." In 1920 the canal was drained to provide a channel for a subway, which was never completed. Today Central Parkway covers the canal and the surrounding area is referred to as "over the Rhine." Courtesy, Cincinnati Historical Society

aggravated the situation. Under such trying hardships, cheap whiskey often became the canal workers' prevalent remedy and consolation. Whiskey dens sprang up around construction sites and, at least in the early years, contractors customarily provided three daily "Jiggerfuls" in order to mollify and retain their crews. Drunken brawls were the "unhappy consequences," frequently between rival Irish clan . . .

Two years to the day after construction began, on July 4, 1827, the canal was completed from Akron to Cleveland. The event was celebrated with even greater ceremony than the initial ground breaking. A convoy of flag-bedecked barges traveled the thirty-six-mile distance with excited residents cheering along the way. At Cleveland a big crowd welcomed the boats and a banquet concluded festivities. Big crowds awaited the canal's completion at every point along the 308-mile route, as well as on the several "feeder" lines. It took three more years to complete the canal to Newark and it was not until 1833 that Portsmouth, the southern extremity, was reached.

Canal boats had a solid and efficient, if not elegant, appearance. Passenger packets were patronized by the wealthy, whereas poorer individuals rode on freight barges. Packets provided separate cabins for men and women and a kitchen, usually in the stern. In fair weather, passengers could escape from the crowded quarters below and gather on deck to view the surrounding countryside. Courtesy, Cincinnati Historical Society

Now the entire state from Lake Erie to the Ohio River could be traversed in eighty hours! Barges were lined up at every lock as the merchandise flowed to the South and Northeast in unprecedented volume. Formerly landlocked communities experienced a sudden birth of affluence. Land values along the canal quintupled in ten years' time. Walter Havighurst described the new prosperity:

At Canal Fulton in Summit County, Canal Street was lined with stores that had rear loading platforms on the water. Barge captains bought provisions and mule feed there, frequently on credit . . . Here on summer days town boys would drop off the overhead bridge onto southbound canal boats, riding to the lock a mile distant. As the return trip, on loaded barges, took twice as long, the boys generally walked back on the towpath. They could stop to swim and catch a few turtles and still beat the northbound boat to town.

One boy, a future president, got his start in life, as legend has it, as a mule driver on the towpath of the Ohio-Erie Canal. James Abram Garfield was his name.

But the colorful Canal Age was almost doomed before it began. The first railroad in Ohio was chartered by the state legislature even before the Ohio-Erie Canal was completed, although the marvelous possibilities of rail transport were only dimly seen then. Though canals were obsolete by the 1850s, they had performed a valuable function by contributing substantially to the growth of the state, both economically and numerically. Cities grew up overnight, a cash economy supplanted primitive barter trade, and the value of goods escalated. Ohio moved into the primal age of industrialism many years earlier than might have otherwise been the case, largely because of its canal system.

In time few people would argue that canals were superior to railroads in speed and volume of goods transported. However, there were various economic objections to railroads during the "period of incubation"—1830-1850—which helped delay their development. Those who had heavily invested in canals saw no good in the iron horse. Turnpike com-

Columbus, which has been called the "Crossroads of America," experienced a big population surge in the nineteenth century. The passage of railroads through the city played a big part in that growth. The city's Union Station, pictured here, was built in the mid-1800s. Courtesy, Ohio Historical Society

panies, tavern proprietors, and farmers in bypassed regions all raised cries of protest. Moreover, serious technical problems prevented the quick triumph of the railroad. Cast-iron wheels and rails were brittle and shattered easily, and no one yet knew how to convert steam power into motive power for the engine. The first steam-powered American locomotive operated successfully in an 1830 experiment, but not until steel rails could be manufactured cheaply after the Civil War would the railroad revolution take place.

Clumsy and unpopular as they were, railroads arrived in the watershed years. In 1830 the first small line in eastern Ohio was chartered, but not built. A wave of charter bills passed the legislature in 1832, including one for the Mad River and Lake Erie line, designed to run from Springfield to Sandusky. Difficulties over financing delayed ground breaking for the Mad River road for several years. In 1837 the legislature authorized the railroad directors to borrow $200,000 on the credit of the state. This plus stock subscriptions from each county through which the road would pass permitted construction to proceed. Sixteen miles of track north of Springfield was opened in 1838. Progress on the Mad River was slow from this point on and Sandusky was not reached until 1848. Meanwhile the Little Miami Railroad was being built south of Springfield to Cincinnati. It was also finished in 1848, which thus provided a continuous rail line across the state from Cincinnati to Sandusky.

During the 1840s other lines were completed, mostly in the northern part of the state. In 1847 the Cleveland, Columbus, and Cincinnati line was chartered, demonstrating the rising importance of Cleveland. The section from Cleveland to Columbus was finished, 149 miles long, in February 1851. The fifty-four-mile stretch from Columbus to Xenia, which linked up with the Little Miami line, was shortly completed permitting through travel from Cleveland to Cincinnati. Various state laws dealing with Ohio railroads were adopted as the network grew and the new constitution of 1851 established more uniform and standardized control over the entire system.

By mid-century Ohio had experienced a major watershed in its history. All parts of the state had been settled, even the swampy regions of the Maumee valley. A transportation network had been built linking all parts of the state and tying Ohio to eastern markets. Industry had expanded. The factory system had been founded and large urban centers dotted the map.

A glance around the state in 1830, a mid-point in Ohio's watershed period, reveals the progress that had been made up to that time. The Western Reserve was still thinly populated with only 1,000 people living in Cleveland, the principal village. But the Ohio-Erie Canal, then under construction, was about to infuse life and vigor into the Lake City. Canton to the south in Stark County was already firmly in place, while its neighbors Akron and Massillon would shortly prosper from the canal. Steubenville was one of the largest towns in the state and boasted an important woolen factory and other industries. In fact, next to Cincinnati, it was one of the leading manufacturing centers in the West.

Among the older cities, Zanesville, another

RICHES, COLUMBUS. O.

FELCH – RICHES.

Facing page, top: This sketch from Martin's 1857 History of Columbus *shows the busy city market-house at the southwest corner of Town and Fourth streets in Columbus. Markets such as the one shown here were often located in a central spot where city dwellers could come to buy farm produce. Cincinnati's own Findlay Market dates from the mid-1850s. Courtesy, Ohio Historical Society*

Facing page, bottom: The state capitol and other government buildings in Columbus are shown here. From left to right are the U.S. courthouse state offices, and the Old State House which served as the capitol building until 1852. Courtesy, Ohio Historical Society

Above: This is how Columbus, south of High Street, looked in 1854 to artist Henry Howe. Note the wide street, laid out in 1816 when Columbus was chosen to be the state's new capital. The street was not paved until after the Civil War. Courtesy, Ohio Historical Society

manufacturing center, was the second largest city in the state in 1830, with a population of over 3,000. Marietta with a population of 1,200 was a lovely town based on shipbuilding and commerce, although some visitors were struck by signs of inactivity and decline. Portsmouth had 1,000 inhabitants and enjoyed a modest prosperity as the outlet for both the Scioto River and the canal. Also the center of the important "Hanging Rock" iron fields, Portsmouth was entering a kind of "golden age." To the north along the Scioto were the old villages of Chillicothe and Circleville where local trade and commerce continued to thrive. Chillicothe alone boasted four cotton mills. Columbus, the state capital, possessed about 2,500 people and was a center for trade and government. Many complained, however, that far too many pigs were permitted to run loose, a criticism made of a number of other places. From what can be gathered Columbus' principal industry seemed to be the state prison.

But without question the first city in every respect was Cincinnati. With an 1830 population of over 25,000, it was the number-one commercial center west of the mountains. Located at the lower terminus of the Miami-Maumee Canal, its prosperity was linked to trade, shipbuilding, and manufacturing. The city intrigued the eye with its beautiful banks, hotels, and private homes. It was a center of culture as well, claiming a university, theater, and museum. One visitor from abroad observed enthusiastically, "Cincinnati is in every respect an extraordinary city; the only one, perhaps, on record, which has in the course of 25 years, sprung up from nothing to be a place of great consequence."

The watershed years marked the transition from what was basically a domestic, small-shop form of industrial organization, to an embryonic factory system. This transition did not occur overnight, nor did it occur simultaneously throughout all fields of business activity. What might be called "factories" appeared early in the nineteenth century. Some of Ohio's early flour mills, textile mills, and iron works possessed many of the features of the factory system. A three-story woolen factory in Steubenville was powered by steam and had 115 laborers on its payroll. An "iron plantation" in Zanesville had 158 workers. Even more impressive was the Cincinnati Steam Mill, a nine-story structure built in 1814, which used steam engines to process wheat, wool, cotton, and pork products for markets as far away as the West Indies. However, the road to a more mature industrial society had not yet been paved.

New inventions, new techniques, and new processes were essential to the growth of the "modern" factory system. Americans contributed two important principles to the sophistication of production processes. One was the idea of the "interchangeability of parts," the other, the idea of "continuous process manufacturing." Eli Whitney is usually given credit for first successfully demonstrating the practicability of interchangeable parts when he manufactured guns for the United States government early in the nineteenth century. Continuous process, whereby a plant is so designed that the product is manufactured by a series of successive smooth-flowing operations—the modern "assembly line"—came later, toward the middle of the century. The early flour mills and woolen mills were not suited to continuous process.

A number of older industries continued to prosper and grow at least until the middle of the century. Take the iron business. The iron forge was almost as vital to the early settlers as the gristmill. Pioneers looked to the forge for tools, utensils, household wares, machinery, horse shoes, and nails. None were built in Ohio prior to statehood. Whatever iron tools and implements the people possessed were imported or made by the blacksmith with his small furnace and anvil. The first large furnace was built in the valley of the Mahoning River, near Poland, by Daniel Eaton. His output measured two tons daily, which was fashioned into kitchenware. The iron forge, which produced a better quality of iron than the furnace, appeared in two places in 1809. That year James Heaton constructed a dam, sawmill, and forge also in the Mahoning valley, at the site of modern Niles. Working the crude pig-iron through a laborious process of heating and cooling several times, Heaton produced a fairly good quality of iron, using charcoal for fuel. Also in 1809 Moses Dillon built a blast furnace and forge near Zanesville. By 1840 some twenty forges had been built throughout the state, fifteen powered by water, and five by steam, which was first used in 1815.

The most famous iron-producing area in early Ohio was the Hanging Rock region of south-central Ohio and northern Kentucky. The picturesque name given to the area, "Hanging Rock," was derived from a suspended rock on a cliff near Ironton. The region, roughly a hundred miles long and twenty-eight miles wide, embraced the Ohio counties of Lawrence, Scioto, Gallia, Jackson, Vinton, and Hocking, plus Carter, Boyd, and Greenup counties in Kentucky. Sixty-nine charcoal furnaces were built from the 1820s through the 1850s.

Iron miners pause after a hard day of mining at the Ohio Furnace in Scioto County. According to the* Ohio Bureau of Labor Statistics *in 1879, miners faced "danger to life and limb . . . added to the awful and hardness and gloom of the coal mine . . . and the inhalation of noxious and poisonous gases [which] blanches the face and impoverishes the human blood." Courtesy, Ohio Historical Society

The needs of the workers of the Hanging Rock furnaces provided a good market for farmers in the area. Some farmers accumulated modest fortunes in selling their goods locally. In addition, iron manufactured at Hanging Rock became a major product of river transportation to Cincinnati, Pittsburgh, and other river ports. Approximately 100,000 tons were shipped annually.

The charcoal furnaces of Hanging Rock continued to dominate iron production in Ohio until the Civil War. The Hecla Furnace in Lawrence County, built in 1833, was the most famous of these, but many others were equally important.

Iron ore was discovered in the extreme northeast in 1812. This "bog iron" was dug from swampy land with a pick and shovel. By smelting, the organic matter was burned off and the ore reduced to iron. Though of low grade, bog iron was a tough material, particularly good for castings. The Arcole Furnace near Madison manufactured bog iron and prospered for about twenty-five years after its founding in 1831, but failed when charcoal became hard to obtain and as the supply of bog ore gave out. The nearby port of Madison Dock (Ellensbury), which prospered during the peak of the bog iron industry, became a ghost town.

As the years passed, new techniques, such as the "hot blast process" for smelting, were introduced. At Hecla and other iron centers in the south, forges utilized waterpower until the 1840s when steam power came into general use. It was more efficient than waterpower and permitted industrial site location far removed from rivers and streams.

Another important innovation in iron manufacture was the use of coal rather than charcoal for furnace fuel. It was responsible for opening up the iron industry in the Mahoning valley. Coal was more efficient in eliminating impurities in iron ore and also preserved timberlands. Mahoning valley's great importance as a center of iron and steel production stems from the late 1840s by which time four coal blast furnaces were in operation.

Coal had been discovered in Portage County and in the southeastern part of the state in the 1820s and production steadily increased in the next two decades. One pioneer merchant, Valentine Dexter Horton, settled in Pomeroy in Meigs County in

The Eagle Iron Works, owned by Miles Greenwood, was established in 1832 and manufactured, among other things, malleable iron castings, house locks and latches, vault and safe locks, shutter fasteners, garden seats, and iron house fronts. During the Civil War, Eagle Iron Works produced more munitions than the National Armory in Springfield. The company received 60,000 old flintlock muskets and converted them to modern weapons at the rate of 800 a day. Courtesy, Cincinnati Historical Society

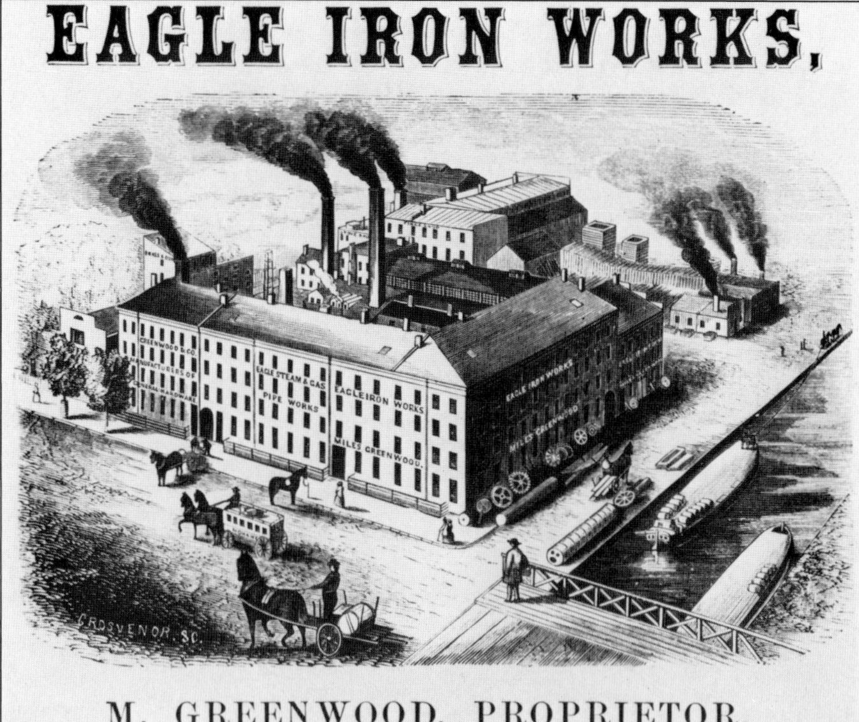

M. GREENWOOD, PROPRIETOR,

Nos. 383, 384, 385, 386 & 396, Corner Walnut and Canal Streets,

CINCINNATI, OHIO.

The Eagle Iron Works was established in 1832, by the present proprietor, in connection with Mr. Joseph Webb, for the purpose of a general Foundry business, although in a limited way, as the means of the proprietors would not admit of an extended business; and the articles of manufacture relied upon principally, were Stoves, Hollow Ware, Sad Irons, Dog Irons, Wagon Boxes, Plow Moulds, and some other ordinary articles in every day use; to which additions were made from time to time, of such things as were generally wanted, or made for special purposes.

The business was continued in this manner, and extended as the demands increased, for eight years, when Mr. Webb withdrew from the firm. The same year, 1840, it was determined to commence the manufacture of

BUTT HINGES.

This undertaking, for a time, met with but little favor from dealers, from whom it was but reasonable to expect a liberal patronage; but builders becoming aware of the superior quality of the Hinges made at this establishment, soon created a demand for them, which placed the manufacture and sales on a substantial basis, and has brought them into general use throughout the country.

1835 and began fairly large-scale operations. He shipped coal downstream to Cincinnati and other river ports. Mahoning valley coal, in addition to fueling the local furnaces around Youngstown, was shipped to both Cleveland and Pittsburgh along "feeder" lines of the Ohio-Erie and Pennsylvania-Ohio canals.

By 1850 Ohio ranked high among all states in certain forms of iron production. In that year it was number two in its output of pig iron and third in iron castings. The Hanging Rock furnaces contributed largely to this performance, shipping nearly 50 percent of its products to the foundries in Cincinnati. Several thousand workers were employed in the factories throughout the state turning out pig iron, castings, and other iron products.

Though Cleveland was growing, its minor industrial importance at the time was evident in its mere handful of factories. The older cities were still the center of most industrial activity at mid-century. Steubenville, for example, located in the heart of the sheep-raising region of the state, continued to be one of the major woolen cloth manufacturing centers in the country with five factories in operation. Zanesville remained the hub of the ceramic industry—about 25 percent of the state's ninety-nine potteries in 1840 were located in Zanesville and its environs—although it would soon surrender its leadership to East Liverpool.

The first pottery in East Liverpool was founded in 1839 by James Bennett, a refugee from the Sheffield plants of England. The town's growth had been slow until the 1830s, when increasing commercial activity along the upper Ohio River instilled new life into it. Bennett, a skilled potter, utilized the rich clay deposits in the area and quickly made a name for himself. His brothers soon joined him, as did many other expert English potters. Soon "Bennett's Liverpool Ware" was selling up and down the river from Pittsburgh to St. Louis. By mid-century there were eleven potteries in the city, with 387 craftsmen producing $175,000 worth of goods annually. With the coming of the railroad, East Liverpool earthenware was being sold in Chicago, New Orleans, and other distant markets.

Rich clay deposits were discovered in Summit County (Akron) as early as 1828. By the 1840s there were so many potteries there that business began to suffer. In order to avoid mass bankruptcies, an agreement was reached among them. Thus a "pool," perhaps one of the earliest business combinations anywhere, was formed in 1841. Although this arrangement may not have lasted very long, it put the pottery business back on its feet. Edwin H. Merrill and his associates and Enoch Rowley and his brothers-in-law made reputations for themselves in the manufacture of different forms of stoneware. Rowley came from Staffordshire, England, as had the Bennetts in East Liverpool, and like the Bennetts, began the successful production of yellow and Rockingham ware.

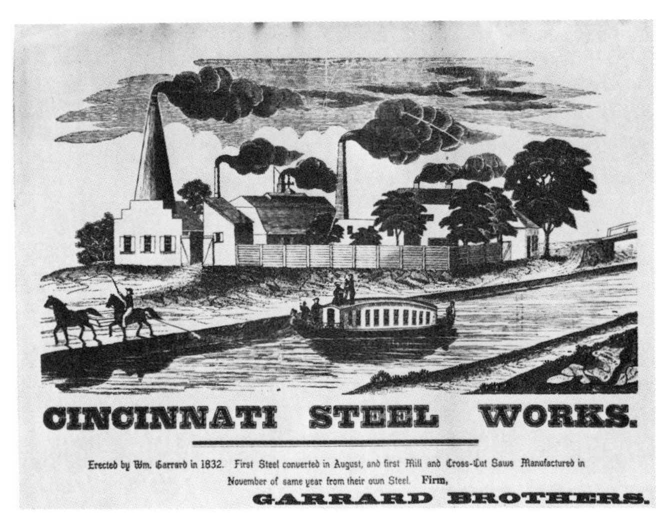

Above: William and John Hill Garrard manufactured crucible steel at the Cincinnati Steel Works Plant. This advertisement shows the steel plant, known for making top quality steel from 1832 to 1837, at its ideal location on the Miami Canal. Courtesy, Ohio Historical Society

Left: Businesses like the Miners' Supply Company sprang up in response to the local economy. This outlet in Coalton provided necessary equipment for the industry and its employees. Courtesy, Ohio Historical Society

Dayton, aided by the completion of the Miami Canal, also enjoyed an age of growth and prosperity during the watershed years. Cotton spinning, agricultural equipment and carpet factories, flour mills, distilleries, foundries, and paper mills were all flourishing there.

Dayton was also the home of many dairy farms. The emergence of the dairy industry occurred during the 1820s. Centered in the Western Reserve, dairying prospered because of the region's rich grassland and the internal migration of practiced New England dairy farmers. As of 1850 the total production of Ohio cheese amounted to twenty-one million pounds, with eighteen million of that emanating from the Reserve, or, as some called it, "Cheesedom." The canals and later the railroads carried cheese from northeastern Ohio to the East, South, Far West, and overseas.

But no matter how prosperous, all other Ohio cities paled before mid-century Cincinnati, which was the dominant commercial and industrial city of

The Cincinnati Butchers' Supply Company opened in 1886 and is still in business today, producing machinery used in the packing industry. For over fifty years, this business was located on Central Avenue, close to the pork packers and slaughterhouses. The wagon pictured here is typical of the company's advertisements describing its equipment. Courtesy, Cincinnati Historical Society

Facing page: In a short period of time Cincinnati became a major manufacturing center. Increasingly dependent on river transportation, many companies, like the Straub Company, were situated close to the Ohio River. Courtesy, Cincinnati Historical Society

the West. About one-half of Ohio's seventeen million dollars of capital investment was centered there. The slaughtering and packing of pork was the major business in this city of many businesses. Although begun only in the early 1830s, the industry in two decades was packing approximately 27 percent of all meat products of the West. So many hogs went to slaughter annually in Cincinnati, that one swinish observer was moved to remark, "that if put into sausages of the ordinary diameter, it would make a girdle long enough to encompass the whole globe along the line of the equator." Cincinnati packers developed a mammoth conveyor system which later manufacturers would adapt for their own assembly lines. The numerous byproducts recovered in the slaughtering process such as lard, soap, candles, and glue, gave birth to new industrial organizations, such as Procter & Gamble.

While pork was the largest industry in Cincinnati, it was by no means the only one. Thousands of workers were employed in foundries, engine plants, boot and shoe and ready-made clothing shops, and furniture factories. Foundries were primarily concerned with stove production and could turn out 1,000 of them in a day. Cincinnati was the major western center for the manufacturing of clothing, using both the factory and "putting-out" systems, the latter occupying the time of 9,000 women working at home. Thousands of pieces of furniture, particularly bedsteads and chairs, were produced annually and marketed in the West and South. Of course, no description of Cincinnati industry in the mid-nineteenth century could neglect breweries and distilleries, which were fueled by the large-scale German immigration of the 1840s. In 1850 Ohio was second in the country in gallons of beer and liquor produced and thirsty Cincinnati was the main reason.

The mid-1830s witnessed another age of wild land speculation in the West, prompted by another wave of "wildcat" banking and indiscriminate issue of state banknotes. This resulted from President Andrew Jackson's removal of federal monies from the Second United States Bank to favored "pet banks." There were nine of these in Ohio. Using these funds as security, state banks began issuing large amounts of notes, much in excess of the federal deposits. The land-office business was far greater than that which preceded the panic and depression of 1819. To stop the rampant speculation, President Jackson in the summer of 1836 issued his famous "Specie Circular," ordering that henceforth only specie would be accepted at government land offices. This had a sharp impact on the national economy, similar to that of the edict of the United States Bank in July 1818 calling for specie payments. Within a year the country had sunk into another lengthy depression.

While Ohio suffered through the next four or five years, the situation was not as critical there as in other parts of the West. Land sales were not great and its economy had attained a greater degree of maturity. The state was also still largely geared to agriculture which softened the blow for many. In

Established 1837

OLD RELIABLE

"QUEEN OF THE SOUTH"

WHEAT FLOURING AND CORN GRINDING

PORTABLE MILLS,

And Mill Machinery Generally.

H. P. STRAUB,

Successor to ISAAC STRAUB,

MANUFACTURER AND PATENTEE.

Double Geared Mill.

PATENTED

March 20th, 1866, and October 18th, 1870.

FIRST PREMIUM

Cincinnati Industrial Exposition.

1872 & 1873.

And La. State Fair, New Orleans,

1872 & 1873.

H. P. STRAUB,

Successor to ISAAC STRAUB,

No. 6 Elm St., bet. Water St. and Ohio River,

NEAR LOUISVILLE MAIL-BOAT LANDING,

P. O. BOX 1063. CINCINNATI, O.

☞ FOR PARTICULARS SEND FOR DESCRIPTIVE CIRCULARS.

Pictured here are the employees of the Jackson Brewery in Cincinnati. Many of these workers were immigrants from Austria. Courtesy, Cincinnati Historical Society

fact, it has been suggested that some Ohioans were not even aware that there was a depression. The pinch was felt most keenly in canal construction. Some projects were temporarily suspended. Money was secured from different sources, but the state's credit was so damaged by 1841 that it was unable to market its bonds anywhere. But one big success was scored. In April 1840 the Pennsylvania and Ohio Canal was completed, providing a clear route from Pittsburgh to Cleveland.

The financial setbacks of 1819-1825 and 1837-1843 had hurt Ohio's economy and delayed growth. But by mid-century these difficulties were all but forgotten as the state rushed forward on many fronts. Better transportation had expanded markets in all directions. New inventions and processes had built the foundation for an industrial complex that would rank Ohio among the country's leaders. The greatest growth was still ahead, but what had been achieved so far was impressive. The total value of manufactured goods tripled between 1825 and 1850. Ohio was still an agricultural state in 1850, but industry was on the march. The watershed years witnessed the origins of this turnaround.

Cleveland's Public Square was the center of the city's community life and was the scene of many important gatherings over the years. In 1865 a pavilion was erected on the square to receive the body of President Lincoln, which was viewed by more than 100,000 mourners. In 1881 James Garfield's body was also brought to the square. Courtesy, Western Reserve Historical Society

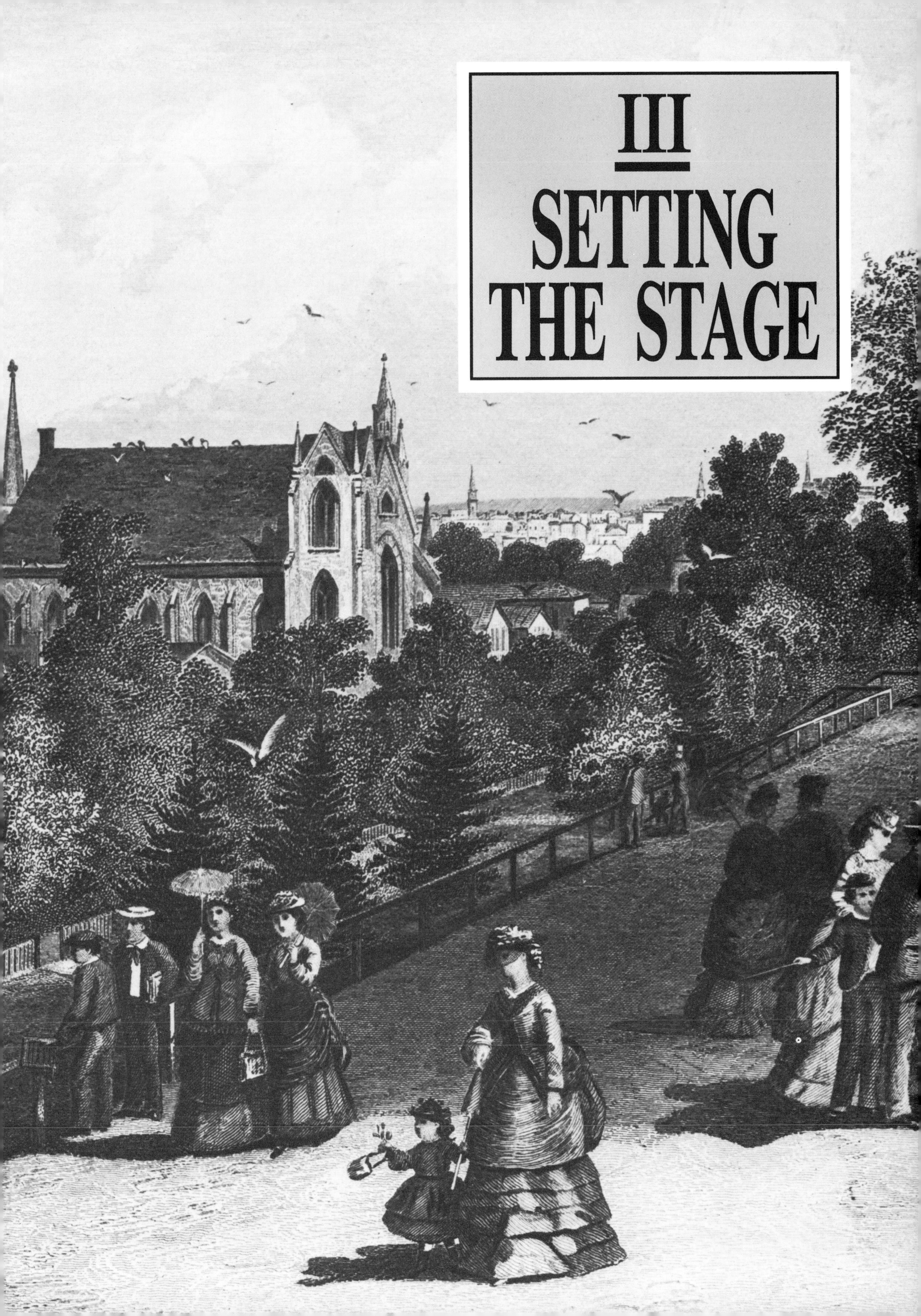

III

SETTING THE STAGE

Cleveland derived its importance from its location on the Great Lakes and at the head of the Ohio Canal. Its railway connections with cities to the east and west aided Cleveland's development. By the 1870s it was rapidly emerging as an industrial center. Courtesy, Ohio Historical Society

Facing page: On September 5, 1862, volunteers marched across a pontoon bridge over the Ohio River to help defend Cincinnati from the threat of a Confederate attack. Cincinnati and its neighbors in northern Kentucky were spared when the Confederates turned back and marched out of Kentucky. Courtesy, Cincinnati Historical Society

While the second twenty-five years of the nineteenth century saw Ohio transformed from a frontier to a settled state, the following quarter-century marked perhaps an even greater watershed in the state's history. Building on the rudimentary foundations of the earlier age, a mighty industrial empire was being constructed, one which would place Ohio among the national leaders.

Prior to this "Industrial Revolution," Ohio, as well as the rest of the country, had to contend with civil war. Though economic historians argue over the affect the war had on industry, the weight of opinion appears to hold that the war neither retarded nor accelerated industrial production. However, it may have stimulated certain industries and impeded others. Ohio wool growers, for example, prospered during the war because of the military need for uniforms and blankets. On the other hand, cotton textiles were severely hurt with the restriction on the cotton trade. A study of wartime industrial progress in the Miami Valley reveals an upsurge of "inventive-innovative" activity with respect to farm equipment, durable consumer goods, and publishing.

Those who argue that the Civil War stimulated industry have only to examine the economic growth of Akron to document their case. The region's second railroad—Atlantic and Great Western—came to town on April 17, 1863. While this road, absorbed by the Erie system in the 1890s, was in financial trouble for many years, it was fundamental to the industrial expansion of the city. Coal also played a part in Akron's growth. Ample supplies of cheap coal, found in abundance in Summit County, gave the local economy a substantial

During the Civil War a German merchant named Ferdinand Schumacher started the German Mills in Akron. After many mergers, the firm became part of the Quaker Oats complex. Courtesy, Cincinnati Historical Society

advantage over other aspiring communities. Ten coal companies were in business there in 1868 and the output of their mines increased steadily in later years.

The heightened demand for foodstuffs during the Civil War stimulated another important industry in Akron—agricultural equipment. Patents for Cyrus McCormick's harvesting machines expired in the 1850s and many new companies were now manufacturing mowers and reapers. The Champion Company of Springfield was an important producer of farm equipment, but Akron boasted two manufacturers in the field. Ball, Aultman, and Company of Canton really started the industry in Akron by opening a branch plant there in 1863. Soon the Akron facility had outgrown its parent. John R. Buchtel and Lewis Miller played central roles in the solid growth of the Buckeye Mower and Reaper Works, by which name the Ball, Aultman offshoot was known. John F. Seiberling, whose son would later create the Goodyear Tire and Rubber Company, founded another mower and reaper plant—the Empire Mower and Reaper Works—in the late stages of the Civil War. While Seiberling's plant had its ups and downs, Buckeye Mower and Reaper grew steadily and by the end of the century was among the largest manufacturers of farm equipment in the world.

Ferdinand Schumacher, a German immigrant, was another Akron resident to prosper directly from the Civil War. He had "invented" oatmeal in the late 1850s, but sold it only locally. Through the intercession of his good friend and fellow German immigrant Erhard Steinbacher, Schumacher received a large order from the army quartermaster for oatmeal for the troops. It proved popular with the men in blue and within a year after the war began, Schumacher was having trouble keeping up with the demand for his oatmeal. The army also needed "pearl barley," and turned to Schumacher to supply it. He built the Empire Barley Mill to meet this need. He also wisely cultivated the civilian market in the postwar years and by 1870 was the unquestioned "cereal king" of the country. In the 1880s, however, other cereal companies were on the scene. To avoid competition a giant "trust," the American Cereal Company, forerunner of Quaker Oats, was formed in 1888 with Schumacher as its head.

Another major Akron industry which blossomed during the Civil War—although apparently independent of wartime economics—was the match business. The architect of this new enterprise bore the improbable name of Ohio Columbus Barber. In 1857, at the age of sixteen, Barber became a salesman for his father's small break-even match plant in Akron. He was a born huckster and by 1863 he and a friend, John K. Robinson, were running the company. Incorporated in 1867, the Barber Match Company began selling its matches under the name "Diamond," because the matchsticks were cut in diamond shapes. By 1871 the company's 150 employees, truly sweatshop laborers, were turning out two million boxes of matches annually. Within another decade the company controled one-fifth of the country's match output. Barber and Robinson, along with other leaders in the industry, in 1881 put together a gigantic trust, the Diamond Match Company, which, according to historian Karl

LEBANON AND CINCINNATI COACH.
An establishment of this kind for the accomodation of the public, will commence running on Monday, the 1st of April, from LEBANON AND CINCINNATI, in the following manner:
Leave Lebanon every MONDAY, WEDNESDAY, and FRIDAY of each week, at 8 o'clock A. M. arrive in Cincinnati at 4 o'clock on the same days: and
Leave Cincinnati on TUESDAYS, THURSDAYS, and SATURDAYS at 9 o'clock A. M. and arrive in Lebanon at 4 o'clock P. M.
FARE—$1 25.
For seats apply in Lebanon, at the store of the subscriber, and in Cincinnati at Dennisen's Hotel.
This COACH is furnished with safe, substantial horses, and with an attentive, sober and honest driver, stopping at Sharonville for exchange of horses and refreshment.
This line connects at Lebanon with the Dayton and Lancaster lines.
WILLIAM SELLERS.

Above: Before the onslaught of the railroad, coaches were often the means of transportation between cities. The trip to Lebanon, roughly thirty miles from Cincinnati, took seven hours, while the return journey took eight. Courtesy, Cincinnati Historical Society

Top: Shown here are hoppers being used to fill waiting trucks with shipments from train cars in the Pennsylvania Railroad yard at Court and Gilbert streets in Cincinnati. Before the building of Cincinnati's Union Terminal, in the early 1930s, each railroad company had its own station. Courtesy, Cincinnati Historical Society

Grismer, held a "virtual stranglehold in the match industry."

Despite his success, Barber exemplified the most exploitive type of nineteenth-century businessman. He employed large numbers of women and children, worked them long hours, and paid them less than subsistence wages. For eleven hours of daily labor men received $1.21, women seventy-seven cents, and children sixty-six cents. At the same time Buckeye Mower and Reaper was paying its employees $2.27 a day. Moreover, work in a match factory was exceedingly hazardous to the laborer's health. Many workers contracted phosphorous necrosis, a painful, degenerative disease of the jaw caused by the yellow phosphorous used in match making. When the victims were forced to quit their jobs, they got no aid, comfort, or recompense from the company. Of course, Barber was no more callous than other employers in this regard. The age of "welfare capitalism" had not yet arrived.

After the Civil War, railroads figured prominently in the changes overtaking the national economy. Though railroads first appeared in the 1830s and 1840s, construction was limited. A number of technical problems inhibited rapid growth and canals were still thought to be a more dependable means of transport. However, the decade of the 1850s marked a sudden explosion in railroad building. Total railroad mileage throughout the country in 1850 was 9,000, but by 1860 the figure had jumped to 30,000. The Civil War brought new construction to a halt, but in the postwar years railroad building was resumed on an unprecedented scale. The demand for transcontinental lines and the availability of the more durable steel rails prompted a large expansion of the railroad network.

Ohio not only reflected the national growth, it may have even been in the forefront of the railroad revolution. In 1850 it possessed only 300 miles of track, but by 1860 the figure had increased to nearly 3,000. At first it was thought that the railroads would be geared to the canal and river systems as an internal feeder network, but it soon became clear that east-west through lines would control the flow. Four such national systems had appeared by the 1880s: the New York Central, the Erie, the Pennsylvania, and the Baltimore and Ohio. One important internal line was the Columbus and Hocking Valley Railroad, built from the state capital to Athens in 1869-1870. This road opened up the coal resources of the Hocking valley in the southeast which would prove so vital to the steel industry developing in the north.

Cincinnati, bypassed by the major east-west rail lines, turned southward and sought to restore its prewar commercial ties with that region. Construction of the Cincinnati Southern Railroad was begun in

This lithograph commemorated the completion of the Cincinnati Southern Railway and a celebration held at Music Hall in March 1880. Cincinnati, sometimes referred to as the "Gateway to the South," had important business ties to the Southern states before and after the Civil War. Courtesy, Cincinnati Historical Society

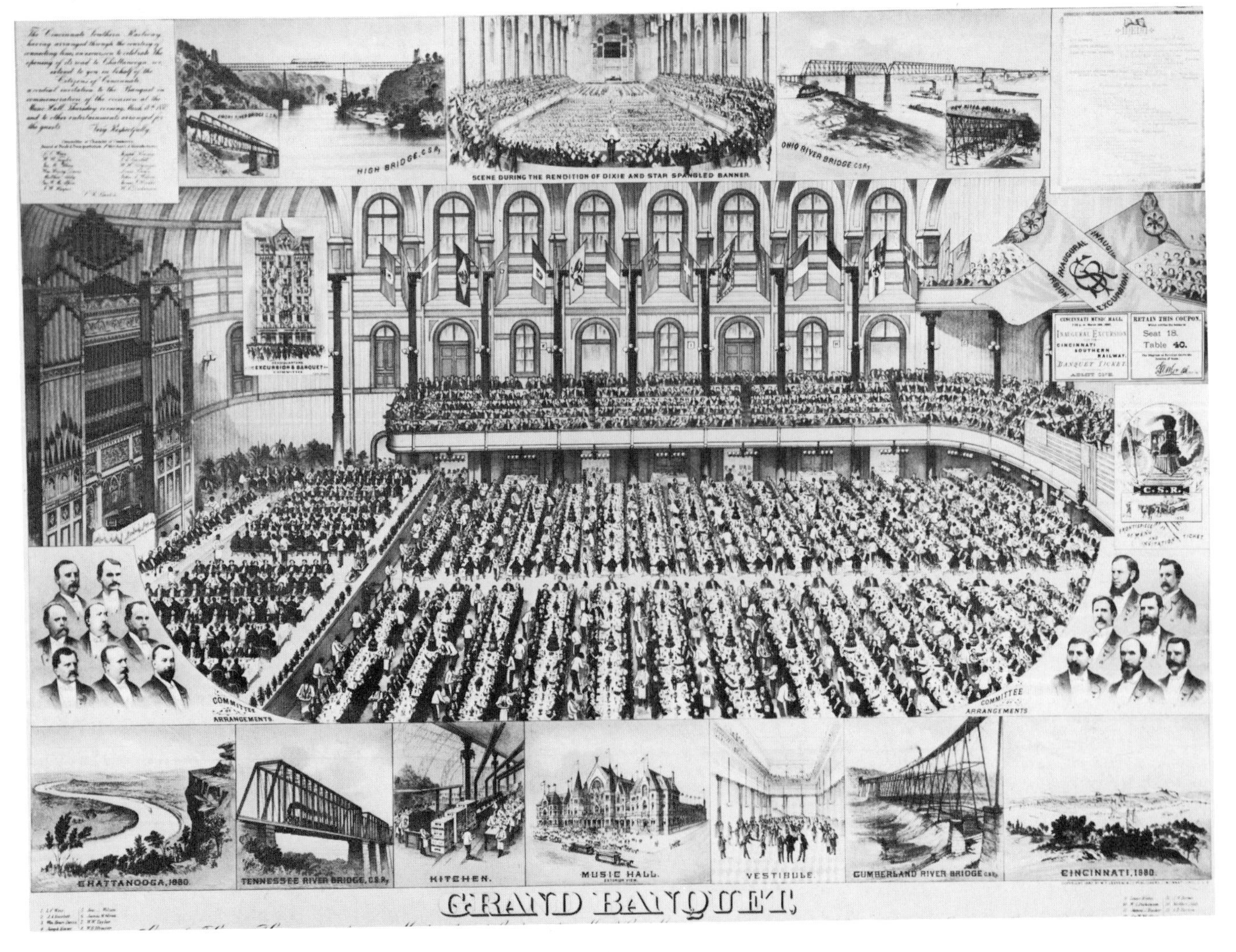

Left: This photograph of Cincinnati was taken in 1865 from the John A. Roebling Suspension Bridge during its construction. Although no fighting took place on her soil, Cincinnati was instrumental in the North's ultimate victory in the Civil War. Cincinnati factories produced a wide variety of goods for the war effort, including shoes, clothing, wagons, harnesses, boats, and guns. Courtesy, Cincinnati Historical Society

Below left: Busy with passenger and commercial riverboat transportation, Cincinnati failed to establish itself as a railroad city in time to keep up with other cities in the state and surrounding areas. Courtesy, Ohio Historical Society

1873 and completed to Chattanooga, Tennessee, 336 miles away, in the next few years. Though the road prospered in both freight and passenger traffic, Cincinnati was partial to river commerce and failed to establish itself as an important railroad city.

Nevertheless, by the 1880s Ohio was crisscrossed by a network of local and interstate rail lines that bound the state more closely together than it had ever been before and integrated it tightly with national markets. The growing pains of the industry, however, troubled Ohio as it did other states. The celebrated abuses of rebates, the "long and short haul" discrimination, free passes to politicians, excessive rates, and the move to monopoly were resented by Ohioans much as they were by western farmers, the chief victims of such practices. Their complaints were by no means satisfied with the passage of the Interstate Commerce Act in 1887, but at least a first step toward ensuring railroad responsibility had been taken.

More visible to the general public than the involutions of rebates, rates, and combinations, were the plethora of railroad accidents, which seemed to occur with frightening frequency. Neither employees, passengers, nor innocent bystanders were spared. Even the introduction of air brakes, automatic couplers, and other safety devices did not slow down the rise in casualty figures. In 1873, 210 deaths and 398 serious injuries resulted from Ohio train accidents. In 1900 more than 500 died from train crashes and the injured list ran to over 7,000. Maimed arms and legs and broken backs were suffered by hundreds of railroad employees caught between or under cars involved in accidents. Probably the worst wreck took place in December 1876 near Ashtabula where a train crashed through a bridge into a gully sixty feet below. Close to 100 passengers were either killed in the fall or in the fire which followed. In addition to human casualties, thousands of cattle, horses, sheep, and pigs

***Right:** As a publicity stunt, the Hocking Valley Railroad staged a wreck on May 30, 1896. Hailed as the "first made to order railway collision," the incident drew spectators to Buckeye Park, twenty-five miles south of Columbus. Several photographs were taken before, during, and after the collision. Courtesy, Ohio Historical Society*

were destroyed by speeding trains.

Closely linked with the rise of railroads and industry was the rise of the city. Ample work forces to man the emerging red brick factories were found in the cities. With businesses located there, cities became the centers for trade, finance, transportation, and government. The rise of urban centers in the last part of the nineteenth century was so spectacular that what little efforts were made to accommodate the mounting multitudes fell far short of what was necessary. Thus while cities mushroomed, the services they supplied for their citizens were grossly inadequate. This was a problem to be faced by the Progressives. But on the emerging industrialists, such matters weighed only lightly. Cities were their playgrounds and production, profits, and power their lodestars.

One can trace the process of the "urban revolution" by an examination of the Ohio scene. The change was most notable in the northeastern part of the state which had been something of a wasteland in the earlier years. True, the canals had given birth to commercial activity in the northeast, but the southern part of the state remained clearly in the ascendant. However, with the rise of the iron and steel industry in the 1870s and 1880s in the Cleveland-Youngstown orbit, a dramatic shift occurred. Cleveland jumped from a population of 17,000 in 1860 to 160,000 in 1880 and more than doubled that figure by 1900 when it reached 381,000, finally passing Cincinnati as the largest city in the state. Meanwhile Toledo, Youngstown, and Akron, which were barely on the map when the Civil War broke out, had moved forward to become the third, sixth, and seventh largest cities in 1900, with populations of 131,000, 44,000, and 42,000, respectively.

Cities of the southeast and southwest, centers of trade and primitive industry in the first half-century of statehood, fell behind the rising metropolitan areas in the north. Springfield became a center for the manufacture of farm equipment while Dayton was a major producer of office machines, but for the most part such historic towns as Marietta, East Liverpool, Steubenville, and Portsmouth grew slowly, if at all, and were overshadowed by the northern cities. Marietta never went above the 16,000 mark in the 200 years after its founding. East Liverpool, still a major pottery producer, grew from 1,600 in 1850 to 5,600 in 1880. Steubenville's figures for those years were 6,000 and 12,000, and Portsmouth's, 4,000 and 11,000. There was growth, but these figures hardly compared with those of Youngstown, Toledo, and Akron. Cincinnati, the most important center of trade and industry in Ohio and the West in 1860, surrendered its position of preeminence to Cleveland, its upstart rival on the shores of Lake Erie.

Ironically, at mid-century there had seemed little likelihood that Cincinnati's grandeur would ever be dimmed. One could hardly have anticipated that the "Queen City" would ever fall behind Cleveland. It should not be inferred from this that Cincinnati had declined as an industrial center in the third quarter of the century. In fact, the city had grown substantially since 1850. By 1880 Cincinnati's industrial plant had practically doubled from thirty years ear-

Above: Located near clay deposits, East Liverpool was one of the country's most important pottery centers. By 1877 pottery making was a major industry, employing thirty-two workers. Pictured here is a construction crew in front of some bottle kilns, few of which remain. Courtesy, Ohio Historical Society

Left: Pictured here are employees of a clay shop in East Liverpool. The pottery industry often employed entire families, including many children under the age of fifteen. Women and children were given menial and routine tasks. Workers endured health hazards such as poor ventilation in buildings, temperature extremes, and overcrowding. Courtesy, Ohio Historical Society

lier. The size of the work force in factories, the value of manufactured goods, and the number of industrial plants were almost twice that in 1880 as in 1850. Through its 3,000 factories spread among 125 different industries, Cincinnati ranked sixth nationally in output and was the most diversified industrial center in the West.

The problem with these promising figures is that the city seemed to be standing still in a period of monumental change. Its major industries were principally the same ones that had marked its rise to supremacy earlier. Cincinnati was still among the national leaders in the manufacture of wagons and carriages, in meat packing and slaughtering, in the number of foundries and machine shops, and in shoes, clothing, and furniture. But these were hardly among the newer heavy industries which were reshaping the national economy. While Cincinnati may have led Cleveland in the number of industrial establishments even after 1900, the value of the goods produced in Cleveland far exceeded that of Cincinnati.

Even in areas where Cincinnati had long been a leader it began to fall behind. Symptomatic of the city's malaise was the pork packing business. Between 1840 and 1860 Cincinnati was the leading pork packing center in the country; it was justifiably called "Porkopolis." In 1840, 1,200 workers in forty-eight packing plants turned out pork and pork products valued at three million dollars. The industry expanded steadily over the next two decades until the annual value of pork and pork products had risen to six million dollars in 1860.

Then something went wrong. Ohio's railroad network which began to take shape in the 1850s did not favor Cincinnati. None of the major trunk lines passed through it. With the construction of the Mad River and Lake Erie line from Springfield to Sandusky, hog farmers in southwestern Ohio began shipping their swine north to the railroad links with eastern markets. It was also more economical to send hogs by rail and they arrived at their destination in better condition than when driven overland to market. Cincinnati merchants and packers failed to recognize the importance of the railroad until new transportation routes and markets had become fixed. The lack of significant growth in the city's economy after the Civil War can be attributed in no small part to its limited railroad structure. Moreover, the corn-growing belt began to shift westward. Corn and hence hogs could now be raised more cheaply in Indiana and Illinois, so hog production in southwestern Ohio declined. This is not to

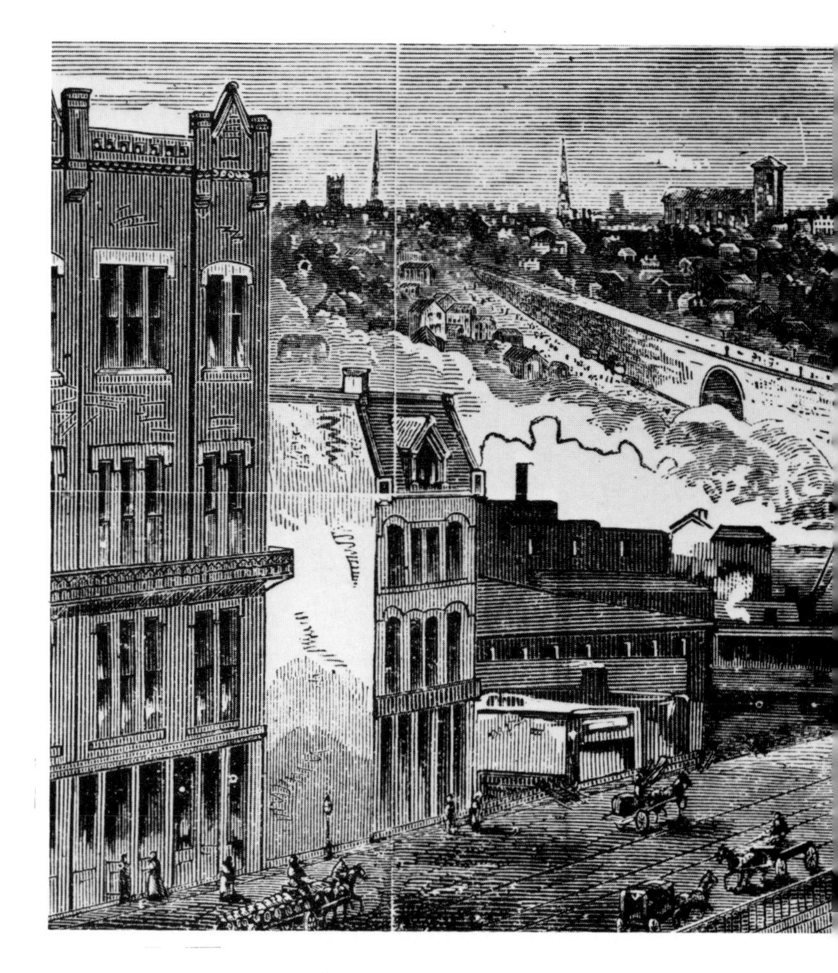

Above: By 1878 in Cleveland's industrial sector, what had once been pastureland was covered with oil refineries and manufacturing plants. An observer pointed out that "blackness, dirt, and decay were visible everywhere." Courtesy, Ohio Historical Society

Right: The first electric trolley car line, owned by the East Cleveland Railway Company, opened in 1884. Citizens of the day expressed concern over the safety of these electrically operated cars. This streetcar traveled along Euclid Avenue in Cleveland, which at one time was home to the city's wealthiest residents. Courtesy, Cleveland Public Library

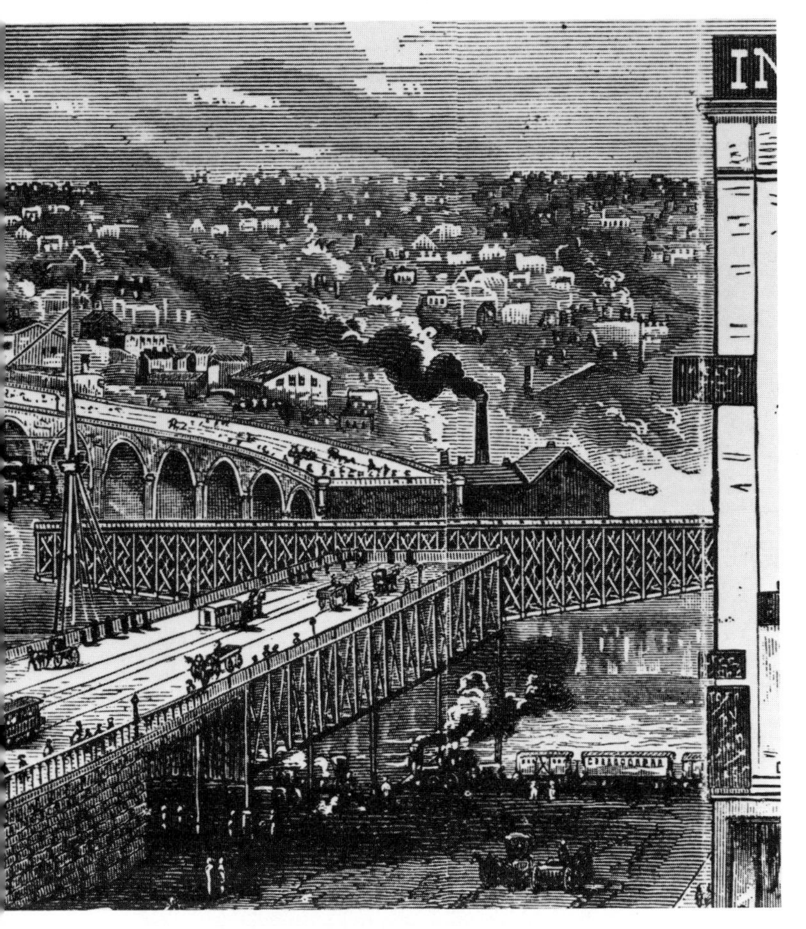

Above: Some of the city's most wealthy and famous residents lived in the grand mansions on "Millionaires' Row" along Cleveland's Euclid Avenue. Some of the residents were Tom L. Johnson; William Chisholm, president of Cleveland Rolling Mill; Sylvester Everett, whose brownstone mansion was said to be the most expensive home erected in Cleveland; nineteenth-century author and Secretary of State John Hay; Amasa Stone; and John D. Rockefeller. Courtesy, Western Reserve Historical Society

say that hog production in Ohio died out. It continued to thrive throughout the state, but no longer did it occupy its once paramount place in the economy. Cincinnati had given way to Chicago as the nation's number-one packing center.

While Cincinnati was experiencing economic problems, Cleveland was being transformed into a major industrial city. Cleveland's rapid rush to a position of leadership in industrial America was due largely to the accident of location. Its prospects had not been bright in the early days. There was even a dispute with Newburg over which town should be the Cuyahoga County seat. But then came the canals, then the railroads, then the iron ore, and then John D. Rockefeller. Rockefeller was not the only great industrialist spawned by the Lake City, but he was the most imaginative one during the oil boom. Then there were the daring entrepreneurs of the steel industry, who sensed that Cleveland could become the happy meeting point for the rich iron ore of upper Minnesota and the plentiful fuel sources of eastern Ohio and western Pennsylvania. Oil and steel, the catalysts of change, elevated Cleve-

land to the industrial forefront.

What was Cleveland like before industry took over? Having only a population of 6,000 in 1840, it was simply a pleasant country village. The center of town was Public Square, which had been set aside by the founding fathers. Whitewashed rail fences marked off the four sections of the square, which were bisected by Superior Street running east-west and Ontario Street running north-south. The business section extended east for several blocks along Superior and then disappeared into the countryside. West of Public Square, the "Flats" along the

Above: This farm scene was common throughout the Ohio countryside in the 1930s. Courtesy, Ohio Historical Society

Top: Cleveland's Tom Loftin Johnson, steel manufacturer and street railway magnate, served as a congressman and then as mayor of Cleveland for eight years. In 1903 he ran an unsuccessful campaign as Democratic candidate for governor. A tribute to him on his statue in Cleveland's Public Square reads: "He found us leaderless and blind. He left a city with a civic mind." Courtesy, Ohio Historical Society

Cuyahoga River, which separated Cleveland from Ohio City on the west bank, were acquiring a busy air. Foundries, soap factories, breweries, and carriage works were a portent of things to come. Canal traffic emptied at the foot of West Superior. Still, Cleveland was only the "capital" of the Western Reserve, the center of a dairy and farming community which gave little thought to an industrial future. Though benefiting from the canal and lake trade, Cleveland had no railroads to speak of and was content being the commercial center of the region.

Yet in thirty years the city was unrecognizable to returning visitors. The tremendous population increase, accompanied by the appearance of a dozen railroads, innumerable steel plants, oil refineries, and sundry other industrial facilities, had totally transformed Cleveland. Smoke and soot clouded the air while shanties and hovels cluttered the ground. The business center had spread out along the main thoroughfares east, southeast, and

Left: By the end of the nineteenth century, Ohio no longer led the nation in agricultural production, but farming was still an important ingredient in the lives of Ohioans. Pictured here is a group of men, women, and children threshing grain in Guernsey County. Courtesy, Ohio Historical Society

Below: By the end of the nineteenth century, Ohio led the nation in the manufacture of farm machinery with products such as mowers, reapers, steel plows, cultivators, and binders. The Champion Company of Springfield, producer of this thresher, became the foremost manufacturer of farm equipment. Courtesy, Ohio Historical Society

By the end of the Civil War and throughout the rest of the nineteenth century, agriculture was Ohio's most important industry. This 1860 diploma from the Ohio Board of Agriculture shows the emphasis placed on agriculture. Courtesy, Ohio Historical Society

west. The view of the "Flats," in the opinion of one observer,

> *though far from beautiful, is a very interesting one. There are copper smelting, iron rolling, and iron manufacturing works, lumber yards, paper mills, breweries, flour mills, nail works, pork packing establishments, and the multitudinous industries of a great manufacturing city . . .*

In contrast to the dirt and congestion of downtown, Euclid Avenue had become "Millionaire's Row," the setting for the city's industrial elite. Amasa Stone, Samuel Andrews, John D. Rockefeller, and Tom L. Johnson, among others, occupied regal mansions on spacious grounds, carefully concealed from the curious proletariat by nicely groomed shrubbery and trees. By the end of the century Cleveland's position as a major industrial center was established.

With the rise of industrial cities such as Cleveland came the demise of agriculture. Though farming still dominated Ohio's economy in 1880, its advantage was lessening. Leading all states in 1850, Ohio dropped to a secondary position in the next twenty years, as the farm belt became firmly fixed in the Great Plains. Agricultural output did increase over the years, but in comparison with industrial production, it fell badly behind.

The post-Civil War years were generally difficult ones for agriculture. Probably the worst farm depression in the nation's history—to that time—struck in the 1880s and 1890s, when prices dropped steadily. The most badly afflicted areas were the Great Plains, particularly the states of Kansas and Nebraska. Exorbitant railroad rates, usurious interest charges, and unfavorable weather had placed the plains farmers in desperate straits. It was during those days, the story goes, that Minnesota farmers found that it was more economical to burn their wheat for fuel rather than ship it to market by rail. The agricultural nightmare gave birth to the Populist Movement, which exercised a significant political influence in the 1890s.

While Ohio suffered from the general decline in farm prices in the late nineteenth century, the problem never achieved the crisis proportions of the western states. For example, Ohio wheat production maintained a fairly stable level during the 1880s and 1890s, although the price per bushel went down continuously. In 1894, the worst year of the depression but a banner year for wheat production —fifty-one million bushels were harvested—farmers got only fifty-one cents per bushel. The other staple for Ohio agriculture, corn, remained at high levels of production throughout most of the period, although the early 1890s were poor years.

Railroads, the principal reason for the westward shift of the farm country, also broke down the regionalism of Ohio farming. No longer was corn produced only in the southwest, wheat in the "backbone," and dairy products in the Reserve. While those regions still led in their specialties, farmers had learned that it was far wiser to diversify their crops. Railroads had overcome the isolation of rural sections and opened up all parts of the state to broader markets. Diversification rather than specialization marked the new age.

Other signs of agricultural change in the post-Civil War era were the advent of new farm machinery, selective breeding of livestock, and the advancement of education. The last point was symbolized by the founding of Ohio State University in 1870 for the purpose, among other things, of promoting agricultural education. Although dirt farmers were slow to accept new academic theories about agriculture, the importance of education finally came across.

In one obvious way the dawning Industrial Revolution proved a boon to agriculture. The manufacture of agricultural equipment and machinery became big business and was instrumental in bringing about more economical and efficient farming practices in the latter half of the nineteenth century. But farming as a way of life had given way to urbanism. No longer was the "sturdy yeoman" of Jefferson's time the bulwark of American society. The great entrepreneurs—the Rockefellers, the Carnegies, and the Morgans—had supplanted the rugged, democratic, independent tiller of the soil as the shaper of the country's future.

With the Civil War over, no distractions barred Ohio's full industrial development. All of the factors essential to a massive leap forward were present. The stage was set. Ohio would figure prominently in the momentous period of economic growth which lay ahead.

IV
STEEL AND OIL

These complex machines were used by the American Steel & Wire Company in the 1930s. This Cleveland firm later became a subsidiary of U.S. Steel. Courtesy, Ohio Historical Society

Facing page: In 1880 Otis Iron Steel Company was the first firm in America organized to produce acid open-hearth steel. Later, the company dropped "Iron" from its name. Pictured is one of the steps in steelmaking, as the finished heat of steel is tapped from the open hearth into a ladle. Courtesy, Cleveland Public Library

The most spectacular event in American history in the last part of the nineteenth century was the Industrial Revolution. An industrial pygmy prior to the Civil War when compared to a number of European countries, the United States advanced so rapidly within the next four decades that by the turn of the century its works dwarfed the accomplishments of all other nations. The Industrial Revolution gave employment to millions of workers, native and foreign born, immeasurably raised the country's standard of living, provided the people with undreamed of conveniences and luxuries, and generated a galaxy of hard-nosed businessmen who would dominate the nation's economic and political life for the next generation and beyond.

What made the United States such "fertile ground" for this revolution? Six factors explain the phenomenon. Several of them may have existed in Europe, but nowhere did all of them prevail, and in such abundance, as in America. "Fertile ground" was certainly one of them. The nation's richness in natural resources—coal, iron, timber, petroleum, and waterpower—was unparalleled. A supply of cheap labor was also a necessity. This was available from the hordes of immigrants pouring into the Atlantic ports. In addition, native inventiveness was needed to solve technical and engineering problems. Yankee ingenuity met this need.

But resources, labor, and creativity were not sufficient in themselves. Imaginative and, yes, ruthless men were required to mobilize the basic ingredients, organize them, push them forward. "Captains of Industry," "Robber Barons," "Great Entrepreneurs," call them what you will, rose to fame and power as they manipulated the

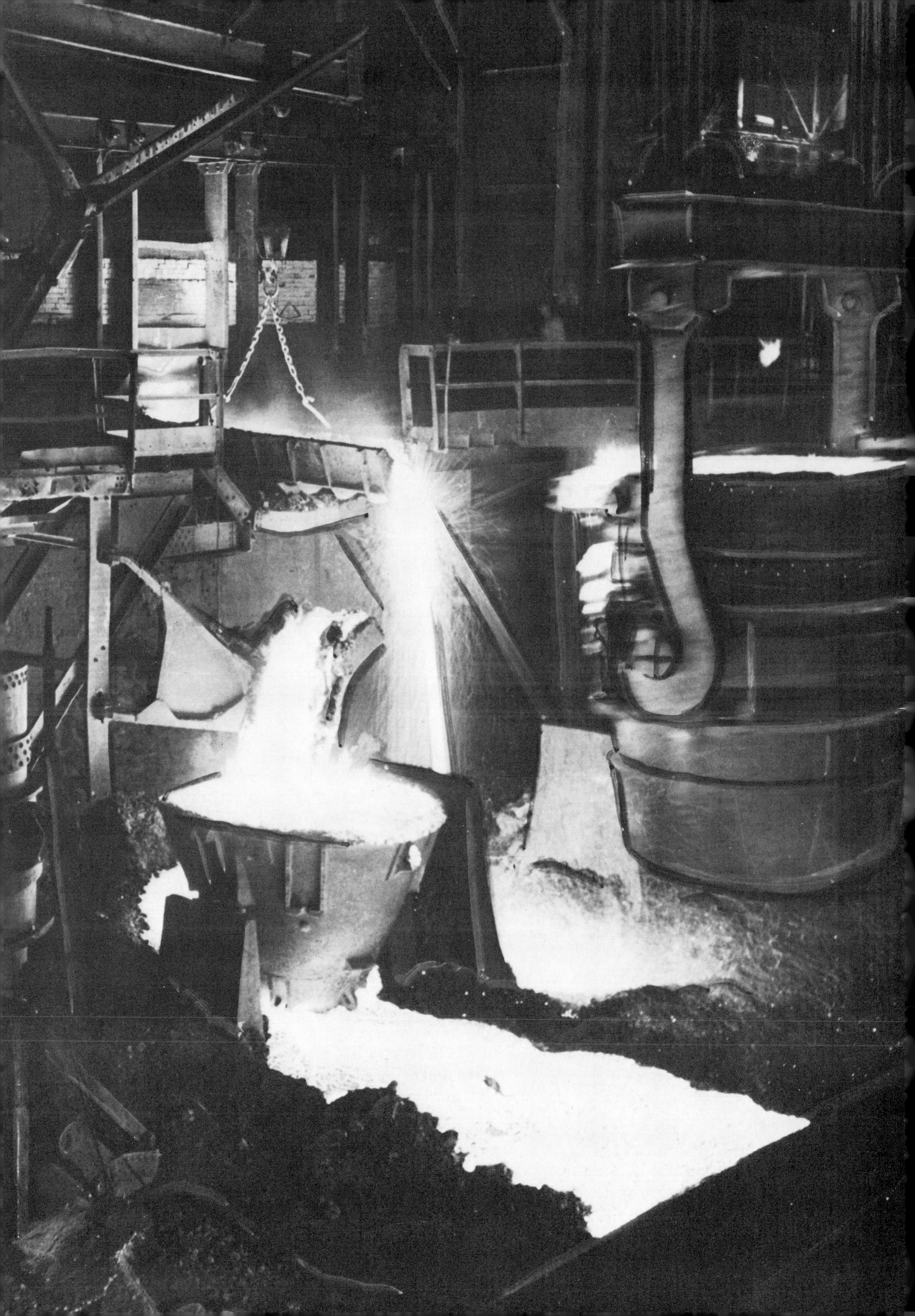

Datus and Irad Kelley made their island, located north of Sandusky in Lake Erie, a thriving community. Kelley's Island became known for its vineyards, peach orchards, red cedar, and a stone quarry, as seen in this picture. Mark Twain also helped immortalize the island when he wrote, "You can't fool me with Kelley Island wine; I can tell it from vinegar everytime—by the label on the bottle." Courtesy, Western Reserve Historical Society

new machinery into high gear. Buyers of the many goods and services were also necessary. Railroads had knit the country from coast to coast, nationalizing markets and tremendously expanding production figures in the process. Finally, the American government was very supportive of industrial growth. Through protective tariffs, railroad land grants, and other favors, industry benefited handsomely at the hands of government.

These six factors forged the Industrial Revolution, and Ohio was blessed with all of them. It had the resources, the labor, the inventors, the entrepreneurs, the markets, and the federal favors. The state was rich in coal, iron, oil, natural gas, and timber. (Actually, much of the iron and oil came from elsewhere, but they were drawn to Ohio.) Among the great inventors were Charles Brush, Thomas Edison, and Charles Kettering. John D. Rockefeller, Marcus A. Hanna, and Harvey Firestone exemplified the entrepreneurs.

Ohio's population figures nearly doubled between 1880 and 1920. A good bulk of the growth was due to immigration from southern and eastern Europe. Whereas prior to 1890 immigrants to the United States were drawn largely from northwestern Europe—Germany, Great Britain, and Scandinavia—from 1890 to 1920 most came from Italy, Greece, Hungary, Bohemia, Poland, and Russia. This was the "new immigration." Because these people arrived without funds, could not speak English, and formed ethnic communities in the large cities, they caused a backlash of nativist opposition leading to the restrictive immigration legislation of the 1920s. Yet these factors made the "new immigrants" an ideal labor source for the burgeoning industries. They could be paid subsistence wages and dismissed if they caused trouble. Most of the immigrants gravitated to the industrial centers. Jobs were available there despite the exploitation, and the newcomers found security among their fellow countrymen who had preceded them.

Cleveland is the best example of the immigrant impact on Ohio. In 1900 it passed Cincinnati to become the largest city in the state. By 1910 its population exceeded the half-million mark and by 1920 reached 796,841, making it one of the largest cities in the country. Because of the city's heavy industry and its easy access to Atlantic ports, large numbers of new immigrants began arriving in the city in the 1880s and 1890s. In 1890, 97,000 of the city's 261,000 people were foreign-born, while another 98,600 were native-born of foreign or mixed parentage. This constituted 75 percent of the total population. This percentage remained constant for the next three decades, although the city's population more than trebled in that time. In the 1905 municipal election, men of forty-four nationalities voted and 36 percent of the electors voting were born in Europe. The only ethnic groups one historian could not find in Cleveland at that time were Australian Bushmen, Hottentots, and Eskimos.

By no means did all new immigrants settle in Cleveland. Youngstown's percentage figures were almost as high for that forty-year period, from 1880-1920. The peak was in 1890, when 70 percent of the city's population of 33,220 was foreign-born and native-born of foreign or mixed parentage. By 1920 the proportion had dropped to 60 percent while its population had increased to 100,000. Toledo and Akron also had large immigrant

Above: Ohio inventor Powell Crosley, Jr., stands in his first WLW studio in 1922. Called "the Ford of the radio business," Crosley not only manufactured radios but experimented with the development of airplanes, invented a four-cylinder auto engine capable of getting thirty-five to fifty miles per gallon, and designed a refrigerator called the "Shelvador" which featured shelves for storage in the door. Courtesy, Cincinnati Historical Society

Above left: Charles F. Brush, 1849-1929, brought electric lights to American streets. In 1879 he demonstrated the use of arc lights for street illumination in Cleveland, his hometown. Courtesy, Ohio Historical Society

Left: Despite his poor eyesight, Charles F. Kettering became an inventor and important figure in the automobile industry. He invented the electric starter for automobiles, introduced ethyl gasoline and quick-drying lacquer finish for auto bodies, and made improvements in the diesel engine. Courtesy, Ohio Historical Society

Above: Thomas Alva Edison, born in Milan, Ohio, in 1847, is foremost among Ohio-born inventors. Although he lived and worked outside the state most of his life, Ohio still claims him as one of her own. Courtesy, Ohio Historical Society

populations. Cincinnati, however, showed a reverse trend. While its population rose only from 255,000 to 401,000 from 1880 to 1920, its immigrant element dropped sharply from 71 percent to 41 percent. Cincinnati remained an important city, but its relative economic influence declined over those years, a point seemingly supported by the immigration statistics. The centers of heavy industry in the northern half of the state were home for the majority of Ohio's new immigrants.

But the growth of large cities was not entirely due to foreign immigration. The latter third of the nineteenth century was marked by a steady influx of young men and women from the countryside. To them, the lure of the city proved irresistible. Its conveniences, its educational and cultural opportunities, its excitement, and, above all, its job prospects, attracted young people in ever-growing numbers. Ohio clearly reflected this national trend. While remaining one of the nation's important agricultural states well into the twentieth century, its rural areas showed little, if any, population increase. Boryczka and Cary observe: "Rural Ohioans outnumbered other Buckeyes for the last time in 1900; indeed, the rural population barely grew at all between 1880 and 1890 and thereafter declined steadily."

By 1920, drawing from both native and foreign sources, Ohio could boast seven cities with more than 100,000 population and a few others approaching that figure.

Ohio, perhaps better than any other state except Pennsylvania, epitomized the flowering of the Industrial Revolution. While the romance of iron, steel, and oil occupied centerstage in the unfolding drama, other industries flourished as well. The manufacture of agricultural machinery and equipment,

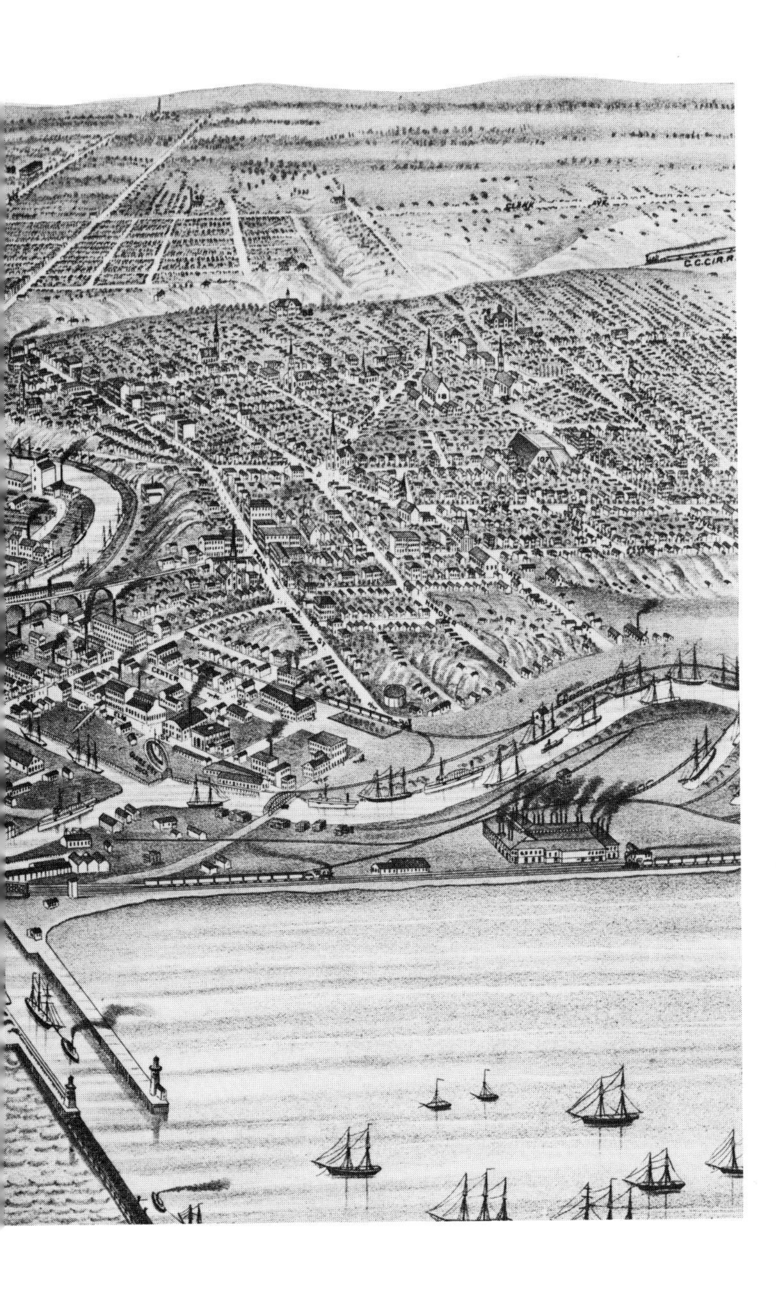

Above: This bird's-eye view of Cleveland in 1877 reveals a bustling riverfront city. Courtesy, Western Reserve Historical Society

Left: Henry A. Schauffler was a pioneer in missionary work among "Bohemians," or Czechs, living in Cleveland. These immigrants settled on Hamm Avenue in the 1880s. Schauffler's schools were mainly to train religious workers, and in 1883 he founded Bethlehem Church to be used exclusively for Slavic mission work. Courtesy, Western Reserve Historical Society

glass and timber products, and office machinery, and the rise of the machine tool, rubber, and automobile industries, only suggest the scope of industrial activity in Ohio. By 1891, when industrialism was gathering momentum, capital investment in Ohio industry amounted to $185 million, while the total value of the products from the more than 12,000 factories was $259 million. These figures multiplied in the decades ahead.

The steel industry was the common denominator for the Industrial Revolution. It was central to all that followed. First, it supplied the strong durable rails so urgently needed for the expanding post-Civil War railroad network. The transcontinental lines linked the East and Midwest with the Far West, and nationalized markets. Prior to the Civil War it was difficult to market one's goods beyond the local setting, unless a river or canal was nearby. Even then, river and canal commerce was slow. Railroads made it possible to sell goods anywhere in the country, quickly and easily. Moreover, steel made possible the manufacture of all kinds of machines, implements, vehicles, buildings, and appliances for commercial and home use. The pace of business and the standard of living improved sharply because of the steel industry.

Steel manufacturing prior to the Civil War was a difficult and costly process, and simply impractical as far as large-scale industrial use was concerned. The knowledge of how to produce steel—by removing impurities from iron—was available, but the technique for doing it was not. The big breakthrough occurred in the mid-1850s when two men, one an Englishman, Henry Bessemer, the other an American, William Kelly, independently invented a relatively easy method of extracting silicon and carbon from iron. Bessemer in 1855 devised a converter into which the molten iron was poured. A violent blast of cold air at the base of Bessemer's converter caused a tremendous fire and minor explosion, which forced out the carbon and silicon. When the converter was tipped, liquid steel ran into the molds. Although Kelly had developed the same method, Bessemer received most of the credit for devising the new process.

But the Bessemer converter was slow to catch on. The first experiments with it failed because, as it turned out, the wrong kind of iron ore was used. Only ore with less than .05 percent phosphorous was suitable for the converter, otherwise the phosphorous spoiled the steel. Lawsuits over patent

Above: This picture shows children playing near Hiram House, Ohio's first social settlement for immigrants. George A. Bellamy, who began the settlement, hoped to encourage good citizenship and improve community welfare. Bellamy was the first to begin Americanization classes in Cleveland. Courtesy, Western Reserve Historical Society

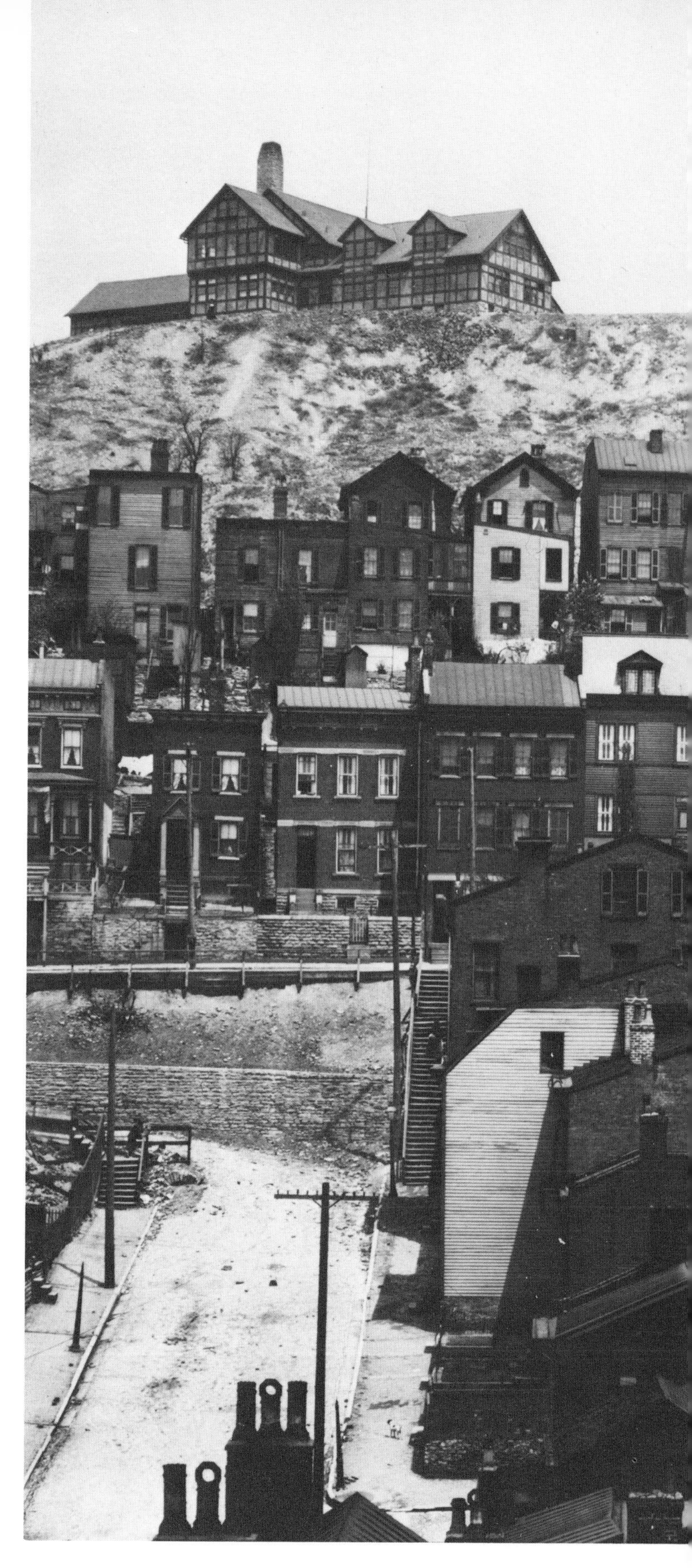

Right: Cincinnati had five inclines which provided cheap and convenient transportation from the downtown basin to the hilltops. The Mt. Adams incline, pictured here, was built in 1876 and continued to operate until 1948. At the top of the hill and to the left of the station stood the Highland House, a popular restaurant and beer garden. Courtesy, Cincinnati Historical Society

STERLING GLASS

Above: It took a lot of hard work to build the railroads across the state of Ohio. The Cleveland Daily True Democrat *wrote about the work that was done on the line between Cleveland and Columbus. "Not far from this city may be seen, and could have been during all the past winter, a solitary man, with pickaxe and spade, digging into the bowels of the earth. Every now and then he would raise his eyes to the task before him and groan in agony." Courtesy, Western Reserve Historical Society*

Above right: The first local railroad ad in a Cleveland newspaper appeared in the Plain Dealer *on June 29, 1850. It advertised the Cleveland, Columbus, Cincinnati Railroad which traveled as far south as Wellington at twenty m.p.h. In 1865 six railroad lines operated daily in and out of Cleveland and by the 1880s, when this photo of the Cleveland and Pittsburgh Railroad was taken, Cleveland was serviced by eleven railroads. Courtesy, Western Reserve Historical Society*

rights further delayed full-scale trials of the process. By the late 1860s these problems had been resolved and the first Bessemer plant in the United States was constructed by the Pennsylvania Steel Company, a subsidiary of the Pennsylvania Railroad. Far more significant was the founding by Andrew Carnegie, America's foremost "ironmaster," of the Edgar Thomson Company outside Pittsburgh in 1873. This marked the first major use of the Bessemer-Kelly method, which would become widely adopted by the end of the century. Carnegie dominated the steel industry for a generation. His company and its subsidiaries were worth more than $400 million at the time he sold out to the newly formed United States Steel Corporation in 1901.

Meanwhile, another steel-making method, the "open hearth" process, had found favor with many manufacturers. The open hearth furnaces took much longer to make a batch of steel than the Bessemer-Kelly method—eight to ten hours compared to fifteen to twenty minutes—but their capacity was much greater. In addition, the extended length of time permitted workmen to regularly test the mix and make any adjustments needed to attain a better quality of steel. This constant checking could not be done under the Bessemer-Kelly process. Whereas the latter remained the most common means of manufacturing steel throughout the nineteenth century, it gradually gave way to the open hearth method in the twentieth.

Ohio moved into the Bessemer age a few years before Carnegie, but not on as large a scale. In 1868 the Cleveland Rolling Mill Company at Newburg installed two six-ton converters. Its main product initially was steel rails, but it expanded the inventory to include wire, screws, and agricultural equipment. Later, an open hearth furnace was installed and the company was absorbed by the American Steel and Wire Company. Bessemer converters were also placed in the Otis Steel Company of Cleveland, the Bellaire Nail Works, and the Mingo Junction works of the Laughlin and Junction Steel Company in the 1880s. Republic Iron and Steel at Youngstown adopted the system in 1901. But by then, the open hearth process had gained adherents. Burgess Steel and Iron in 1871 was the first to install the new system, followed by Otis in 1875. Canton and Portsmouth firms adopted the method in 1880 and by 1905 at least a dozen open hearth furnaces were operating in Ohio.

Coincidental with the development of improved ways of manufacturing steel came the discovery of vast new iron ore deposits in northern Michigan and Minnesota. Whereas Ohioans had played no role in developing the Bessemer-Kelly and open hearth processes, they had a great deal to do with the finding of the untapped lodes in the north country. These Ohioans were mostly Clevelanders involved in Great Lakes shipping, eager to improve their commercial prospects. Lake Superior iron ore made Cleveland, Youngstown, and Pittsburgh the greatest steel domain in the world.

The first news of important mineral reserves around Lake Superior reached Cleveland in the 1840s. The famous local geologist Charles Whittlesey published several papers based on his findings which greatly intensified interest on the subject, particularly in Cleveland. Fifty-two tons of copper ore arrived in Cleveland from the Upper Peninsula in the summer of 1848. Cleveland developers unearthed several million dollars worth of ore containing silver and copper by the mid-1850s. However, the discovery of vast lodes or iron ore directed attention away from silver and copper.

Pictured here is the Van Dorn Iron Works in Cleveland, which manufactured products varying from garden furniture to jail cells. Van Dorn also made ornamental ironwork, streetcar vestibules, bicycle parts, and metal office furniture. Courtesy, Western Reserve Historical Society

The first major iron range was developed at Marquette, Michigan. Clevelanders were soon on the scene. The Cleveland Iron Company, formed in 1849 and reorganized as the Cleveland Iron Mining Company in 1853, played the most important role in the early days. Samuel L. Mather and W.J. Gordon, prominent Cleveland businessmen, were the principal organizers of the company. They built forges on the shores of Lake Superior, cast the iron into ingots and blooms, and shipped them back to Cleveland. Very soon, however, it was found more economical to send the ore directly to Cleveland and let blast furnaces there make the pig iron and derivative products. This decision was abetted by the construction of a canal at Sault Sainte Marie in 1855, making it possible for larger ships to travel from Lake Superior to Lake Erie.

As more mines were opened, more mining and

shipping companies appeared. An important new mine was opened at Menominee, Michigan, in 1870, but by far the richest and most productive lodes were those at Gogebic (opened in 1884) and in Minnesota at Vermilion (1884) and Mesabi (1892). As the ore poured forth in ever-increasing volume, bigger ships were needed to carry the cargoes. The locks at the "Soo" and adjacent rivers were deepened and widened to accommodate the heavier flow. The Cleveland Iron Mining Company, as it expanded its holdings, added steadily to its fleet of ships—from wood to iron to steel—and later, as the Cleveland-Cliffs Company, became the foremost organization in Great Lakes shipping. Mark Hanna, after marrying into the Daniel Rhodes family, which was rich from a prosperous Cleveland coal and iron business, soon took over the company, expanded its operations, and became another Great Lakes shipping magnate. Samuel Mather and Colonel James Pickands formed the Pickands Mather Company in 1883 to exploit the new mines to be opened at

Below right: After 1880 iron works along Lake Erie shifted from the production of steam boilers and machinery for wooden vessels to the construction of iron- and steel-hulled ships. This ship under construction belongs to the Cleveland Shipbuilding Company, which in 1897 began to build the largest dry docks on the Great Lakes at Lorain, Ohio. Courtesy, Western Reserve Historical Society

Below: Cleveland's position as a port on the Great Lakes, its service by trunk line railroads, and its nearness to coal, limestone, and oil deposits had much to do with the city's emergence as Ohio's premier manufacturing city. Today, Greater Cleveland extends 100 miles along the shore of Lake Erie and more than forty miles inland. Pictured here is a ship being loaded on the Cuyahoga River before heading out on the Great Lakes. Courtesy, Western Reserve Historical Society

Gogebic. Pickands Mather also developed its own fleet of lake ships, a subsidiary known as the Interlake Steamship Company. Most of these ships were built by the American Shipbuilding Company of Cleveland, one of the largest firms in the country.

Greater Cleveland's rise to industrial supremacy was due to its location. The city's growing importance as a commercial center and lake port had resulted from the coming of the canal, followed swiftly by the railroad in the 1850s and 1860s. Now it was a major entrepot for Lake Superior iron ore. Pittsburgh, 130 miles to the southeast, had become the nation's number-one steel manufacturing center as a result of Andrew Carnegie, who secured his ore from regional and eastern sources and his coke fuel from the Connellsville area. Youngstown, too, midway between Cleveland and Pittsburgh, had a long history of iron production although its local sources had been depleted. It is no mystery, then, that a natural iron and steel nexus was formed along the Cleveland-Youngstown-Pittsburgh line. Jones and Laughlin, Republic Steel, and Youngstown Sheet and Tube were only the best known of the major steel companies established on the Ohio-Pennsylvania frontier.

An important advance in steel production was the introduction of, first, coal, and then coke for fuel. Charcoal had been the principal fuel in the glory days of Hanging Rock, but its relative inefficiency and total dependence on timber stands, which were vanishing, necessitated a substitute. Coal was burned in eastern iron mills in the 1830s and its use spread west of the mountains with the discovery of coal reserves in western Pennsylvania and eastern Ohio. It was found that coke, derived from coal, provided a better fuel for smelting iron. After the Civil War, coke came into favor throughout most of the iron and steel industry. Early in the twentieth century Ohio had established itself as the second state in the country, next to Pennsylvania, in both iron and steel production. One authority on the subject, Bert S. Stephenson, writing of the Ohio scene in 1905, observed that Cincinnati was

> *. . . a maker of machine tools and heavy machinery. Columbus became famous for its malleable castings, its car couplers, chains, mining and hoisting machinery. Dayton and Columbus developed large car building plants, turning in later years to the manufacture of the all-steel car. Youngstown and the Mahoning Valley built up immense works for the production of*

Above: A worker at Youngstown Sheet and Tube directs the pouring of molten iron into an open hearth furnace. Youngstown has been called the "prototypical industrial city" because it was dependent upon steel production for its existence. Courtesy, Ohio Historical Society

Top: The Jones and Laughlin Steel Corporation merged with Otis Steel in 1942, thus uniting America's two oldest steel companies. Pictured is the entry end of an eighty-four-inch tandem temper mill at the Cleveland Works of Jones and Laughlin. This highly mechanized machine was used to facilitate production. Courtesy, Cleveland Public Library

Above: Among Cleveland's fifteen ranked manufacturing plants in the 1880s was the Bowler Foundry, pictured here. Courtesy, Western Reserve Historical Society

Right: This photo, taken underground in a Hocking Valley Coal Mine, is possibly the first "flashlight" photograph of a mine. Mining in this coal-rich area was dangerous work. Miners toiled in gloomy environments, rarely seeing the sun because of their work schedules. In 1873 more than 250 Ohio miners were killed, and 750 suffered injuries in mining accidents. Courtesy, Ohio Historical Society

sheets, plates, and steel rails and a string of prosperous establishments for the working of steel into finished and semi-finished forms eventually stretched along the Ohio River. Almost every city of size now has its important iron, steel or manufacturing works, and Ohio products in these lines have won for themselves more than a nation-wide reputation.

The impact of iron and steel on Cleveland is reflected in city directories for the boom years of the late nineteenth century. On the eve of the Civil War only a handful of companies were connected with the industry, which employed well under a thousand workmen. It was quite different in the 1890s, as Harlan Hatcher reports:

Above: Railroads facilitated the movement of goods across the state. Buckeye Coal depended on trains to ship coal to its customers. Coal was moved along on the conveyor to the building where it was loaded into waiting train cars. Courtesy, Ohio Historical Society

Left: Mining companies built communities for workers because coal mines were often located in remote areas. Unfortunately, these houses, only meant to provide temporary shelter, were usually built rapidly and poorly and soon deteriorated into shanties. Courtesy, Ohio Historical Society

The list covered pages. There were 462 establishments, a heavy percentage of which were working with iron and steel. The Cleveland Rolling Mills employed 5,000; American Wire Company, 463; Ohio Steel Works, 623; Globe Iron Works and Shipyard, 543; Cleveland Malleable Iron Company, 550; Union Rolling Mill, 335; the Central Blast Furnace and the Riverside Blast Furnace, 323—to mention samples of the transformation wrought in these few years. By 1910 . . . there were 14 large iron and steel works and rolling mills, and 231 foundries and machine shops in the city doing $76,000,000 worth of business annually. Cleveland had become the first ranking industrial city in Ohio.

* * *

The oil industry began at the same time as the steel industry and almost at the same place. Western Pennsylvania was the birthplace of both and nearby Ohio cashed in on the fruits of both. For years prior to the Civil War, rivers and creeks in the region of Titusville, eighty miles north of Pittsburgh, had been exuding a greasy, scummy substance, which local farmers skimmed from the surface of the water and used as both a medicine and lubricant. At length an enterprising man named George H. Bissell decided to learn if this "petroleum" possessed commercial value. He sent a sample of the stuff to the celebrated Yale chemist Benjamin Silliman. In 1855—the very same year of Bessemer's patent—Silliman published a paper in which he said that

Above: The Cleveland Rolling Mill, a family business started by Henry Chisholm, was incorporated in 1863. Manned by Welsh, Irish, and Scottish workers, the company paid inside men and rollers between $3.50 and $7 a day and laborers $1.65 a day. William Chisholm took over as president after his father's death on May 9, 1881. Courtesy, Western Reserve Historical Society

Right: This picture shows trains being assembled at the Lima Locomotive Works. The company, originally called the Lima Machine Works, turned out its first three locomotives in 1879 and in 1893 exhibited its 450th locomotive at the World's Columbian Exposition. Courtesy, Ohio Historical Society

petroleum would make an excellent illuminant, and that a number of valuable byproducts, such as naphtha, kerosene, paraffin, and lubricating oil, could be recovered from it. Encouraged by this report, Bissell raised the necessary funds and hired an engineer, Edwin L. Drake, to sink the first well at Titusville. It was August 1859 and the oil industry was born.

In contrast with steel, the oil industry had no mass market. Gasoline automobiles would not appear in significant numbers for another half-century. In spite of that, however, oil boomed. Following Drake's successful gusher, there was a "gold rush" descent on the oil country. Visions of instant wealth flashed through the minds of hundreds drilling for oil around Oil City, Titusville, and their environs. Fortunes were made, lost, and remade almost overnight. Crossroad villages mushroomed into crowded, boisterous, money-mad centers of wealth, with gambling, drinking, and other kinds of dens. As quickly as they had risen, many such places died out as the oil dried up. Lucky farmers on whose property gushers were struck became rich beyond their dreams if they went into the oil business. The conservative ones no doubt regretted having sold out to budding entrepreneurs.

In Trumbull County the crossroads village of Mecca struck oil in 1860 not long after engineer Drake had begun the business. The word quickly got out—"Thar's oil in Meccy!" Within several months 700 wells had been drilled and the town was booming. Three post offices were required to handle the mail. The boardinghouses, hotels, saloons, and gambling halls echoed with talk of quick wealth. The overflow of speculators and prospectors filled the hotels of nearby Warren. Alas, it was only for a moment. The oil simply was not there. The boom ended and most everyone left. A few houses were moved to Warren, while others were abandoned to the elements.

The domain of oil rapidly spread to southeastern Ohio and panhandle West Virginia. Within a dozen years the 4,000-square-mile tri-state area dominated the industry. By 1872 forty million barrels had been pumped from the wells there and oil had become a major product in the national economy—number four on the list of exports. Because of the oil fever in Marietta, during Civil War years local papers regularly ran stories of people going into the oil business and of new wells being drilled. Oil news was not as important as war news, but it was a matter of intense interest.

Crude oil must be refined before it is commercially usable, much as iron ore must be smelted. Refineries appeared in the oil fields almost as soon as the oil. Most of them, however, were ill-suited for the purpose. Under-financed and poorly situated for transporting the oil to major markets, the field refineries could not hold their own against larger competitors in big cities. Pittsburgh and Cleveland became the two principal refining centers for the oil industry and small refiners were driven out of business. Pittsburgh appeared to have an advantage because of its proximity to the field, but Cleveland gradually pulled ahead. Early in 1865 thirty refineries producing coal oil, gasoline, paraffin, kerosene, and tar were operating in Cleveland. The number doubled within a year. By the early 1870s the race for supremacy had been won by the Lake City. The reason for Cleveland's success lay in its superior transportation links to eastern markets. Whereas in Cleveland the New York Central and Erie railroads, plus the Erie Canal, provided competitive routes, Pittsburgh relied solely on the Pennsylvania Railroad.

Industrialist and philanthropist John D. Rockefeller, 1839-1937, established the Standard Oil Company in 1870. By the time he retired in 1897, he was the world's richest man with a fortune estimated at $1 billion. After his retirement Rockefeller devoted much of his time to setting up endowment funds and is said to have given away $550 million in his lifetime. Courtesy, Ohio Historical Society

The man who capitalized on Cleveland's competitive advantage was not necessarily unique in the annals of industrial history, but he became the most celebrated entrepreneur or "Robber Baron" in America. John D. Rockefeller was born in Upstate New York in 1839, the son of a sharp, somewhat irresponsible traveling patent medicine salesman. The family moved to Cleveland in the early 1850s when young Rockefeller was thirteen. He finished his common schooling and became a clerk in a local produce commission firm, an early wholesale house. Possessing a shrewd, calculating mind and an observant eye, he quickly mastered the basics of bookkeeping and the mechanics of business management. His passion for thrift, economy, and efficiency, inherited from his mother, was quickened in this early business experience.

Growing to maturity in Cleveland just when the oil refining business was being established there, Rockefeller had a ringside seat at the unfolding of the Industrial Revolution. He had no intention of missing out on the opportunities available to an industrious young man with sense and vision. Having carefully husbanded his earnings, he formed a produce commission partnership with a man named Clark in 1863. The business was quite successful, grossing nearly half a million dollars in its first year, returning more than 100 percent on the original investment. Rockefeller's mind, however, was on oil. Using proceeds from his firm, he formed a new partnership in 1865 with Stanley Andrews for the purpose of refining oil. The organization did well in the

This 1928 photo of a clean and bright Standard Oil of Ohio (SOHIO) truck was made by Palm Brothers, a Cincinnati firm specializing in decalcomania. Courtesy, Cincinnati Historical Society

next five years, adding steadily to its resources, expanding operations, and taking on new partners, such as Henry Flagler. By 1870 the partnership was prepared for the next step.

In January of that year Rockefeller and his associates announced the formation of the Standard Oil Company of Ohio. Capitalized at one million dollars, the new firm was the largest refiner in the largest refining center in the world. It produced initially about 1,500 barrels of oil daily, one-seventh of the output of all Cleveland refineries. With his passion for economy and efficiency, Rockefeller recognized the need to build up large cash reserves in the event of a depression, or if an inviting opportunity for growth appeared. Hard times struck very soon, in 1873, and small refiners were poorly fixed to weather the difficulties facing them. On the other hand, Standard Oil was in a position to buy up the weaker refineries at bargain prices until it had a near monopoly on Cleveland's refining business. The company could now organize its operations on such a broad scale that costs for refining and distributing oil were reduced substantially below those of their competitors.

Further steps to drive out competition involved the use of rebates, drawbacks, and kickbacks in the shipping of oil. Standard Oil was not the first company to employ these devices, but it was the first to manipulate them to the great disadvantage of its rivals. The "rebate" was simply the return to the company of a portion of the shipping charge it paid to the railroad. Because Standard Oil's business was so vast, it was a matter of some consequence that the railroads not lose it. Any favors might help. Standard officials persuaded the railroads to grant their company rebates while denying them to other oil refiners. The company also convinced the railroads to grant it "drawbacks," or a percentage of the shipping charge paid by other refiners. "Kickbacks" to railroad officials sweetened to some degree the unpalatable necessity of making rebates and drawbacks to Standard Oil.

Through such practices, Standard Oil by 1880, ten short years after its founding, was in sole control of 90 percent of the refined oil business in the United States. One by one, its competitors, lacking the resources to withstand these cutthroat methods, had fallen before it. By 1875 Standard Oil's cash resources had climbed to thirteen million dollars, and by 1882 the figure had reached forty-five million. Over eleven million dollars had already been paid out in dividends. The ruthless techniques employed by the company in destroying its competition—rebates, drawbacks, and kickbacks were but a few of many—can hardly be defended by even its most sympathetic critics. However, other "Robber Barons" were doing the same things in the violent dog-eat-dog world of modern business. No rules existed by which to play this new game, so most of its practitioners resorted to any method they could think of to destroy their competition.

So vast had become the Standard Oil empire, extending far beyond the boundaries of Ohio, that a new plan of organization was needed. Thus in 1882 the Standard Oil Trust was established, although the public knew nothing about it for several years. By this device, stock in all Standard companies—numbering around twenty—was transferred to nine trustees, in exchange for twenty trust certificates for each share of stock. This permitted the trust to manage all Standard Oil properties as a single unit, providing the centralized control so dear to Rockefeller and his fellows. Greater economy and efficiency was attainable now than when the companies operated independently. The Standard Oil Trust, capitalized at seventy million dollars with annual earnings of about ten million dollars, became the prototype for the trust movement

Blacksmiths were important and necessary craftsmen before the advent of automobiles. This photograph, taken in the 1890s, depicts a blacksmith shop in Portsmouth. Courtesy, Ohio Historical Society

which ran rampant throughout American business over the next decade. The very term "trust" has become a part of our language, implying a massive monopoly.

Trusts were outlawed by the Sherman Anti-Trust Act of 1890 and the Standard Oil Trust was dissolved in 1892. For seven years the company's leaders—Rockefeller, Andrews, Flagler, H.H. Rogers, John D. Archbold, and others—ran the organization much as they had the trust, under a "gentleman's agreement," an informal arrangement whereby all decisions were made in concert. In 1899 they came up with another device which would shape the course of American business organization for much of the twentieth century: the holding company. By this scheme Standard Oil of New Jersey bought controlling stock in all other Standard Oil companies and the entire empire was run through Standard Oil of New Jersey. Centralized management had again been achieved. In 1911, however, the United States Supreme Court ordered the dissolution of the Standard Oil holding company as it caused unreasonable restraint of trade under the Sherman Act. The empire was thereupon broken up into its constituent companies.

The breakup of the Standard Oil empire in 1911 gave birth to another large, independent oil company in Ohio. The discovery of oil in 1885 in the northwestern part of the state led to the formation of the Ohio Oil Company in 1887. The company's energies were devoted chiefly to the production of oil rather than the refining and marketing ends of the business. At the time Standard Oil was extending its activities into the area and was impressed by the efficient operations of Ohio Oil. It was so impressed, in fact, that in 1889 Standard Oil bought out Ohio Oil. With its headquarters now located in Findlay, Ohio Oil in the next few years was producing 50 percent of all the oil in Ohio and Indiana.

Granted considerable autonomy under Standard Oil ownership, Ohio Oil moved into the newly opened oil fields of Illinois and by 1908 had a pipeline running from the Mississippi River to the Pennsylvania border. The company was looking well beyond the Mississippi to the Rocky Mountains and Texas for new oil fields when the Supreme Court issued its dissolution order against Standard Oil. Thus on December 9, 1911, Ohio Oil once again became an independent organization. For another decade it confined itself to oil production, but in the 1920s it began to revamp its structure toward total integration—production, refining, and marketing. In 1962 the Ohio Oil Company became the Marathon Oil Company.

By the time of the dissolution, Standard Oil had played an important part in the nation's history and its Ohio origins were almost forgotten. The oil business had expanded far beyond the fields of Pennsylvania and the refineries of Cleveland with the discovery of great new reserves in Texas, California, off the Atlantic and Gulf coasts, in South America, and in the Middle East. New companies were organized which would in time rival and surpass Standard Oil as drillers and refiners of oil. Nevertheless, Standard Oil of Ohio remained a prominent Ohio corporation, and its claim to being the first company in one of the world's major industries assured it a special place in history.

UNIO
DWYER
RESTAURANT
ICE CREAM SODA
PRICE'S
CAFE
PRICE'S CAFE
DENTIST
BRICE
BARBER
CIGARS

V

RUBBER AND THE REST

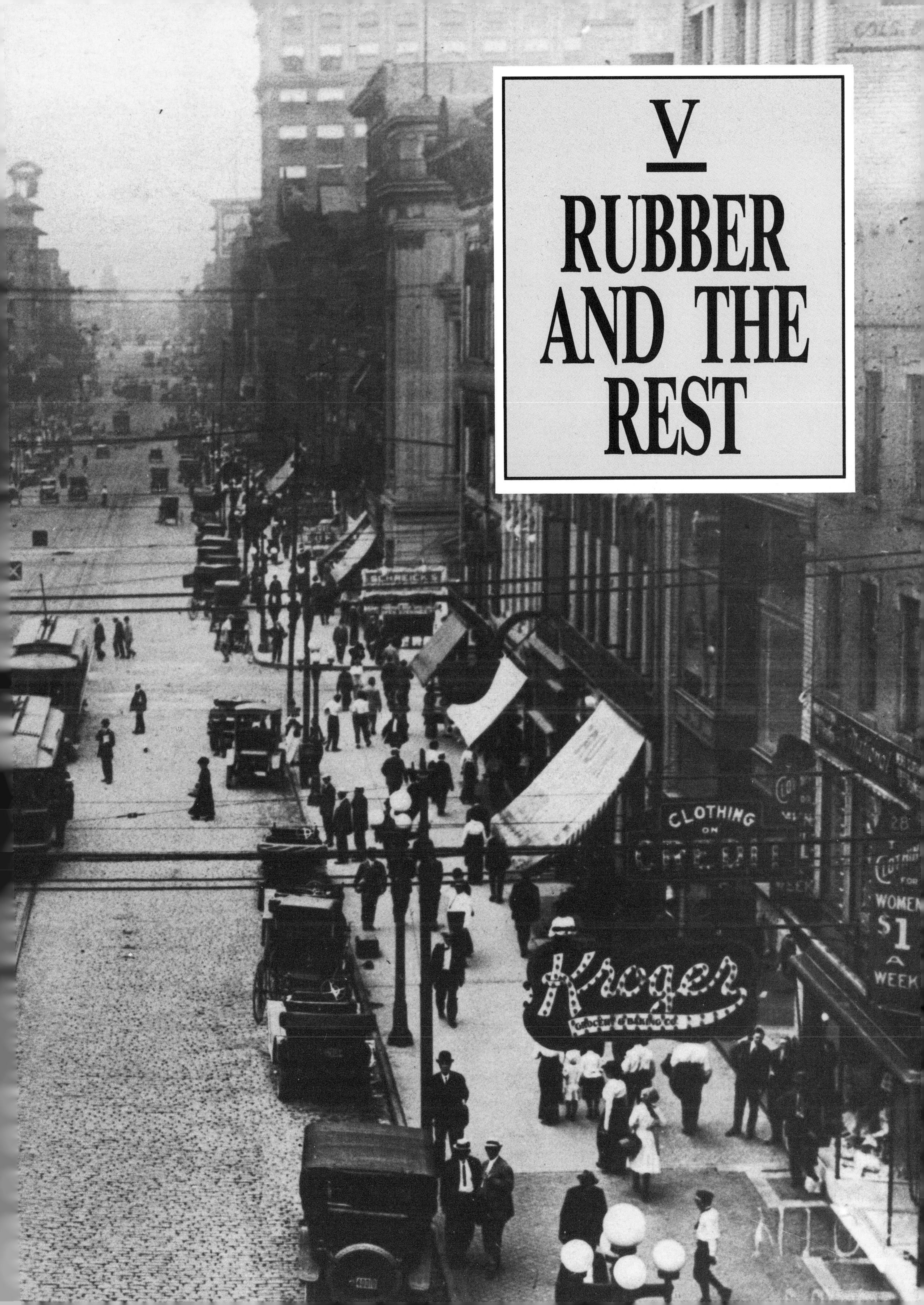

This picture, looking north on High Street, shows busy downtown Columbus. By 1914 Columbus ranked among the top forty industrial cities in the country. Transportation has been a basis of the city's industry: Columbus was home to buggy and wagon factories, and has manufactured railroad, automotive, and airplane parts. Courtesy, Ohio Historical Society and the Columbus Dispatch

Facing page: This eye-catching ad for nonskid "quick detachable clincher" tires, designed by the Firestone Tire and Rubber Company, appeared in the October 22, 1910, issue of The Outlook.

While John D. Rockefeller and Standard Oil were going national, another Ohio industry was being founded, one which would forever retain its Ohio identity. In fact, this industry would always be identified with one particular Ohio city. There was no special reason why Akron should become the "tire capital" of the world. Cleveland, Youngstown, and Pittsburgh were suitably situated to form the heart of the iron and steel business, but why did the rubber industry come to Akron? Rubber manufacturing required crude rubber, coal, cloth, and ample supplies of water, but these were not indigenous to Akron; many places had them. Akron was chosen because of one man, who deliberately selected the city as the site of his rubber plant.

Benjamin F. Goodrich arrived in Akron in November 1870. He knew something about the area having attended Cleveland Medical College (now the Case Western Reserve School of Medicine) before the Civil War. After the war, he stopped practicing surgery, worked briefly in the Pennsylvania oil fields, and then, in 1867, opened a real estate business in New York City. Two years later he exchanged $10,000 worth of real estate for $14,000 in stock in the Hudson River Rubber Company at Hastings-on-Hudson and moved the plant to Melrose, north of Albany. While the company's products were of high quality, Goodrich found that eastern competition in the rubber business was keen. After learning that there were no rubber companies west of the mountains, Goodrich decided to look for prospects in Ohio. While visiting friends in Cleveland, he saw a circular put out by the Akron Board of Trade extolling the city's bright promise for

"Firestone"

NON-SKID
TIRES

QUICK DETACHABLE CLINCHER MFD. BY FIRESTONE TIRE

ENSURE
SAFETY
ON SLIPPERY
STREETS

THE FIRESTONE TIRE & RUBBER CO.
AMERICA'S LARGEST EXCLUSIVE TIRE MAKERS, AKRON, O.

"I can make a hose which will stand up under any test," said B.F. Goodrich, a doctor who went on to open the first rubber factory in the Midwest. Within a few years the Goodrich Company was among the leading industries in Akron, the soon-to-emerge "Rubber Capital of the World." Courtesy, University of Akron Archives

future industry. He decided to check it out.

Goodrich liked what he saw in Akron. He spoke with a local businessman about relocating his rubber company there and was invited to address a large group of civic leaders at an evening meeting. He discussed his own history and explained why he wished to move his plant to Akron: there was plenty of coal and water, good transportation links, and a sizeable, available work force. And since no rubber companies existed west of the mountains, the market potential was good. Where would he get his supplies? The rubber would come from Brazil, the cotton from textile mills in the East. What would he make? Many products could be made from rubber, but what he was most interested in were fire hoses. He had seen a neighbor's house burn to the ground because a fire hose had burst. His promise was simple: "I can make a hose which will stand up under any test. It will sell—and sell at good prices. I'm sure of it."

The rubber industry was a fairly new one. It dated only from 1839 when Charles Goodyear perfected the vulcanization process, making it possible to work the rubber more readily, enhancing its practical usage. But the industry developed slowly because rubber's usefulness was underestimated. Raincoats, shoes, overshoes, hot-water bottles, and caps were the principal items made. Rubber tires had been used but infrequently. Queen Victoria supposedly had solid rubber strips glued onto the wheels of one of her early carriages, and an Englishman had designed a primitive pneumatic tire in 1845, but it was of no real value.

The breakthrough in the rubber tire business occurred in 1888 when an Irish veterinarian named John B. Dunlop developed a clumsy pneumatic for his son's bike. Displeased with the heavy, solid rubber tires which slowed the bike's speed, he wrapped a tube of rubber around the tire rim, inserted a valve, and encased the whole tire in strong cloth. He inflated the tube and the experiment worked. The tire provided a smoother, faster ride. Pneumatic tires, first manufactured in the United States in 1891, ignited the bicycle mania of the 1890s. Everyone who was anyone had to have a bicycle on which he could enjoy the soft ride provided by the pneumatics. Manufacturers had trouble keeping up with the demand and popular songs were composed about the new fad.

Akron's business community, seeking to lure industry to town, was impressed with Goodrich. The president of the Board of Trade traveled to Melrose to make sure all Goodrich had said was true and found that it was. Goodrich needed $15,000 in financial backing. His new friends were able to collect only $13,600, but Goodrich decided to go ahead anyhow. The Melrose plant was dismantled and the machinery shipped to Akron. The new factory opened in March 1871 with a work force of twenty. A local newspaper announced that the company was ready to manufacture a host of items, including billiard cushions and fruit jar rings. As promised, though, Goodrich specialized in fire hoses.

Business was not good at first. The company was not well known and did not push its products aggressively. The depression of the mid-1870s led to a crisis in 1875 when bankruptcy threatened. George T. Perkins, one of Goodrich's original

As tire manufacturing progressed from manual methods to semiautomatic processes, employees at the Goodyear tire plant in Akron often faced pay cuts or lay-offs. Their discontent resulted in the great Akron rubber strike in 1913, which lasted a month and a half. Courtesy, Goodyear Tire and Rubber Company Archives

backers, supplied sufficient capital to keep the company functioning until 1878 when an even more serious crisis faced the company. On this occasion another early backer, George W. Crouse, guaranteed the company's financial stability and the worst was over. From then on the company grew steadily. In 1880 it was incorporated as B.F. Goodrich Company, capitalized at $100,000. Although Goodrich died in 1888, the organization was so firmly established that the transfer of control to others went smoothly. By 1891 Goodrich had risen to fourth place among Akron companies. The following year, the company, with about 400 employees, reported sales of $1,413,000, and profits of over $250,000.

Despite this good financial report the next few years were not easy ones for Goodrich. The nation's worst depression until that time struck within a few months and the demand for most rubber products dropped off sharply. However, offsetting this decline was the growing call for pneumatic bicycle tires. By 1896 business had so improved that the company was making more money than it had before the depression. Goodrich during these years continued

"We could build them cheaper, but we won't. We would build them better, but we can't." So went the motto of the Diamond Rubber Company, founded by former Goodrich employees in 1894. This ad appeared in 1912, the same year the company was absorbed by its rival, the B.F. Goodrich Company. Courtesy, The Outlook, *1912*

to market solid-rubber tires for the carriage trade, but this was not a major money-making branch of the business. The first agreement for a pneumatic automobile tire, a field which would revolutionize the tire business, was made with the Winton Company of Cleveland. The owner, Alexander Winton, blew one of the tires when he was out driving and patched the hole with molasses. Too much molasses went into the tube and it blew again, decorating Winton with a complete coat of the sticky stuff. Molasses and all, Goodrich had produced the first set of pneumatic automobile tires and a milestone had been reached. The big business, however, was still in bicycle tires.

Many other rubber manufacturing firms were now responding to the demand for pneumatic bicycle tires. One of these plants, the Diamond Rubber Company, was built literally next door to Goodrich. Diamond Rubber had purchased a building recently abandoned by the Diamond Match Company which had moved to Barberton. Capitalized at $50,000 when it opened in March 1894, Diamond Rubber was founded by former Goodrich employees (ex-Goodrich workers were prominent in many of the new rubber companies). Diamond had difficult times in the depression of the 1890s, and went through several reorganizations. But forceful leadership and innovations in rubber research put it on a solid financial footing. Goodrich's major competition came not from Diamond, however, but from two "new kids on the block"—Goodyear and Firestone.

The Seiberling family had long been active in Akron's business and civic affairs. John Seiberling had owned agricultural machinery, flour milling, and traction companies during the 1870s, 1880s, and 1890s. He had been one of the backers of Goodrich's rubber company in 1871 and even organized his own rubber company. But financial problems during the depression in the mid-1890s forced him to dispose of all his properties. However, one of John's sons, Frank, who had worked with his father, had gotten the rubber "itch." In 1898 while in Chicago selling his father's Empire Mower and Reaper Works, he learned of a vacated factory complex in East Akron which was up for sale. He raised $56,000 to acquire and renovate the abandoned building and to purchase equipment. With an additional $93,000 to begin operations, raised through a stock sale, Frank Seiberling was prepared to start up his own rubber company.

Frank named his new company for Charles Goodyear, whose vulcanization process had made possible the growth of the rubber industry. The Goodyear Tire and Rubber Company was incorporated on August 29, 1898. Operations began in early December. Specializing in pneumatic bicycle and carriage tires, Goodyear had sales of $508,000 in 1899 and doubled this figure in 1900.

But things are not always what they seem. From the very outset Goodyear was plagued with bitter legal controversies over patent rights. Goodyear applied for a license to use the "Grant patent," which involved a method of securing a carriage tire to the wheel rim. The company's request was turned down, even though others who had applied for the license had received it. As a result Goodyear made a modification in the Grant process and pro-

As time went on, Firestone diversified its production and began to manufacture other items besides tires. Pictured here are women at work in the Firestone Spark Plug Factory in Akron. Courtesy, Ohio Historical Society

Above: The B.F. Goodrich Company made products other than tires, as seen in this ad for Goodrich Trouser Guards. The ad guarantees that the trouser guards will not rust or "soil the pantaloons." Courtesy, University of Akron Archives

Above right: The Seiberlings provided financial backing for Melvin Vaniman's airship, pictured here at Atlantic City on July 2, 1912, before taking off on a trans-Atlantic flight. The airship met with tragedy when it later burst into flames, taking the lives of all five passengers, including Vaniman. Courtesy, University of Akron Archives

ceeded to manufacture the tire on the theory that its method was different. This was at once challenged in court. Goodyear was allowed to continue manufacturing the tire while the litigation proceeded, but all revenue from sales was held in escrow. In May 1902 a federal appeals court ruled for Goodyear and the escrow funds were released.

Harvey Firestone, born in 1868 on a farm in eastern Ohio, attended a business college in Cleveland and obtained a job with the Columbus Buggy Company. He learned about the tire business in 1892 when he was the company's representative in Detroit. Later he was a partner in a small rubber company in Chicago. He sold out for a nice profit and with the boom in bicycle tires reaching a peak he decided to enter the business. Since Akron was a rising tire town and near his home he set up shop there. The Firestone Tire and Rubber Company was chartered in August 1900. The tires were actually manufactured in Chicago, but the marketing was

handled by Firestone. Although business was good all the profits went to the Chicago manufacturer. Thus the company was reorganized in 1903 and Firestone went into the tire manufacturing business for itself.

Firestone entered the tire business at the dawning of the automobile age. Early auto tires were not of a very high quality. The life of a tire was about 1,000 miles at best and frequent punctures or blowouts meant frequent changes. Most tires at the time were "clinchers," which were very difficult to remove after a puncture. What was needed was a tire which a motorist could remove, repair, and reinstall while on the road without exhausting himself. Goodyear and later Firestone both came up with a new type of rim and "straight-side" tire which was easier to handle. This advance led to Goodyear's supremacy in auto tire manufacturing, but it also gave a great boost to Firestone.

By 1910 Firestone's sales were in excess of five million dollars, returning a profit of over one million dollars. The work force had grown to 1,000. Since this extensive growth was well beyond the company's original capacity, buildings were added. But this enlarged complex was still inadequate. A new four-story plant opened its doors on June 8, 1911. Within another year or so some 2,900 workers were turning out 7,500 tires daily.

Meanwhile Goodrich and Goodyear were rapidly moving forward. Goodrich's sales had risen more than five times between 1900 and 1911, increasing from $491,000 to $27,406,700. Profits had quintupled over the same period. In 1912 Goodrich absorbed its friendly neighbor and rival, Diamond Rubber. While Goodrich made products other than tires, Goodyear had moved to the front as the country's leading tire manufacturer. In 1912, with a work force of 6,880, Goodyear's sales had reached $25,232,000 with profits of $3,000,000. Goodrich, Goodyear, and Firestone were the giants in the rubber and tire capital of the world, but there were a dozen or more lesser firms in the rubber business in the Greater Akron area.

Again the question is asked: Why did Akron of all places become the heart of the rubber industry? Karl H. Grismer, who has written an excellent history of Akron and Summit County, provides some clues. He points out that Akron's prosperous future could hardly have been predicted in 1890. Of ninety-four rubber plants across the country at that time, Akron possessed only B.F. Goodrich. However, economic conditions in the city in the mid-1890s made it fertile ground for any kind of new industry. Many companies had gone out of business and there were a host of empty factory buildings about town. "Every new concern," Grismer writes, "which started between 1894 and 1902 located in buildings once occupied by companies which had gone bankrupt or had left the city. In every case the buildings were acquired at prices far below the cost of construction."

The empty factories left a large number of unemployed workers who were ready to work at almost any wage. This large pool of cheap labor was readily seized upon by the rubber companies. Not that they were ruthless exploiters of labor—in fact, all of them later developed substantial programs providing for the workers' well-being. Yet when the rubber companies were fighting for survival they needed cheap labor. Grismer reports that Akron firms paid their workers about 20 percent less than their competitors in other places. This gave them an obvious advantage with respect to production costs. In addition, the ample supply of coal and water and Akron's convenient location were important assets. The Cuyahoga River came down from the north and the Erie Railroad came in from the east. Of course, being adjacent to Detroit would be an unexpected bonus.

The managers of the rubber companies were all very smart and talented men, each trying to gain an advantage over his rivals. Grismer writes that

> *they fought constantly for leadership in sales, in profits, and even in such minor matters as amateur athletics. Every one of the rubber barons strove constantly to produce a better tire than his competitors—a tire he could crow about at the country club and in his national advertising. He stopped at no expense in employing top-flight chemists and physicists for his research laboratory, and in making countless experiments. All the leading companies had fleets of test cars barreling through the country, day and night, in all kinds of weather and over all kinds of roads, to determine in what respects their tires were weak or strong and how much mileage they would give. Whenever one company came out with a new tire, the others immediately got samples to tear apart in their laboratories and find out how they were made. To keep track of what their competitors were doing, they allegedly employed "spies" who got jobs in the rival plants and carefully reported all tidbits of information pertaining to new developments. Because of this intense rivalry, the quality of Akron-made tires improved steadily, and shortly became better than the tires made by firms in other cities. Motorists everywhere began demanding Akron tires —and in the race for supremacy in the rubber industry other cities dropped by the wayside.*

With the growing demand, new techniques were perfected, production increased as costs were cut, plants expanded, and thousands upon thousands of workers were hired. The city population jumped from 27,600 in 1890, to 42,700 in 1900, to 69,000 in 1910, to 208,000 in 1920. All this seems to explain why Akron became the "tire city," the "rubber capital of the world."

But the rubber industry would never have blossomed as it did without the automobile. At first considered an impractical plaything, then a luxury for the rich, and finally a necessity, the automobile transformed America in the twentieth century. The automobile industry not only zoomed to the top as the nation's number-one business, providing thousands of jobs to workers in auto and auto-related industries, it changed the lifestyle of America. The automobile brought the country to the city and the city to the country. No, life was never quite the same after the arrival of the automobile.

The gasoline auto appeared after considerable experimentation with other methods of locomotion. Autos powered by steam were manufactured by many companies in the 1890s, the most famous being the Stanley Steamer. Burning kerosene heated the tank of water and the resultant steam energized the motor. It took too long to raise a head of steam, however, and steam cars disappeared around World War I.

Developed at about the same time as the steam car was the electric automobile. Some 35,000 of these were manufactured in the United States between 1896 and 1915. The electric car was popular, especially with ladies because it was easy to handle and made little noise. The problem with the electric was that it could not attain speeds much above twenty miles per hour and the battery required frequent recharging. Gas autos were not bound by these limitations and electrics disappeared shortly after the steamers. But the Electric Vehicle Association did not lose hope, urging as late as 1913 that "before you buy any car, consider the electric."

Very few gas cars were on the road in 1900, but as inventions and refinements expedited manufacture and lowered the cost of cars, sales picked up rapidly. Ransom E. Olds designed a primitive assembly line in 1901 and within two years was manufacturing over 5,000 cars annually. Henry Ford developed a moving assembly line and brought out his first Model-T in 1908. By 1916 he was selling the car for under $400. The Model-T was discontinued in 1927 to make room for the Model-A, but in that twenty-year span over fifteen million of them were sold, over half the total number for all companies. Auto sales were off in World War I, but the boom resumed after the war, with almost two million being sold in 1920.

Although Detroit quickly asserted leadership in automobile manufacture, in the early years of the industry Ohio ranked next to Michigan in the output of cars, auto bodies, and auto parts. For a time it competed on an even basis with Michigan for first

Left: With the advent of the automobile came the gasoline station. This early Columbus station offered drive-in service. Courtesy, Ohio Historical Society

Below: Pictured here is an advertisement for the Buckeye Buggy Company of Columbus, boasting the largest selection of carriages in the state. Companies that began manufacturing carriages typically progressed to making automobiles years later. Courtesy, Ohio Historical Society

***Right:** Baker Electric Vehicles, often called the "Aristocrat of Motordom," boasted in 1902 that its electric car was the "most elegant automobile made." Thomas A. Edison, a good friend of Walter C. Baker, is reported to have bought the first Baker car. Courtesy, Western Reserve Historical Society*

***Facing page:** Peerless Motor Car Company used slogans such as "All That the Name Implies" and "The Car for Aesthetics." The cars were in such heavy demand that in 1913 the company offered an incentive plan: buyers were given a $100 discount if they were willing to wait thirty days for delivery. A $200 discount was given if the customer agreed to take delivery in sixty days. Courtesy, Western Reserve Historical Society*

place in car production, but fell behind when Ford brought out his Model-T.

Many Ohio auto companies grew out of electric car, carriage, and bicycle companies. The Winton Company of Cleveland went from the bicycle to the carriage, and then to the gas auto. The Columbus Buggy Company manufactured carriages, then electrics, and finally gas machines.

Two famous Cleveland firms never got beyond the electric stage. The Rauch and Lang Company started making carriages before the Civil War, turning to electrics at the end of the century. This company was not interested in the assembly-line philosophy, boasting that it required ninety days to make a single car. But the end product was worth it, the public was assured, for the car was absolutely safe and so simple to drive that a twelve-year-old could handle it. The Baker Motor Vehicle Company of Cleveland also specialized in electric cars. Claiming to be "the oldest and largest manufacturers of electric motor cars in the world," Baker called itself "the aristocrats of motordom." It was asserted in 1909 that one battery charge was good for 100 miles. By 1911 the figure had improved to 244.5 miles per charge. At the peak of its popularity, Baker Electrics sold for $3,000 while Henry Ford's Model-T cost only $500.

Cleveland's three largest automobile manufacturers, three of the largest in the state, were Peerless, White, and Winton. Peerless, whose slogan was "all that the name implies," manufactured six-cylinder cars, both open and closed models, in addition to a line of trucks. The cars were not cheap, averaging between $4,300 and $7,200. The company stressed silence and comfort as the hallmarks of its product.

The White Motor Company began turning out steam automobiles in 1899 and continued to make them for about ten years. They boasted of their superiority over gas cars and pointed with pride to their victory in an endurance run against gas autos

The 1908 Peerless
All That The Name Implies
is fitted for the roughest work
and proportioned to satisfy the keenest
sense of refinement and comfort.
A larger Tonneau, longer wheel-base, slightly
longer springs and a double ignition system
are simply the 1908 slight developments of the
principles of past Peerless construction.
They like it best who know it most intimately.
Write for our 1908 Catalogue "O" which fully
describes and illustrates the Peerless Models.
PEERLESS MOTOR CAR CO., 2445 Oakdale St., Cleveland, O.
Member A.L.A.M.

Above: Assembly of automobiles at Willys-Overland in Toledo originally took place in individual stalls, but by 1913 the plant had developed assembly lines. Here a worker guides an auto body onto a frame. Courtesy, Ohio Historical Society

Below right: With the advent of the automobile, accidents became inevitable. Several curious boys gathered to view the damage done to this vehicle in 1920. Courtesy, Western Reserve Historical Society

at Harrisburg, Pennsylvania, in May 1908. By 1910, however, they were extolling the virtues of their gas engine cars, although they still produced some steam cars. In two more years they were exclusively into gasoline cars. To assist women in learning how to drive their fashionable "town cars," the company prepared "a dainty booklet for dainty women." White was now manufacturing trucks and taxicabs as well as cars. It became famous in World War I for its trucks, which earned the Croix de Guerre from the French government. The statement put out by the company read:

> *The Croix de Guerre has been awarded the First and Second Groupments of the Great Headquarters Reserve No. 1 of the French Army, each operating 500 or more White Trucks. Citations for distinguished service accompanied the order, supplemented by a later citation to the entire Reserve No. 1, operating 2,500 White Trucks. This is the first and only instance on record of motor transport formations in any army receiving this honor. The White trucks were all veterans, many in continuous service since 1914.*

Winton got started as a bicycle company in 1890 and progressed onward to the gas automobile after the turn of the century. In 1896 and 1897 their "12 stylish models" of bicycles were selling for $100. As the bicycle mania ebbed and the automobile mania grew, the Winton Bicycle Company became the Winton Carriage Company and then the Winton Motor Car Company. Its principal product was the "Winton Six," an open touring car which sold in 1910 for $3,250. Winton got plenty of free publicity in 1903 when Tom L. Johnson, Cleveland's famous mayor, drove his Winton around the state during his campaign for governor. The company may not have been happy about this publicity, however. The "Red Devil" ran into trouble outside of Ravenna in early September. The weather was bad and the machine went off the road into a ditch. Johnson and his party eventually made it to town on the back of a hay wagon. A week later the car's battery went dead near Newcomerstown and a local farmer came to the rescue. In another week the mayor drove the machine into a stone culvert while trying to take a cigar out of his pocket. Finally, near the end of September, the "Red Devil" suffered a general breakdown at Georgetown on the Ohio River and

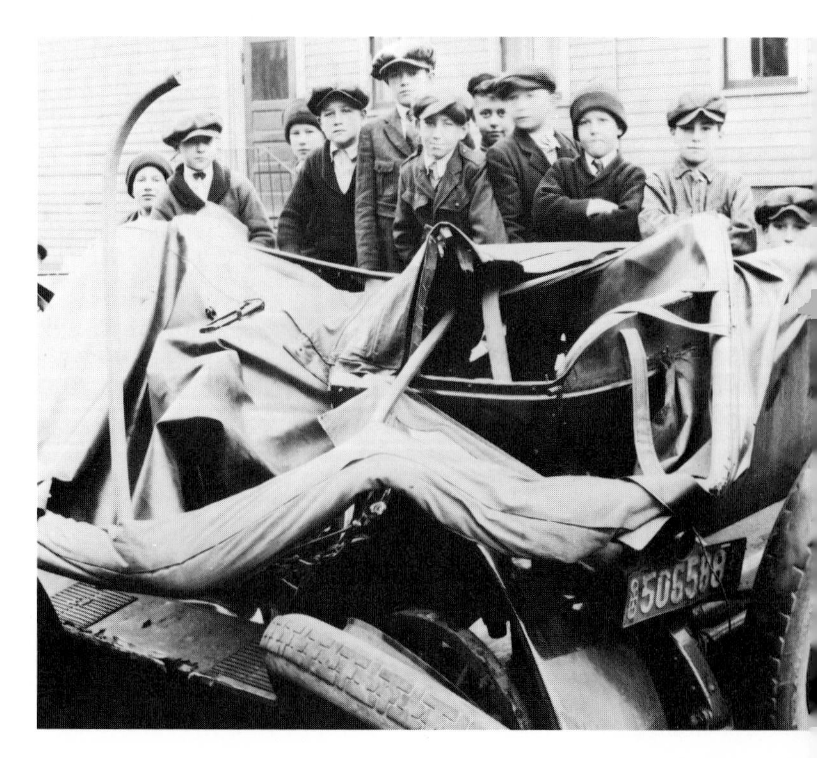

Left: Toledo's proximity to Detroit helped its auto-related industries, like the Electric Auto-Lite Company, which manufactured batteries, ignitions, and lighting systems for automobiles. Pictured here is the metallurgical and chemical laboratory at Electric Auto-Lite in 1933. Courtesy, Toledo-Lucas County Public Library

Below left: A famous Toledo trademark is the Toledo scale. Developed by Allen DeVilbiss, Jr., the first springless automatic computing scale made Toledo famous around the world. In this photo a Toledo scale truck is shown ready for delivery. Courtesy, Toledo-Lucas County Public Library

had to be abandoned. Driving an automobile in those pioneer days may have been an exhilarating experience, but it could also be an exasperating one.

Another famous Ohio car was the Willys-Overland of Toledo. Toledo had come a long way since its incorporation in 1835. Growth was great after the Civil War, in particular, with railroads and iron ore stimulating industrial activity. One of the companies established by the turn of the century was Pope Motor, which was purchased by John Willys in 1909. A native of New York State, Willys had grown up in the bicycle business, but quickly recognized the possibilities of the automobile. Under his leadership Willys-Overland became Toledo's number-one business concern and its product was well regarded throughout the auto business. Within two years it was manufacturing twenty-two low-priced models. Its promotional literature boasted that its five factories were the best equipped in the world and that there were "20,000 delighted owners" of Overland cars.

Toledo boasted not only Willys-Overland, but other important industries, some related to the automobile business, some not. One of the most famous was the Champion Spark Plug Company, run by the Stranahan brothers, Robert and Frank. By the late 1920s Champion was turning out fifty million plugs a year, which supplied two-thirds of all autos and airplanes throughout the world. Another concern which rose to a dominant position in its field was the Electric Auto-Lite Company, which produced batteries and ignition and lighting systems for automobiles. Other companies manufactured auto parts and auto supplies. Proximity to Detroit helped Toledo's auto-related industries.

Perhaps Toledo's most famous industry in the twentieth century resulted from the discovery of a large natural gas field in northwestern Ohio in the 1880s. In 1888 Edward D. Libbey, a successful New England glass manufacturer but beset with labor problems, came to Ohio to explore the prospects of relocating his company. Attracted by the community and cheap fuel, he founded the Libbey Glass Company in Toledo. Within a decade his high quality "Libbey Cut Glass" was known at home and abroad. An inventor, Michael J. Owens of Newark, Ohio, joined the company in the 1890s. In the next

These were employees of the Federal Glass Company of Columbus, which was started by George and R.J. Beatty, descendants of a family prominently identified with the glass industry since 1848. They manufactured mainly household glass and initiated the process of making handblown glassware from continuous tanks, rather than from clay pots. Courtesy, Ohio Historical Society

few years he developed a machine which produced bottles, tumblers, and glass chimneys. While putting many skilled glassblowers out of work, Owens' machine greatly increased Libbey revenues. In addition to cut-glass pieces, bottles, containers, and window glass, Libbey also was manufacturing "shatterproof" windshields for the growing auto industry. Akron may have been the "tire capital of the world," but Toledo was the "glass capital of the world." After World War II Toledo's professional baseball team was even given the unlikely nickname of "Glass Sox."

Like Toledo, Cincinnati also had a highly diversified economy throughout the Industrial Revolution. The city never was caught up in iron and steel or rubber as was the northern part of the state. It simply continued on its way manufacturing carriages, furniture, machine tools, paper, clothing, soap, and other sundries, much as it had before the Civil War. It could claim having more industries than any other city in the state, although they were

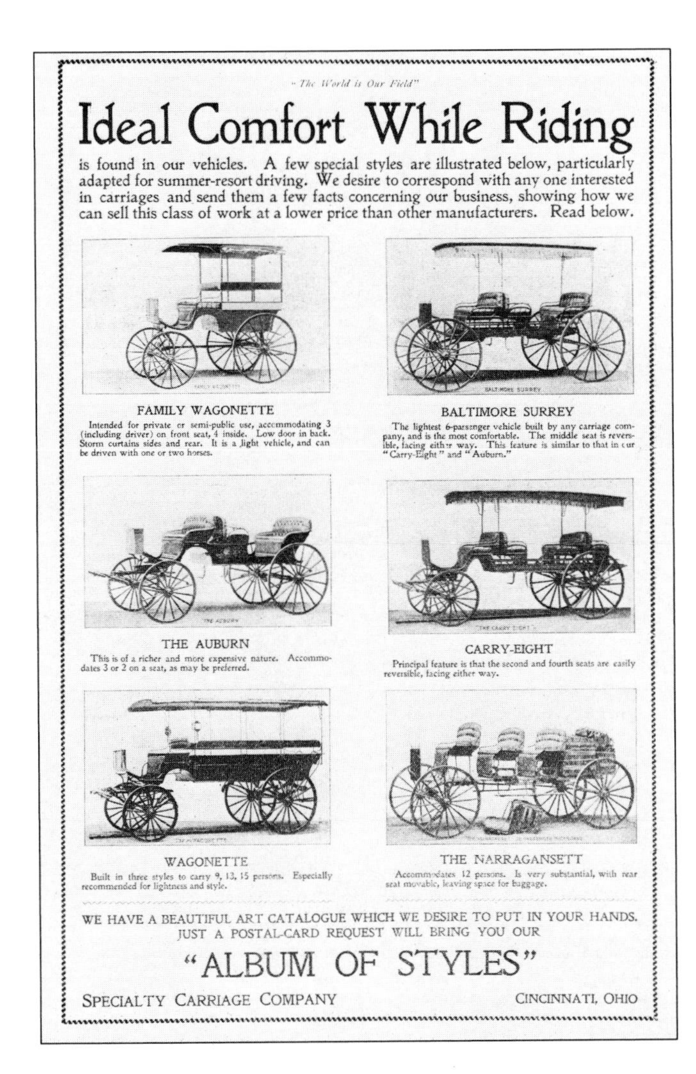

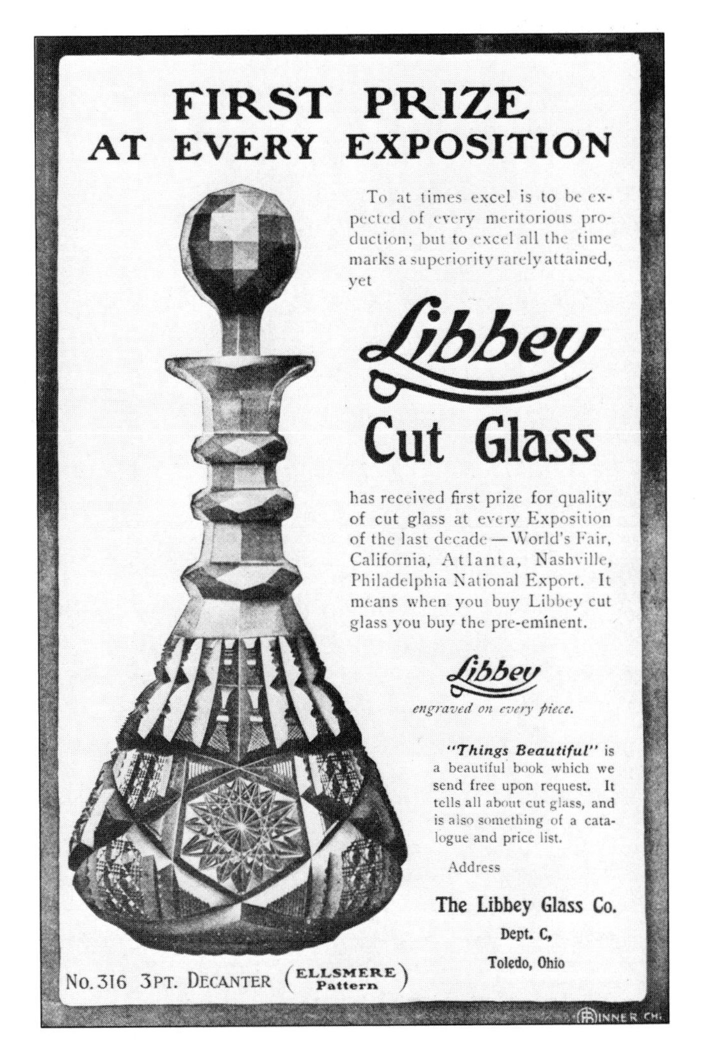

not among the so-called "heavy" industries. Cincinnati missed out on the automobile much as it had missed out on the railroad. Both Henry Ford and the Packard brothers of Warren, Ohio, had tried to raise funds for their experimental cars in Cincinnati because of its strength in the carriage industry, but they were turned down and shifted their attention to Michigan. When the carriage business declined, Cincinnati had no automobile industry to replace it, as it might have had.

But Cincinnati did not miss out on soap. Procter & Gamble, the world's premier soap maker, was founded in 1837 by two young immigrants from Great Britain. James Gamble arrived in Cincinnati a very sick sixteen-year-old lad in 1819. The family, late of County Fermanagh, Ireland, had come to the United States hoping to improve their prospects at Shawneetown, Illinois, which developers had proclaimed an "El Dorado." James' illness from fever compelled the family to stop at Cincinnati, and they liked the place so much they decided to stay. In 1821 James became apprenticed to a soap maker, a position he held for eight years. In 1829 he formed a soap and candle partnership with Hiram

Above: The Libbey Glass Company was founded by Edward Libbey, a New England glass manufacturer. Soon Libbey Cut Glass was famous around the world and, as this 1901 ad proudly proclaims, it took first prize at every exposition it entered. Courtesy,* The Outlook, *1901

Above left: The carriage and wagon industry began in Cincinnati in the early 1800s. Before the end of the century, Cincinnati led the world in the manufacture of wagons and carriages. This ad in the April 23, 1896, issue of* The Outlook *illustrates six styles of carriages available from the Specialty Carriage Company in Cincinnati.

Knowlton and in 1833 married Elizabeth Ann Norris. Meanwhile, William Procter, whose woolens shop in London had been destroyed by fire, left England in 1832 planning to settle in Louisville. His wife was stricken with cholera as their boat reached Cincinnati, and she died within a few days. With some experience in candle making in England, Procter saw a need for candles in the city and set up a shop on Main Street. He made the candles, packaged them, and delivered them personally to his customers. In 1833 he married Olivia Norris, sister of Elizabeth Ann.

After four years of carrying on their respective businesses, and upon the urging of their father-in-law, the two young men formed Procter & Gamble Company to make soap and candles. It was not the most propitious moment to go into business with a financial panic sweeping the country. But they were not expecting great things and worked long hours to put their business on a firm foundation. Gamble ran the "factory" while Procter minded the "office." Early every morning Gamble would make

Above: Procter & Gamble's Central Avenue factory in Cincinnati was situated next to the Miami and Erie Canal. Built in 1850, the factory was close to the city's slaughterhouses, which provided it with the necessary raw materials for candle and soap making. The Central Avenue building burned down in 1884, and Procter & Gamble relocated to St. Bernard, close to the railroad lines. Courtesy, Cincinnati Historical Society

Left: This interesting ad for Ivory soap appeared in the September 1884 issue of **Harper's Young People*****. Such a depiction of the Procter & Gamble product is quite different from the "Ivory Girl" image. Courtesy, the Procter & Gamble Company***

Above: This is a typical Procter & Gamble advertisement for Ivory soap. This soap is said to be gentle and pure, appropriate for this beautiful woman and young girl. Courtesy, the Procter & Gamble Company

the rounds of the packing plants to collect meat scraps and fat essential for making soap. Expected or not, the company grew steadily. In 1850 the factory moved into a complex of buildings on Central Avenue and four years later the company offices were transferred to a five-story building on Second Street at the corner of Walnut. By 1859 it was one of the largest companies in Cincinnati with annual sales in excess of one million dollars.

By the 1880s the second generation—three Procter and three Gamble sons joined the firm—was in full control as the company continued to expand. It was now the recognized national leader among 432 soap manufacturers, with sales in the millions and profits in the half-millions. In 1890, in keeping with the popular new form of business organization, the company was incorporated.

Prior to reorganization, in 1881 Harley T. Procter had sold his brothers and cousins on the advantages of large-scale advertising. He argued that notices in store windows, billboards, and newspapers were insufficient and urged that they get their message into nationally circulated magazines. Within a decade Procter & Gamble was advertising in *Ladies Home Journal, Good Housekeeping, Outlook,* and *Harper's Weekly.* One product, in particular, had become a household name through advertising and proved a turning point in the company's history. The successful promotion of Ivory soap, which had been submitted to professional chemists for testing and proven to be "99 and 44/100 per cent pure," substantially stimulated Procter & Gamble's reputation and revenues and marked a new stage in commercial advertising.

The Ivory soap ads implied that the product was not only useful but necessary in whatever job, business, or pastime in which one might be engaged. The new homemaker, the world traveler, the

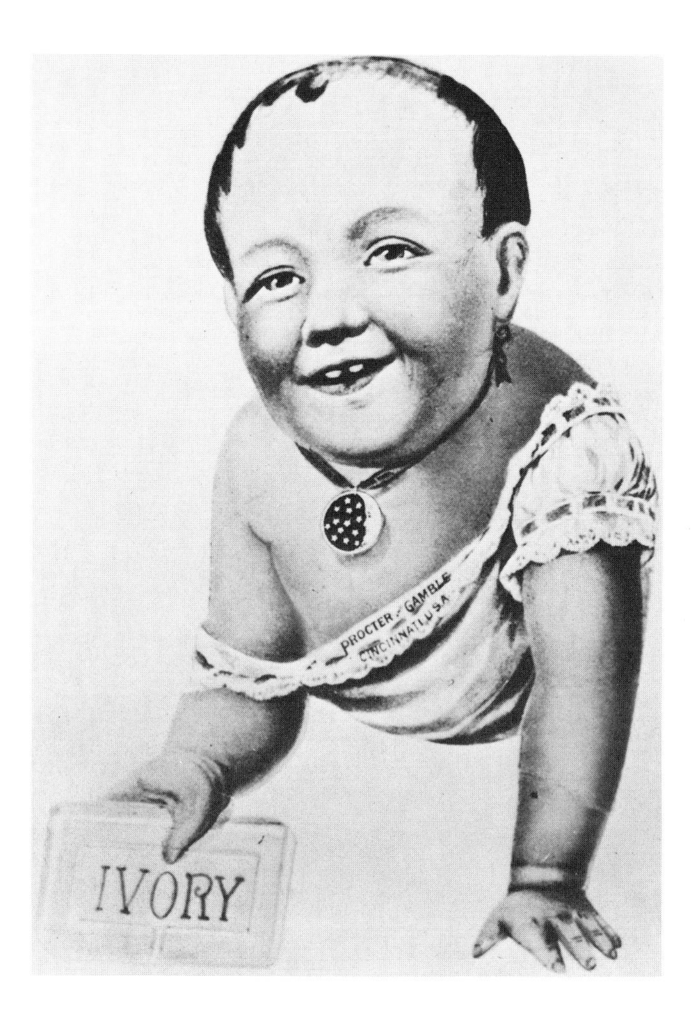

***Above:* The Procter & Gamble Company was a firm believer in the importance of advertising. Pictured here is the first Ivory baby, clutching a bar of Ivory soap and wearing the company's logo on a necklace. Courtesy, Cincinnati Historical Society**

***Right:* This photo shows workers leaving the Ivorydale plant, so named because of the popular soap manufactured there. Production began in 1886 at the plant north of Cincinnati in St. Bernard. The company, known worldwide, became very important to the economy of the Cincinnati area. Courtesy, the Procter & Gamble Company**

ostrich farmer, the new baby, and the factory worker all needed and used Ivory soap. One ad pictured a soldier in France tossing a cake of soap into a tub of water and as it rose to the surface an unbelieving mademoiselle shrieked in delight, "Il flotte!" Little ditties frequently accompanied an ad, such as this one in which a mother is tucking her tiny one in bed:

A bath in cleansing, sweet and mild
As "Ivory" makes it, always seem
To bring such comfort, that the child
Drops fast asleep with happy dreams.

When Procter & Gamble developed Crisco, its revolutionary vegetable shortening, in 1911, the product got a big send off in the advertising pages of major magazines.

While Cincinnati had no heavy industry, it was considered by some to be the most important manufacturing city in the state. It remained in the forefront of the machine tool industry, which had developed during the halcyon years of the river trade. As a major port on the Ohio River, Cincinnati possessed many shops to manufacture, replace, and repair steamboat boilers, engines, and gears. The city ranked sixth in the country in the manufacture of ladies' shoes and remained high on the list in its output of men's clothing. There were no more carriage makers, but Cincinnati was still a major furniture manufacturer. Globe-Wernicke was wellknown for its line of desks, filing cabinets, bookcases, and other office furniture. Hartwell Furniture specialized in chairs, rockers, and tables for the home. Peck-Williamson was noted for its warm-air furnaces and steam and hot-water boilers. And the "Queen City of the West" had the largest playing card factory in

The Procter & Gamble Company began marketing Ivory soap, "the pure soap that floated," in 1879. The men pictured here, with a wagon and Ivory soap signs, distributed free samples of the soap. Courtesy, Cincinnati Historical Society

Right: Pictured here is Barney Kroger's shiny red delivery wagon. The Kroger Grocery and Baking Company was incorporated in 1902, when the store became the first to bake its own bread. Soon after, Kroger began to sell meat in addition to bread, fruits, and vegetables. Courtesy, Cincinnati Historical Society

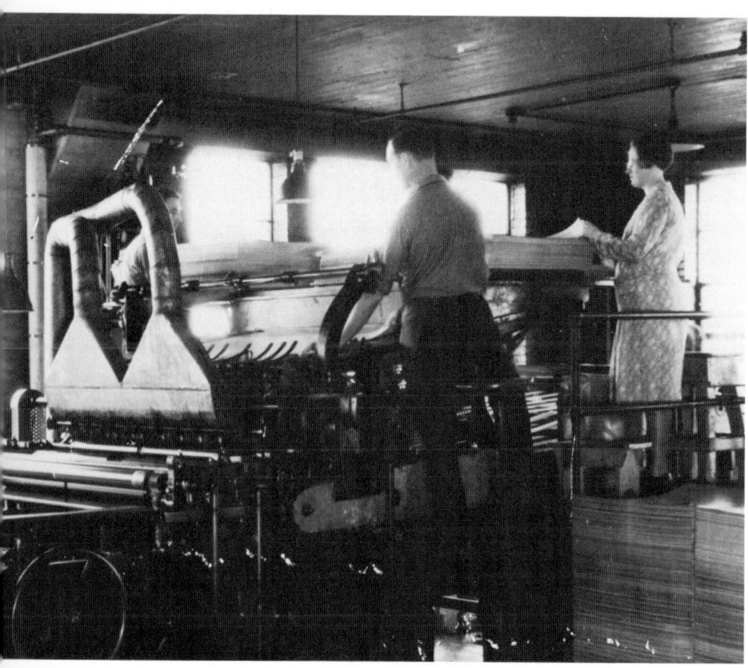

Below: Cincinnati companies printed not only textbooks, religious books, and greeting cards, but also playing cards. The U.S. Playing Card Company was the nation's largest playing card factory. Pictured here is the printing of large sheets of cards not yet cut. Courtesy, Cincinnati Historical Society

the country, the United States Playing Card Company, founded in 1880.

The turn of the century saw many other Ohio cities prospering from the Industrial Revolution. Marion, fifty miles or so northwest of Columbus, never was a large town, but it produced Warren G. Harding and the Marion Steam Shovel Company. Marion shovels have been used worldwide for the most strenuous digging demanded by man. Founded in 1884, the company was instrumental in railroad construction throughout the American and Canadian West. Following the acquisition of the Panama Canal Zone in 1903, Marion shovels were used to dig the canal, and Marion became known as the "city that built the Panama Canal." Steam shovels gave way, as automobiles were doing, to electric and then gas-powered machinery. After World War I, Marion Shovel manufactured the largest shovel ever built and in the 1930s came out with an even bigger one. This weighed three million pounds and required forty-six freight cars to ship. Road building and strip mining were the major uses for these mammoth shovels between the wars. By this time several other Marion shovel companies were also doing a good business.

Springfield's Champion Machine Company was the major manufacturer of agricultural machinery at the turn of the century. Two thousand workers produced one reaper every four minutes. However, as the corn and wheat producing areas gravitated toward the Great Plains, the farm machinery business went with it and Springfield lost its lead. Yet it remained an important center for the industry well into the twentieth century.

Another industry in which Springfield was a leader was publishing. The Crowell-Collier Company was an outgrowth of the agricultural machinery business. John Crowell, a printer from Louisville, began publishing *Farm and Fireside* in 1877 to push the sale of cultivators. Later *Woman's Home Companion, Collier's Weekly, American Magazine,* and other national magazines were added to the list. Several thousand employees worked for Crowell-Collier during its most prosperous years.

Canton was part of the iron and steel complex of the northeastern part of the state. Republic Steel had a plant there. Among other things produced in Canton were auto bodies and roller bearings. The Timken Roller Bearing Company was founded there in 1900. The nationally known Hoover vacuum sweeper was made in North Canton. Safes and watches were also manufactured in Canton. After the Deuber-Hampden Watch Works came to town in 1887, lured by $100,000 and free land, thousands of people also moved to Canton, hoping to work in the plant. By 1880 the population had jumped from 13,000 to 26,000. Deuber-Hampden boasted that its watches "were accurate to the second" and would not accidentally reset in one's pocket as the "common" ones did.

Columbus was not a major manufacturing city like Cleveland, Youngstown, Akron, or Toledo. It remained primarily a center for commerce and government. Among the industries for which Columbus was noted were paper making, publishing, and shoe manufacturing. One of the nation's major steel castings companies was also in Columbus. Buckeye Steel Castings began business on a small scale in 1881 making iron castings. Progress was slow until it began producing automatic couplers for railroads.

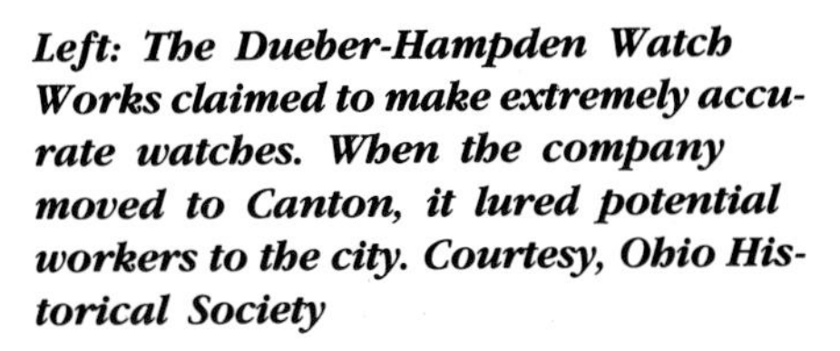

Left: The Dueber-Hampden Watch Works claimed to make extremely accurate watches. When the company moved to Canton, it lured potential workers to the city. Courtesy, Ohio Historical Society

Below left: Barney Kroger's first store, the Great Western Tea Company, opened in 1883. Within the year, Kroger bought out his partner and named the store after himself. Within ten years the first grocery chain had expanded to include seventeen stores. By 1912 the number of stores had grown to 157. Courtesy, Cincinnati Historical Society

Right: In 1857 the Ohio state government moved into the new capitol building which was under construction when the old State House burned down. Originally the new building was to cost $400,000 and take six years to construct; however, it took twenty-two years and some $1.6 million to complete this Greek Doric structure. Courtesy, Ohio Historical Society

Below right: Businesses of Columbus used motorized vehicles for making deliveries and often advertised their products on the sides of delivery trucks, as seen in this 1910 photo of Capitol City Products. Courtesy, Ohio Historical Society and the Columbus Dispatch

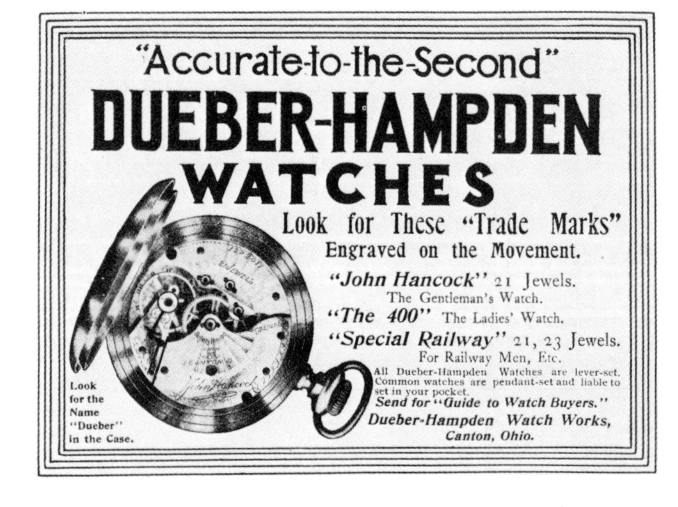

Below: The Dueber-Hampden Watch Works was an important business in Canton for many years. This ad from an issue of The Outlook *in 1900 expounds the virtues of the Dueber-Hampden Watch, which is lever-set and will not "set in your pocket." Courtesy,* The Outlook

Above: In 1916 Buckeye Steel Castings Company claimed to have the world's largest steel foundry manufacturing steel casting for railroads. Located in Columbus, the company made automative couplers which linked railroad cars together. Courtesy, Ohio Historical Society

Left: This Columbus business firm offered an interesting combination of services: undertaking and livery. Courtesy, Ohio Historical Society and the Columbus Dispatch

This collage shows production, from the drawing board to the factory, at the Sidney Machine Tool Company, established in 1904. Courtesy, Ohio Historical Society

As steel came in, Buckeye went to steel couplings. That was in 1902. A new factory was built in 1916 by which time the company was claiming that it was "the largest steel foundry in the world . . . devoted entirely to the manufacture of steel castings for railroad work." Two major reasons for the success of Buckeye Castings were its early utilization of the principles of "scientific management" and adoption of employee welfare programs.

Among the smaller towns, Sidney, Ohio, had a remarkable record of industrial success. In the late nineteenth century Sidney artisans made wooden parts for carriages and other products. The Wagner Company which made cast-iron parts and ventured into aluminum ware was also in Sidney. Sidney was noted for its community support of local firms. The most important industry in town was Monarch Machine Tool Company. Citizens of Sidney induced Monarch, then a small machine shop in Detroit, to move to their city in 1909. It prospered greatly during World War I with the huge demand for machine tools. The plant was enlarged after the war. In promoting home industry, Monarch purchased castings for its lathes from a neighbor firm next door.

An account of another world industrial leader will close this selective catalog of Ohio industry. The National Cash Register Company of Dayton was founded by John Patterson in 1884. A Dartmouth graduate, Patterson was a toll collector on the Miami and Erie Canal who was troubled by the inexact method of counting fares. When he and his brother opened a retail shop at Coalton in the late 1870s, dealing in coal and miner supplies, they had the same problems. John Patterson read about a cash register which did all the counting of all transactions and ordered two of them. The registers cut debts and saved money. In 1884 he bought controlling interest in the same cash register company, which had been failing, and the National Cash Register Company was born.

Patterson was a humorless, tough, single-minded man, determined to make the company succeed. He had little patience with inefficiency or insubordination. The people he fired or who left under pressure constitutes a "Who's Who" in American business leadership. Charles F. Kettering and Thomas Watson are two of the more memorable names. Between 1910 and 1930, "an estimated one-sixth of the top executives in the nation's companies were former NCR executives," proclaims a company brochure.

Patterson pushed his product with a driving intensity. His salesmen were carefully trained. They had to memorize a 450-word primer on selling techniques and were fired if they could not. Patterson made frequent "flying trips," unannounced, to check up on his people. He established a training school for the agents and converted annual conventions into instructional seminars. He believed strongly in advertising, but in contrast to Procter & Gamble which sold its product through national magazines, Patterson favored mailing his own publications, one of which was called the "Hustler," directly to potential buyers.

Patent fights and legal battles marked the first twenty-five years of NCR history, as they did with most other large corporations. In one case Patterson was fined and sentenced to jail, but the ruling was overturned on appeal. There was no stopping NCR's growth and eventual domination of the industry. Construction of a vast new complex of buildings was begun in 1906. The number of employees had increased from 13 in 1884 to 7,000 by the end of World War I, while cash register sales leaped from 359 to 1.5 million dollars.

One of the world's great paint companies was founded in Cleveland in the years following the Civil War. Henry Sherwin's career, to a point, paralleled that of John D. Rockefeller. Arriving in Cleveland as a teenager from Vermont in the 1850s, Sherwin avoided war service and got a grounding in business by working in a produce commission house. He was keenly aware of several new fields of business enterprise just opening, but where Rockefeller chose oil, Sherwin chose paint. In 1870, the same year Standard Oil was launched, the unschooled Sherwin and a Western Reserve Ph.D., Edgar P. Williams, formed the Sherwin-Williams Company.

In those days, paint manufacturers merely supplied the ingredients for the paint while buyers mixed the batch they wanted themselves. A few ready-mix paints appeared on the market in the 1870s, but Sherwin-Williams came out with the first quality ready-mix paint in 1880—Sherwin-Williams Paint. The acquisition of the Calumet Paint Company outside of Chicago in 1888 marked an important advance in the company's fortunes. Calumet's strategic location was well-suited to the growing paint market in Pullman and other railroad cars, farm equipment, and carriages. Over the years the company expanded into Canada, South America, and Europe. In 1905 it adopted its famous "Cover the Earth" logo, which well-reflected its rise to preeminence in the industry.

Without question Ohio made a major contribution to the Industrial Revolution which, between the Civil War and World War I, forever changed America. Many of the large business organizations which made the United States an industrial giant had some links with the Buckeye State. Great Ohio corporations, prominent Ohio "captains of industry," and well-known inventors played key roles in transforming the nation's rich resources into necessary goods and luxury items which significantly improved the way Americans lived. True, the Industrial Revolution had its negative side, but all things considered, as historian George Knepper put it, "these were good years for Ohio."

By 1895 Smith's European Hotel was beginning to enjoy its heyday in Columbus. The New York Oyster House, on the first floor of the hotel, was located near the corner of Broad and High. Courtesy, Ohio Historical Society

VI
BOOM AND BUST

The 1939 strike at the Fisher Body plant in Cleveland erupted into violence during its final days. In response to management's refusal to negotiate, union leaders called for a walkout of selected skilled workers in strategically located plants. Thus, the plants were handicapped while other employees were able to work, draw their wages, and support their striking coworkers. Courtesy, Ohio Historical Society

Facing page: By 1930 a number of companies had merged into Republic Steel, strengthening Cleveland's position in the iron and steel industry. Problems arose in the summer of 1937, however, when a clash between strikers and nonunion workers at Republic's Corrigan-McKinney Plant left one man dead and sixty injured. In 1945 Republic was one of the largest single employers in the city, with 9,000 people on its payroll. Courtesy, Western Reserve Historical Society

The rise of big business transformed the United States in many ways. Although the standard of living was improved, wealth and power became concentrated in the hands of the very few. The exercise of this tremendous power was not always in the best interests of society. Exploitation of laborers and farmers and the disregard of the public welfare were commonplace. The *laissez-faire* philosophy had created a massive imbalance within the system. In 1900, according to one writer, one-half of the population possessed nothing, while one percent owned 54 percent of the national wealth. Fewer and fewer corporations controlled more and more of the country's industrial might. In 1897 the total capitalization of all one-million-dollar corporations totalled $170 million. In 1900 this figure had increased to five billion dollars; in 1904 it had escalated to twenty billion dollars.

This monopoly movement occurred, ironically, in the wake of passage of the Sherman Anti-Trust Act of 1890. This act was designed to prevent "trustification," yet within fifteen years huge monopolies had appeared, creating a national scandal. One reason for this was the ambiguous wording of the statute, which allowed federal courts, unsympathetic to antitrust regulation, to interpret the Sherman Act very narrowly. While monopoly provided efficiency, economy, and centralized control—desirable goals in business management—it also provided such unrestricted power that abuse was an inevitable consequence. The masters of the great corporations felt that they alone had the right to determine how their business should be managed and strongly opposed any attempts by legislative bodies to regulate them.

This arrogance excited the interest of a legion of investigative

In April 1887 Procter & Gamble announced an agreement to share profits with its employees. To maintain the employees' enthusiasm, the company held Dividend Day Celebrations twice a year. Pictured here is the 1926 celebration at Cincinnati's amusement park, Coney Island. The tradition continues, but now the celebrations are only held once a year. Courtesy, the Procter & Gamble Company

Facing page: Workers pose in front of the Xenia Machine Works factory. Wages were generally low and working conditions poor for the predominantly black female laborers, such as those pictured here. Courtesy, Ohio Historical Society

reporters, called "muckrakers." Beginning in 1903, articles began to appear in national magazines exposing abuses by the great railroads and corporations. These included bribery of legislators, price-fixing without reference to cost, forcing competitors out of business, blacklisting troublemakers among employees, and closing plants where unions had been formed. When these stories began to attract national attention, the most activist president in American history sat in the White House. Theodore Roosevelt, upset by the monopolization trend in business, gained fame as a "trustbuster." While he never "busted" too many trusts, he did focus attention on the situation.

But how should these "captains of industry"—or "robber barons"—be judged? Until the middle of the twentieth century historians dealt harshly with them. The classic view holds that they were men who devoured the nation's wealth, plundered its resources, and controlled its political institutions. They may have helped develop the economic system, but the road was strewn with the wreckage and waste of human and natural resources. More recently, however, this interpretation has been challenged. Allan Nevins, the famous Civil War scholar and biographer of Rockefeller and Ford, was one of the first historians to question the earlier judgement. While conceding that the behavior of many business leaders was indefensible, Nevins pointed out that the Industrial Revolution created an unprecedented economic environment for which no established code of ethics existed. Business leaders were fighting for survival in an atmosphere which demanded extreme measures to avoid destruction. Had they acted in a "moral" manner, they would have been eliminated and others, employing the ruthless tactics they had abjured, would have triumphed.

Moreover, these men created the mightiest industrial empire in the world. In addition, by the time this structure had been built, the great entrepreneurs had developed a social conscience, a recognition that perhaps they did have an obligation to society. Andrew Carnegie was the first of his generation to sense this. His "gospel of wealth" was not as well known as his libraries, but it marked new directions in corporate philanthropy. Establishing universities, cultural complexes, and foundations were other means by which robber barons/captains of industry bequeathed their fortunes for the betterment of mankind. In balance, holds the current view, the good they did outweighed the evil.

Along with the great entreprenuers appeared

great forces of laborers who manned the machines and plants. As large factories with their thousands of workers emerged, no particular thought was given to the workers' well-being or safety. Under hallowed *laissez-faire* doctrine, the worker was free to labor for an employer, or leave, if he so wished. The employer bore no responsibility for his welfare. As the system grew and as job competition intensified, the worker's freedom was restricted. Theoretically, he could still come and go as he pleased, but in reality this was not the case.

Working conditions were bad. Hours were long, work was hard, and the machinery was generally unsafe. During the famous strike at Carnegie's Homestead works near Pittsburgh in the summer of 1892, it came out that steelworkers were paid fourteen cents an hour for a twelve-hour day, six days a week. Since there was no lunch hour, food was eaten on the job. Some workers never went home, sleeping beside their machines. Because of the long hours and high noise level, the men's reaction time slowed down and they became prone to serious injury. Mutilation of hands and arms was common. Three hundred and eighty-one deaths occurred in Pittsburgh mills alone in 1891. Work in coal mines was also dangerous, not only because of cave-ins but because of the inhalation of bad air. Bad air was a problem also in the rubber plants, in Akron. Far more publicized were the miserable conditions in the packing houses, immortalized in Upton Sinclair's 1906 *The Jungle*.

Dissatisfaction with wages, hours, and working

***Bottom:** The United Mine Workers of America, founded in 1890, gathered in Columbus at its first convention. The union claimed to represent all workers in and around the mines. In 1898 a strike by the UMW won workers an eight-hour workday. After that grand victory, the number of union members doubled within two years. Courtesy, Ohio Historical Society*

***Below:** On December 8, 1886, the Ohio State Journal announced the opening of the Columbus convention which led to the formation of the American Federation of Labor (AFL). The new organization, with Samuel Gompers as its leader, was basically a loose affiliation of autonomous craft unions, not a strong, centrally organized body. Courtesy, Ohio Historical Society*

THE FEDERATED TRADES.

OPENING OF THE SIXTH CONGRESS.

The Relations of the Unions with the Knights of Labor – Preparing to Amalgamate with the Labor Union Conference.

The sixth annual Congress of the Federation of Organized Trades and Labor Unions of the United States and Canada was called to order by President Gompers in Druid's hall, South Fourth street, at noon yesterday. D. P. Boyer, chief organizer of the International Typographical union, introduced Grafton Pearce of this city who, as the representative of the Columbus Trades assembly, delivered an excellent address of welcome, in which he ably discussed the objects to be attained, urged harmony, deliberation, freedom from politics and the wisest course of procedure.

President Gompers returned the thanks of the congress for the cordial welcome, referred to the mistakes of organized labor in the past, the good it had done and the purposes for the future. He discussed the eight-hour law, the struggles of the past year, and urged harmony in all meetings and co operations.

conditions was responsible for the rise of trade unionism during the Industrial Revolution. Since Ohio was one of the most heavily industrialized states in the country, an active union movement developed there. The most powerful national labor organization, the American Federation of Labor, was founded in Columbus in 1886. Another important national union which was very prominent in Ohio labor matters was the United Mineworkers of America. Other active unions in the state were in steel, rubber, glass, and the skilled trades. Because of the continual struggle between employers and employees, hundreds of strikes broke out in Ohio between 1886 and 1905.

One of the most bitter strikes which occurred in Ohio involved the rubber industry. Serious trouble erupted early in 1913 at Firestone over the installation of laborsaving machinery. With a cut in the piece-rate wage the income for tire-finishers declined and a number of them stayed away from work. When Firestone fired the absentees, unrest spread to other departments in the plant and by mid-February engulfed other plants in the city. The strikers, who numbered almost 75 percent of the 22,000 Akron rubber workers, demanded an eight-hour day, a minimum hourly rate, and double pay for overtime. The companies rejected the demands. Refusing to negotiate with union representatives or impartial mediators, the employers built barricades, harassed picketers, imported strikebreakers, caused the arrest of strike leaders, and launched an extensive propaganda campaign to win over public opinion. This pressure, combined with developing internal conflict, weakened the strike front as February gave way to March. With their leaders either in jail or chased out of town, the strikers caved in by the end of the month. It came out later that most of the union leaders had been paid informers.

A good portion of the general public also believed that there was something un-American

about unions, but it was the "captains of industry" who had to deal with the issue. In their view, unions had no place in the factory. These men insisted that any improvements in working conditions that were made must be made on the company's terms and not dictated by workers or unions. Paternalistic "welfare capitalism," as this was called, characterized the new trend.

The subtitle of Samuel Crowther's 1923 biography of NCR's John Patterson is *Pioneer of Industrial Welfare.* Patterson had a good claim to the distinction. Like most successful businessmen, he personally went immediately to the source whenever serious problems arose. In 1894, $50,000 worth of equipment was returned to the company as unusa-

Above: Rubber workers at the B.F. Goodrich Company protested the plant manager's threat to move from Akron. These protestors were members of the Industrial Workers of the World, a radical strand of the American labor movement founded in 1905. Although these "Wobblies," as they were often called, advocated irradication of the capitalist system, most workers who joined the union were more interested in higher wages and improved working conditions. Courtesy, University of Akron Archives

Left: Joseph and Feiss, one of the largest clothing concerns in the U.S., grew out of an earlier company, Kock and Loeb. Involved in the wholesale apparel field, Joseph and Feiss purchased, cut, and sent cloth to small contract shops to assemble. Pictured is a company library where Joseph and Feiss workers could go to read and check out books. Courtesy, Western Reserve Historical Society

ble. Patterson at once relocated his office to the factory floor. In addition to learning what had gone wrong with the returned cash registers, he found that working conditions for his employees were not satisfactory. This incident marked the beginning of a massive program directed to improve the workers' welfare.

The factory was cleaned up, bathrooms and restrooms were installed, and wages increased. Special privileges were extended to women. Workers were given a shorter work day, fifteen-minute breaks in the morning and afternoon for exercise, lunch at company expense in a special lunch room was provided, and a half-day holiday each week and a one-day holiday each month was granted. In addition, a new factory was built in 1894, which was equipped with "first class baths and locker rooms, and restrooms for the women, hospitals and first aid stations, medical inspections, and free, clean aprons

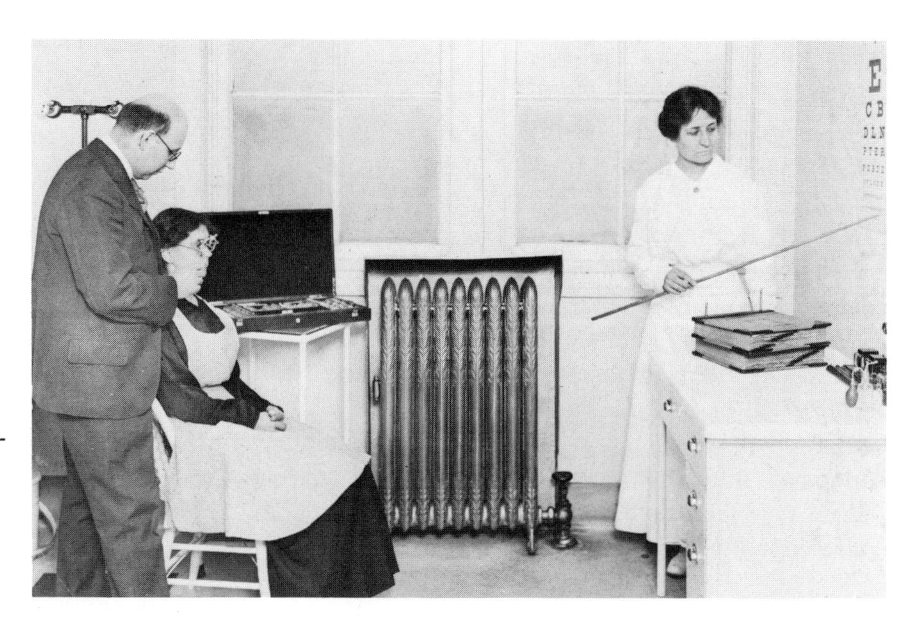

Right: Displaying an early interest in social welfare, Joseph and Feiss developed special services for its employees. Pictured are a doctor and nurse testing the eyesight of a clothing worker in 1915. Courtesy, Western Reserve Historical Society

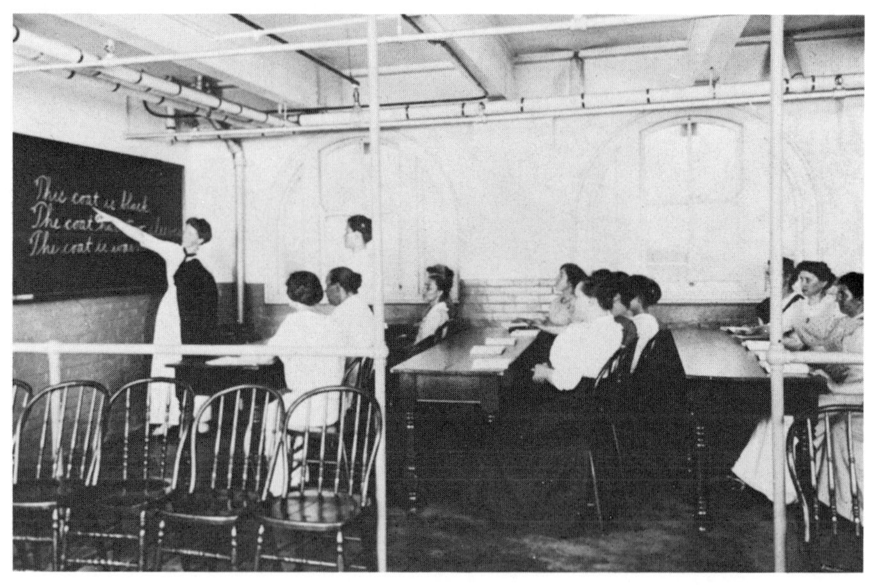

Below right: Joseph and Feiss hired a large number of immigrants and offered educational classes for its employees. These women were enrolled in a 1916 English class. Courtesy, Western Reserve Historical Society

and sleevelets for the women."

NCR was located in a deteriorating neighborhood, called "Slidertown," which had an adverse impact on the company's image. Patterson saw the relationship between company and community and concluded that something should be done to improve the image of the former and the condition of the latter. A landscape architect was hired to improve the grounds and a young woman, Lena Harvey, was employed to win over the residents. Boys who had devoted most of their leisure hours to flinging rocks through NCR windows, were formed into clubs. The boys' clubs planted gardens and learned both technical and business skills. A number of them would later become valued employees at NCR.

Patterson's concern extended beyond the immediate environs of the factory. The women's Century Club set up coffeehouses for female workers throughout Dayton. The Men's Welfare Work League, founded in 1904, worked closely with local educators to upgrade the school system. None of Patterson's actions prevented the bitter strike of 1901. After putting down the strike, Patterson instituted changes in management and a program of welfare capitalism which would lead to a healthier work atmosphere in the future.

Procter & Gamble may have trailed NCR in several aspects of welfare capitalism, but in one particular area—profit sharing—it was well ahead. W. Cooper Procter, grandson of the cofounder, joined the firm, fresh out of Princeton, in 1883. He learned the business from the ground up and in 1907 became president of the company. In his first years young Procter labored side by side with the workers at a time when the Knights of Labor were recruiting members in the Cincinnati area. To blunt this campaign he proposed to his elders that all employees be given Saturday afternoons off with pay. A revolutionary idea for 1885, it was accepted by the company. This by no means resolved the labor unrest in the plant. Strikes broke out periodically and worker turnover averaged 50 percent annually.

In searching for an answer to the problem, Cooper Procter at length determined to experiment with profit sharing. The idea was not popular in business circles and he had no easy time convincing father, uncles, and cousins of its virtues. He contended that sharing company profits with the workers would give them a stake in the company's fortunes and lead to greater job satisfaction and improved performance. The plan was instituted in 1887. Dividends were paid from company profits twice a year to each worker. The first dividend day in October was celebrated with a party, entertainment, and a speech by Procter. He urged the employees to work as hard as they could, so the company would prosper and there would be more profits to share.

The plan did not work as intended. The workers came to view the dividends as simply a semiannual bonus unrelated to job performance. Procter

Above: William Cooper Procter, grandson of the co-founder of Procter & Gamble, was instrumental in the introduction of the profit-sharing system. This memorial to him is carved in stone outside the company building at Ivorydale: "William Cooper Procter, 1862-1934. He lived a life of noble simplicity believing in God and the inherent worthiness of his fellow men." Courtesy, the Procter & Gamble Company

Left: Sherwin-Williams, organized in 1870, has become the world's largest manufacturer of paints, lacquers, varnishes, insecticides, and other associated products. The company's trademark, "Cover the Earth," is included in the lower corners of this 1913 advertisement. Courtesy, **The Outlook**

struggled with the plan for a number of years and at length arrived at a workable solution. In 1903 he revised the entire system by tying profit sharing to stock ownership in Procter & Gamble. To receive any profits an employee had to own company stock, and the amount he received was linked to the amount of stock he owned. Stock purchases were spread over a period of time and the company more than matched the employee's contribution. The plan worked. While not every employee bought company stock, well over half of them did.

The Cleveland Chamber of Commerce, organized in the 1890s, gave a boost to welfare capitalism in the big city. Under its leadership close to eighty companies, including several of the more important ones such as Cleveland Trust and Sherwin-Williams, had instituted welfare programs during

the first decade of the twentieth century. The chamber's purpose, like most companies which supported welfare capitalism, was to promote a healthier atmosphere within the industrial community and to avoid labor strife. M.A. Hanna Company, for example, adopted a life insurance program for its employees in 1914. The rubber companies were also active in promoting worker welfare. Paul W. Litchfield, a twenty-five-year-old MIT graduate, came to Goodyear in 1900 as factory superintendent. Instrumental in establishing Goodyear's employee welfare programs, Litchfield in 1909 helped create

***Above:** Goodyear provided buses to transport workers back and forth between Goodyear Heights and the Goodyear factories. To walk from the housing subdivision to the factories took about ten to fifteen minutes. Goodyear Heights covered 350 acres, with approximately 1,000 homes that were fifty feet by 115 feet. Courtesy, Summit County Historical Society*

***Left:** This photograph shows the construction of company-sponsored housing for employees of Youngstown Sheet and Tube. This two-year project began in 1915 with a plan to build 500 dwellings; these would be sold to workers in an attempt to increase loyalty to the firm. At the same time, because of wartime shortages of labor and housing, the company was building a labor camp, complete with central dining hall and barracks, to house newly recruited workers. Courtesy, Ohio Historical Society*

***Above:** Aside from condoning the nation's newly established welfare system and providing medical care for its employees, Buckeye Steel Castings Company took an interest in its employees' social and recreational lives. The Buckeye Steel baseball team, pictured here, played on a baseball field adjacent to its factory. Courtesy, Ohio Historical Society*

the Goodyear Relief Association. This fund was designed for the benefit of injured or ill employees. In 1912 he founded the first employee publication, the *Wingfoot Clan.* The following year he established an employee development program, the "Flying Squadron," in which talented employees learned more of the company's total operations and enhanced their opportunities for advancement.

Frank Seiberling developed a unique employee housing plan for Goodyear workers in 1912. The idea was to reduce the commuting time to work and to allow employees to become homeowners at a moderate price. A large piece of property east of the plant—a ten-minute walk away—was acquired and the workers were given the option of purchasing three different types of structures: a single unit, double unit, or a bungalow. No down payment was required and modest monthly fees financed the purchase, which averaged about $3,500. All the services for a self-sustaining community were provided. By the spring of 1914 ninety homes were occupied and within two more years all lots were sold.

World War I stimulated company welfare programs because of the desire to increase production and keep workers happy. While it did not always achieve these goals, welfare capitalism became quite popular in the war years. Buckeye Steel Castings in Columbus, another pioneer in welfarism, set up a medical dispensary in 1903 within a year of the company's founding. By the time of World War I the dispensary had become a hospital, and the company had built washrooms, locker rooms, and a kitchen. Buckeye sponsored annual picnics, and a baseball field was laid out adjacent to the factory. An employee life insurance policy was instituted in 1917 and later the same year 108 acres of land were acquired and $143,000 appropriated for employee housing near the plant. Buckeye began cosponsoring technical courses with the Columbus YMCA through which employees could improve their knowledge and skills. Athletic teams participated in YMCA leagues and social and recreational programs included musical performances, movies, and refreshments. Buckeye went out into the community and its officers provided financial assistance and leadership for Columbus' philanthropic endeavors.

* * *

For more than two and one-half years after war began in Europe in August 1914 the United States sat on the sidelines. Whatever the country's official stance, Americans were distinctly pro-Allies in sentiment and the industrial community began supplying France and Britain with the sinews of war. Exports to Europe jumped from one and one-half billion dollars at the time war began to four billion dollars in 1917 on the eve of America's entry into the conflict. Business, recovering from a pre-war decline, boomed, although it was a somewhat chaotic expansion. Planning came quickly following the declaration of war. The massive mobilization of manpower and resources required by the war effort could not be undertaken by an unregulated economy. Hence a host of national agencies were created to coordinate and maximize industrial, fuel, food, and transportation resources. Probably most central to the complicated network of agencies was the powerful War Industries Board, under the direction of the prominent Wall Street broker Bernard Baruch.

Coordinating American industry was not a simple task and countless problems and bottlenecks developed. Nevertheless the economy expanded and the job of winning the war was accomplished. Plant facilities of auto and steel companies grew at such a rate that they were well prepared for further expansion after the war. American steel production

The women's suffrage movement was important to Ohio women, many of whom contributed greatly to Ohio industries in World War I. Pictured here are women representing counties throughout the state at a 1914 rally in Columbus. Courtesy, Ohio Historical Society

attained forty million tons annually during the war years, far in excess of the output of all the Allies and Central Powers combined. Income in the manufacturing sector climbed from $8.7 billion in 1916, to $13 billion in 1918, to $16.8 billion in 1920. Profits skyrocketed in many industries.

Ohio, like most states, had its own wartime councils which worked with the national bodies. The Council of Defence was a branch of the War Industries Board, while state fuel, food, and employment agencies similarily were geared to their federal counterparts. A yeoman's task was the lot of Fred C. Croxton, who chaired both the defense council and food administration. The council's membership included leaders from both management and labor; the public and agricultural sectors were also represented. The council strove to coordinate the state's economy to minimize food and fuel shortages and to channel labor where it was most needed. With the demand for goods and services at a record peak and manpower mobilization in full swing, labor shortages continued throughout the war.

Not surprisingly, Ohio's contribution to the nation's industrial effort during the war was substantial. Steel for tanks, trucks, weapons, and munitions poured forth from the mills of the Mahoning and Cuyahoga valleys. Coal production reached an all-time high. Akron's rubber factories produced "hundreds of thousands of tires for the army, a tremendous number of gas masks, countless miscellaneous articles, and hundreds of blimps and observation balloons." Economically, this was Akron's greatest age of growth. Marion Steam Shovel produced tanks and shovels "that could crawl over marshy places." Machine tool makers thoughout the state—especially in Cincinnati—were also busy. White Motor Company in Cleveland became famous in World War I for its trucks, and, as mentioned, earned the Croix de Guerre from the French government.

Operating a large industrial plant is never easy, but it is particularly difficult in wartime because of shortages of materials, labor, and transportation. George King, president of Marion Steam Shovel, reviewed these problems in his annual report of January, 23, 1917. While the country appeared to be prospering economically, he commented, difficulties caused by shortages had drained away most of the company's profits. "With few exceptions," he observed, "we are paying more for all materials than was necessary a year ago. Labor has not only been scarce and high-priced, but of very low competency. The floating laborer has hindered us a great deal because of his short period of employment."

Labor, indeed, was "feeling its oats" during World War I. Not since the movement had emerged as an influential force had labor been so in demand. Jobs were for the asking, wages were good, and the federal government generally supported the workers in disputes with employers. Good times usually find labor more aggressive than when the economy is on the downslide. From 1914 onward the strike spirit intensified. The outbreak of war initiated a wave of labor disputes across Ohio. Cary and Boryczka report that

> *among those striking in 1914 were Portsmouth and Cincinnati shoe workers, Canton phone operators, retail clerks in Zanesville, buffers and polishers in Wooster, clay workers in Empire and Toronto, miners in Dillonvale. In 1915, the list of 115 strikes included paper makers in Middletown, molders in Hamilton, machinists in Cincinnati and Columbus, and munitions workers in Youngstown. The following year 276 strikes swept the state.*

Among the latter number were violent disputes at Youngstown's steel plants. As grievances mounted some 16,000 workers finally lashed out in fury and frustration, leading to a million dollars in property damage and the summoning of 2,000 National Guard troops.

Once the United States entered the war, the workers' bargaining position improved dramatically as the national government pressed for a maximum production effort. The National Defence Council, which became the War Industries Board in 1918, included members from organized labor. As the eruption of strikes across the land escalated in 1917 a War Labor Policies Board was created. The board worked actively to nip labor disputes at their outset through mediation, although strikes continued to occur during the war. Union membership doubled under the favorable wartime conditions. The years following the Armistice, however, were marked by a backlash against unionism.

* * *

The decade following the end of the war was a gold mine for the social historian. With the

Pictured here are employees at the Crooksville China Company in 1919. Crooksville, like Roseville, East Liverpool, and areas in Perry County, is rich in clay deposits and therefore important to the thriving pottery industry. Courtesy, Ohio Historical Society

popularization of the automobile, the appearance of the radio, and improvements in movies and phonograph recordings, the lifestyle of millions of Americans was irreversibly changed. The 1920s is also a fascinating period for business historians to examine. Capitalism had matured with the quest for stability and systemized planning supplanting the prewar thirst for experimentation and innovation. Management tended more to mirror an impersonal bureaucracy than a daring wildcatter. The federal government was firmly in the hands of the friends of business and the *laissez-faire* spirit stimulated a period of economic growth. As an older textbook put it, "It was an age of unprecedented prosperity."

Before the arrival of prosperity, however, there was a sharp break in the economy in the summer of 1920. Conditions had been fairly good for over a year after the Armistice, but then the canceling of war contracts, the demobilization of more than two million men, and the loss of European grain markets made their impact. The rubber industry was hard hit at this time and before the dust had cleared one of the major figures in the business had been driven out of his own company. Frank Seiberling, who had founded Goodyear, though a fine engineer was not very good in the front office. The sudden break in the economy in 1920 found the company with a huge inventory, few buyers, and practically no cash. The work force was cut back from 34,000 to 8,000 and Seiberling went hat in hand to Wall Street.

Wall Street was not interested at this time, however, and Goodyear's crisis worsened. By the end of 1921 bankruptcy and receivership were imminent. Now Wall Street came to the rescue. Dillon and Read assumed the task of refinancing and reorganizing the company and were able to raise sufficient funds to restore Goodyear to a sound footing. However, both Frank and Charles Seiberling would have to go. Frank Seiberling with the help of friends was able to establish a new tire factory, under his own name, in Barberton, and within a few years was again one of the top tire manufacturers in the country.

In the early days of Standard Oil Company, horsedrawn tank wagons, built in the company's wagon works in the Cleveland Flats, made the rounds to farms, groceries, and hardware stores. The wagons, pictured here, were still in operation in the early 1920s, before the company began to use motorized tank trucks. Courtesy, Western Reserve Historical Society

Under new leadership and banker supervision, Goodyear slowly fought its way back. Ruthless cost-cutting practices prevailed for several months as the new managers were determined to eliminate the debt. Sales gradually picked up and furloughed employees began to come back. Litchfield, one of two top men to survive the shakeup, now moved full speed ahead to again make Goodyear competitive with its rivals. Meanwhile, the company's overseas operations had expanded. By 1928 the work force, at home and abroad, had climbed to 40,000. Goodyear was again the number-one tire manufacturer and the number-one rubber company in the world.

Goodyear was not the only rubber company to suffer in the postwar depression. Firestone, too, was in trouble. Prices for tires were cut drastically and employees were fired. Goodrich had good relations with New York financiers and was able to pull through the crisis with less discomfort than the others, although its entire advertising department was abolished.

Contributing to the refinement of corporate operations during the 1920s were both managerial and technical advances. Perhaps the wide adoption of the "scientific management" idea of Frederick W. Taylor was the most important of these. However, research and development divisions, standardization of products, and cost accounting methods all played an important role in increasing efficiency. Diversification of products and establishment of overseas plants were other new features of this maturation period. Mechanization of industry moved forward, unfortunately contributing to the rise in "technological unemployment." Installment buying—"buy now, pay later"—became popular, stimulating consumer purchases of a vast array of products. Statistics reveal that between 1920 and 1930 the value of Ohio's major manufacturers grew 18 percent. At the same time the national growth was 14 percent. The steel industry increased its production by 31 percent and production of motor vehicles and parts was up by 64 percent. The only major industry which experienced a loss in the 1920s was rubber, down 9 percent.

The automobile, plus installment buying, was the catalyst for the boom years of the 1920s. In 1921 one and one-half million cars were manufactured. By 1929 the output was up to four and one-half million, by which time there were some twenty-three million vehicles on the road. Automobile manufacturing, now the biggest industry in the land, comprised 12.7 percent of the total of all manufactures.

Significant improvements in the functioning of the automobile were the work of the famous inventor from Dayton, Charles F. Kettering. Graduating from Ohio State with an engineering degree early in the century, Kettering went to work for NCR. There he mastered the process of applying electrical power to the cash register, making obsolete the laborious hand crank. Later he established the Dayton Engineering Laboratories Company (DELCO). His major achievement took place in 1911 when he successfully operated a self-starter on a Cadillac. In 1916 Kettering's company was absorbed by General Motors and incorporated in its research division. His other contributions to the auto industry were the development of antiknock gasoline and refinements in the diesel engine.

Ohio's auto industry had declined with the rise of Detroit, although there were several plants in Toledo and Cleveland. The production of bodies, parts, tires, glass, and other car accessories was big business in the state. Among other Ohio industries which prospered during the decade were petroleum refining (up 58 percent), bread and bakery products (up 54 percent), paper and paperboard production (up 46 percent), chemicals (up 42 percent), and newspaper publishing and printing (up 126 percent). A more modest increase was scored by the machine tool industry (up 8 percent).

As has been mentioned, internationalization and diversification were prominent characteristics of the 1920s. NCR was an exponent of both. Actually, overseas plants had been built earlier, in Berlin, Germany, in the early 1900s and in Toronto, Canada, in 1918. Sales offices were established in the 1920s in South Africa, India, Colombia, and the Soviet Union. Its first effort at manufacturing something besides regular cash registers was in the early 1920s with the successful launching of the Class 2000 accounting machine. This was a "sophisticated cash register that printed data on inserted forms and provided 30 totals rather than half a dozen." The Statler Hotel chain adopted the Class 2000, but it was such a complicated machine with its 20,000 hand-assembled parts, that for awhile NCR had to have a repairman stationed at every Statler Hotel. In 1929 NCR acquired the Ellis Adding-Typewriter Company, and came out with its Class 3000 accounting machine, useful in "the preparation of payroll, stock records, billings for utilities and insurance companies, and in cost accounting operations."

NCR was one of the first large corporations anywhere to institute a personnel department for promoting better employee-employer relations. This was done shortly after the 1901 strike. Corporate personnel offices became quite common in the years after World War I. Marion Shovel joined the ranks in 1921 when it established a Department of Personnel Training, to provide training for workers in different aspects of the business. Announcing the new program, the company noted that the manufacture of sophisticated machinery had become increasingly complex. Employee training could no longer be permitted to take place on the job. I.B. Shoup was lured away from Westinghouse, where for four years he had been the director of vocational education, to head the new department.

Another feature of the economy of the 1920s was the shifting of production from industrial to consumer goods. With the industrial plant constructed, attention was focused on the wants and desires of the general public. The decade saw an outpouring of not only automobiles, but washing machines, refrigerators, vacuum cleaners, radios, tin cans, and a host of household conveniences. Many such machines and appliances were manufactured in Ohio and it took the genius of an Ohio inventor to make the consumerist revolution possible.

John Butler Tytus, born in 1875 near Middletown, took his Yale degree in English literature and returned home to work in the family paper mill. After the company was sold, Tytus sought a position with Middletown's new (founded in 1901) American Rolling Mill Company (ARMCO). No office jobs were available, so he worked in the sheet mill, "one of the lowest, hottest, and hardest jobs in steel making." He picked up the basics of steel work in a hurry and began to move up through the ranks.

As he observed the workers clumsily dragging heavy sheets of steel through the rollers, Tytus could not help but think of the big papermaking machines he once worked with which converted wood and pulp into one long continuous sheet of paper. If the principle could be applied to a sheet mill it would relieve workers of backbreaking drudgery while producing a much better and cheaper product. But steel was quite different from paper. United States Steel had already failed twice to construct continuous-sheet steel mills. Tytus confided his idea to several of his associates, but they doubted its feasibility. Yet he never lost hope and continued to study the matter. He examined carefully the steel sheets to determine what effects the rollers had on them. He made mathematical computations and collected scientific data. In a 1916 article he discussed the problem and concluded that the difficulty lay with the rollers which changed shape with each passage of the steel through them.

In 1921 ARMCO purchased the Ashland Iron and Mining Company in Ashland, Kentucky, for the purpose of constructing traditional sheet mills. Tytus recognized that this was the moment to proceed with the continuous mill. He and his supervisor, Charles Ruffin Hook, took the proposal to the board of directors. How much would it cost? Ten million dollars. If it failed, they were told, it might ruin the company and cost thousands of people their jobs. Would you recommend it, Hook was asked? "Yes." The directors gave Tytus the green light, recognizing full well the risk involved. But they had faith in the vision as well as the technical expertise of the English literature scholar from Yale.

Construction began in October 1922 and was completed about a year later. The special engineering office in Middletown was moved to Ashland and by late December 1923 all was ready for the first trial. Fourteen "stands of rolls" set in a straight line were prepared "to reduce red-hot, five-inch thick

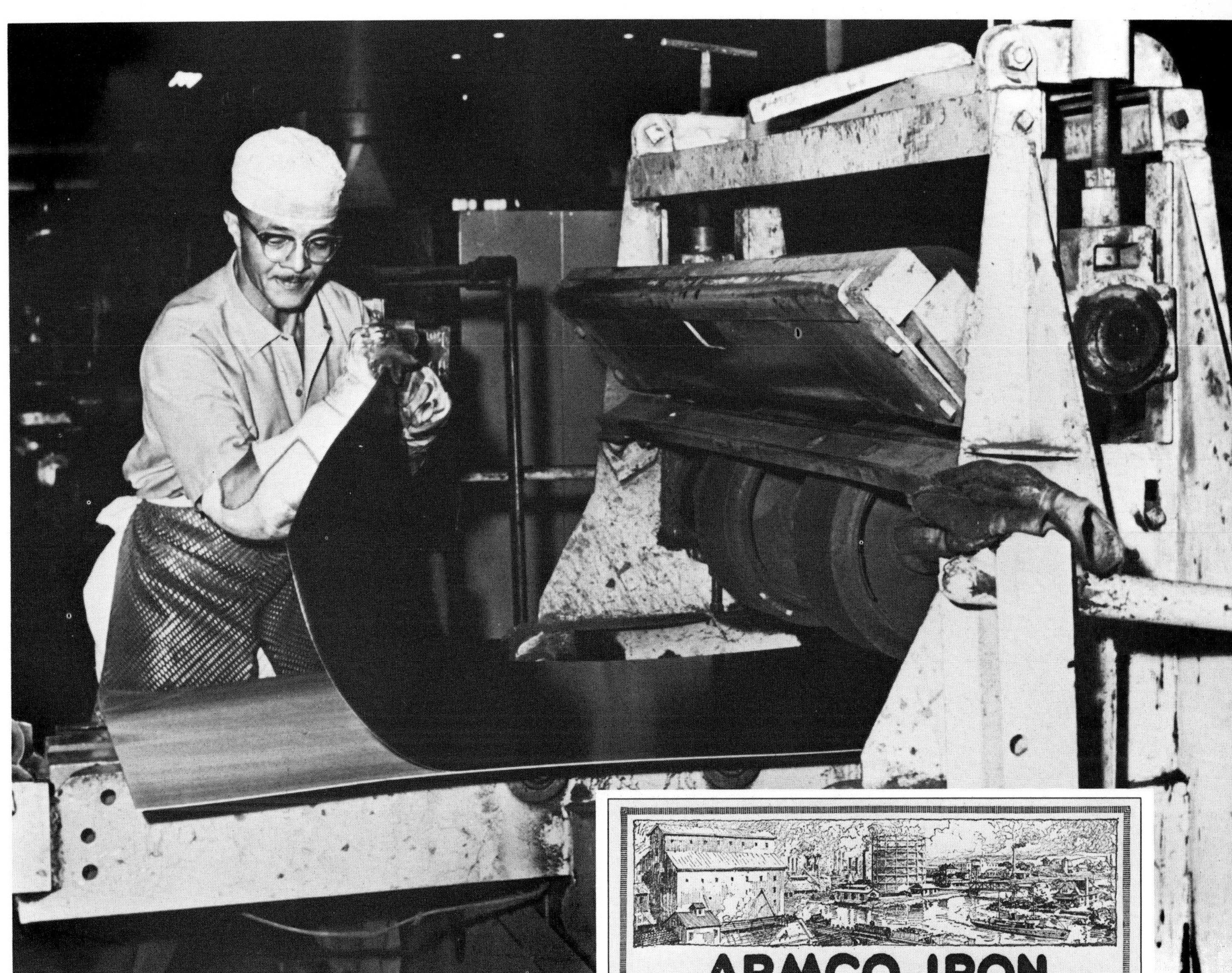

Above: The American Rolling Mill Company was famous for its continuous hot strip mill. Shown here is an employee at work in the Zanesville plant. Courtesy, Ohio Historical Society

Right: This American Rolling Mill Company advertisement appeared in The Outlook, *a weekly magazine, in September 1914.*

ARMCO IRON
Resists Rust

About ten years ago, Government scientists discovered that impurities such as carbon, silicon, sulphur, manganese, copper, etc., make metals rust. When impure metals are exposed to moisture, an electrical action corrodes either the impurity or the metal itself. Inversely, they found that pure iron is an almost perfect resistant to rust. Pure iron, ten years ago, was not made on a commercial scale. Steel was so cheaply made that metallurgists said pure iron couldn't be made to compete with it. But we believed it could be done.

Armco is the Purest Iron Made

After patient research, spending thousands in equipment, we finally produced pure iron—this pure iron is called Armco or American Ingot Iron. Armco Iron is purer than the iron made a hundred years ago by laborious refinement and forging.

Armco Iron resists rust, not only because it is the purest iron made, but because it is of uniform texture and strength, is free from stresses and strains. It has a smooth surface that takes a very high polish.

Its Purity Makes Possible Perfect Galvanizing

Armco Iron shows practically no dissolution when the zinc is applied in galvanizing. Therefore, the coating is purer and lasts many times longer than galvanizing does on ordinary iron or steel.

AMERICAN ARMCO INGOT IRON

The trade mark ARMCO carries the assurance that iron bearing that mark is manufactured by The American Rolling Mill Co. with the skill, intelligence and fidelity associated with its products, and, hence, can be depended upon to possess in the highest degree the merit claimed for it. It has behind it the guarantee of that company concerning the purity of the iron and the accuracy and thoroughness with which each step in its manufacture has been conducted.

Armco Iron is most serviceable for:

Roofing-Siding, Refrigerators, Smoke-stacks, Motor Boats, Window Frames, Stoves-Furnaces, Metal Lath, Water Tanks, Railroad Cars, Flumes, Wire Fencing, Metal Cars

Armco Old Style Tin Roofing or Terne Plate, with its base of rust-resisting Armco Iron coated with pure tin and lead, makes roofs that last like those of our grandfathers' time.

Armco—American Ingot Iron—has withstood the ravages of salt water and salt air, the fumes of brimstone, all kinds and conditions of weather.

How to Get Armco Iron

Armco Iron is sold in sheet form through distributors all over the country. It is specified by architects and engineers and is used for making sheet metal products by many manufacturers. You can obtain Armco Iron products from your hardware store or tinner. If you have difficulty in getting Armco Iron, write to us for the names of dealers and manufacturers who use Armco. For example: Page Woven Wire Fence Co. use Armco Iron; General Fireproofing Co. make Herringbone lath of Armco Iron; Imperial Spiral lath and several other styles are made of Armco Iron by us.

Write for FREE Copy of "Defeating Rust"

Whether you are manufacturer, sheet metal dealer, roofer, civil engineer, architect, contractor, housewife—you cannot afford to be without this book. Learn the truth about sheet metal. Our Service Department will make any test if requested to determine the adaptability of Armco Iron to your needs.

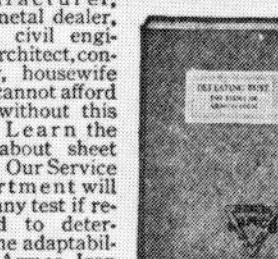

THE AMERICAN ROLLING MILL CO., BOX 510, MIDDLETOWN, OHIO

Licensed Manufacturers under Patents granted International Metal Products Company

District Sales Offices of The American Rolling Mill Co.

CHICAGO, 1266 People's Gas Bldg. PITTSBURGH, 1832 Oliver Bldg. DETROIT, 901 Ford Bldg.
NEW YORK, 551 Hudson Terminal Bldg. ST. LOUIS, 814 New Bank of Commerce Bldg.
CLEVELAND, 952 Rockefeller Bldg. CINCINNATI, 2101 Union Central Bldg.

The first controlled, powered flight took place at Kitty Hawk, North Carolina, on December 17, 1903. Victory thus came at last to the Wright brothers, the Ohio inventors who had been trying to fly at Kitty Hawk since late September. Courtesy, Department of Archives and Special Collections, Wright State University

slabs into thin steel sheets." On the first attempt one of the rollers broke down. Within the next few weeks other breakdowns occurred. But Tytus patiently corrected the flaws, and ordered bigger and stronger rollers, and the continuous mill began to work. Whereas the old rollers turned out 130 tons of steel weekly, the continuous mill within three years was producing 40,000 tons each month. By 1927 the experiment was over, the process perfected. Steel executives were invited to attend a demonstration of the mill that spring and went away in awe and admiration, having seen the smooth functioning of a plant they believed impossible to build.

ARMCO licensed its patents for the continuous mill to other companies, and it was not long before the revolutionary process was being used in all plants. The cost of sheet metal was cut in half just at the time consumer demand for cheap steel was rapidly increasing. The trade publication *Iron Age* observed that the "ARMCO continuous mill at Ashland is epoch-making . . . a monumental example of the scientific approach to a major manufacturing problem." When a critic complained to Tytus that his machine had taken away men's jobs, the inventor quickly replied, "Did you ever try your hand at the kind of work it eliminated?"

One of the great industries of the twentieth century—aviation—came of age in the 1920s and 1930s. Again Ohioans were central figures. By tradition aviation history began on the sand dunes at Kitty Hawk, North Carolina, on December 17, 1903, when the brothers from Dayton, Orville and Wilbur Wright, made the "world's first sustained, controlled power flight." It lasted twelve seconds and the plane traveled 120 feet. Work on improving the speed, load, and altitude of aircraft progressed over the next few years. In February 1908 the brothers contracted for their first military plane with the United States government. During 1909, 1910, and 1911, they conducted numerous aerial exhibitions which brought increasing recognition to the novel form of transportation.

The first successful commercial flight, as with many "firsts," was not spectacular by modern standards, yet it marked a milestone in aviation history. In November 1910 Philip O. Parmalee, one of the Wrights' exhibition pilots, flew two packages of Salome Silk, weighing 200 pounds, from Dayton to Columbus, a distance of about seventy miles. Flying at 2,000 feet, the wind cutting him to the bone, Parmalee made the trip without incident in about an hour. He nonchalantly debarked, commenting, "Well, that was going some." The popularization of commercial aviation, however, would have to await further advances in the field.

Military aviation progressed slowly after the army's purchase of its first plane from the Wrights in 1908. With the outbreak of war in Europe, the aircraft industries of England, Germany, and France were forced to grow; thus the United States lagged behind when it entered the war in 1917. A facility was developed at McCook Field in Dayton, where an engineering force was assembled and buildings and runways were constructed. There was little time to produce planes, however, and most of McCook's efforts were devoted to the redesigning of British planes for American use. More importantly, McCook became a center for testing and experimentation. Even though the end of the war slowed down operations, the engineering division continued functioning, developing and refining aircraft design. Numerous records for speed and maneuverability were set there during the 1920s. The celebrated Jimmy Doolittle was one of the record setters.

By the mid-1920s over thirteen million dollars

Above: The Wright brothers participated in a number of aerial exhibitions, drawing many eager and curious spectators. The inventors were frequent guests of European nobility, as seen in this pictures taken at Pau, France, in 1909. Courtesy, Department of Archives and Special Collections, Wright State University

Left: The Wright brothers made several attempts to fly before they finally succeeded on December 17, 1903. Wilbur Wright is seen here at the controls. Courtesy, Department of Archives and Special Collections, Wright State University

Above: The Dayton Wright Airplane Company built this plane, ready to take off for France in 1918, during World War I. Courtesy, Department of Archives and Special Collections, Wright State University

Right: Orville Wright is seen here flying a single propeller pusher plane over his hometown, Dayton, in 1912. Courtesy, Ohio Historical Society

Left: Wilbur Wright and his wife Katherine are pictured here in Pau, France. Although Katherine tied down her skirt to keep it from billowing up during flight, the look became fashionable and the "hobble skirt" was born. Courtesy, Department of Archives and Special Collections, Wright State University

Below: To give the city a lift from the worries of the Depression, the Women's Art League of Akron hosted a Rubber Ball. Everyone who attended was required to wear a costume made of rubber. C.W. Seiberling, of the Goodyear Company, was crowned king of the First Rubber Ball. His queen was an elevator operator from a local department store. Courtesy, University of Akron Archives

had been invested in McCook Field. However, by then the aircraft industry had outgrown the field's capabilities and the government was seriously considering relocating the plant to Langley Field in Virginia. But aware of its rich aviation history, the people of Dayton raised sufficient funds to acquire land east of the city which was then donated to the government for a new facility. Construction began in 1926 and in October 1927 Wright Field was dedicated. In ten years McCook Field had, in the view of one historian, "helped lay the foundation for the aircraft industry and had aided in the development of civil aviation in the United States." Wright Field continued this work and contributed substantially to the aircraft industry's future military and civilian growth.

While the nascent aviation industry was prospering, one ancient industry was not. The problem had little to do with the economy, but much to do with a band of militant crusaders. The temperance movement had a long history, predating the Civil War. Its ultimate triumph was hastened by World War I when it was concluded that drinking was harmful to military personnel. Resulting from the massive propaganda efforts of the Woman's Christian Temperance Union and the Westerville-based Anti-Saloon League, the politicians finally surrendered. Congress approved the Eighteenth Amendment, by which the "manufacture, sale, or transportation of intoxicating liquor . . . within

the United States . . . is hereby prohibited." It was ratified in 1920. The Volstead Act, passed in 1919, barred the manufacture or sale of any beverage with more than one-half of one percent alcoholic content.

Naturally, this was a blow to brewery interests and Cincinnati, long one of the nation's best beer towns, suffered accordingly. It had over twenty breweries before Prohibition. When repeal came in 1933, Bruckmann's was the only one remaining. However, plenty of people experimented with "bathtub gin" and "home brew," and frequented speakeasies. By the late 1920s, 3,000 beer parlors were doing business in the city. Bootlegging was big business, too. In 1929, the busiest year, 490 bootleggers were jailed. But enforcement proved

Right: ***Originally situated in an old German neighborhood, the Wolf Ledge Brewery became the property of Wilhelm Burkhardt in 1879. After his death, his wife changed the brewery's name to Burkhardt, and the business remained in the family until the 1950s. Burkhardt, in the center of the first row, posed for this photograph with his employees. Courtesy, Summit County Historical Society***

Below right: The men in this photo were cutting tobacco, which would later be hung to dry and then stripped. Tobacco was an Ohio industry that gradually diminished over the years. Courtesy, Ohio Historical Society

impossible, not only in Cincinnati but every place else, and the cry for "repeal" became more strident. Repeal came with the New Deal in 1933. Cincinnati's brewery industry recovered slowly, however, and it was not until 1940 that sales regained the 1918 level.

Farmers, like brewers, did not do well in the 1920s. They had enjoyed plush times during the war. With European farmland ravaged, a premium was put on American grain, particularly wheat. Anything that could be grown could be sold—and at good prices. With greater income, farmers invested in new homes, machinery, equipment, and blooded animals, and began living a life of "unnatural ease." Then the war ended. The European market evaporated and prices began a sharp decline which was not arrested until the New Deal era.

If breweries went out of business and farmers had their backs to the wall, the decade of the 1920s was still considered one of "unprecedented prosperity." But was it really? In the fall of 1929, soon after the stock market collapse but before the Depression had set in, writer Stuart Chase published an economic study of the previous decade. It was a period of only limited prosperity, he argued, and to illustrate his point he used an onion to represent "the total economic life of the United States." He began peeling off one layer after another, each one signifying a weak spot, a sick industry, in the economy. After stripping away eleven layers of the onion, including farmers, a portion of the middle and professional classes, the unemployed, coal miners, shoemakers, and shipbuilders, the core still remained, but it was not as big and healthy looking as it had once been. Illustrating Chase's argument, in Ohio coal production dropped over 10 percent during the decade, one out of every four miners was discharged, and for those who retained their jobs, yearly earnings declined by 21 percent.

The decade following the First World War was a mixed one, economically speaking, for organized labor. In an effort to retain wartime gains in the face of the country's desire to cut back, a wave of bitter strikes broke out in 1919 and 1920, which resulted in a series of setbacks for labor. Business, while not opposed to what it considered labor's legitimate rights, remained steadfast in its opposition to collective bargaining and the closed shop. Welfare capitalism expanded and company unions were instituted in many plants. As the "prosperity" of the 1920s spread into more sectors of the economy, working classes began to share a bit in the bounty. The combination of employer pressure, adverse court rulings, and spreading affluence had a debilitating effect on militant unionism. Union membership declined.

These shadows were cast by men standing in line for jobs during the Great Depression. The sign overhead warns that "dirty men will not be sent out." Scenes like this one from Cincinnati were repeated all over the state of Ohio. Photo by Paul Briol. Courtesy, Cincinnati Historical Society

The story of the Great Depression has filled many books. Looking back one can readily see that much was amiss with the economy in the years before the collapse. Rather than reducing prices of goods or raising workers' wages, corporations either plowed their huge profits back into plant expansion or gambled them away in the skyrocketing stock market. Between 1922 and 1929 profits rose by 83 percent, while the real income of the laboring man rose only about 20 percent. In the words of one economist, "the future was oversold." Far more was being produced than could be consumed.

One of the most cruel ironies of American history is that the man in the White House when the capitalist bubble burst was an exemplary product of that very system. Herbert Hoover had risen from humble origins to fame, fortune, and political favor by virtue of his intelligence, energy, business skill, and engineering talent in a society which richly rewarded such qualities. A more perfect specimen of the American success story would be difficult to find. Now Hoover had to preside over the collapse of the system to which he was indebted for his success. It is not surprising that he had problems accepting the fact that the free enterprise system had failed.

Slightly over a year after Hoover had said, "We in America are nearer to the final triumph over poverty than ever before," the stock market collapsed. "Black Tuesday," October 29, 1929, witnessed the worst percentage drop in market history and the decline which set in would continue uninterrupted for over three years. The supply of investment funds dried up, business confidence was shaken, production was cut back, and unemployment spread rapidly. By the winter of 1932-1933, when the nation's economy was practically at a standstill, the value of all stocks traded on the New York Stock Exchange had dropped from their 1929 high of eighty-seven billion dollars to only nineteen billion dollars.

Hoover's response was to encourage voluntary help for the needy and to urge the hard-pressed to help themselves. Times were hard, he conceded, but the system was basically sound and would bounce back. He continued to support budget balancing and other deflationary policies when what

Women often ran machines at the Williams' shoe company, while men worked in other parts of the company, such as the cutting room. Courtesy, Ohio Historical Society

was needed was massive federal spending. In 1931, under pressure from Democrats who gained control of the House of Representatives in 1930, he signed into law spending measures for public works projects, but they were hardly adequate to deal with the crisis. Unemployment grew, local welfare resources became exhausted, and the country settled into an abyss of gloom and hopelessness. An estimated fifteen to seventeen million were on relief by 1932.

While no state escaped the harshness and horror of those Depression years, Ohio suffered unduly because of its large population and industrial character. Production dropped 24 percent in the 1930s, while nationally the figure was 19 percent. As a consequence, the state's factory work force declined 20 percent. The number of industrial workers unemployed statewide in 1930 was 307,000; in 1931, 576,000; and in 1932, 869,000, over 37 percent of all Ohio workers. The large industrial centers suffered the most. By the time the economy struck rock bottom in 1932 Cleveland's unemployment figure had reached 50 percent, Akron 60 percent, and Toledo 80 percent. As for particular industries, construction was hit the hardest with a 67 percent decline, with manufacturing next, down 44 percent.

Statistics cannot convey the degree of human suffering visited on millions of workers without jobs. People starved to death; families evicted from their homes moved in with overcrowded relatives or set up in ramshackle lean-tos; miners gained "sustenance" from blackberries and dandelions; former millionaires subsisted by selling apples on street corners; furniture was burned for fuel; the hungry grubbed through garbage cans like alley cats; children could not learn in school because they were hungry, cold, and ill-clad; thousands rode the rails and suffered in shantytowns, or "Hoovervilles," along railroad sidings.

Most large corporations weathered the Depression. The Cincinnati Milling Machine Company (since 1970 Cincinnati Milacron) exemplifies how one of them pulled through. Cincinnati Milling, founded in 1884, had become one of the nation's foremost machine tool manufacturers. The demands of World War I greatly stimulated demand for its milling machines, but the end of the war meant a sharp cutback. The work force dropped from 1,223 to 922 within a year of the Armistice. The burgeoning auto industry, however, picked up some of the slack. But another setback came with the 1920-1921 recession. Sales

The Cincinnati Screw and Tap Company became the Cincinnati Milling Machine Company in 1889. The company kept that name until 1970, when it changed its name again, to Cincinnati Milacron. It has long been an important employer in the Cincinnati area. Courtesy, Cincinnati Milacron

dropped 70 percent and employment fell off 75 percent. Management salaries were reduced, stock holdings in other firms were sold, and cash reserves were depleted. Recovery was slow. As late as 1926 the work force was only about 50 percent of its wartime high. Then, spurred by an order from the Ford Motor Company for ten "centerless" grinding machines, the company by 1927 had secured title to all American patents for the centerless grinding process. Because of this and other new machines, new markets opened up and by the late 1920s Cincinnati Milling had become the largest machine tool producer in the country. In 1929 sales exceeded ten million, while the work force numbered 2,300.

Oddly, 1929, the year of the stock market crash, was the company's best year and there were great hopes for 1930. Sales reached $2.3 million in the first quarter of 1930, but then the cancellations began coming in and only $3.6 million sales were recorded during the remainder of the year, a 42 percent drop from 1929. By 1933 sales had declined to only 20 percent of the pre-Depression figures. Occasional large orders assisted in the difficult years. Such an order came from Ford at Christmas time in 1932. "I can keep 100 men on for three more months with that order," cried a happy Frederick A. Geir, company president. To help the unemployed, the Mutual Aid Committee, an employees' assistance organization set up in 1916, was transformed into a relief agency. The committee purchased food and clothing, which was distributed without charge. It helped out in paying rent and utility bills. Fringe benefits were continued by the company.

Cincinnati Milling instituted a number of innovations during the bleak years, which would serve it well when better times returned. In 1931 it began sending its own salesmen into the field, abandoning the use of manufacturers' representatives. It also adopted the "scientific management" plan. In 1934, by which time business had begun to pick up, a branch plant was opened in Birmingham, England. Thanks to overseas and export operations, sales improved, surpassing the ten million mark in 1936. The work force now numbered more than 200 over the 1929 figure. Sales improved to $13.6 billion in 1937.

It did not work out the same way with the Van Sweringen brothers, Oris Paxton and Mantis James. Their rise and fall was as meteoric as any in the annals of American history. Born in rural Wooster in 1879 and 1881, the boys moved with their family to Geneva, Ohio, in the early 1880s and after their father's death in 1886 relocated on Cleveland's east side. Dropping out of school in the middle grades, they held various jobs and displayed an obvious flair for business. The boys, who never married, had a closer personal relationship than most brothers and conducted all of their affairs as a unit.

One of the trademarks of the Van Sweringens was the purchase of property without the investment of their own funds. They used this tactic first in the real estate business in the early 1900s. In 1905 they took an option on a small lot southeast of Cleveland, where the Shaker society had once built a communal farm. They continued to buy up additional lots over the next ten years and by 1916 had developed a beautiful suburban community called Shaker Heights replete with broad boulevards, landscaped lots, lakes, and a golf course. Shaker Heights, remote from downtown Cleveland, needed a transportation system to connect it with the metropolitan area.

The Van Sweringens planned a "rapid transit" street railway line to the Public Square in downtown Cleveland, where they had already purchased land for a railroad terminal. However, they still needed five miles of right-of-way, on which to bring their line into the center of town. At this very time, in 1916, the New York Central had been ordered by the Interstate Commerce Commission to divest itself of the Nickel Plate Railroad. Its right-of-way ran along the route needed by the Van Sweringens to complete their rapid transit system. On July 15, 1916, they bought the entire Nickel Plate line to get that five-mile stretch.

Once in control of the Nickel Plate, the brothers got the itch to buy more rail lines. They studied railroad maps avidly as they plotted their moves. Oris Paxton once said that his favorite book was the Rand-McNally atlas. In 1922 they acquired the Lake Erie and Western, and the following year, the Toledo, St. Louis and Western, both of which were merged with the Nickel Plate. Later in 1923 they bought the Chesapeake and Ohio, while in 1924 they added the Erie and Pere Marquette.

By the late 1920s, while the Van Sweringens had amassed a railroad empire covering 9,000 miles and valued at more than three billion dollars, they had also amassed a huge debt. It grew larger with each new purchase. A Morgan bank loan of forty million dollars in 1926 was the first of several such transactions, but it barely scratched the surface of the debt. However, the financial mood of the country was a bullish one in the late 1920s. The general feeling was that the old cycle of boom and bust was over and that economic conditions would continue to improve without end. As long as business prospered the brothers would be all right.

The beginning of the end arrived with their purchase of the Missouri Pacific in 1928 and 1929. The brothers' plan was to extend their railroad holdings into the Southwest and to the West Coast. By the spring of 1929 they had control of the Missouri Pacific but it was to be their last purchase. The stock market crash that October hit them very hard. Prices of their holdings dropped sharply, earnings fell off, and creditors demanded repayment of loans. They managed to secure another forty-million-dollar loan in 1930, but this was totally inadequate to

The Ohio Relief Production Units provided jobs for Ohioans during the Depression. The Cleveland Unit made suits, pants, and hosiery for men and women. The girls shown in this photo are working at "looping" machines, sewing up the toes of hosiery. Courtesy, Cleveland Public Library: Newspaper Enterprise Association

ward off disaster. When that loan fell due in 1935 the brothers were unable to redeem it and on September 30, 1935, their assets were auctioned off—what was left of their assets, that is, for they had already lost a great deal and were having difficulty meeting their annual living expenses of $150,000. Worn out from work, stress, and disillusionment, the brothers died in quick order—Mantis James on December 13, 1935, aged fifty-four, and Oris Paxton on November 23, 1936, aged fifty-seven. The Van Sweringens never did anything illegal, they never stole from their companies, and they stayed at their desks through the worst of times to salvage something from the disaster which had struck. They had simply gotten in too far over their heads.

American Greetings Corporation represents a happy fulfillment of the "American Dream" which even the Depression could not erase. Jacob Sapirstein emigrated from Russian-controlled Poland in 1905 to avoid becoming cannon fodder for Tsar Nicholas II's armies then engaged in war with Japan. Although he arrived in this country penniless and unable to speak English, by 1906, at age twenty-two, he was in business for himself. He sold postcards, imported from Germany, to drug stores and candy shops. Studying the market closely, Sapirstein gradually expanded his business, operating out of his own home. Driving a horse and wagon he called personally on all of his customers. One day a woman driving a Buick ran into the wagon, but Sapirstein was now able to buy a brand new Model-T Ford in which to make his visits.

World War I stopped the importation of German cards, but, oddly, the war gave birth to the greeting card business. American manufacturers began to produce specialty cards which recognized birthdays, holidays, and other such events. The market was ripe for this innovation and Sapirstein cashed in. He was able to move his business out of his home and into a regular office, although it was only a garage on East 95th Street. When the Depression struck, the greeting card business continued to thrive, simply because people who were no longer able to give presents on special occasions could still give greeting cards. In 1932, during the depths of the Depression, Sapirstein and his three sons, who had entered fully into the business, decided to break with the past and manufacture their own greeting cards. They were immediately successful in this new departure; more office space and more employees were soon needed. In 1938 the Sapirstein Greeting Card Company became American Greeting Publishers. It went public in 1952 and today is the largest public-owned greeting card corporation in the world. (It ranked 296th on the *Fortune* 500 1986 list.) Jacob Sapirstein is still living at the time of this writing, a venerable 102.

A new approach toward the problems of the Depression was apparent when Franklin D. Roosevelt took office as President on March 4, 1933. Abandoning the deflationary philosophy of the Hoover administration, the New Deal plan was to spend as much money as necessary for the relief of the unemployed and the recovery and reform of

This photo taken by a WPA photographer shows employees running a calendar stacker at the Champion Paper and Fiber Company in Hamilton during the Depression. Thanks to the efforts of the WPA, valuable documentation of life during the 1930s is available. Courtesy, Ohio Historical Society

the economic system. Relief was the immediate concern and through the numerous alphabet agencies funds were parcelled out through the states to those in need. Relief funds were expended in two forms: direct relief, or the "dole;" and work relief where the recipients were employed on public works projects.

Ohio made a brave effort to bring unemployed workers and idle industrial plants together when it organized the Ohio Relief Production Unit in the spring and summer of 1934. Between July 2 and November 19, twelve empty factories were reopened employing about 1,000 persons. The largest companies were Sun-Glo Industries of Mansfield (furniture), Toledo Garment (clothing), Moore Shirt in New Philadelphia (work shirts), and Comer Manufacturing in Dayton (coats and windbreakers). The plan did not work. Too many clothes and not enough other necessities were produced. Payment was in scrip which could not be used to buy most things the workers needed. The shortcomings of the plan became apparent within a year or so and all the plants were closed in May 1935.

The most massive of all federal relief programs—the Works Progress Administration, or WPA— was launched in the spring of 1935. It lasted until 1942 when World War II made it no longer necessary. All projects were screened and approved and workers were certified as relief recipients. From the time the program began until World War II between 200,000 and 300,000 Ohioans were on WPA. Up until October 1938, federal funds spent in the state amounted to fifty-five million dollars. In that month Ohio had the largest number of people on WPA among all states.

It is no doubt an understatement to say that the business community was not happy with the New Deal. Its spending and deficit financing policies, for one thing, violated all that had been sacred to the "masters of capital." More offensive, however, was its attitude toward labor. The National Industrial Recovery Act (NIRA), passed in 1933, was intended to bring about a maximum cooperative effort from industry to revive the economy. As a price for the suspension of antitrust laws, business had to recognize the legitimacy of trade unions. This was a bitter pill and numerous companies would not swallow it. The Supreme Court invalidated the NIRA in 1935, but Section 7a of that act, which authorized and encouraged trade unions, was salvaged and elaborated in the Wagner Act, which was adopted shortly after the NIRA was thrown out. Not only did the Wagner Act recognize the right of unions to organize and bargain collectively with employers, it also created a National Labor Relations Board to conduct elections and investigate charges of unfair employment practices.

Encouraged by this legislation, labor went on an organizing orgy. The main body of the conservative AFL was not much interested in this, but the militant industrial arm of the AFL, the Committee for Industrial Organization, was. Led by the outspoken head of the United Mineworkers, the bushy-browed John L. Lewis, the committee broke away from the AFL in 1936 and founded the Congress of Industrial Organizations, or CIO, for the purpose of recruiting hundreds of thousands of industrial workers shunned by the AFL. The CIO's membership crusade led to repeated clashes with corporations which were dead set opposed to outside control of their workers.

A bitter strike broke out at the Autolite plant in Toledo in 1934, where the new local of the United Auto Workers demanded recognition. Violence erupted in May as thousands of unionists and allies reacted angrily to the use of strike-breakers, tear gas, and the efforts of company and municipal police to rout the picket lines. Federal mediators finally were able to bring the two sides together and tensions eased. Concessions were made to the union, but it did not gain the bargaining rights it had demanded. Workers in the rubber industry contributed the sit-down strike to the arsenal of union pressure tactics. In February 1936 a series of sit-downs at the major plants in Akron halted all production. The United Rubber Workers won a partial victory and union membership rose.

The sit-down strike at Cleveland's Fisher Body plant of General Motors in December 1936 initiated the most memorable confrontation between labor and management during the New Deal era. The strike spread to other GM plants and soon the entire organization was at war with the auto workers. The main combat zone was at the Fisher Body plant in Flint, Michigan. Having made no progress in the negotiations, the company turned off the heat in the plant and ordered police to storm the building. They were beaten back by the strikers. Eventually, due to the intervention of Michigan Governor Frank Murphy, GM agreed to recognize the union. The forty-four-day strike of 44,000 workers, which had tied up sixty plants in fourteen states, was labor's greatest victory in history. In the wake of this success, Lewis and the CIO turned next to the steel industry. To the amazement of everyone, United States Steel surrendered without a whimper and the rest of "Big Steel" went along, recognizing the steelworkers' union as the bargaining agent for their employees.

It was not the same with "Little Steel," however,

The Nickle Plate Railroad, organized in 1881 to run from Buffalo to Chicago, brought its first passenger train through Cleveland in August 1882. Pictured is the Nickle Plate under construction at Broadway Avenue. Courtesy, Western Reserve Historical Society

represented by Inland Steel, Youngstown Sheet and Tube, Republic Steel, and Bethlehem. These companies, which had plants in six Ohio cities —Cleveland, Youngstown, Massillon, Canton, Warren, and Niles—refused to follow the example of U.S. Steel. Union organizing attempts in May and June 1937 were met with bitter resistance, as policemen and National Guard troops struggled with strikers. A battle at Massillon led to the death of one man and the wounding of twelve others. At the Warren plant of Republic Steel 1,000 strikers clashed with 250 policemen; one striker was killed and fourteen injured. Little Steel won out and the CIO was defeated in these unionization efforts. However, four years later, in a calmer atmosphere, and under National Labor Relations Board auspices, the steelworkers won elections in all of the plants where they had suffered defeats just a few years before. Militant unionism subsided after 1938. Major victories had been achieved and a time for consolidation of the gains was necessary.

* * *

The period of boom and bust, the 1920s and 1930s, closed out on an up note. Despite the recession of 1937-1938, business was reviving. Conservative critics denounced the New Deal for its massive spending without having ended the Depression, since ten million were still unemployed in 1940. Yet the economy had improved. In most industries sales were much better and workers were going back on the job. Although business was not pleased with the new role of government in the lives of Americans or with the maturing of the labor movement, it was reluctantly adjusting to the new dispensation. But now more pressing matters were at hand. With the outbreak of war in Europe in September 1939 and with eventual American involvement, industry and labor needed to work together to provide the materials of war to bring down the Axis powers.

Pictured here is the Republic Steel plant in Cleveland. By 1930, after merging with several companies, Republic Steel Corporation had greatly strengthened its position in the iron and steel industry. Courtesy, Cleveland Public Library: Newspaper Enterprise Association

Road and mileage signs give clues to the location of this small Ohio town. Urbana, in Champaign County, looks serene as the country emerges from the throes of the Depression. Courtesy, Ohio Historical Society

MARTIN
U.S.A

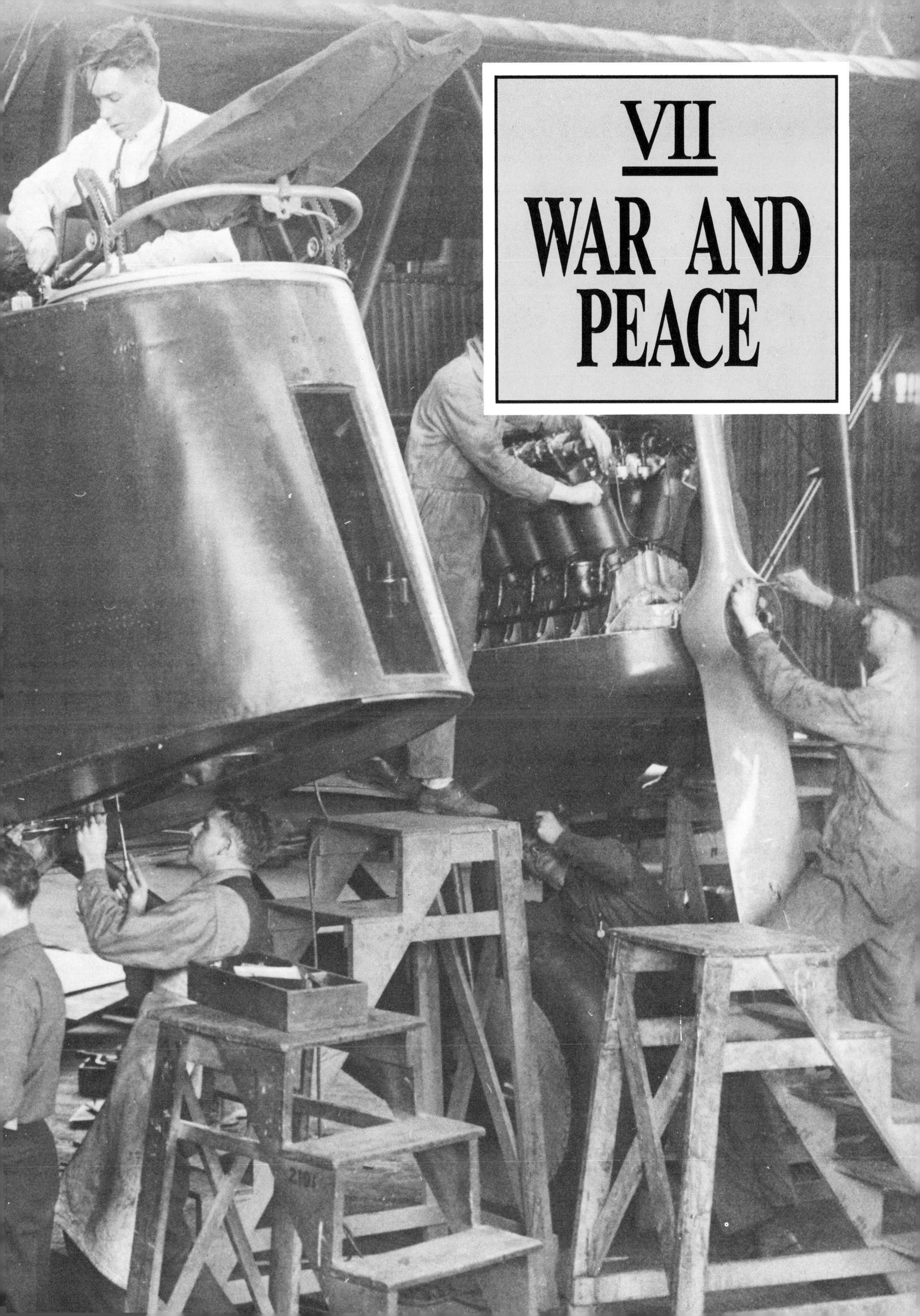

VII
WAR AND PEACE

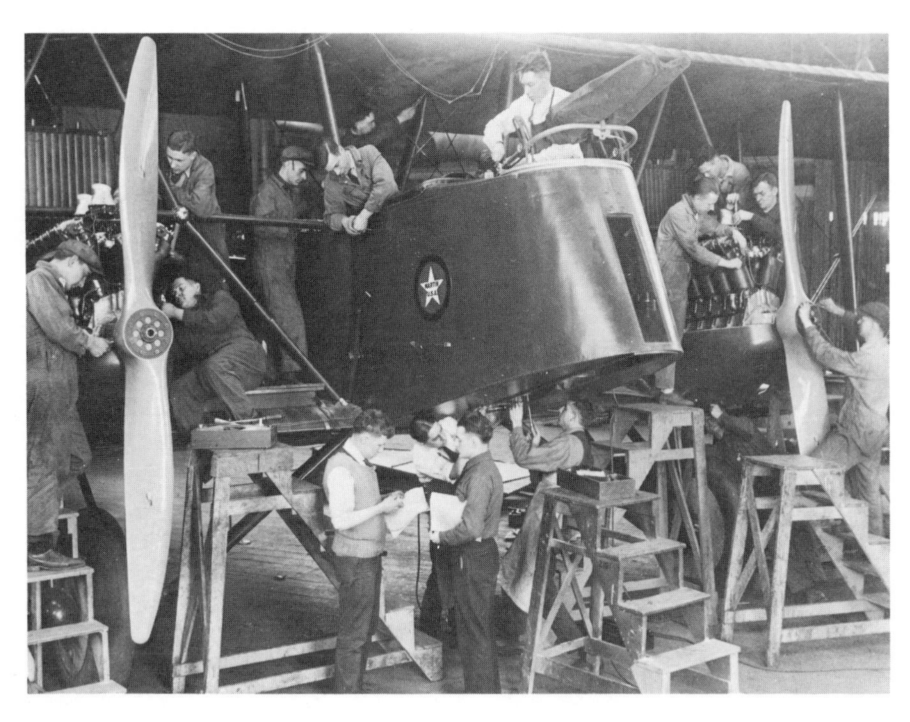

The Glenn L. Martin Company of Cleveland received a government contract in January of 1918 to build six Martin bombers to accommodate the famous Liberty Motor. Pictured is the final assembly of the MB-2, a plane designed to hold 2,000 pounds of bombs carried by a special bomb-dropping device, in addition to a 1,700-pound Mark VII navy torpedo. Courtesy, Western Reserve Historical Society

Facing page: The Hoover Company, the oldest and most widely known manufacturer of vacuum cleaners in the world, ceased producing vacuum cleaners in order to concentrate its manufacturing capabilities on the war effort. Advertisements such as this one appeared nationwide during World War II, urging women to share their Hoover cleaners with those who did not have one. Courtesy, the Hoover Company

It took America well over a year after the Japanese bombed Pearl Harbor on December 7, 1941, to get its war machine in full running order. Once operating, it turned out an incredible number of tanks, aircraft, ships, artillery pieces, guns, grenades, bombs, and all the other needed instruments of war. Twenty-five thousand planes a year were being produced by 1943 and early the following year the production of American war plants was double the amount of the Axis countries. As a major industrial state, Ohio was expected to contribute substantially to the war effort. It did. From the outbreak of war until V-E Day in May 1945, eighteen billion dollars in war contracts were let to Ohio companies. The most important contracts were in aircraft, ordnance, and shipbuilding. Cleveland, Cincinnati, Akron, and Dayton were the busiest cities. The number of workers in Ohio manufacturing plants during the war jumped from 755,000 to almost twice that number. Wages went up by 65 percent.

But while war stimulated the economy and eliminated unemployment, all was not happy in the work place. To maximize production and reduce labor-management friction, the government created the War Labor Board in 1942. The WLB proposed a plan whereby, on the one hand, wages would be frozen except for cost-of-living increases and labor would agree not to strike. On the other hand, in order to conciliate labor leadership, the government would guarantee that union members could not withdraw from their unions. Hardly an equitable arrangement, but it was sufficient to secure national union approval. The rank and file, however, did not approve. Their dissatisfaction surfaced in countless work stoppages, which made

The Neighborly Spirit of Sharing

These are days when many good, old-fashioned virtues are coming back into their own—Neighborliness . . . Sharing what we have.

The common enemy has given us a new appreciation of our homes, our friends, our country and the way we live.

We are giving each other many little "lifts."

A great cause has made America a nation of neighbors again.

The Hoover Company is no longer making cleaners; it is completely engaged in making precision products for America's fighting forces.

If you are fortunate enough to have a modern Hoover Cleaner, your cleaning problem is answered for many years to come.

But there are times when all of us must be interested in the other fellow, too; when we want to spread our blessings and give the lifts in our power to give. The woman who wants clean clothes for her family can't get the washing machine she needs. Her next door neighbor has a washing machine and uses it only once a week. Other appliances, other needs, other friends. Why not share?

Some relative of yours, some near-by neighbor or some close friend down the street or across the hall may have been unable to get a cleaner. Your Hoover Cleaner is husky enough to clean for you and her too. Why not share? Incidentally, she may have some household appliance that you have been unable to get.

You can help her, she can help you. That's how sharing works. That's how America is looking at things these days —one for all—and all for our country!

HOW TO MAKE YOUR HOOVER SERVE LONGER

Empty bag after each cleaning. A clean bag will help keep your cleaner operating at top efficiency and prolong its life.

Do not wind the cord tightly. Coil it loosely around the cord clips. *Pull* out *plug*—never *jerk* cord —to disconnect cleaner. When using cleaner, avoid running over the cord.

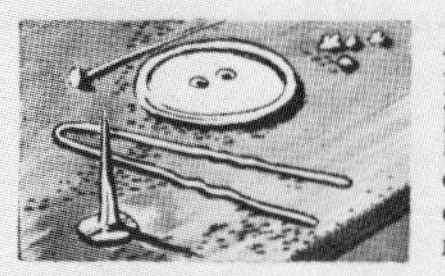

Do not try to pick up pins, hairpins, tacks, pebbles or other hard objects with cleaner. These may damage belt or other moving parts.

Have your Hoover inspected once a year. To be sure of obtaining genuine Hoover parts and service, register your cleaner with your Hoover Factory Branch Service Station (*consult classified telephone directory*) or dealer. If you cannot locate either, write: The Hoover Company, North Canton, Ohio.

Remember, do not discard any worn or broken parts. They must be turned in to secure replacements.

THE HOOVER *IT BEATS . . . AS IT SWEEPS . . . AS IT CLEANS*

a farce of the "no-strike" pledge. In 1943, 300,000 Ohio workers were involved in 467 wildcat strikes and although in 1944 the number of strikers dropped to 216,000, work stoppages increased to 549. In 1943 a massive coal strike so disrupted the operations of Hanna and other coal companies that the federal government took over management of the mines.

Local union officials were caught between the militant demands of the workers and the insistence of their national leaders that discipline be maintained. Factional disputes erupted within many unions such as at the General Tire and Rubber plant at Akron over wildcat walkouts in 1943 and 1944. At the Willys-Overland factory in Toledo, workers belonged to four different unions and jurisdictional fights repeatedly broke out. Disputes also developed between locals of the same union, such as among electrical workers in Dayton. Bitter union wrangling reached all the way to the top, particularly between John L. Lewis' United Mineworkers and the Ohio CIO.

One significant breakthrough on the labor front brought about by World War II was the infusion of large numbers of women into the work force. Because of the heavy demands on manpower for the military, the need for laborers in war plants grew proportionately. Millions of homemakers donned slacks and caps and went into the factories. "Rosie the Riveter," the title of a popular song of the day, symbolized the American woman during wartime. (Cincinnati Milling claimed it had a "Millie the Machinist" before there was a "Rosie the Riveter.") From May 1942 until late 1943, the number of female war workers increased almost fourfold. As the war progressed, the number continued to grow until over one-third of all workers in war plants were women. The Ohio state legislature abolished age and occupation restrictions on women working in industry. In time not only were many single women working in war plants, but many married women including some grandmothers had also

A riot broke out during a strike at the Goodyear Tire and Rubber Company in Akron. Police are shown here advancing on a throng that surrounded the plant's main gate. More than 100 persons were injured in the clash between 200 officers and strikers. Courtesy, Acme Photo and the Ohio Historical Society

entered the work force. Female workers were discriminated against in wage and seniority matters, which caused occasional wildcat stoppages, such as at Libbey-Owens-Ford in 1943.

But despite the labor unrest throughout war plants, production of the necessary material accelerated and Ohio industry played an important role in the ultimate Allied victory. One of the remarkable aspects of industry during the war, and Ohio's industries were no exception, was the speed and relative ease with which companies retooled their plants for war production. Firms which specialized in nonmilitary products already had the physical plants, engineering expertise, and labor skills that could be adapted to the needs of the moment. But quite a few companies did not have to retool, as they were already manufacturing products needed in war.

Cincinnati Milling Machine, a producer of machine tools, was in a particularly advantageous position. As with other machine tool plants, it did not need to retool. It simply had to produce more machines which could make the tools of war. Well

Before there was Rosie the Riveter, the Cincinnati Milling Machine Company had "Millie the Machinist." This company, as well as others, depended on women to work in its plants during World War II. There was a seven-day standard work week during the war that consisted of eleven-hour days. More than 2,000 Cincinnati Milling Machine employees entered the military, with thirty-one losing their lives. Courtesy, Cincinnati Milacron

before Pearl Harbor, the company's management anticipated that war would come and began expanding its facilities and increasing its labor force. This head start proved vital as the orders for machine tools began pouring in following America's entry into the war. Not that Cincinnati Milling alone tooled the country for war; the entire industry turned out more machines between 1940 and 1943 than in the previous forty years. Yet by 1942, when the demand for machine tools peaked, Cincinnati Milling had manufactured 17,511 machines, one-twelfth of the national output.

By 1942 and 1943 the demand for machine tools had abated, the job of supplying war plants with the needed machinery having been accomplished. In the last year of the war only 40 percent of Cincinnati Milling's capacity was devoted to machine tools. Hence it was necessary to produce specific war goods if it was to keep its inflated work force occupied. Among a number of such products that the company manufactured were parts of B-29 landing gears, parts for tractors, transmissions for amphibious landing craft, radar components, dies for ammunition makers, and artillery fuse setters.

Thompson Products in Cleveland also did not need to retool as it was already into aircraft parts and products which were readily adapted for tanks, trucks, and tractors. Existing plant capacity was increased to meet the demands of the American as well as the British military. The federal government, even before Pearl Harbor, subsidized the construction and operation of a new plant known as the Thompson Aircraft Products Company, or TAPCO, in the Cleveland suburb of Euclid. By 1943 the factory, which operated seven days a week, twenty-four hours a day, had 16,000 employees. Engine parts for airplanes remained a much more important component in Thompson's product line after the war than it had been before. In addition to helping the country arm for war, the company enjoyed a profit boom as sales skyrocketed by 700 percent by 1945.

Another company which was not required to retool for war was the Austin Company of Cleveland, builders of big buildings around the world. Austin specialized in aircraft plants, but as company historian Martin Greif reports, Austin also constructed "numerous shipbuilding facilities, machine tool factories, two major penicillin plants, an air base in Alaska, several factories for the manufacture of electronic instruments and devices . . . the design of special Naval facilities, and America's largest wind tunnel . . ." However, perhaps Austin's greatest contribution was the design and construction of "con-

Above: Ohio's lake ports buzzed with activity as the demand for iron and steel grew, resulting from U.S. involvement in World War II. Here, an ore boat is towed up the Cuyahoga River in the early 1940s. Courtesy, Ohio Historical Society

Facing page, bottom: The Hanna Coal Company has been a major coal producer in Ohio. Although coal mining has been quite successful throughout the years, the industry has had its share of strikes. A massive strike in 1934 brought the federal government in to manage the mines. Courtesy, Ohio Historical Society

trolled condition" plants, which were windowless, insulated, and under constant temperature controls. The buildings also met wartime blackout needs. In 1939 the company built such a plant for General Motors for the manufacture of Allison liquid-cooled aircraft engines. This led to contracts for controlled-conditions factories for Grumman Aircraft's fighter and torpedo planes. During the war Austin built eleven blackout plants for the aircraft industry as well as many traditional aircraft factories.

The company was proudest of three controlled-conditions plants. At Fort Worth, Texas, and Tulsa, Oklahoma, it built twin-bomber assembly facilities for Consolidated-Vultee and Douglas Aircraft. The insulated fiberglass and steel-panel walls and the light-reflecting white concrete floors made these plants unique. These features provided advanced and improved air-conditioning and lighting conditions. The Fort Worth building was later expanded and became, next to the Pentagon, the largest air-conditioned structure in the world. In 1943, when steel was in short supply, Austin designed a "breathing" masonry wall for its Oklahoma City Douglas Aircraft plant. Seventeen and a half million bricks were substituted for the steel walls.

One concern which had to retool was Hoover Company of North Canton. Vacuum sweepers were of little use in winning the war, so their production ceased shortly after Pearl Harbor. Machines for manufacturing vacuum sweepers were removed from the plant and machines for war production were installed. According to a company brochure, Hoover

Right: The Austin Company of Cleveland had an interest in the quality of its work environment. Pictured here are men working under fluorescent lighting, in an air-conditioned room, to help reduce the strain of their work. Courtesy, Cleveland Public Library

Below right: The Hoover Company became an active participant in the war effort. The company ceased manufacture of new vacuum cleaners in order to devote its facility to the production of helmet liners, parachutes for fragmentation bombs, parts for the variable time fuse, and turret motors. The War Department ordered Hoover to remove its name from their buildings to prevent the company from becoming a target during an air raid. Pictured here are women working in the parachute department. Courtesy, the Hoover Company

secured war contracts for the production of "helmet liners, parachutes for fragmentation bombs, propeller pitch control motors, turret motors, and amplidynes for bombers." Most important, perhaps, was its production of the variable time or "proximity" fuse, critical in the detonation of artillery shells and bombs.

National Cash Register was in a somewhat similar position as Hoover. The manufacture of cash registers also ceased soon after Pearl Harbor, by which time the conversion to war production was well advanced. Military items made by NCR included bomb fuses, parts of artillery shells, rocket motors for five-inch antiaircraft rockets, carburetors for B-29s, and "analog computer gunsights" for aircraft defense systems. During the war years, government contracts paid the company's overhead costs, while the rebuilding of old machines brought in a little profit.

The fact that NCR had extensive overseas operations led to strange and amusing wartime incidents. NCR personnel, men and women, served in the armed forces of their native countries in Great Britain, Europe, Africa, the Middle East, and the Far East. They served on both sides in the conflict and some, including a future president of the company, spent time in prison camps. As German forces entered Paris in 1940, a tank thundered to a halt outside the NCR office on the Champs Elysees. An officer dismounted and knocked on the door, which was opened tentatively by an apprehensive employee. "Hello," said the smiling German. "I am from National Cash Register in Berlin and I am wondering if you made your quota last year? We made ours." Five years later an American tank rumbled by the ruins of the NCR office in Berlin where employees were digging through the rubble. A grinning GI called out: "Hi, I'm from NCR-Omaha. Did you guys make your quota last month?"

Goodyear by no means abandoned tire production during the war, but it devoted more attention to aircraft production. It entered the aircraft business before Pearl Harbor when on December 5, 1939, it contracted with the Glenn L. Martin Company to manufacture parts for the B-26 Marauder. Goodyear Aircraft Corporation was incorporated at that time to handle the aircraft parts business and the Goodyear Airdock, idle since the collapse of the dirigible industry, was reactivated for a production facility. In the fall of 1940 Grumman and Curtiss-Wright contracted with Goodyear for the Avenger torpedo bomber and the P-40 Warhawk fighter. The navy ordered patrol and training blimps. Orders for additional airplane parts in 1941 led to the construction of two new plants near the airdock and a third in Litchfield Park in Arizona. Sales ran to $330 million for 1941, 52 percent over the previous year.

With American entry into the war, Goodyear built on the solid base already established for the manufacture of aircraft parts. In February 1942 it signed an agreement to produce the navy Corsair fighter plane, the one complete plane to be built by the company. It subcontracted 40 percent of the job to plants large and small throughout the country and the first Corsair taxied out of the factory one year later, in February 1943. Before the war's end, over 4,000 Corsairs went into naval service. In addition to the Corsair, the navy ordered a large number of blimps from Goodyear to patrol both Atlantic and Pacific coastal waters. One hundred sixty-eight blimps had been manufactured by the spring of 1944 when, because of the decline in need, production was halted.

With the loss of natural rubber sources from Southeast Asia by 1941 it was imperative to develop a synthetic substitute. The federal government called on the major rubber companies to expedite their research so that something would be available when the stockpile of natural rubber gave out. By 1943 the formula had been developed and produc-

Goodyear Aircraft produced this Corsair fighter plane for the navy during World War II. The navy also used Goodyear blimps to patrol the Atlantic and Pacific coastal waters. Courtesy, Goodyear Tire and Rubber Company Archives

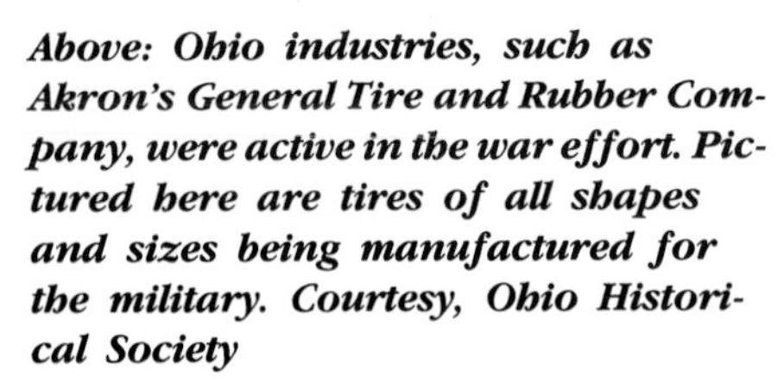

Above: Ohio industries, such as Akron's General Tire and Rubber Company, were active in the war effort. Pictured here are tires of all shapes and sizes being manufactured for the military. Courtesy, Ohio Historical Society

Above right: World War II rubber manufacturing focused on products for use in the war effort. With the cut-off of rubber shipments from Southeast Asia, the development of synthetic rubber was a top priority. By the end of the war, rubber companies reverted to civilian tire manufacturing. Courtesy, University of Akron Archives

tion of synthetic rubber was well underway. Goodyear produced the first synthetic rubber tire early in 1943, but all of the tire companies were soon in the business. Firestone, Goodrich, Goodyear, and General Tire each had three or four plants scattered from Akron to Texas. Tires for military vehicles were the primary products in the early war years, but later on the companies began to shift back to civilian production. Goodyear's Jackson, Michigan, plant stopped tire manufacturing when the war began, retooled, and by late 1942 was turning out antitank cannons. Within another year or so it had re-retooled and was back to manufacturing tires.

Marion Shovel did not need to retool as it was called upon to dig and excavate all across the country. Its powerful cranes were employed to handle materials for the Austin Company in the erection of the twin bomber plants at Fort Worth and Tulsa. It played an important role in the excavation and construction of ordnance plants. Marion Shovels moved two million cubic yards of dirt and rock prefatory to the building of an electrical power facility for the Aluminum Company of America in the Tennessee Valley. In Idaho men using four Marion cranes, the company proudly proclaimed, "poured 24 concrete igloos in a 24-hour period," which were used to store explosives. Marion shovels dug coal, copper, and iron ore from the nation's mineral beds. Its huge stripping shovel had a thirty-five-cubic-yard capacity with a monthly output figure of over one million yards, which helped increase Ohio's wartime coal production by 82 percent.

Perhaps the greatest American hero of World War II was not a man but a machine. Willys-Overland in 1938 hired Delmar G. "Barney" Roos, an engineer with long experience in various automobile factories, to work on improving a light, four-cylinder car. Roos determined to develop a more powerful, more durable, and more long-lasting engine for the car. Beginning with a forty-eight horsepower engine at 3,400 rpm's, which ran for only four hours, Roos in two years' time had increased the engine's performance to sixty-five horsepower at 4,400 rpm's with a continuous running time of 150 hours. Numerous other refinements lessened the weight and increased the strength of the car.

At this same time, the United States Army was searching for a tough, light, all-purpose vehicle; a machine with four-wheel drive, capable of speeds as low as three miles per hour, with substantial pulling power, and not weighing over 1,600 pounds. Bids were requested by the army but only

***Left:** Willys-Overland, after suffering problems during the Depression, recovered with its production of the Willys Jeep. The company produced over 650,000 of the rugged multipurpose machines. Courtesy, Toledo-Lucas County Public Library*

***Below:** Clevelanders witnessed a horrifying event on October 20, 1944, when an explosion hurling flames at the East Ohio Gas Company devastated a section of East 61st and 62nd streets. In the stricken area, which had an estimated population of 22,468, homes and stores were in ruins and 130 people were dead. Courtesy, Western Reserve Historical Society*

Willys and American Bantam responded. In tests the Willys car outperformed the Bantam, but it was too heavy, weighing 2,400 pounds. Revised specifications increased the weight limit to 2,175 pounds. Roos either had to scrap his engine or streamline his vehicle. He went for streamlining and the modified machine won army approval. Thus was born the famous "jeep."

Willys produced over 650,000 jeeps during the war and their achievements were legendary. They could climb steep grades and cross sandy deserts. They could accelerate quickly up to sixty miles an hour. The jeep was a multipurpose machine as well. With mounted machine guns it became a tank, with stretchers it became an ambulance, with a radio it became a command post, and with flanged wheels it became a locomotive. It became the subject of Bill Mauldin cartoons and soldier anecdotes: A corporal was in tears in his bombed out jeep. "Don't worry, you'll get another one," he was comforted. "But you don't understand," was the tearful reply. "I loved *this* one."

Sherwin-Williams continued to manufacture paint in World War II, but it also manufactured shells and bombs. The company built a munitions plant in Carbondale, Illinois, which at one time employed 15,000 workers. More than ten million artillery shells, millions of antitank mines, and a million 500-pound aerial bombs were turned out at this facility without rejects, and more important, without any fatalities. Along its traditional product line, Sherwin-Williams also manufactured camouflage paints for the military. One story has it that the Allied invasion of North Africa in November 1942 was delayed because of the late arrival of camouflage paints.

Although Cincinnati was no longer the pork-packing center that it once was, the industry continued in the city. Pictured here are women working at the Kahn's Company, the city's largest packing plant. Courtesy, Ohio Historical Society

Many Ohio companies other than those mentioned played their part in the Allied victory in World War II. It is not possible to name them all or to catalog their contributions. By looking at a few of the major ones, however, one can sense the ferment and pulsating beat of wartime America in one of the most important industrial states in the Union.

War ended in Europe in May 1945 as the Allied noose finally strangled Hitlerite Germany. A few months later in August, Ohio's Colonel Paul Tibbetts piloted the *Enola Gay* over Japan, dropped the atom bomb, and the war in the Pacific came to an end. Now the massive task of demobilization and reconversion was at hand, a challenge hardly less formidable than the original one of gearing up for war.

Despite the joy and relief when the guns stopped firing and the bombs stopped dropping, the future state of the economy generated considerable concern. The abrupt termination of billions of dollars worth of war contracts and the labor glut prompted by the return of millions of service men and women to the work force, led to predictions of a massive depression. Yet countervailing forces were at work, which blunted the impact of the expected economic decline.

The two factors most responsible for this unexpected turn of events were the large pent-up buying power of Americans, and the continued high level of government spending. Because of price controls, high wages (due to overtime work), and shortages of consumer goods, potential spending resources of private persons and corporations had climbed to $200 billion toward the end of 1944. With the end of the war the sudden pouring of these funds into the economy had a stimulating effect on peacetime production. Moreover, federal budgets continued to rise after the war as more and more public monies found their way into social and economic programs begun under the New Deal and continued under the Fair Deal of President Harry Truman. While serious problems of reconversion did occur and while a number of violent labor disputes broke out, there was no postwar depression.

As the country rushed onward, it became apparent that conditions were going to be quite different from what they had been before 1940. New technology, new processes, and new products marked what was coming to be called the "postindustrial society." Basic industries of the Industrial Revolution were giving way to a service-oriented economy. The standard of living of Americans would rise to unanticipated heights in this new "Age of Affluence." American life in the 1950s and 1960s displayed a new face. It featured plastics and Pampers, suburbs and supermarkets, environmentalism and ecology, aerobics and robotics. It was an age of interstate highways and fast food restaurants, motels and discount houses, television and computers, nuclear power and aerospace exploration, shopping centers and health spas. The scientific research upon which this new society was built received a major impetus from World War II. Two good examples of this are nuclear power and numerical controls, or computer systems. Prior to the war, research and development was confined chiefly to the electrical, chemical, rubber, petroleum, and automotive industries. After the war, research and development divisions became key departments in all industrial plants. Expenditures on research and development jumped dramatically between 1947 and 1968. And whereas industry had shouldered most of the financial burden for research and development in earlier times, the federal government steadily increased its contribution in this area. The following figures reflect the increase in and sources of research and development funds for the different years in millions of dollars:

	1947	1955	1960	1968
Federal Government	500	3,490	8.720	14.972
Industry	1,515	2,510	4.510	8.941
Other	85	270	480	1.170
Total	2.100	6.270	13.710	25.083

Diversification, decentralization, and internationalization were other characteristics of postwar industry. None of these were new departures, but their degree of acceleration was far greater than before. Shifting markets, population migrations, changing consumer appetites, and labor difficulties all were prominent factors in causing companies to diversify, relocate, and internationalize.

Diversification was accomplished in two ways, either by creating new divisions within the corporate structure or by acquiring businesses producing other products. This generally led to the decentralization of manufacturing centers and the appointment of autonomous heads to manage the new operations.

Particularly by acquiring other plants, diversification led to the "age of the conglomerate" in the 1950s, 1960s, and 1970s. By applying sophisticated management techniques, a parent company could transform an undervalued business concern into a real money-maker. Gulf and Western and ITT were among the more successful early large-scale conglomerates. Two big Ohio steel companies, Republic and Youngstown Sheet and Tube, were absorbed by Ling-Temco-Vought (LTV) in the 1970s and 1980s. LTV began as Ling Electric in 1958 with about seven million dollars in sales. By 1968, after acquiring twenty-five or so companies, its sales were over three billion dollars.

Meanwhile the image of the corporate manager was changing. No longer was the highly visible "captain of industry/robber baron" dominant on the business scene. Instead one began reading more of "organization men" and "men in gray flannel suits." An antiseptic sameness characterized the new industrial leader and his middle-management underlings. Rather than coming up through the "school of hard knocks," the new executive had his MBA from a distinguished university, lived in a prosperous suburban community, and played the corporate game. Those who would rise to the top usually had to accept transfers from plant to plant with the inconveniences that such frequent moves entailed, as they mastered all phases of the business. It was not as glamorous a life as it seemed to outsiders, but for those who paid the price the rewards were ample.

Dana Corporation of Toledo illustrates several of the trends noted above, although Dana is not a conglomerate. Founded in 1904 as the Spicer Company in Plainfield, New Jersey, the organization specialized in manufacturing universal parts for the burgeoning automobile industry. World War I gave a big boost to its business with the sharp increase in truck production. Charles A. Dana, related to the famous newspaperman, poured a large amount of needed capital into the company in 1914 at a time when it was in difficulty. Dana played a growing role in the company in the 1920s and 1930s, buying up companies producing universals, axles, and auto and truck frames. In 1929, to be closer to the heart of the auto industry, Dana relocated the Spicer Company to Toledo. The company name was changed to the Dana Corporation in 1948. Fifty years after its founding, Dana had become dominant in its field as a supplier of automotive components with annual sales of $153 million.

A new regime headed by Jack Martin took over the company at this time. A tough, demanding executive, Martin had a solid grounding in industrial management in steel, ordnance, and rubber-tire plants. He came to Dana in the late 1940s as executive vice-president and was named president in 1953. Martin opposed diversification but favored the acquisition of companies producing automotive parts, and moved heavily into the replacement-parts business. Perfect Circle and Aluminum Industries were added in 1963, giving Dana a strong foothold in the automotive "aftermarket." Three years later Victor Manufacturing and Gasket Company were acquired to further strengthen the company in this field. In the twenty years following his elevation to chief executive officer at Dana, Martin had increased the company's replacement parts sales from a few million to $309 million.

Following the acquisition of Perfect Circle, Dana went to decentralized control. Starting with five divisions, each maintaining its own manufacturing, engineering, finance, and sales force, the company expanded to twenty-one divisions by 1975. Martin also pressed actively for internationalization. In 1958 auto manufacturing outside the United States for the first time exceeded that within the country, so it was essential to develop overseas affiliates. By 1975 the network embraced 166 facilities managed by forty-five affiliated corporations in twenty-one countries in Europe, Asia, Africa, and South America. Dana owned from 33 percent to 49 percent of the stock in the affiliates, which were managed by nationals of the particular country. International operations were carried on before Martin's time, but between 1965 and 1975 investment abroad grew from $175 million to $430 million.

Austin Company was in the international market as early as 1914 and gained widespread recognition with its construction of the automobile plant in Nizhni Novgorod (Gorky) in the Soviet Union in the early 1930s. It built airplane plants in China in 1933 and opened its London office in 1938. Following the Second World War its international operations expanded greatly with subsidiaries located throughout Europe, in Asia, and in South America. Each subsidiary was a completely integrated and autonomous operating unit. As with its American offices, the subsidiaries were staffed with their own planners, architects, engineers, accountants, supervisors, and field workers.

Austin played a significant role in changing the face of America in the postwar world by building research laboratories, shopping centers, banks, computer facilities, television studios, college dormitories, hospitals, food-processing plants, department stores, and much more. In doing this, the company's engineers were in the national forefront in the suburbanization of industry. With superhighways and suburbs, corporations began relocating their plants from congested and deteriorating downtown quarters to spacious, attractive grounds in the city's outskirts. In this new setting came the adoption of the single-story, straight line, controlled-conditions plant, developed and popularized by Austin.

An example of the company's contribution to the suburbanizing of industry was the Northlake, Illinois, factory of Automatic Electric, a division of General Telephone Corporation. Business had increased so rapidly in the 1950s at Automatic Electric, which manufactured equipment for the telephone industry, that new quarters were a must. The company's facilities occupied seventeen different buildings in the Chicago "loop." Austin was commissioned by Automatic Electric to survey Chicago's outlying areas and recommend a new site. In addition it was authorized to design a new plant layout which would provide for maximum efficiency. Austin engineers selected the Northlake site and eighteen months after ground was broken the 1,520,000-square-foot, integrated, single-story, straight line plant went into operation. The ideal for a unified office and manufacturing facility had been attained.

Timken Company in Canton extended its international operations after the war, but did not diversify in the traditional way. It preferred to expand its own operations into related fields of steel manufacturing. Founded in 1899 in St. Louis by Henry Timken as the Timken Roller Bearing Axle Company, the concern produced a new kind of tapered roller bearing to eliminate friction in the carriage and infant automobile industries. In 1909 Timken moved operations to Canton for the same reason as Dana moved to Toledo, to be near the heart of the auto industry. To insure a high quality of steel, Timken built a plant in Canton in 1916, becoming the only bearing company to operate its own steel facility. In 1932 it expanded its operations by developing a percussion rock bit for mining, quarrying, and blasting operations. Before World War II new plants had been located in Columbus and Wooster as well as in Canada, Great Britain, and France.

Following the war, rock bit operations were centralized in a new plant at Colorado Springs and an automated bearing facility was opened in Bucyrus. Other bearing factories were built in nearby New Philadelphia and in faraway South Africa, Australia, and Brazil. Research was a top priority at Timken in the 1960s and considerable effort was devoted to improving the company's steelmaking capacity. With growing national concern over pollution and the environment, improvements were undertaken to eliminate the noxious gasses and wastes, normal byproducts of large manufacturing concerns. Since roller bearings had not been the company's sole product for over half a century, the name was changed in 1970 to simply the Timken Company.

Mead Corporation, the venerable Ohio paper and paper products company in Dayton, practiced internationalization and diversification, but also engaged in some de-diversification. Founded in 1846 by Daniel Mead, the company almost went broke in the years following Colonel Mead's death in 1891. After reorganization, it grew steadily in the first half of the twentieth century. Prior to World War II, Mead had acquired and built paper mills in Kingsport, Tennessee, Brunswick, Georgia, and Escanaba, Michigan. It also began to diversify, before the war, by getting into paperboard manufacturing, but these operations were greatly expanded in the decade after the war. By the late 1960s Mead had acquired several recycling plants which turned out "specialty boards" for a number of industries.

Mead began its move toward the "billion dollar club" in the 1950s and 1960s by extensive diversification. Corrugated shipping containers, multiple-packaging systems, and specialty papers were related to the company's basic product. But in 1958 Mead acquired Data Corporation, which put it in the electronic storage and retrieval business. Mead Data Control developed systems known as Lexis and Nexis, which have become, according to a company brochure, the "world's leading computer-assisted legal research service" and "leading full-text search and retrieval service for news and business information," respectively. In 1968 Mead also bought the Woodward Company which manufactured iron castings and rubber products, and mined metallurgical coal. In 1977 it purchased a pipe, valve, fittings, and electrical supply company, Gulf Consolidated Services.

But bad times lay ahead. In the late 1970s a five-year $1.5-billion modernization plan was instituted to replace obsolete and worn-out machinery. Close upon this came the economic decline of the early 1980s, leading to an $86-million loss for Mead in 1982. Retrenchment was a necessity and the corporation began unloading several of its non-forest companies, such as Gulf Consolidated, a portion of the Woodward holdings, and a good chunk of the container operations. Twenty percent of Mead's assets were unloaded in 1982 alone. Confining itself to paper, paperboard, pulp, and electronic retrieval, the company made a solid comeback in the next few years.

Hoover got right back into the vacuum sweeper business as soon as World War II ended and has largely confined its domestic operations to that product. However, new buildings have been constructed in the industrial park north of North Canton and the latest technical advances have been employed in the plants. Efficiency and productivity have been improved by the use of computer terminals, robotics, lasers, and microprocessor technology. Self-operating cleaners, portable cleaners, and rug and floor conditioners have been marketed around the world. Hoover also manufactures refrigerators, freezers, dishwashers, and washing machines in its overseas factories. It has plants in Wales, England, Scotland, Australia, South Africa, Colombia, Portugal, and Canada.

Cincinnati Milling established a "Committee of Five," composed of its top executives, to plan post-war readjustment. It was well that it did because

This 1947 photograph shows new automobiles being transported on the Ohio River. Today, Cincinnati still uses the Ohio for river transportation, as well as for recreation. Courtesy, Cincinnati Historical Society

there was a slump in the milling business when the guns stopped firing. The Committee of Five insisted that Cincinnati Milling must diversify if it was to survive. Cincinnati Milling acquired a lathe company in 1945 and got into the chemical business when it purchased the Carlisle Chemical Company in 1948. Its work in chemicals opened the door to the field of reinforced plastics in the 1950s. Between 1945 and 1950 other ideas for diversification were experimented with—zippers, brushless shaving cream, automatic telegram recorders—most of which were abandoned. Among new products which worked out well were Cimcool (a synthetic cutting fluid), abrasive grinding machines, and centerless grinders for making bearings.

The computer revolution of the 1950s and 1960s impacted heavily on industry. Although the origins of the computer have been disputed, it is immaterial to enter the debate or to become involved in the technical aspects of the computer revolution. Suffice it to say that in 1946 a 150-man team of scientists at the University of Pennsylvania produced ENIAC, a mammoth thirty-ton computer which carried out mathematical calculations thousands of times faster than any existing mechanical device. The early computer consisted of large banks of vacuum tubes and mechanical switches that filled three normal-sized rooms. Advances in the next ten to fifteen years brought about a steady reduction in the size of the component parts and with it a greater efficiency in output. The biggest breakthrough came in the 1960s with the development of miniaturized integrated circuits. Further improvements brought greater miniaturization of controls, more accurate control, and greater memory, all at reduced cost.

Cincinnati Milling welcomed the computer. In 1955 it was one of several companies awarded Air

Force contracts for the manufacture of computerized machines. The technology for developing a method of numerical controls for milling machines was available, but Cincinnati Milling proceeded to develop its own. In 1958 it shipped its first machine to the Air Force. In another year it was applying the technology to other machines. Engineers at the company were also groundbreakers in the field of software production and CINAP was among the first numerical control packages available on the commercial market. The company developed a "machining center," which had the capability of changing tools for different cutting operations by computer control.

The advent of miniaturized circuits in the 1960s, as noted, signaled a major step forward in computer technology. Until this time Cincinnati Milling, although it had been making some progress, appeared to be falling behind in the field. However, it now pressed ahead and in 1966 came out with Acramatic IV. The idea had originally been developed for use in the government's Minuteman Guidance system; however, the company adapted it to commercial use and stole a march on its competition. It boasted that "each tiny IC (integrated circuit) in the Acramatic IV replaced as many as 90 discrete components. IC's made it possible to increase control reliability by a factor of ten while shrinking the size of the control unit itself."

In 1968, after three years of research, Cincinnati Milling engineers developed a computerized system to automate the production of machine parts. Called a "flexible manufacturing system" (FMS), it incorporated a central computer which controlled the routing of workpieces to individual numerical control machines. While it was slow to catch on, the flexible manufacturing system might be viewed as the initial step in designing the "factory of the future." Thus through diversification and computer technology Cincinnati Milling had broken sharply with its prewar history. In fact, its name no longer suited its product and processes. In January 1970 the Cincinnati Milling Machine Company became Cincinnati Milacron.

It was a different story up in Dayton at National Cash Register. In the early 1950s the company's president, Stanley C. Allyn, acknowledged that NCR was at a fork in the road with the advent of computers. It could either stay with its original mechanical products with the prospect of only limited growth, or it could forget the past and move fully into computers and risk the financial dangers common to any uncharted field. Not everyone in the company believed that the future was necessarily wedded to computers. Business with the mechanical machines had been so good in the twenty years since the war that it was not easy to let go. Therein lay the dilemma. NCR tried to combine the new with the old and got into trouble.

NCR did go into computers, all right, and may have even recorded a few "firsts." As early as 1952 the company acquired a young California firm, Computer Research Corporation, which became NCR's Electronics Division. In 1957 the company came out with the NCR 304 data processing system, which was installed at the Marine Corps base at Camp Pendleton, California, and later at Marine headquarters in Washington, D.C. A smaller system, the 390, announced in 1960, became widely used for payroll processing by the Air Force and Navy. To accommodate medium-to-small present and potential customers, NCR installed data processing centers at half a dozen cities both in this country and abroad. In 1962 NCR was among the first companies to use the Telstar satellite for data transmission. A year later it introduced the 315, a full on-line system for banking operations. NCR took its most important step into the computer market in 1968, with its two-part Century Series.

However, throughout the 1950s and 1960s NCR never gave computers a very high priority. Demand for mechanical registers, accounting machines, and other traditional products remained high during this period and most of the company's attention was focused upon them. Plant facilities were expanded and sales offices were added. In 1960 NCR employment throughout the world totaled 52,000 and revenues were close to $500 million. New products were introduced regularly, in addition to cash registers and accounting machines. Kits were prepared to help workmen modify older machines in India, Pakistan, and South Africa, then shifting to the decimal system. The prosperity which the traditional machines were bringing the company apparently clouded management's view of the broader picture. Robert Oelman, who became president in 1960, continued the policies of his predecessor. That is, while expanding computer production, the chief emphasis remained on the manufacture and marketing of mechanical business machines. The bulk of NCR's income was derived, by a substantial margin, from the traditional market throughout the 1960s.

But problems began to emerge during that decade, which would soon bring the company to the brink of extinction. One was the escalating costs of its computer rental service. Another was the difficult position company salesmen found themselves in as they attempted to peddle both computers and mechanical machines, the one competing with the other. Moreover, as noted, management preferred improving the mechanical machines rather than developing new ideas. As an example, as late as 1967 NCR brought out a brand new mechanical register, the Class 5. It could do all kinds of things, but not as many as a computerized machine could do more economically. As the Class 5 contained thousands of parts it was an expensive machine to manufacture. So it was with most of the mechanical machines: they sold well, but costs were eating up profits. Revenues doubled from $458 million in 1958 to $1.1 billion in 1968, but profits did not go up accordingly. NCR was eighty-ninth in revenue in *Fortune* 500's 1968 list, but 334th in profits. Even the company's biggest plunge into computers, the Century Series, had been costly to produce and developed performance problems.

The cumulative effect of rising manufacturing costs for old products, marketing difficulties with new products, inflation, recession, and higher unemployment led to a drop in sales in 1970 and 1971. Orders were cancelled and NCR was forced to cut back production and to fire workers. While 1970 revenues were 12 percent above those of 1969, earnings dropped from forty-six million dollars to thirty million. The worst was yet to come. In 1971 earnings dropped to $1.3 million. A bitter strike of 8,500 workers idled the Dayton plant from October 1971 through January 1972 and contributed to the poor earnings report for 1971.

Summoned to the rescue was a man who had headed up NCR's successful Japanese operation. William R. Anderson had joined NCR in 1945, soon after his release from a Japanese prison camp, where he had spent the previous four years. After service with the Hong Kong branch he took over the Japanese office in 1960. It was the number-one overseas facility when in 1972 Anderson was called to Dayton. He was in his early fifties at the time. The new president stated quite clearly that the company's future depended on its total commitment to the computer. He eliminated old mechanical machine operations and began converting the various plants to the new mode. In addition, he decentralized manufacturing and instituted vocational marketing. Although recovery was slow, NCR eventually got back on the road to economic health. When Anderson retired in 1984, NCR was among the world leaders in electronic and computer systems.

One Cleveland-based firm which rose to the front ranks of major industrial concerns after World War II was TRW Inc., formerly known as Thompson Products. Founded in 1902 as a manufacturer of valves for automobiles, the company grew up with the auto industry. It benefited handsomely from an early agreement with the Winton Company and improved its condition during World War I. In the 1920s it developed the Silcrome valve which was important for the aircraft, as well as the automotive, industry. In 1926 it became Thompson Products Inc., honoring the man who had nursed the company from infancy to maturity, Charles E. Thompson.

The Depression hurt Thompson Products, but the company returned to health in the late 1930s under the leadership of its new president, Frederick C. Crawford. World War II boosted the fortunes of the organization as most of its products were easily adapted to military usage. Reconversion to peacetime presented no problem for the company as sales rose steadily from $64 million in 1946 to $125 million in 1950. During the Korean War the figure more than doubled to $327 million.

The "quantum leap" forward came in 1953 when Thompson, poised to press on to new frontiers, backed an infant California company, the Ramo-Wooldridge Corporation. Dean Wooldridge and Simon Ramo, brilliant Cal Tech Ph.Ds., specialized in ballistic missile design at a time when the United States was deeply immersed in competition with the Soviet Union in this new field. In 1955 their company became the technical advisor for a $17-billion ballistic missile program for the Air Force. Within two years this program grew to such dimensions that it involved 220 major contractors and thousands of subcontractors. The work force exceeded 3,000 and revenues were over twenty-eight million dollars. In 1958 Thompson absorbed Ramo-Wooldridge thereby forming Thompson Ramo Wooldridge. In 1965 the name was changed to TRW Inc.

In the 1950s and 1960s TRW began to diversify heavily and expand its overseas operations. It acquired auto parts, oil field equipment, and electronic companies. It pushed into markets throughout Europe, Asia, and South America. International sales currently bring in 30 percent of all revenues. Its three main divisions today are Car and Truck, Electronics and Space Systems, and Industrial and Energy. For research and development, the company built its Space Park in Redondo Beach, California. Of the 17,000 scientists employed there, 750 have Ph.D. degrees. By 1977 sales cleared the $3.2-billion figure. In 1985 TRW ranked fifty-ninth on the *Fortune* list with revenues in excess of six billion dollars.

In Canton another company, somewhat unique, adjusted well to the economic climate of postwar America. Perhaps its uniqueness was a factor. Diebold Incorporated, founded in Cincinnati in 1859, manufactures industrial security systems. These include bank safes and vaults, alarm systems, cash and record protection equipment, and information retrieval and material handling systems. Diebold had no second thoughts about computerizing its diverse product lines as soon as the technology was available.

The terrible Chicago fire of October 8, 1871, the year before Diebold moved to Canton, gave a big assist to the company's fortunes. Diebold had 878 safes installed in banks and other buildings in the Windy City. Despite the awesome destruction wrought by Mrs. O'Leary's thoughtless cow, all 878 safes survived the holocaust with contents intact. The free publicity afforded by this led to a flood of orders for Diebold safes and vaults. And the company has built some big ones. In 1874 Wells Fargo ordered the largest vault ever built up until that time. It required forty-seven railroad freight cars to ship the monster to San Francisco. The Detroit National Bank ordered the biggest vault for a commercial bank in 1921, only to be outdone by one commissioned by the Union Trust Company in Cleveland three years later.

From the company's inception, Diebold's engineers have had a running battle with resourceful bank robbers. To frustrate burglars who possessed duplicate keys, combination locks were devised. To foil kidnappers of bank cashiers who knew the combinations, the automatic time-lock came into being. When burglars started using TNT to blow up time-lock vault doors, Diebold pioneered in the manufacture of manganese steel doors which withstood TNT. Decades of experience with bank robbers have caused Diebold engineers to develop sufficient knowledge and expertise to design vaults which are virtually impregnable today.

Postwar architectural trends in business and industrial design stressed cleanliness, spaciousness, and style. Diebold caught the spirit with its Basic Vault Door in 1951. Without compromising security, the vault, whether it was open or shut, blended in nicely with the building's decor and became the interior showcase of the bank. A revolutionary wedge-lock door introduced in 1956, which was installed in many banks, similarly was designed to be architecturally harmonious with the environment.

The Armco plant in Hamilton, a city in the lower Miami Valley, was described in* The Ohio Guide *in 1940 as follows: "Here amid a welter of long buildings, giant smokestacks, tracks, and large cranes, are the furnaces and pits in which iron ore is changed into all types of steel." Courtesy, Western Reserve Historical Society

Diebold began diversifying in 1938 when it made its first tentative step into information retrieval. Work in this area was intensified after World War II and the engineers developed highly sophisticated processes for easy storage and quick recovery of vast amounts of data. With the acquisition of the Herring-Hall-Marvin Safe Company of Hamilton, Ohio, in 1959, Diebold moved into the bankteller counter equipment field. Drive-in banking caught on in the early 1950s, but many of the early systems were not practical. Diebold devised a plan whereby closed circuit television and an intercom network brought customer and teller close together. The company even manufactured a drive-in unit which extended itself outward to meet the reach of a customer who had parked too far away.

Unlike Diebold, Parker Hannifin Corporation of Cleveland, one of the leaders in the manufacture of fluid drive systems, had a bumpy postwar adjustment. Arthur Parker founded the Parker Appliance Company in 1918, but it failed in 1919. He started it up again in 1924 and, by linking the firm closely to the nascent aviation industry, was able to carry it through the Depression. With the outbreak of World War II, Parker Appliance was well-fixed to secure government contracts. During those years it became the world's largest manufacturer of hydraulic connecting and flow control devices.

The problem with this was that all of Parker's business was with the federal government and once the war ended, all contracts were cancelled. Employment dropped from 5,000 to 300 within a few months of the war's close. The plant was idle and the family—Arthur Parker had just died—was ready to abandon the business. Stubborn Mrs. Helen Parker, however, said "no," and resolved to rebuild. New but experienced corporate managers were brought in and under their guidance the company's condition improved. Fluid power technology was the basis for the company's successful return to industrial respectability. Parker's position was enhanced in 1957 with the acquisition of the Hannifin Manufacturing Company of Des Plaines, Illinois. The corporate name was changed at this time to Parker Hannifin.

Goodyear enjoyed many good years in postwar America. The new age was marked by advanced product lines and stepped-up emphasis in marketing and public relations. But perhaps the company's outstanding achievement was the globalization of its operations. By 1955 Goodyear production facilities had been expanded to include seventeen countries in Europe, Asia, and South America. In 1957 Goodyear International Corporation was created as an umbrella management organization for overseas facilities. That same year, the Goodyear Technical Center-Europe was opened at Colmar-Berg in Luxembourg, which in time became a mammoth center of research and development and the second largest employer in the country. Within the next ten years, European operations were accelerated with the opening of new plants in France, Italy, and West Germany. In the early 1970s the company opened the first tire-making factory in Zaire.

Following the war, rubber consumption in the United States was divided between the natural and synthetic varieties, although in Europe natural rubber had a commanding lead. While Goodyear possessed large sources for natural rubber, it remained the biggest American producer of synthetic rubber throughout the 1950s. In 1954 Goodyear produced its first tubeless tire. But the most important breakthrough in tire construction came from France with Michelin's radial in 1948. The radial caught on quickly in Europe in the next two decades, but was resisted in the United States. Goodyear developed what was called a "transitional" tire in the 1960s, something halfway between the traditional and the radial, but the future was obviously with the radial. Following Michelin's all-out invasion of the American tire market by 1970, Goodyear and the others recognized that they had better regroup and go to the radial.

Through its experience in aviation, Goodyear early entered into the aerospace business. In 1963 the Goodyear Aircraft Corporation was renamed the Goodyear Aerospace Corporation. The company produced parts for missile, guidance, and radar systems, ground support equipment, flight simulators, and space satellites. Air-conditioning and heating systems were installed in the Apollo 11 and Apollo 12 spaceships, which carried out the first two moon landings. The two-wheeled rickshaw which astronauts Alan Shepard and Ed Mitchell piloted over the moon's surface on Apollo 14 was equipped with Goodyear tires. Flotation bags used to flip over upside-down spaceships as they landed in the ocean were also made by Goodyear.

Goodyear had sponsored racing cars as a promotional tool in its early years, but had dropped the practice after World War I. However, following World War II sports car sponsorship became an important advertising weapon. The increase in auto racing as a spectator sport and the great success Firestone and Dunlop were enjoying in promoting their tires could not be ignored. A prestige factor was involved as well. The manufacturers of tires of winning cars had a big advantage over other tire companies. Goodyear inconspicuously began sponsoring entrants in major races in the mid-1950s and within a decade had attained parity with other companies. The first Goodyear driver to win the Indianapolis 500 was A.J. Foyt in 1967.

Goodyear began advertising on television even before it got back into racing, sponsoring "The Paul Whiteman Revue" in 1949. "TV Playhouse" was another program sponsored by the company during television's first decade. An important promotional project was the widespread use of the Goodyear blimp at sporting and ceremonial functions around the country. In 1958 only one blimp was in service and it was about to be mothballed when a new and enterprising public relations man, Robert H. Lane, recognized its advertising possibilities. By the midsixties a number of new blimps had been built and were in great demand, particularly by television networks, to serve as aerial camera platforms for football and baseball games, yacht races, golf matches, auto races, and world fairs. Television audiences came to expect to see the "Goodyear of goodwill" at sporting events.

Goodyear faced some problems in this era of growth and globalization. First, there was an upsurge in tire imports from abroad in the last half of the 1960s. Foreign auto and truck imports jumped from 3 percent of the American market in 1965 to 9 percent five years later. Cheaper labor costs, differential tariffs, and government subsidies all contributed to the less expensive foreign products. The growing demands from environmentalists for pollution controls led to a battery of rules and regulations, with which all industries had to comply. The threat of the radial hung overhead, while the company delayed entering the competition. The energy crisis of 1973-1974 sparked by the sharp rise in oil prices impacted on the entire economy, but especially on auto-related industries, such as tire manufacturers. Finally, labor unrest, which developed during the "age of protest" in the late 1960s and early 1970s, led to massive strikes.

Despite these difficulties, Goodyear's sales and earnings proceeded steadily upward. In 1952 it was the first tire company to exceed $1 billion in annual sales. By 1958 sales were up to $1.3 billion and in the mid-1960s broke through the $2-billion barrier. In 1969 Goodyear was the first rubber company to pass the $3-billion mark in sales. Strikes in the auto, rubber, and trucking industries in 1970 caused a drop that year, but from 1971 through 1982 there were regular increases in both sales and earnings. Foreign subsidiaries showed a similar steady growth during the same period.

Like other "smokestack" states, Ohio's heyday of industrial glory had passed. Heavy industry, as spawned by the Industrial Revolution, was giving way to a new type of business activity, one which supplied the consuming public with the countless goods and services its enhanced economic condition demanded. The nation's industrial plant, you might say, had been built. What was now needed were the refinements, the frills, and the luxuries that an affluent society could afford. Thus there emerged sometime after World War II the "post-industrial age," a time when "service" industries moved to the forefront, rivaling, if not surpassing, the once vaunted industrial giants that had made the United States a formidable economic power.

The American Ship Building Company, formed through the merger of the Cleveland Shipbuilding Company, Globe Iron Works Company, and the Shipowners Dry Dock Company, is shown here celebrating its 50th anniversary. Within five years of the company's formation, it had constructed 181 vessels and was involved in the construction of more ships for the Allied effort during WWI and WWII. Courtesy, Western Reserve Historical Society

VIII

THE POST-INDUSTRIAL AGE

As in the past, the Ohio River remains the major artery for an economically thriving state. Photo by Deborah E. Sarabia

Facing page: This ad for Procter & Gamble's new washing product was placed in newspapers in 1946. At first only available in six U.S. cities, Tide was a great success for the Cincinnati-based company. Courtesy, the Procter & Gamble Company

The later postwar era has become associated with the rise of "service" industries. *Fortune* initiated this new classification in 1983, although the distinction had been commonly recognized for many years with the development of the "postindustrial" society. A service company is a nonindustrial concern, with 50 percent or more of its revenues derived from nonmanufacturing. The chief subcategories of service organizations are diversified financial, diversified service, commercial banking, insurance, retailing, transportation, and utilities. In the mid-1980s Ohio ranked fifth nationally in headquarters for service corporations with twenty-five, being surpassed by California, New York, Texas, and Illinois. As for cities, Cleveland was eleventh nationally, Columbus tied for eighteenth, and Cincinnati tied for twenty-second.

Statewide, Kroger is by far the largest company in retailing, while Roadway leads in transportation, Ohio Casualty in diversified financial, Nationwide in insurance, American Electric Power in utilities, Super Food Services in diversified service, and National City Corp. in banking. What is intriguing about this list of service leaders is that four of the seven—Kroger, Ohio Casualty, Nationwide, and American Electric Power—are located in Cincinnati and Columbus, cities which lagged behind during the glory days of heavy industry. They appear to symbolize the postindustrial era.

Burger King, McDonald's, Hardee's, Taco Bell, Long John Silver's—all have become familiar names along the "fast food freeways" of most American cities. Although a later development in the changing postwar American scene, the fast food restaurant is now such a part of the lives of Americans that we sometimes wonder how

From Procter & Gamble's Great Laboratories-
JUST RELEASED
A Revolutionary New Washday Miracle!
IT'S TIDE
. . . you've never used anything like it!
TIDE is a completely NEW washing product—the most revolutionary washday help that ever came out of a package! Discovered during Procter & Gamble's wartime research, Tide does what's never been done before—washes clothes cleaner than any soap, yet leaves colors brighter! The first time you put Tide in water you'll know you're using a brand-new product! The amazing suds look different...they even feel different!
GUARANTEE
Procter & Gamble guarantees that Tide will do everything claimed for it in this advertisement. If you are not completely satisfied, return the unused portion of your package to your dealer and the purchase price will be refunded.
NO OTHER WASHING PRODUCT KNOWN CAN MAKE THIS STATEMENT
Tide
GETS CLOTHES CLEANER THAN ANY SOAP MADE
—yet actually
LEAVES COLORS BRIGHTER
Procter & Gamble
ONLY Tide DOES ALL FOUR!
1. Washes clothes cleaner!
Yes, cleaner than any soap made! Everything comes cleaner with Tide—even heavily soiled work clothes! Tide leaves clothes free, not only from ordinary dirt, but from gray, dingy soap film as well. No soap can get clothes as clean as Tide!
2. Actually brightens colors!
Tide is not only safe for dainty washable colors, but it actually brightens soap-dulled colors. Brightness perks up almost like magic as Tide makes dulling soap film disappear!
3. Never "yellows" white clothes!
Tide can't turn them yellow, no matter how often they're washed or how long they're stored! Tide-washed clothes stay dazzling white week after week.
A Hymosol Product
4. Gives more suds!
Faster suds! Kind-to-hands suds! Test Tide in your dishpan. Tide washes dishes cleaner than any soap! No scum in the water! No greasy ring round the pan! No cloudy film on dishes and glasses! That's why they rinse and dry so sparkling clear.
New washing miracle
Tide
Oceans of Suds
white CLOTHES, sparkling DISHES
TIDE'S IN—DIRT'S OUT!
Copyright, 1946 by The Procter & Gamble Company
TIDE is available only in WICHITA. If your dealer is sold out because of the tremendous demand for TIDE, he will have more soon.

we ever got along without them. Indeed, it has been frequently said that by the year 2000, Americans will be eating the greater proportion of their meals outside of the home.

One of the most famous fast food restaurants is Columbus-based Wendy's International Inc., founded in 1969. R. David Thomas, born in Atlantic City, New Jersey, in 1932, always "wanted to be in the hamburger business." Orphaned at an early age, he traveled about the Midwest as a teenager with his adopted father, a construction worker. He worked in several restaurants during World War II, entering military service in 1949. Still a teenager, he was the youngest soldier to manage an NCO club. In the mid-1950s, a civilian again, Thomas worked at the Hobby House Restaurant in Fort Wayne, Indiana, which held an early Kentucky Fried Chicken franchise. He worked with and learned much from Colonel Harland Sanders. In 1962 he took over the operations of four failing Kentucky Fried Chicken restaurants in Columbus and turned them around. But he still wanted to get into hamburgers.

On November 15, 1969, the first Wendy's Old-Fashioned Hamburgers restaurant was opened in Columbus. The name was taken from Thomas' eight-year-old daughter, Melinda, called "Wendy" by her brother and sisters. In charge of his own place, Thomas was now able to apply a few of the ideas he had gathered in the fifteen years or so of his apprenticeship in the business. He insisted on the use of "100 percent pure American beef," served fresh daily rather than being prepackaged and heated by a lamp. He also offered customers a broad array of condiments to season their hamburgers. Made-to-order hamburgers and the novel pick-up window, in the view of the company historian, "revolutionized the fast service restaurant industry and sparked Wendy's rapid growth across the nation in the early to mid-1970s."

It was one full year later, in November of 1970, before the second Wendy's restaurant was opened. This was also in Columbus. From that point onward the chain expanded rapidly throughout the Midwest. On June 25, 1975, the 100th restaurant was opened in Louisville, Kentucky. One and one-half years later the 500th restaurant opened in Toronto, Canada. At the end of 1985, 3,442 restaurants were scattered throughout all fifty states and eighteen foreign countries. In just over fifteen years, R. David Thomas' brainchild had become the world's fourth-largest restaurant chain, with annual sales well over $2.5 billion.

Wendy's rapid growth and success were linked to its energetic television advertising campaign. Beginning in 1973 the company ran ads on local radio and television stations. In April 1977 it went national with a "Hot N' Juicy" ad. The commercial ran for three years and, according to a marketing official, "put Wendy's on the map." It ran on breaks during Monday Night Football and the Tonight Show, and earned the Clio Award for creativity. In 1980 the company introduced both its salad bar and

Bob Evans shows a grill cook the proper procedure for frying sausage. Evans began making his own sausage in the late 1940s because he couldn't obtain sausage of comparable quality in the Midwest. Bob Evans Farms employs more than 12,000 workers and sells its sausage in nineteen states. Courtesy, Bob Evans Farms, Inc.

chicken sandwich, which were featured in its "Wendy's Has the Taste" ad. In 1984 Clara Peller's "Where's the Beef?" query perhaps more than anything made Wendy's a household name.

Although not as well-known nationally in the food business as Wendy's, but perhaps more "Ohioan," is Bob Evans Farms Inc. Born on a farm in rural southeastern Ohio in 1918, Bob Evans began putting together his "sausage empire" in 1946, soon after his return from military service. That year he opened the twenty-four-hour Bob Evans Steak House just outside Gallipolis. The breakfasts were popular, especially with truck drivers, but there were complaints about the sausages. Bob Evans decided to make sausages using hogs from his own farm in nearby Bidwell. The sausage was sold in retail stores in southeastern Ohio as well as at the Steak House. So well-received were Bob Evans' sausage products that in 1953 a second plant was established near Xenia. Later, additional plants were opened in Hillsdale, Michigan, Galva, Illinois, and Gallipolis.

Evans bought another farm at Rio Grande, about twelve miles west of Gallipolis, in the early 1950s, which over the years has become a tourist attraction and showcase for many activities. People began visiting the farm in such numbers that in 1962 a small restaurant was opened to accommodate them.

Above: Bob Evans is pictured here at his Rio Grande farm, posing with his mare and colt. Built in 1824, his home was once used as a stagecoach stop and inn. Courtesy, Bob Evans Farms, Inc.

Left: Bob Evans' 1,100-acre Rio Grande farm in southeastern Ohio has become a tourist attraction, hosting special events from April through October. Courtesy, Bob Evans Farms, Inc.

David Frisch bought the first Big Boy franchise in the 1920s and opened his first restaurant in Norwood. Today there are 105 company-owned Frisch's restaurants, plus numerous franchises. This picture shows the thirteen original Frisch's Big Boy Restaurants. Courtesy, Cincinnati Historical Society

In 1969 a third restaurant was opened in Columbus. The number of restaurants grew steadily, although the total never reached that of Wendy's chain. In the mid-1980s over 165 "family" restaurants had been spawned from Michigan to Florida, from Pennsylvania to Missouri. In addition, the five pork-packing plants were delivering fresh pork regularly to 7,600 retail outlets in nineteen states throughout most of the eastern part of the country.

People kept coming to the farm. In 1970 it was decided to hold a farm festival and 10,000 visitors arrived. The festivals became so popular that twenty are now held each summer—including an International Chicken Flying Meet, a Country Music Convention, Homesteading Days, and a 4-H Fall Roundup—which culminate in a kind of Oktoberfest every autumn. Various outdoor activities—horseback riding, canoeing, and hiking—are available to guests at the 1,100-acre plantation. Cattle are bred, horses are raised, and tobacco, sugarcane, corn, and wheat are grown. Bob Evans, his sausages, and his restaurants have become an Ohio institution.

Although Wendy's is the largest fast food company headquartered in Ohio, it is not the only one. A Columbus competitor is Rax Restaurants, which made its first appearance in *The Ohio Roster* in 1986. Other major Ohio restaurant systems are Ponderosa, based in Dayton, and Frisch's in Cincinnati.

Speaking of food, the largest Ohio corporation according to earnings is Kroger Company of Cincinnati. The latest revenue figures for the multistate supermarket chain exceed seventeen billion dollars. It ranks fourth nationally in *Fortune*'s list of retail organizations and first in *Business Week*'s list of food retailers. Other large Ohio supermarket chains, although not to be compared to Kroger, are Big Bear (based in Columbus), Fisher Foods (Cleveland), and Seaway Food Town (Toledo). Super Food Services of Dayton is a large food wholesaler with sales close to $1.4 billion. J.M. Smucker is a more modest diversified food manufacturer in Orrville.

Rubbermaid, with corporate headquarters in Wooster, began as the Wooster Rubber Company in 1920, a manufacturer of toy balloons. Rubber dustpans first appeared in 1934, a central turning point in the company's history. From then on, as a major producer of rubber and plastic products for household use, Rubbermaid began the growth which has placed it in a commanding position in the field. The name Rubbermaid was adopted in 1937. The company has never gone in much for diversification, staying primarily with rubber and plastic goods. In those areas it has done well, despite being a relatively small organization. About 5,400 employees man Rubbermaid facilities throughout the United States, Canada, and Europe, manufacturing many varieties of sinkware, bathware, food containers, "roughneck" containers, and microwave cookware.

The coming of age of the automobile in the 1930s, 1940s, and 1950s not only led to the decline of the railroad, but contributed directly to the rise of a major postwar industry—trucking. And one of the top trucking companies in the country is headquartered in Akron. It was in 1930 that a young Akron attorney, Galen J. Roush, formed Roadway Express. He recognized the need for a direct means of transport between his hometown tire center, the auto center in Detroit, and other major cities. Within a couple of years Roadway terminals dotted

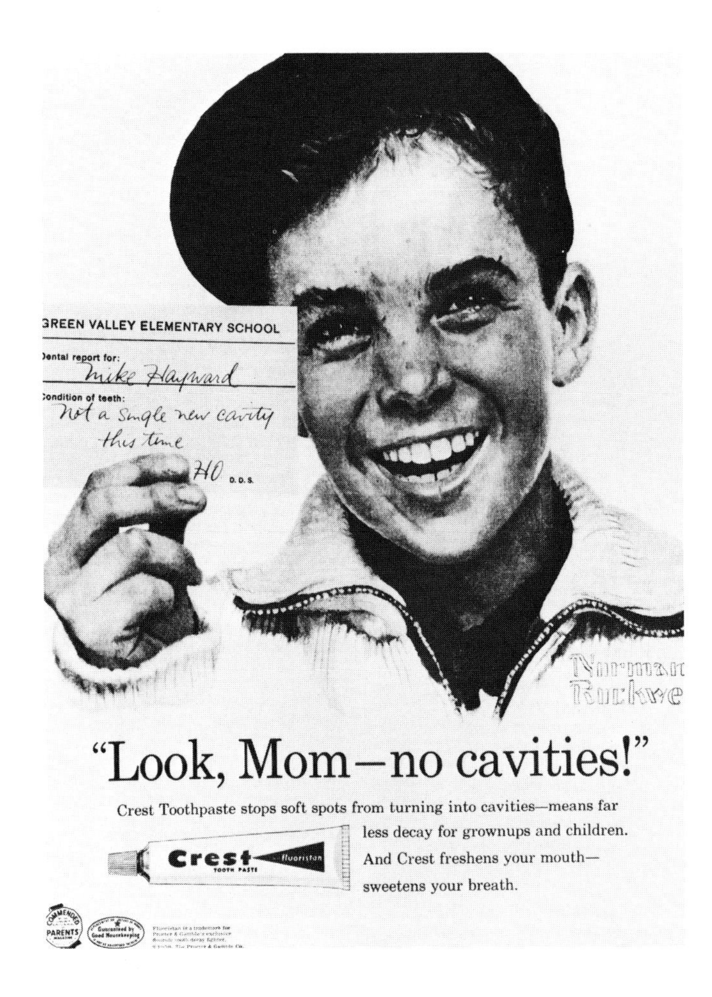

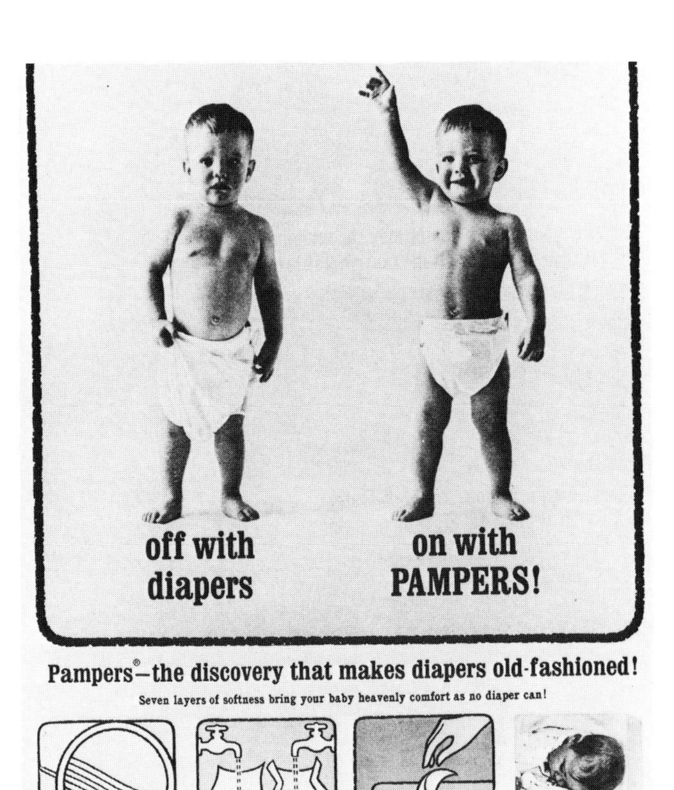

Above: Pampers disposable diapers has been a successful product from the time it was first marketed by Procter & Gamble in the 1960s. Courtesy, the Procter & Gamble Company

Above left: Norman Rockwell painted this 1957 advertisement for Crest toothpaste. When Procter & Gamble finally obtained the American Dental Association's endorsement of Crest, the toothpaste became the best--selling brand in the country. Courtesy, the Procter & Gamble Company

the map throughout the East and South. Originally, the drivers operated their own trucks under a franchise arrangement with Roadway. In 1945, however, the company acquired its own trucks and equipment.

At the end of the war Roadway introduced a novel distribution system, beneficial to small communities. The company's trucks would carry less-than-full loads from tiny towns to large central "break-bulk" terminals for consolidation and distribution. Similarly, less-than-full loads would be transferred from the break-bulk centers to satellite terminals in small places. Over 500 Roadway terminals are scattered across the country today, mostly in the Midwest, East, and South. Break-bulk terminals are to be found in places like Chicago, Kansas City, St. Louis, Toledo, Cincinnati, Columbus, Memphis, Nashville, Winston-Salem, Atlanta, Buffalo, and Phoenix. Forty-two thousand communities are served in this fashion.

The importance of trucking in postwar America is readily seen from an examination of Roadway's growth. In 1951 the company had only fifty-two terminals. This figure increased to 178 in 1971 and to 506 in 1982. For these same years revenue grew from about $50 million to $400 million to $1.2 billion. Income followed a similar path upward: $2 million, $24 million, and $78 million. Roadway can also be classed as an international corporation since it ships across the borders into both Mexico and Canada. With its 18,000 employees, the company operates a fleet of 23,000 tractors, trailers, and trucks.

An old familiar name, Procter & Gamble, made important contributions to consumer-oriented, post-World War II America. Within fourteen years the soap-making company came out with three products which forever changed the lives of housewives and consumers, to say nothing of brand new babies. In 1947 it was Tide, in 1955 it was Crest, and in 1961 it was Pampers. Interestingly, only one of these three products had anything to do with soap.

Research advances during the 1930s and World War II led to the development of a heavy, multiduty laundry detergent. However, test-marketing had to be delayed until the war was over. But when Tide was put on trial it was a smashing success. Nothing before had ever been able to wash clothes cleaner, leave colors brighter, make better suds, make clothes whiter, and eliminate hard-water problems all at the same time, as did Tide. The new product overwhelmed all other soap products. Along with the advent of the automatic washing machine, it immeasurably eased the burden of homemakers. Ironically, it destroyed almost half of the company's market for traditional soap products and made obsolete a sizable bulk of its soap-manufacturing equipment.

Procter & Gamble had some experience in toiletries as early as 1933, but it was not until after the war that we heard about Prell Concentrate, Lilt-Home Permanents, and Gleem Toothpaste. Soon the company was into therapeutics. Working closely with researchers at Indiana University, the company developed a fluoride compound which became the basis for an anticavity toothpaste. Crest was successfully test-marketed in 1955, but was not the instant success that Tide had been. It was more difficult to quickly demonstrate the benefits of a dentifrice than it was with a detergent.

To give its new product credibility, Procter & Gamble went to the American Dental Association, which had made a practice of not endorsing toothpastes. For five years ADA scientists tested and evaluated Crest. In August 1960 it reported that "Crest has been shown to be an effective anticaries [tooth decay preventive] dentifrice that can be of significant value when used in a . . . program of oral hygiene and regular professional care." This was the recognition the company needed and within two years Crest was by far the best-selling toothpaste in the country.

Building on the success of Crest, Procter & Gamble moved further into the health-care field and by the mid-1980s had become the largest manufacturer of over-the-counter drugs in the United States.

But what put young mothers into the company's debt was Pampers. Developing a highly absorbent pad that could be encased in a plastic wrapper was not only unpleasant, but complicated. "We had to design the entire production line from the ground up," said one of the engineers. At length the problems were overcome and test-marketing began in Peoria, Illinois, in late 1961. One of the early users of the disposable diaper was Beverly Greenhall of Peoria. She first used Pampers on her daughter, Vickie, who was born December 10, 1961. In 1986 Procter & Gamble held a twenty-fifth anniversary party in Peoria, and twenty-four-year-old Vickie, now Mrs. Williams, was one of the honored guests. Her eighteen-month-old son Andrew naturally was equipped with Pampers.

Three other Ohio companies illustrate the range of service industries and further emphasize the significant role Cincinnati and Columbus play in the consumer-oriented economy of the modern day. In fact, many well-known national retail stores are actually parts of Federated Department Stores and United States Shoe Corporation, both of Cincinnati, and The Limited of Columbus.

Federated, one of the largest department stores in the country, was founded in the late 1920s when five independent stores—Lazarus, Shillito's, Filene's, Abraham and Straus, and Bloomingdales—were brought together under one large umbrella. Fred Lazarus assumed control of the combine in 1945 and commenced an acquisition policy by which he built an empire of fifteen "divisions" by 1970. Among the acquisitions were Foley's (Houston), Bullock's (Los Angeles), I. Magnin (San Francisco), Rike's (Milwaukee), Goldsmith (Memphis), and Burdine's (Miami). Pursuing a strategy of strong divisional autonomy in which "upside-down" or buyer management plays a significant role, Federated has risen to its preeminent position in the retail field. In the mid-1980s *Fortune* listed it eighth among all retail stores by sales and fifth by income.

United States Shoe is a good example of a company which came into being to do one thing, but which over the years evolved into a service industry. It was founded at a most unlikely time, 1931, by the merger of two small Cincinnati shoe manufacturers. Growth was slow but steady. Expansion

The Lazarus Company, a part of the Federated Department Stores, Inc., began in 1851 when Simon Lazarus opened a men's clothing store in Columbus. Over the years the store expanded its merchandise to include women's clothing, furnishings, and sporting goods. In the 1960s the first Lazarus branch store opened, and in the early 1970s the company opened a branch in Indianapolis, Indiana. Courtesy, Ohio Historical Society

resulted largely from acquisitions of other shoe companies, but also from the construction of several new factories. Until 1962 United Shoe was strictly a manufacturer of footwear, but that year, with the purchase of Wm. Hahn and Co., it entered the retailing field. Then in 1970 it acquired Casual Corner, a retailing chain specializing in women's apparel. Other specialty shops were added, catering to young women, "misses," "petite misses," and young men. Lenscrafter optical has been a more recent addition, marking United States Shoe's entry into the health-care field. A recent annual report notes that the company has 2,267 retail stores, 1,894 of which specialize in apparel, soft goods, or eyewear, while only 373 handle footwear.

The Limited of Columbus, the largest retailer specializing in women's clothing, is another billion-dollar-plus corporation. Leslie H. Wexner, the owner, ranks sixth in *Forbes*' collection of billionaires. The 43,000 employees of the company man such stores as Victoria's Secret, Lane Bryant, Lerner's, and Henri Bendel. Wexner started out with one store, but by acquiring failing chain groups he built an empire. Recently he has decided to open up a number of men's apparel shops. The Limited was ranked forty-eighth according to stock value in *Business Week*'s 1986 1,000 list.

A common feature of American suburbia from the 1950s forward has been the shopping center —that mammoth aggregation of retail outlets, grouped together, which sell almost anything anyone would ever want to buy. The founder of the shopping center was Youngstown billionaire Edward J. DeBartolo, Sr. A graduate of Notre Dame and a World War II veteran, DeBartolo first worked for his father, a paving contractor. He thought of building shopping malls in 1949 and plunged boldly ahead with the untested idea. It was a great success and in the next decade he built over 100 shopping centers. Seeking new fields, DeBartolo sold most of the plazas and turned his attention to enclosed shopping malls in the 1960s. DeBartolo became the largest mall developer in the country and currently operates fifty-five of them.

From what has been written to this point, the postwar economic picture would appear to be a prosperous one. Many companies expanded, diversified, globalized, and made a lot of money. Numerous new enterprises also did very well. Ohio continued to rank among the top states in the country in manufacturing, services, and financial institutions. It has had its share of corporations among *Fortune*'s elite 500. The state's location is still a good one, serviced as it is by interstates and airports. Its natural resources are not as plentiful as they once were, but they remain an important component in the industrial scene. Still many things have changed, which, to a degree, have blunted Ohio's industrial progress.

From the end of the war until the 1960s, the

state's economic growth continued unabated. Yet there was an uneasiness about this growth. The decline in manufacturing jobs had proceeded steadily despite increased production. Automation was beginning to take its toll. In the late 1960s, for the first time in Ohio's history, the number of workers engaged in services exceeded those in manufacturing. By 1970 the figures were 54 percent in services and 46 percent in manufacturing. The postindustrial age was at hand.

Because of liberal concessions to trade unions, workers' wages and benefits increased steadily. These high labor costs led to developments that were not good for either labor or the state. For one thing, strikes accelerated the trend toward automating plant facilities. For another, where unions proved intransigent to making changes or concessions, plants were sometimes closed down. For still another, companies with labor difficulties found it simpler to move to the "Sun Belt," where unions were less strong than in the northern "Rust Belt." As a corollary to this, when stories about the militancy of Ohio labor got out—not that such reports were new—the natural tendency was for companies to look elsewhere when planning to build a new plant. Moreover, excessive labor costs led directly to a flood of foreign imports, particularly automobiles, which could be produced more cheaply than the American product. "Buy American" has a noble ring, but in an age of heavy inflation, Americans will shop for lower-priced goods.

Honda of Japan was one of the first foreign companies to "invade" the American auto market with a cheaper product. At the time of the 1973 oil embargo Honda introduced into the United States its fuel-efficient Civic. Honda expanded its offerings in the next several years and the response was so good that in 1977 it decided to build an American

Like its neighboring state, Kentucky, Ohio recently attracted foreign car manufacturers. A Honda of America Manfacturing facility is headquartered in Marysville and abides by the company's motto, "Accept no bad parts, make no bad parts, and pass no bad parts." Pictured here is a quality assurance inspection. Courtesy, Honda of America Manufacturing, Inc.

The Honda of America Manufacturing auto plant in Marysville has all manufacturing operations located under one roof. Here in the welding department, the body of a Civic sedan is checked, cleaned, and inspected prior to painting. Only three years after beginning production at Marysville, Honda of America became the fourth largest auto manufacturer in the United States. Courtesy, Honda of America Manufacturing, Inc.

assembly plant. It chose Marysville, Ohio, about twenty-five miles northwest of Columbus, as the site. Honda already had a prosperous motorcycle factory in Marysville and the auto plant was to be built next to it. The first automobile rolled off the assembly line in 1982 in time to circumvent the quota on imported Japanese cars. So successful has this operation been that Honda constructed an engine plant in Marysville and is planning a second assembly plant there. An instrument panel factory is being constructed in Sabina.

The Marysville facility is unlike the typical American automobile factory. The workers are not unionized, although they are paid well and receive fringe benefits. They also operate under a "democratic discipline" that the United Automobile Workers would have difficulty living with. Other Japanese automakers have been quick to follow Honda's example in building American plants—Nissan built a facility at Smyrna, Tennessee, and Toyota at Georgetown, Kentucky.

But other factors contributed to the malaise of Ohio business in the 1960s and 1970s. Industrially speaking, Ohio was an out-of-date state. It was deep

Right: This Honda employee is using a computer-aided probe system to check quality before the blocks are passed to assembly. This engine plant, located in Anna, can turn out 90,000 engines per year. Courtesy, Honda of America Manufacturing, Inc.

Below right: Honda's 260,000-square-foot plant in Marysville was the company's first motorcycle facility in the United States. Opened in 1979, with a production capacity of 60,000 cycles per year, the plant adheres to the philosophy that "Honda quality is built in, not inspected in later." Pictured here is a step along the assembly line of the Gold Wing motorcycle. Courtesy, Honda of America Manufacturing, Inc.

into heavy industry, particularly steel and autos, which was not the wave of the future in the post-industrial age. Though steel and autos were still important, technological change had significantly altered American thinking as to what should be manufactured and how it should be manufactured. The new "hi-tech" engineering had centered itself in the newer states of the South and West. Old-fashioned Ohio had little appeal in this regard. Many Ohio industries were still operating their original plants, which were becoming obsolete.

But even new plants built in Ohio by American companies were not always the answer to the problem. A case in point is the Lordstown "state-of-the-art" factory, built by General Motors west of Youngstown in the mid-1960s. Rather than labor's traditional "gut" issues of wages, hours, and conditions, the problems at Lordstown were psychological. Management's tough policy toward absenteeism and union arrogance, and its determination to maintain maximum production levels, generated a rising resentment among the workers over the humdrum routine of the assembly line. "Alienation" and "depersonalization," new words for work place conditions, characterized the "blue-collar blues." A long strike in 1972 received national attention, as the "new worker"—young, antiauthoritarian, assertive—challenged the traditional management. The workers did win minor concessions, but Ohio's struggling economic image had been struck another blow.

Two other related problems which have plagued industry, not only in Ohio but across the land, are in-plant health hazards and environmental pollution. A strike broke out at the Columbus Coated Fabric plant in February 1974 which lasted well into the summer. Whereas alienation was a factor, as at Lordstown, health safety was perhaps more important. Environmental pollution can only be dealt with by extensive renovation of old plants and the installation of costly antipollution equipment. It was not unusual for some factories to budget over one-third of their resources to clean up the facility. Even the modern Bruce-Mansfield plant devotes nearly half of its annual operational budget to pollution control.

Unemployment figures suggest the ups and downs of the Ohio industrial work force in recent times. Between 1969 and 1977, particularly following the oil crisis of 1973-1974, the eight most industrialized counties lost on the average over 15 percent of their jobs in manufacturing. Dayton (Montgomery County), Youngstown (Mahoning County), and Cleveland (Cuyahoga County) suffered job losses well above the 15 percent figure. Something like 140,000 jobs in all were eliminated. The crisis in steel and rubber brought the problem into sharp focus. Two of the oldest and most hallowed industries in the state were dealt near-lethal blows because of plant obsolescence, technological advances, labor costs, and foreign imports.

Steel appeared in good shape until 1959, although there had been some slippage in employment. But a 110-day industry-wide strike that year was a turning point. Plant closings marked the

This steam engine provides a nostalgic glimpse into Ohio's past, when lifestyles were slower and less complicated. Recently the Cuyahoga Valley Train Line introduced a twenty-two-mile excursion between Cleveland and Akron through the Cuyahoga Valley National Recreation Area. A 1918 Mikado Steam locomotive pulls the train and its passengers along on a trip into yesterday. Courtesy, Western Reserve Historical Society

1960s and 1970s, culminating in the shocking shutdown of Youngstown Sheet and Tube's massive works in the late 1970s, which cost thousands of steelworkers their jobs. Conditions were no better in Akron. The oil embargo hit the auto industry hard with a rippling effect on tire manufacturing. The United Rubber Workers, fearful of losing hard-fought gains, conducted their longest strike in history, 141 days, in 1976. While gaining substantial wage and cost-of-living increases, the union really won only a "pyrrhic victory." In four years' time the major tire producers closed their Akron plants and transferred manufacturing operations elsewhere. Incredible as it may seem, no automobile tires are manufactured in Akron today.

* * *

The Central Trust Building in downtown Cincinnati stands over a thriving city of industry. Photo by Andrey Gibson

For some years now Ohio has been the object of abuse and ridicule for its supposed economic decline and other shortcomings. It is not an easy matter to sort out the assets and liabilities on such a nebulous balance sheet. Certainly, unemployment has been high and companies have left the state. It is true that the Cuyahoga River caught fire and that Cleveland went bankrupt. Of course, New York City practically went bankrupt at one point and unemployment in Detroit has been high with the slump in automobile production. Many communities across the country have been visited by economic hardship.

Yet when all is said and done, some surprising facts emerge. Ohio remains the fourth-ranking manufacturing state in the Union, a position it has maintained throughout most of the 100 years since the beginning of the Industrial Revolution. It is sixth in population and possesses seven major market regions with populations in excess of 500,000. Its central location puts it within a day's motor reach of all of the Midwest and most of the East and South. Ohio is among the top-five states in volume of freight trucked over its numerous interstate highways. Early in the book, Ohio was described as the "Gateway State," the gateway to the West. Today it might well be called the "Gateway to all of the United States."

Corporate industry likes doing business in Ohio, whatever the state's detractors might say. Roughly forty Ohio industries regularly appear on the *Fortune* 500 list and the state has its share of companies among the ranking "service" institutions. Ohio is third among the states in hosting corporate headquarters for the 500 industrials and is fifth for the 500 services. The October 1986 edition of *The Ohio Roster* reports that business has recovered substantially from the recession of the early 1980s. "This continued strong performance confirms that Ohio businesses are holding their own in a highly competitive business environment and a low inflation economy," says Gary Pildner, author of *The Ohio Roster.*

It is not the purpose of this survey of Ohio business to judge the past or predict the future. The purpose has been to describe the origin, growth, and maturation of industry in one of the most important states in the Union. Yet the thrust of this book suggests that Ohio has contributed significantly to America's rise to industrial greatness. It is a story which has needed telling and one which must ignite a spark of pride in those who call themselves "buckeyes."

Compliments of the STANDARD SEWING MACHINE CO
CLEVELAND, O.
STANDARD
ROTARY-SHUTTLE

Previous page: This advertisement was for one of Standard Sewing Machine Company's biggest selling item, the Rotary Shuttle.

Right: Cincinnati became famous in 1811 for the production of beer. With the arrival of more German immigrants to the city, the brewing industry thrived in the 1840s and 1850s. The first lager beer was produced in 1853 by Christian Moerlein, and by 1892 Cincinnati exported 600,000 barrels of lager beer. Pictured here is the Bellevue Brewing Company, formed in 1878, which met its end during Prohibition. Courtesy, Cincinnati Historical Society

vue Brewing Co. Cincinnati, O.

HARDWARE CO.

Above: Founded in 1812, Columbus is the seat of Ohio's government and is also an important center for numerous industries. Photo by Kevin Fitzsimons

Left: The highrises of downtown Cincinnati tower over the Ohio River. Photo by Rick Dieringer

CENTRAL
TRUST
PROV IENT

Left: The Hulman Building and the Dayton Power and Light corporate office buildings make up part of this Dayton skyline. Photo by Connie Girard

Facing page: The Cincinnati skyline, with Riverfront Stadium at the right, is shown at dusk. Photo by Connie Girard

Below left: This Hyatt Regency Hotel, in Cincinnati, is a popular spot for conventions and out-of-town visitors. Photo by Connie Girard

Below: The wide variety of architectural styles shown here reflect the history and diversity of Dayton. Photo by Connie Girard

The Ivorydale Building of the Procter & Gamble Company stands as one of the significant companies in Cincinnati. Photo by Deborah E. Sarabia

Facing page: Seen in the distance are the twin towers of the Procter & Gamble Company. Photo by Connie Girard

Right: Telecommunications is among the many research projects at the Ohio State University in Columbus. Photo by Kevin Fitzsimons

Below right: Research in pharmacy is pictured here at the Ohio State University in Columbus. Photo by Kevin Fitzsimons

Below: This water tower stands in Eden Park, in the southernmost part of the state. Photo by Kay Shaw

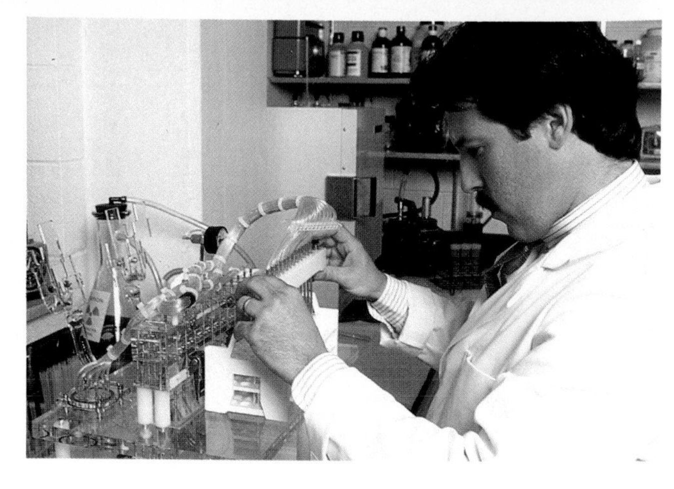

Left: The processing and fabricating of chemicals as seen in this picture, is done at the Shepard Chemical Factory. Photo by Rick Dieringer

Below left: This worker investigates a step in production at the Mead Corporation Paper Plant in Chillicothe. Photo by Kevin Fitzsimons

Below: This vivid picture was captured at the Sawbrook Steel Mill in Cincinnati. Photo by Rick Dieringer

Left: At the Timken Research facility, steel is developed and tested. In this picture technicians analyze the characteristics of a "melt" after the addition of various elements. Courtesy, the Timken Company

Fountain Square, located in downtown Cincinnati, was dedicated to the people of this prosperous city. Photo by Kay Shaw

These flags wave on 48th Street in Columbus. Photo by Mark E. Gibson

Left: Strawberry pickers get a day's work in at this farm in Urbana. Photo by Audrey Gibson

Below: This picture shows the agricultural region of Urbana, in the midwestern part of the state. Photo by Mark E. Gibson

Dramatic lights reflect off the Roebling Bridge. Photo by Mark E. Gibson

IX

PARTNERS IN PROGRESS

Ohio historians would hardly mention Max Morehouse in the same breath as Thomas Alva Edison, Harvey Firestone, or Neil Armstrong. But in his own way Morehouse captured and held aloft for a brief moment the entrepreneurial spirit that has blessed the Buckeye State and its people.

Morehouse was a Columbus dry goods merchant, the proprietor of Morehouse-Martens—The Home Store. His small mark in history was made November 7, 1910, when he sponsored Phillip Parmalee to fly two packages of silk from Dayton to Columbus, the first air cargo flight.

Although Morehouse did not set the world on fire, many others from Ohio did. It is hard to imagine a world today without the pioneering spirit of Ohioans that began with the first settlers in the Northwest Territory. From the beginning they were blessed with natural abundance. The mighty Ohio River, which provided a route for the French explorer Robert La Salle and the pioneers that followed, is still one of the nation's great commercial waterways.

To the north Lake Erie fostered industrial growth unsurpassed by any state in the Union. All manner of industry came to life along its shores, lined with harbors for vessels bearing iron ore, coal, and grain. Later the St. Lawrence Seaway offered the giant ships access to the open sea.

In between the river and the lake was a natural wealth that put food on the nation's table and muscle on emerging industry. Ohio's great seal highlights the state's rich and varied agricultural heritage. Ohio agriculture is still a major and competitive force in the markets of the world.

It is doubtful that the Buckeye State's renowned economic strength would have prospered without the water, coal, iron ore, natural gas, and crude oil found within its borders. These basic resources contributed to the commercial development of so many industries: steel, glass, automotive, rubber, paper, petroleum, chemical, and hundreds of others.

Ohio's partners in its remarkable progress have been adventurers and leaders of vision. Foremost among these, perhaps, have been the eight presidents of the United States from Ohio. Others, such as astronauts John Glenn and Neil Armstrong, have stepped out of this world for their place in history.

But there are many buckeye entrepreneurs who have made their mark through vision, courage, and leadership: the Wright brothers of Dayton; Edison, the unsurpassed inventor; Charles F. Kettering, the automotive genius who invented the self-starter; John D. Rockefeller, a self-starter himself who began penniless, founded Standard Oil, and became the world's richest man; W.A. Otis of elevator fame; and Dr. B.F. Goodrich and Harvey Firestone, pioneers of the tire industry.

Today's entrepreneurs, whose stories are found on the pages that follow, continue to add to Ohio's rich and diverse history, and they have chosen to support this important literary and civic project. Some have been a part of the Ohio scene for more than 100 years; others are relative newcomers, who have built on the vigor and prosperity of their predecessors. Ohio can be proud of the achievements of these innovators.

OHIO CHAMBER OF COMMERCE

On November 15, 1893, after the election of William McKinley as governor and a new delegation of legislators to the Ohio House and Senate, a group of forward-looking Ohio businessmen met in Cleveland to discuss the severe economic depression the nation was facing. That meeting resulted in the founding of the Ohio State Board of Commerce, which later became the Ohio Chamber of Commerce, a voluntary organization of business people working to make Ohio's economic climate one in which business and industry could succeed.

According to old records of the Cleveland Chamber of Commerce, the preliminary steps to the founding of the Ohio State Board of Commerce were taken at a meeting in Cleveland on March 7, 1893. Apparently the months between May and November 1893 were devoted to planning and making arrangements for a statewide commercial conference held on November 15 in Cleveland. Called by the Cleveland Chamber, the conference was attended by 55 representative businessmen, delegated by the leading commercial bodies from around the state. The conference brought together in one meeting the state's local commercial associations and the leading companies to promote, by unity of action, the commercial, industrial, and financial general business interests of Ohio.

During World War II the U.S. Army occupied the Huntington Bank Building where the Ohio Chamber had offices. The Ohio Chamber continued its work from temporary offices on the corner of Fourth and Broad streets.

After 31 years of effective but essentially limited programs, there came a call for a reorganization of the Ohio State Board of Commerce. The reorganization, started in January 1924, was fully implemented by 1926.

Three significant features of the reorganization changed the Ohio State Board of Commerce. First, there was to be a broadening of representation on the board of directors; second, the establishment of a systematic effort to secure the membership of local chambers of commerce and other organizations; and third, a change in the name of the organization to the Ohio Chamber of Commerce.

Since that reorganization, the Ohio Chamber of Commerce has moved to the capital city of Columbus, and has expanded and broadened its activities and services to business to the point where it is now regarded as one of the largest, most influential, and greatly respected state business organizations in America.

The Ohio Chamber serves as the only statewide business organization representing a broad spectrum of Ohio business and nearly 300 local chambers of 70 state trade associations. The chamber is governed by a volunteer chairman and board of 100 directors selected from business and professional leaders from various sections of the state, representing all types of business interests. Business can receive guidance and service from the Ohio Chamber of Commerce on many public issues, and government officials look to the organization for well-informed opinions on problems and issues affecting business.

The chamber employs full-time lobbyists who deal with specific issues in the legislature. These lobbyists are kept busy during legislative sessions, giving testimony on bills vital to business, providing information to legislators, and interpreting the impact of legislation on business.

Ninety-four years after its formation, the chamber is still guided and supported by volunteer businessmen and -women. Members of the chamber are involved in setting its policies, or issue positions and goals through serving on committees or by serving on the board of directors. Seven standing committees, with a combined membership of more than 500 key business executives, focus on specific business problems and present recommendations for the board of directors' policy decisions. Policies are then communicated to governmental leaders by chamber members, staff, and many of the volunteers themselves.

Since its formation, the Ohio Chamber of Commerce has consistently changed and expanded to meet its members' needs and to better relay business concerns to legislative leaders. As part of that change, the organization formed a council in 1985 to specifically deal with concerns of small-business owners. The Ohio Small Business Council (OSBC) has become a statewide network of small-business owners united for legislative action.

As the Ohio Chamber of Commerce builds toward a full century of service, it will continue to fulfill the purpose laid out by the group of businessmen in 1893—to work to make the economic climate in Ohio one in which businesses and industries can succeed.

VULCAN TOOL COMPANY

A small group of toolmakers founded Vulcan Tool Company in 1916 by establishing a shop at 418 East First Street. In 1917 the late Lee Amos Jones purchased control of the firm from this group, and the company continued to grow throughout World War I.

In 1927 Lee Amos Jones moved the operation from East First Street to 213 North Beckel Street, where both the tool and design rooms were enlarged. In 1933 the late Lee Warren Jones, son of the founder, joined the company and in 1939 founded Tube Products Company, which is located north of Dayton in Troy, Ohio. Today Tube Products operates plants in Troy and also in Louisville, Kentucky. Both of these plants produce auto and truck exhaust systems.

Although the economy was stagnant during the early 1930s, the past performance and quality workmanship of Vulcan's skilled craftsmen kept the firm afloat.

During World War II Vulcan designed and made the tools and dies needed to change U.S. manufacturing facilities into producers of war weapons. At the end of World War II Vulcan purchased the Dayton Tool and Engineering Co. and moved to the expanded plant and offices at 730 Lorain Avenue in East Dayton where the firm remains today.

Diversification became a necessity with the changing times. The creative minds of Vulcan invented the Vulcanaire grinder, which became Vulcan's first proprietary product in 1949. Diversification continued in 1956, when Vulcan entered into an agreement with Steel Products Corporation for the right to manufacture Brehm Shimmy® dies and also acquired the rights to the Brehm® Tube Cutter shortly thereafter.

In 1959 Howard H.H. Jones, Vulcan's current president and grandson of the founder, established Production Tube Cutting, Inc., with branches in France and England. In the late 1950s and early 1960s Vulcan displayed its new products at machine shows throughout the world, and by the mid-1960s both the Vulcanaire and Brehm® Tube Cutter were being sold worldwide.

In the late 1960s and on through the 1970s, Vulcan continued to improve its proprietary items. In 1976 Vulcan developed a unique tube-cutting machine, the Ringmaster. This makes Vulcan one of the largest manufacturers of tube-cutting equipment in the country. In 1964 the firm purchased the assets of Arbor Tool of Iowa and established Vulcan Tool of Iowa. This acquisition included Dubuque Industrial Supply, a tool supply distributor. Finally, in 1973 Tube Products merged with Vulcan Tool Company to form Vulcan Tool Corporation. With the continuous upgrading of its equipment, Vulcan has become one of the most modern tool rooms in the country.

From its humble beginnings in 1916, Vulcan Tool Company now operates plants in three states and employs more than 300 people. One of the largest tool and die manufacturers in the country, Vulcan will be servicing industry for years to come from its birthplace—Dayton, Ohio.

***Left:** The excellent craftsmanship of German immigrant toolmakers contributed to the early success of Vulcan Tool Company.*

***Below:** The staff poses outside the original facility at 418 East Street in Dayton shortly after its founding in 1917.*

PIZZA HUTS OF CINCINNATI, INC.

For Pizza Huts of Cincinnati, pizza is just part of a growing business that includes real estate, construction, interior design, landscaping, and maintenance.

Owner Anthony J. "Jack" Nickert and his stepson, Stephen King, have brought the Cincinnati firm from a one-store operation in 1968 to more than 25 stores in greater Cincinnati and northern Kentucky in 1987. They also own as a joint venture 20 stores in the Pittsburgh area. The corporation hopes to expand by seven stores each year until it saturates the market at 45 stores in the 1990s.

Nationally, Pizza Hut opened its doors in the late 1950s, when two brothers, Frank and Dan Carney, decided to develop a family restaurant based on pizza and a few other Italian food items. The company got its name because, after the word "Pizza," there was room for only three more letters on the sign—and so was born, Pizza Hut. The Carneys' first restaurant was so well received that a second was opened within the first year. By 1959 the first franchise was awarded to Dick Hassur in Topeka, Kansas.

Nickert was selling prefabricated restaurant buildings at a franchise convention when he and Hassur met and formed a partnership that led to the development of Pizza Huts of Cincinnati. Originally Hassur handled the operations and Nickert took care of the real estate and site locations. In 1974 Hassur's share of the business was bought out by three area businessmen; three years later Nickert bought their shares and became sole owner and president of Pizza Huts of Cincinnati.

After buying out the other partners Nickert decided to use his experience in manufactured construction to benefit Pizza Hut. He formed Jan Builders in 1980 to construct Pizza Hut stores. Just about all the firm's construction work is done directly for Pizza Hut accounts. Jan Builders also has an interior design, landscaping, and maintenance arm that services Pizza Hut restaurants. Using his own building and design and maintenance services, Nickert has been able to capitalize on his experience and use it to keep his overhead costs lower and assure quality.

Nickert's stepson, Stephen King, began his career at age 14 as a busboy in his stepfather's first store on Compton Road. He obtained his real estate license at age 19. As a result of his work, the company now owns several million dollars in real estate in choice high-traffic retail areas throughout the greater Cincinnati area.

King, at age 30, was named one of the top 10 young entrepreneurs in America. Persons on the list are ranked according to the gross revenues of their companies as determined by the Association of Collegiate Entrepreneurs and the Young Entrepreneurs Organization. In addition to coming up "through the ranks" of the pizza business, King has a bachelor of business administration degree from the University of Cincinnati with a major in finance.

Together Nickert and King have developed a business that, although founded and best known for its family-style restaurant, is making its profit not only in this business but also in construction and real estate. However, both men know that their business would not be a success without two other important components—their staff and their customers.

The company has grown to employ more than 1,500 full- and part-time workers. Some, like King, started behind the counter in high school and have moved up to operational and store management positions. A number of employees have been with the firm for more than 10 years, while many college students return and work summers and holidays even after they graduate from high school.

Although the company emphasizes "quality, service, cleanliness, and atmosphere," Nickert and King recognize that what their customers want most is a well-made, quality product. Over the years Pizza Hut has innovated its product line with the institution of pan pizza, Italian pies, turnovers, and other new products that have changed the face of the industry. Pizza Hut Inc. also pioneered new techniques in preparing and cooking pizza to eliminate the perception of pizza as a "slow food" in a fast-food marketplace.

Pizza Hut franchisees have always contributed to the communities they serve through support of local charities, tours for youth groups, and, most important, with jobs for young workers.

With national leadership in product development and local operators such as Nickert and King, Pizza Huts of Cincinnati, Inc., is looking to further growth well into the 1990s.

Owner Anthony J. "Jack" Nickert (right) and his stepson, Stephen King, have brought the Cincinnati firm from a one-store operation in 1968 to more than 25 stores in greater Cincinnati and northern Kentucky in 1988. They also own 20 stores in the Pittsburgh area as a joint venture.

THE STOUFFER CORPORATION

When Abraham and Mahala Stouffer opened their dairy bar under the steps of the old Arcade in downtown Cleveland in 1922, their goals were to earn a living and help their sons get a college education. Little did they realize that their buttermilk stand would someday evolve into the nation's leading producer of premium-quality frozen prepared foods, and a chain of about 80 restaurants and 34 luxury hotels stretching from coast to coast.

It turned out that son Vernon, fresh from the Wharton School of Business at the University of Pennsylvania, had a host of new ideas and nationwide plans when he joined the family business in 1924. He talked his father into investing $15,000—a sizable sum in those days—in a new restaurant on the corner of Euclid Avenue and East Ninth Street. Called Stouffer's Lunch, the restaurant served five types of sandwiches—including toasted cheese and bacon, lettuce, and tomato—buttermilk, coffee, and open-face Dutch apple and lemon meringue pies.

Success grew out of Abraham's genuine interest in guests, Mahala's fine cooking and family recipes, and Vernon's innovative management and high standards. Soon the family added a dinner menu, which offered a small steak dinner, including baked potato, rolls with butter, and beverage, for 67 cents. Within a year they opened other restaurants in Cleveland and Detroit, and the following year yet another in Pittsburgh.

Founder Vernon Stouffer tasted reheated frozen and freshly prepared entrées side by side and insisted that they taste and look the same.

Left: Employees at the Woodland Avenue plant—Stouffer's first plant for preparing frozen foods. Then and now all employees at all plants meet face to face with top managers each quarter to learn about new developments and ask questions.

To preserve quality while expanding, Mahala and Vernon became super-tasters. To preserve harmony between management and employees, the company's managers worked out a formula for multiunit operations. Son Gordon, who joined the business on a full-time basis in 1929, brought to the team insight in personnel selection, training, and team organization. Early on the firm took steps to ensure that "everybody is somebody at Stouffer's." By pleasing both customers and employees, Stouffer's continued to grow, launching its first venture in New York during the height of the Depression. Expansion halted during World War II but resumed in 1946, when the company opened its first suburban restaurant at Shaker Square in Cleveland—a daring move at the time.

It was at Shaker Square that manager Wally Blankinship began freezing menu items at the request of customers wanting to dine at home. Soon he opened an adjoining outlet store called the 227 Club. By 1954 the volume of business had grown so much that a pilot processing plant employing 25 people was opened on Woodland Avenue to prepare spinach soufflé and other favorites. Two years later it expanded fivefold, and Stouffer Foods was officially incorporated.

In the early 1960s a marketing team headed by Vernon Stouffer and James Biggar figured out how to sell their line to supermarkets. They understood that their entrées could not compete on the basis of volume, so Stouffer's became the first company to use selective distribution. The firm

Above: Abraham Stouffer's original buttermilk stand, circa 1922, in the lower level of the old Arcade in downtown Cleveland.

Stouffer's Tower City Plaza, the 70-year-old hotel on Cleveland's landmark Public Square, has been restored to its original beauty. Inside are a marble registration desk and the second-largest ballroom between New York and Chicago.

placed its 25-item line only in high-income areas of major markets, and guaranteed stores a certain level of profit. By the mid-1960s the company could not keep up with the demand for its frozen prepared foods. After opening a highly automated food plant in Solon, Ohio, in 1968, Stouffer's sold the line nationwide and at U.S. military commissaries worldwide. Regarding the last frontier—outer space—Stouffers handled, at NASA's request, the quarantine feeding of Apollo 11, 12, and 14 astronauts returning from moon trips. Meanwhile, Stouffer's restaurant operations continued to grow in the 1950s by branching into the suburbs and diversifying. One proposal, made by founder

Below: An early view of Stouffer Foods' operating and sales headquarters in Solon, Ohio, a Cleveland suburb. The Solon plant opened in 1968 and now employs more than 2,000 people in the production and distribution of frozen prepared foods, including entrées, side dishes, French bread pizza, soups, crepes, and Stouffer's popular Lean Cuisine line of calorie-controlled entrées.

The 227 Club, where the first Stouffer's frozen foods were sold, was next door to Stouffer's Shaker Square restaurant (now Vernon's) in Cleveland.

Stouffer's Lunch, the first official Stouffer restaurant, opened for business in May 1924 on the corner of East Ninth Street and Euclid Avenue in downtown Cleveland.

Vernon Stouffer, called for restaurants atop skyscrapers to give diners a view. This led to the "Top" series of restaurants, including Top of the Town in Cleveland.

Stouffer also anticipated the need for hotels in the late 1950s, as travel was coming into vogue. Seeing the potential, he purchased Stouffer's first hotel property, Anacapri Inn, in Ft. Lauderdale, Florida, in 1960. After a trial period, other Stouffer hotels followed.

In 1967, in the midst of these developments, the publicly owned and traded Stouffer Corporation lost its independence. It was bought by Litton Industries, which in turn sold the firm in 1973 to Nestle S.A. of Vevey, Switzerland, the world's largest multinational food company. Nestle's purchase marked the start of Stouffer's greatest period of growth.

The following year Stouffer's celebrated its 50th anniversary. A month after the celebration, the entire organization mourned the death of Vernon Stouffer. His creativity and high standards in both product and management laid a solid foundation for Stouffer's future success.

By 1981 the Stouffer Hotel Company consisted of 18 hotels. Since then, with the guidance of William Hulett, hotel president, the firm has become identified with the top segment of the hotel industry.

The Stouffer Hotel Company has acquired the historic Mayflower in Washington, D.C., just four blocks from the White House, and has spent $65 million for renovations. It also has acquired the AAA five-diamond-rated Wailea Beach Resort in Hawaii and has built the concourse properties adjacent to Denver's Stapleton International Airport and Los Angeles International Airport. Other acquisitions include four Wyndham properties in Dallas and Austin, Texas; Orlando, Florida; and St. Thomas in the Virgin Islands. The newest hotels to join the chain are the Stouffer Nashville Hotel and Harborplace in Baltimore's Inner Harbor complex. In all, there are four AAA five-diamond-rated properties and 22 four-diamond-rated units, placing the Stouffer Hotel Company among the top four in the top-quality hotel business.

The 1970s and 1980s brought rapid growth and many new theme restaurants, such as J.B. Winberie, Cheese Cellar, James Tavern, Parker's Lighthouse, and the Pier series of restaurants. The acquisition of Borel Restaurant Corporation (1976) brought the Rusty Scupper chain of restaurants under Stouffer management. In the same period a few "traditional" restaurants were updated to become the Chicago Bar & Grill and The Whole Grain. John Quagliata is president of the Stouffer Restaurant Company.

Stouffer's greatest growth has been in its frozen-food operations. Since its 1981 introduction of the Lean Cuisine line, the company has occupied the number-one position in store freezer sections. To supply the more than 100 items in its frozen prepared foods line, the firm opened a second plant in Gaffney, South Carolina, in 1980, and a third in Springville, Utah, in 1987.

Today The Stouffer Corporation is headquartered at a 42-acre complex in Solon, Ohio, just southeast of Cleveland. James Biggar, a 28-year veteran, is president and chief executive officer. In 1984 he also became responsible for all Nestle Enterprises' food operations in the United States. As a result, Biggar, from his Solon office, oversees not only Stouffer Foods Corporation, Stouffer Hotel Company, and Stouffer Restaurant Company, but also Nestle Foods Corporation, Hills Bros. Coffee, Inc., Beech-Nut Nutrition Corporation, Wine World, Inc., Nestle Puerto Rico, Inc., and L.J. Minor Corporation.

KASTLE ELECTRICAL CONTRACTORS

Technology has changed the face of the world since 1923, and nowhere is it more evident than in electrical contracting.

When Karl Kastle opened the doors of Kastle Electric Company in 1923, he worked out of his garage and installed mostly knob and tube wiring to light Dayton's homes. Electric refrigerators, irons, stoves, washers, and dryers were just making their way into working class homes with some regularity. Business, too, had few electrical needs. Typewriters and copiers—essentials of everyday life today—were powered by hand.

But as our way of life started to change in those early years of the affluent Roaring Twenties, Dayton residents joined their neighbors nationwide in finding more and more uses for electrical energy. Through the 1920s and the Great Depression of the 1930s, Kastle Electrical Contractors grew slowly. By the time the firm moved to its current location at 809 Xenia Avenue, Dayton, it had grown to 12 employees and was working all over the city.

After World War II the baby boom, the economic boom, and the boom in new technology and products spurred growth at Kastle Electrical Contractors. Karl Kastle was not satisfied to just supply power for the new, expanding line of electrical time-savers—he wanted to sell them as well. As a result, the office space on the first floor became a showroom, the family moved out of the upstairs, and the offices and warehouse moved to the upstairs and the garage.

In 1947 Jack Stuhlmiller was hired by the aging Kastle to learn the business and succeed him as company president. The firm, with Kastle as president and Stuhlmiller as vice-president, was incorporated that same year and continued to develop its residential customers.

It was Stuhlmiller, seeing great changes in American business and technology, who moved the company toward providing electrical contracting for business. When Kastle retired a few years later, Stuhlmiller took over the firm and continued to be a part of the changing face of Dayton business and industry. He phased out the appliance sales area to concentrate on new projects springing up all over Dayton.

One of Kastle's largest contracts during the 1950s was the wiring on the Town and Country Shopping Center near Kettering, one of the first centers in the Dayton area. By that time the firm had dropped most of its residential wiring and concentrated on the more intricate needs of Dayton business.

By 1965, when current president Richard Prass joined the organization, Kastle Electrical Contractors was well known for both its public and private industrial work on substations and distribution stations.

As the city's skyline changed throughout the 1960s and 1970s, Kastle Electrical was there, installing the wiring and the technical systems that made the buildings light up the night as well as meet customers' needs during the day. It was no longer good enough to install the needed energy—the installations had to be energy efficient as well.

Each new building or project brought about its own special design needs so Kastle Electrical added engineers to its reliable technicians and began not only installing but also designing systems. Today the company installs only a portion of the design work completed by Kastle Electrical engineers. Cargill, the NCR world headquarters, St. Elizabeth Medical Center, Kettering Tower, and Gem Savings are only a few of the corporations served by Kastle Electrical.

As the 1990s dawn Kastle Electrical Contractors is on the cutting edge of the newest technology, designing systems and installing wiring to last at least another six decades.

Top: The Kastle Electrical Contractors staff on the occasion of the company picnic in 1948 (standing, from left): Dick Gray, Frank Burkhart, Clarence Blatz, Tom Rattliff, Karl Kastle, Jack Stuhlmiller, and Kern Frank. Seated (from left) are Dick Quinn, Paul Woeste, Joe Schmid, Art Nolan, Bob Smith, Art Nicholson, and Red Gilmore.

Richard Prass, chief executive officer.

SAINT LUKE'S HOSPITAL

Left: Cleveland General Hospital, predecessor of Saint Luke's Hospital, boasted a progressive staff and offered free medical care to the poor.

Above: Francis Prentiss, Cleveland businessman and longtime president and benefactor of Saint Luke's.

Cleveland in the 1890s was a city where great commercial might and wealth coexisted with poverty and disease, where children represented 50 percent of the annual deaths. Growing awareness of these contrasts, and the desire to apply advances in bacteriology, cell theory, and nursing, led in 1894 to the opening of Cleveland General Hospital, the predecessor of Saint Luke's Hospital.

Located on Woodland Avenue, Cleveland General soon made a name by caring for the indigent and founding a nursing school that would train the first public health nurses in the area. The 75-bed hospital boasted a young, progressive staff, up-to-date facilities, and a dispensary for the needy. Described as the busiest place in town, the dispensary brought the hospital to financial collapse and foreclosure by 1905, as the medical staff could not bring itself to reduce its work for the poor.

Fortunately, a group of distinguished Cleveland businessmen stepped in with financial and administrative aid. One member of the group, Francis Prentiss, assumed the presidency, and the group worked out an agreement with the Methodist Church. Renaming the facility Saint Luke's Hospital Association of Cleveland, the businessmen and religious leaders made it clear that the Methodists had not joined this enterprise for glory, but to help carry forward needed philanthropic work.

Funds for a new 120-bed hospital were raised, and construction at 6606 Carnegie Avenue was completed in July 1908. The new facility was commended by *The Plain Dealer* as "one of the nearly perfect institutions for the care and cure of ailing humanity in the United States." To attract the carriage trade, it offered private rooms elegantly furnished by donors with linens, silverware, china, and fine rugs. The facility also reflected the newest in medical technology, with rounded corners and nonporous tiles used extensively to aid the maintenance of cleanliness. Surgery was made as antiseptic as possible with shower rooms and wash basins. This, combined with skillful use of a nitrous-oxide painkiller, established the hospital's reputation for safety and comfort in childbirth.

Further improvements throughout the medical world in pathology, X-ray technology, and other areas, coupled with an exploding population, soon increased the demand for services. By 1926 new facilities became necessary, and a site was proposed at its present 11311 Shaker Boulevard address. The new hospital was completed in 1927.

Two weeks before the statue of Saint Luke was unveiled in 1929, however, Black Tuesday hit, and $25 billion in paper values vanished. The hospital, unable to collect on its pledges, cut its staff and expenses, while visits increased 55 percent. However, with government assuming some responsibility for medical welfare and gradual economic recovery, the hospital returned to financial health by 1934.

When Prentiss died in 1937 after 31 years as president, he left Saint Luke's more than $4 million. His widow, Elizabeth, was elected president—the first woman to hold such office. She promptly revolutionized hospital administration with reforms, called in a hospital consultant, and started

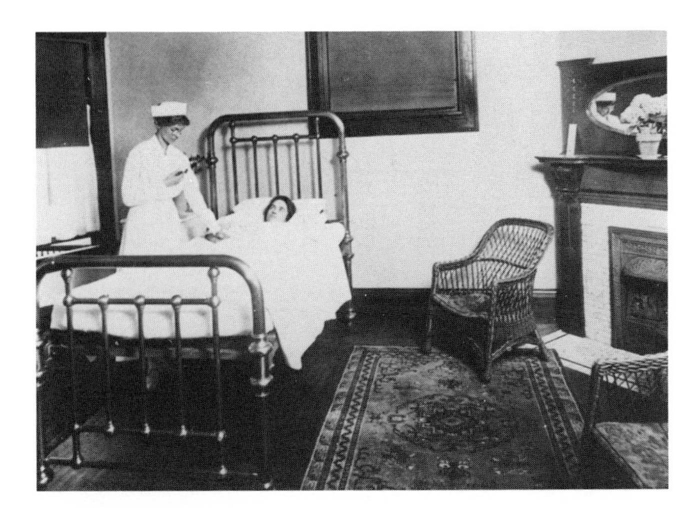

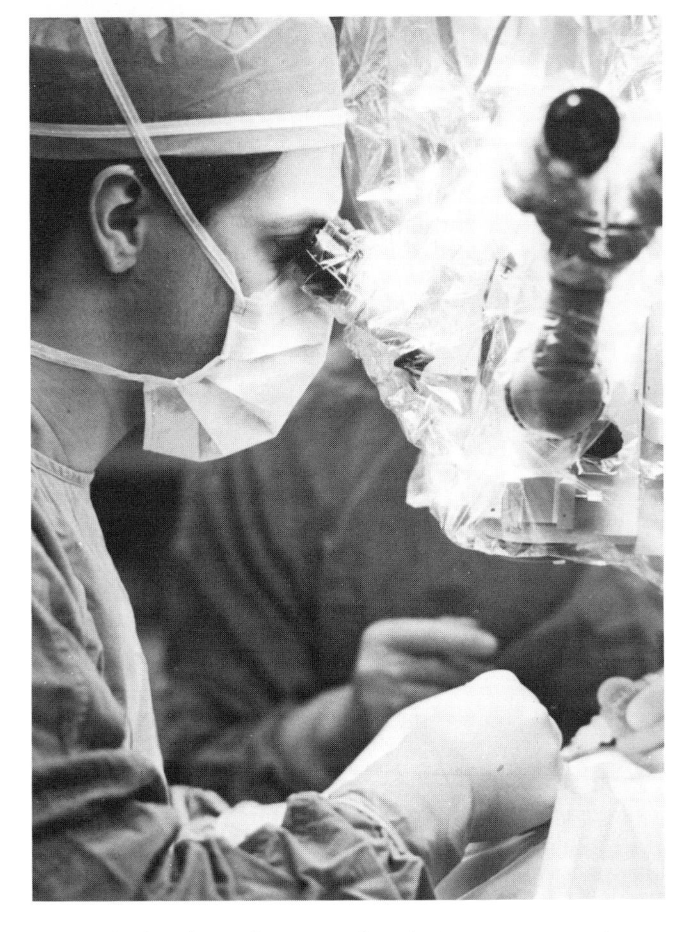

***Top left:** Saint Luke's offered private rooms elegantly furnished with linens, silverware, china, and fine rugs to appeal to the carriage trade.*

***Above:** Dr. Ursula Kringle, Dr. Frederick Cross, and Bill Coggins conduct tests on the heart-lung machine in the surgical research lab. The first working heart-lung machine was developed at Saint Luke's in the 1950s by Doctors Frederick Cross, Earl Kay, and Richard Dell Jones, Ph.D.*

***Left:** A surgeon performs microsurgery using a microscope to see to reconnect blood vessels, do delicate eye operations, and carry out other refined procedures at Saint Luke's.*

a search that brought in Frederick Carter as superintendent. Among the nation's most progressive hospital administrators, Carter began a program of modernization, establishing a personnel department to make salaries equitable and to handle grievances. He began a patient education program and advanced plans to expand the facility in anticipation of war.

During World War II military demands created a severe shortage of physicians and nurses. Saint Luke's nursing school, the largest of its kind in Ohio, was expanded. Peacetime brought a baby boom, as well as overcrowding and pressure to turn over patients quickly.

In the 1950s medical technology exploded, stimulating an active interest in research. Saint Luke's investment in research would be rewarded by the development of the first working heart-lung machine by Doctors Earl Kay, Frederick S. Cross, and Richard Dell Jones, Ph.D. The team built a machine that met the requirements of artificial lungs. It was finally used on January 18, 1956, at Saint Vincent Charity Hospital in a three-hour surgery to repair a pulmonary valve in a six-year-old girl. The operation's success stimulated developments in heart and vascular surgery around the world.

In recent years Saint Luke's Hospital responded to the increased demand for emergency room medicine by equipping a certified Level I trauma center—one of two in Cleveland. The center is staffed 24 hours a day with a team of specially trained nurses and surgeons. With the growth of competition among hospitals, Saint Luke's has focused attention on some special needs. It offers a nationally recognized center for adolescent chemical dependency, a program totally devoted to the treatment of depression, and a spine center that specializes in treating adult curvature of the spine (scoliosis). Its next challenge is to care for an increasingly older population, and provide special services for women.

COLUMBIA GAS OF OHIO

Columbia Gas of Ohio, one of six distribution companies in the Columbia Gas System, today serves some 1.1 million customers in 548 communities scattered throughout 62 Ohio counties. More than 3,250 employees work for "the gas company."

Those impressive numbers are a far cry from the genesis of oil and gas exploration in Ohio in the early 1800s. In fact, the early wildcatters looked upon gas as useless waste until harnessing it for cooking and heating became a reality and financially feasible in the mid-1800s.

Many of the wildcatters knew little of finance—and had little in finances to know about. Consequently, history shows that more often than not they would be out of business almost as quickly as they got into it, unable to continue exploration or production, which eventually expanded to all of Ohio's 88 counties. Many of the early wildcatters either went belly up or were merged into larger concerns.

Above: A pipeline construction crew near Springfield in 1900 used tongs and wooden levers to install line.

Left: The headquarters of Columbia Gas of Ohio in downtown Columbus.

Among those who were able to manage their partnership with a conservative bent were George W. Crawford and T.N. Treat. They had been in business together for 16 years when they formed the Ohio Fuel Supply Company in 1902.

Beginning in central and southern Ohio, the partners began to expand through the acquisition of oil and gas properties that showed promise but needed capital. Local companies in Zanesville, Nelsonville, Corning, Mt. Vernon, Gambier, New Bremen, Roseville, and Cambridge were acquired early in the partnership.

In 1922 Crawford and Treat had a gas operation that served 65,000 customers in more than 100 communities in 31 Ohio counties. They also controlled some 1,500 gas wells and 3,600 miles of pipe from Lake Erie to the Ohio River, and had about 750,000 acres of leaseholds. It was time, they believed, to reorganize the company.

In December they divorced the gas business from the oil operations by forming the Ohio Fuel Gas Company. When the Ohio Fuel Corporation was incorporated in 1924 with Crawford as president, it acquired the stock of Ohio Fuel Gas. Two years later indirect control passed to the Columbia Gas and Electric Corporation, which subsequently became Columbia Gas System Inc.

Columbia Gas and Electric set up five operating groups, one of which was the Columbus group. It consisted of the Ohio Fuel Gas Company; the Preston Oil Company, which had acquired the oil properties of Ohio Fuel Supply; and the Logan Gas Company, acquired by Ohio Fuel Gas in 1929. Another major Ohio Fuel acquisition occurred in 1942, when nearly 80,000 Toledo customers of Northwestern Ohio Natural Gas Company came into the fold.

On January 1, 1964, a new company, Columbia Gas of Ohio, assumed responsibility for Ohio Fuel's distribution operations, although transmission and production functions remained under Ohio Fuel's control until 1971.

The 1960s were a period of tremendous growth. By 1965 sales had doubled those of 1955 and were more than six times the 1945 volume. A milestone—one million customers—was reached in November 1970.

Columbus serves as the headquarters for the Columbia System's six-state distribution companies and for Columbia Gas of Ohio, which moved into a new headquarters building in downtown Columbus in 1983.

What with today's new generation of energy-efficient appliances for residential and commercial use as well as new technologies and gas-burning applications for industry, Columbia Gas of Ohio faces the opportunity for continued service and growth in a competitive marketplace.

BATTELLE MEMORIAL INSTITUTE

The history of Battelle Memorial Institute is the story of a man, of an idea, of an organization that grew out of that idea, and, most important, of a long line of achievements that have added human value to scientific knowledge.

The man central to the story of the institute is Gordon Battelle, who possessed amazing foresight and believed in the usefulness of scientific research. After Battelle died in 1923, his will provided that the bulk of his estate be used to create "a Battelle Memorial Institute . . . for the encouragement of creative research . . . and the making of discoveries and inventions." The facility was to serve as a memorial to his family—pioneers in Ohio and its early steel industry.

Battelle's original building in Columbus, completed in 1929, houses the corporate offices of the international, technology-based research organization.

Following the incorporation of Battelle in 1925, the institute's trustees acquired a site of about 10 acres in Columbus adjacent to The Ohio State University. There the facility's first laboratory opened in 1929. At that time the institute had a staff of about 30 people. Research expenditures in the first year totaled $71,000.

While the institute's research activities throughout the 1930s were primarily directed to materials technology, an effort to broaden its capabilities was constantly at work. This led to nuclear research, for example. Because of its international reputation in the field of metallurgy, Battelle became involved in the Manhattan Project in World War II, studying the fabrication of uranium. As a result, Battelle became one of the nation's outstanding centers for nuclear research. Also during that period Battelle pursued the development of xerography, a duplicating process that would later have a far-reaching effect on Battelle, the Xerox Corporation, and the world of business.

The postwar years saw Battelle's presence established outside the United States. Research centers were built in the early 1950s in Frankfurt, West Germany, and in Geneva, Switzerland.

In the 1960s the institute was selected by the U.S. Atomic Energy Commission to operate the former Hanford Laboratory in Richland, Washington. Thus, in January 1965, Battelle acquired 1,959 new staff members at what was designated Battelle's Pacific Northwest Laboratories.

In the 1970s the institute undertook a much-expanded research effort in energy, environmental work, and the life sciences. And, in 1978, the U.S. Department of Energy authorized Battelle to manage a major program on commercial nuclear waste isolation.

As the institute moved into the 1980s, it continued to invest in facilities and people to keep it at the forefront of technology. With a staff of about 8,000, Battelle has been undergoing a process of renewal to more closely match its resources with a changing marketplace. While broadening the range of the services it offers industry and government—from conceptual research to commercial product—Battelle Memorial Institute also has been defining more clearly its areas of major thrust. These include advanced materials, biological and chemical sciences, biotechnology, engineering and manufacturing technology, electronics, and information systems.

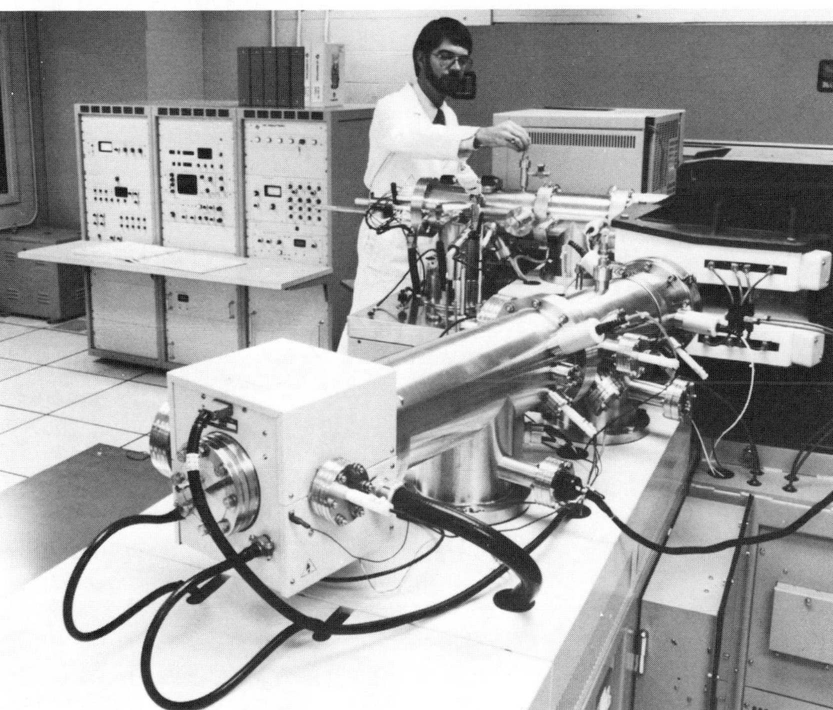

Exemplifying Battelle's state-of-the-art facilities is this high-resolution tandem mass spectrometer used in pharmaceutical and environmental research.

BARDES CORPORATION

Diligence and diversification have been the keys to success for the Bardes Corporation of Cincinnati—79 years young and still growing. Founded by Edward Henry Bardes in 1908 as the E.H. Bardes Range & Foundry Company, it has diversified its product line through the years to include electrical connectors, well strainers, street gratings, plumbing fixtures, and elbows for downspouts.

Edward Bardes was the general manager of the Kruckemeyer Retail Stove Store when he decided to strike out on his own. He bought an existing foundry, the John Schulte Grey Iron Foundry and Factory in Cincinnati, and changed the name.

Bardes stoves were used throughout the area, and many Cincinnatians remember the huge cast-iron stoves that sat in a few neighborhood stores run by another Cincinnati entrepreneur, Barney Kroger. Many Bardes castings can still be seen on area streets, especially in Mariemont, where Bardes had the contract for all the municipality's castings.

Edward Henry Bardes, who founded the E.H. Bardes Range & Foundry Company in 1908.

Oliver Louis Bardes, son of the founder, served as sales engineer, general manager, and took over as president upon the death of his father in 1943.

An early believer in advertising, Bardes coined the slogan "Bardes Ranges are Good—Very Good," and for years his friends called him "Very Good Eddie." A large mail-order business was added early on, contributing to the firm's general prosperity.

Seeing a specialized market, Bardes began concentrating on heat-resistant castings. The company was one of the first to melt grey iron electrically in making these special-duty castings.

During World War II an emphasis was placed on modernizing the foundry to make machine tool castings, primarily for the Cincinnati Milling Machine Company—today known as Cincinnati Milicron. Bardes also produced castings for tractors, most notable those used by Caterpillar Tractor.

Upon his father's death in 1943, Oliver Louis Bardes took the reins of the company. He had worked at his father's

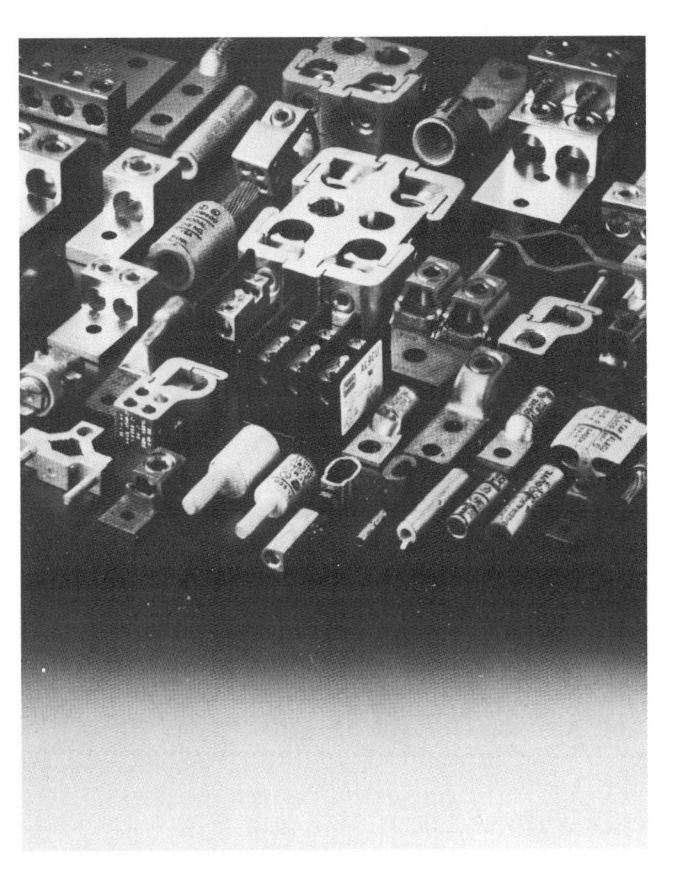

***Left:** The Bardes foundry on Colerain Avenue in Cincinnati (top) and a 1924 Bardes range.*

***Above:** A cross section of the Ilsco connector product line.*

factory on Saturdays and vacations since the age of 10. He graduated from Massachusetts Institute of Technology and served in the U.S. Navy. His education at the Bardes Corporation was from the ground up, making molds and pouring metal.

Returning from MIT as an engineer, Bardes worked his way up from sales engineer to general manager before becoming president. When he took over, the firm's chief product was metal castings for heavy industrial and farming machinery. However, there was change in the air. New products and new techniques for making them threatened the company and its customers. In 1949 Bardes closed down his foundry and spent six months evaluating the needs of his current and future customers.

He started business again by incorporating Cincinnati Elbow Company, a manufacturer of galvanized and aluminum elbows. A short time later Bardes purchased A.D. Cook, Inc., of Lawrenceburg, Indiana. He sold the pump division and foundry to Borg Warner and moved the well strainer operations to Cincinnati. Bardes Corporation continued to grow with the purchase of Chicago Steel & Wire Co. and Wheel Trueing Tool Company, Detroit, Michigan. These companies are no longer part of Bardes Corporation.

In 1954 Bardes purchased Ilsco Cooper Tube & Products and renamed it Ilsco Corporation. That year the present factory was built on Madison Road. In 1956 Bardes started Ilsco of Canada in Toronto to manufacture connectors for the growing Canadian market. Ilsco has expanded its operations with the addition of the Glenmoor Company, a large screw machine plant in Harrison, Ohio, as well as by the acquisition of Kentucky Connector Corp. in Glasgow, Kentucky, and Kupler Corp. in Connecticut. Ilsco is a leader in the manufacture of electrical connectors in the United States and Canada.

In 1968 Bardes purchased approximately 1,200 acres in Pinellas County and incorporated Bardmoor Properties, a Florida land development company. Today Bardmoor Country Club offers one of the best recreational communities on the West Coast of Florida.

Oliver L. Bardes died in 1977, leaving the company to his wife, Olivia, and two daughters, Merrilyn and Brittain. Bardes Corporation presently continues its family tradition under the direction of the Bardes daughters.

WORTHINGTON FOODS, INC.

The feeling at Worthington Foods, Inc., that a new day is dawning for the company was perhaps best illustrated by an item that appeared recently in the nationally syndicated advice column by Ann Landers. She mentioned the availability of a free cholesterol education booklet published by the Citizens for Public Action on Cholesterol and supported, in part, by Morningstar Farms®, a major Worthington Foods product line. In less than one week nearly 250,000 requests for the booklet were received.

Obviously, health-conscious Americans are looking for ways to reduce their cholesterol levels, which is right up Worthington Foods' alley. Since 1939 the company, located in the Columbus suburb of Worthington, has been developing innovative products for those with particular dietary needs or preferences.

Worthington Foods literally began with peanuts in a small frame house adjacent to the modern 150,000-square-foot production plant of today. With $5,000 in borrowed funds, Dr. George T. Harding, Sr., founded the business—then called Special Foods, Inc.—with the idea of providing vegetarian food products to meet the dietary and health needs of the Seventh-day Adventist Church, of which he was a member. Harding's first two peanut-derivative products were Proast and Numete, and after two years sales had reached $20,000.

Things really began to happen in 1941 when 29-year-old James L. Hagle joined the company. As general manager, Hagle sought to expand the market for the firm's new products. Choplets®, developed just before World War II, were snapped up by the general consumer when meat was rationed. Sales had jumped fifteenfold by 1945, when the company was renamed Worthington Foods, Inc.

At about the same time a Ford Motor Company research scientist, Robert Boyer, was trying to synthesize wool from soybeans, believing that a filament of soy protein could be spun in the same manner nylon and rayon were produced. Although never made into cloth, the substance did resemble the muscle fiber of chicken, lamb, and beef. That eventually led him to Worthington Foods, whose own research team, headed by Warren E. Hartman, determined that it could be used for meatless products if it was frozen rather than canned.

The company's entry into the frozen meat analog market in the early 1950s put it years ahead of its competitors. Today Worthington Foods is one of the world's largest producers of textured vegetable protein.

The decade of the 1960s saw the acquisition of the Battle Creek Food Company, founded by Dr. John Harvey Kellogg, and the Madison Foods plant in Madison, Tennessee. Worthington Foods itself was acquired in 1970 by Miles Laboratories, which then greatly expanded the plant and research facilities.

A dozen years later Hagle and a group of investors repurchased Worthington Foods, but not before Miles had established what has become the firm's most popular product line: the Morningstar Farms® brand of cholesterol-free foods sold nationally in supermarkets. Another brand, Worthington®, identifies the vegetarian products generally acceptable to Seventh-day Adventists, and a third brand name, Natural Touch®, is aimed at health food store patrons.

As Worthington Foods, Inc., heads into its second 50 years, it can look back on a half-century of contributions from many men and women in addition to Harding and Hagle, who is now chairman of the board. Among them were Allan R. Buller, who succeeded Hagle as general manager and later served as president until 1986, and his successor, Dale E. Twomley, former dean of the School of Business Administration at Andrews University, Berrien Springs, Michigan.

***Bottom:** James L. Hagle, former president and current chairman of Worthington Foods, in front of the company's food-processing plant in the mid-1950s.*

***Below:** Worthington Foods was the first U.S. company to produce frozen meat analogs. Here former president Allan R. Buller stands beside one of the firm's early delivery trucks.*

ERNST & WHINNEY

In 1903, just a few months before the Wright brothers sent aloft the first motorized aircraft, fellow Ohioans Alwin C. Ernst and his older brother, Theodore, launched in Cleveland the only major U.S. accounting firm founded in Ohio. Known then as Ernst & Ernst, it has grown into a worldwide professional services firm known as Ernst & Whinney.

The organization's service-oriented approach of producing information to interpret, control, and enhance the operations of a business was as novel then as the Wrights' flying machine. Today it is a standard in the accounting profession.

A.C. Ernst devoted little time to bookkeeping, the profession's mainstay. Instead, he focused on auditing and the practical application of accounting theory, believing that accounting and business would draw closer together out of necessity. Also, he believed accounting could be vital to helping enterprises succeed in an increasingly competitive economy. He espoused the advantages of keeping the right records in the right form and what the results would tell about the business itself.

The firm's first-year income was $9,831.33, which included $573.38 for "special services" to clients such as the Cleveland Trust Company (now AmeriTrust) and Cleveland Cap Screw Company (now TRW Inc.). Rapid growth followed, especially in Ohio. Offices were established in Cincinnati (1911), Toledo (1918), Canton and Columbus (1920), Youngstown and Dayton (1921), and Akron (1922).

In 1923 the firm established ties with the venerable United Kingdom predecessor of Whinney Murray & Co. By 1932 Ernst & Ernst had offices in 46 cities across the United States and Canada, plus this United Kingdom affiliation. Over time the firms' cooperative practice, known as Whinney Murray Ernst & Ernst, expanded into other parts of the world. In 1979 they formed a single worldwide partnership under the name Ernst & Whinney.

Continued expansion through both internal growth and mergers has brought Ernst & Whinney to its present 120 U.S. offices and its total of 400 offices in 80 countries. Its eight Ohio practice offices, plus the National and North Central Region offices in Cleveland, boast more than 1,700 of the firm's 14,000 U.S. staff members. Worldwide, its more than 32,000 staff members provide accounting and auditing, tax, and management consulting services to more than 65,000 clients. Its 12,000-plus audit clients include more than 1,400 Securities and Exchange Commission registrants.

Ernst & Whinney continually reaffirms its founders' commitment to provide technical excellence through teamwork and to be responsive to clients' needs and expectations. That commitment is expressed in the firm's philosophy: Quality In Everything We Do.

A.C. Ernst, the 21-year-old founder, at his desk in the firm's first office at East Ninth Street and Euclid Avenue in Cleveland.

EBCO MANUFACTURING COMPANY

Oasis. It's a word that conjures up a vision of a cool and refreshing way station in an arid land. It also can be defined as something serving as a pleasant relief.

No doubt the late Lee Love had these thoughts in mind when, in 1941, he suggested the word "Oasis" for a line of electric water coolers his employer was producing. The name selection was one of many milestones the Ebco Manufacturing Company has passed on the road to becoming one of the world's largest in its field.

Every day thirsty millions use an Ebco product, although very few would be able to link that product to the Columbus company. They may not even spot the firm's name on the cooler. What they probably have seen during the past 65 years is a wide variety of trade names: Kelvinator, Frigidaire, General Electric, Crosley, Philco, Norge, and many others. All wanted their label on Ebco's product. And, yes, there was even an Ebco label, but the best, and most famous, brand name for the company has been Oasis.

Before there was Ebco Manufacturing there was the D.A. Ebinger Sanitary Manufacturing Company, a Columbus enterprise that was a spin-off from Columbus Heating and Ventilating Company. Ebinger made a wide variety of special plumbing fixtures, primarily for use in public buildings. In 1913, three years after the firm's birth, it added the Ebco line of water and beer coolers, which had ice capacities ranging from 25 to 200 pounds.

A dozen years later Ebinger produced its first electric water cooler and began selling it to such customers as Frigidaire, Westinghouse, and Kelvinator. As time passed, however, the Ebinger company perhaps extended itself too far—restroom partitions, urinals, and kitchen sinks were among the lines it tried. By 1935 it was in the hands of a bankruptcy court, and a receiver, W.H. Bodurtha, was appointed to run the firm until a buyer could be found.

Enter A.R. Benua; his uncle, Frank Benua; a cousin, Ellsbury Benua; and a friend, Don Hess, who got together to buy Ebinger. A.R. and Frank Benua had had many years of experience, each having owned the Triumph Brass Company, which made brass valves and faucets and other machined fittings. Ebinger was a valued customer.

An interesting sidelight is that Triumph's history began inside the walls of the Ohio State Penitentiary in Columbus. The name then was the Patton Manufacturing Company and, as was the custom at the turn of the century, it employed convicts. Later the firm moved outside the walls and was known as the Ohio Pump and Brass Company before it became Triumph.

Late in 1935 A.R. Benua became president of the reconstituted Ebinger, renamed the Ebco Manufacturing Company. "We started with 28 employees," A.R.'s son, Louis, was to recall years later. "The group at the foot of the steps for my Dad's first 'encouraging talk' didn't make a very big crowd."

Louis P. Benua, who succeeded his father as president in 1963 and served until his death in 1987, knew how tough times were for the fledgling company. "Bodurtha had sold some of the machinery and equipment to meet payrolls. We were out of everything and had used up all ready cash to buy the place."

Nevertheless, A.R. Benua persevered. Hess left the company, and Frank and Ellsbury Benua were bought out with

Right: Thomas R. Benua, Jr., president.

Below: Ebco Manufacturing Company's plant near Port Columbus International Airport.

the help of a $70,000 loan from Ohio National Bank.

Toilet partitions, urinals, and sinks fell out of the product line as Ebco began to concentrate on its electric water coolers. The introduction of Ebco's refrigerated electric water cooler in 1924 was an industry first.

As noted, an early customer was Kelvinator, which, in 1941, put the manufacturing and the sales of its water coolers in Ebco's hands. "Some years later Kelvinator went completely out of the commercial refrigeration business," Louis Benua remembers. "We were forbidden to sell water coolers to any Kelvinator zone, and they were far and away our biggest customer at the time. We were crushed."

According to Louis Benua, the "sop" to Ebco was that it could use Kelvinator's name and sell to distributors, not zones, in return for a 2-percent royalty to Kelvinator. "The business . . . is still with us. It helped us prosper," he says.

Right after the creation of the Oasis brand name, World War II broke out, and the company turned its production to supplying military installations and defense plants. But once the war ended, Ebco—and Oasis—took off.

Louis Benua's brother, Tom, got the organization unexpectedly moving in a new direction in 1947. Tom had a damp basement in the clothing store he operated and asked his brother if he could come up with a cure. "The funny machine I threw together for him is still in the museum's corporate headquarters, and it still works," Louis recalled more than 35 years later. "This was our first dehumidifier, or air dryer, as they were called then."

Above: The Oasis wheelchair cooler design is one of Ebco's most popular products.

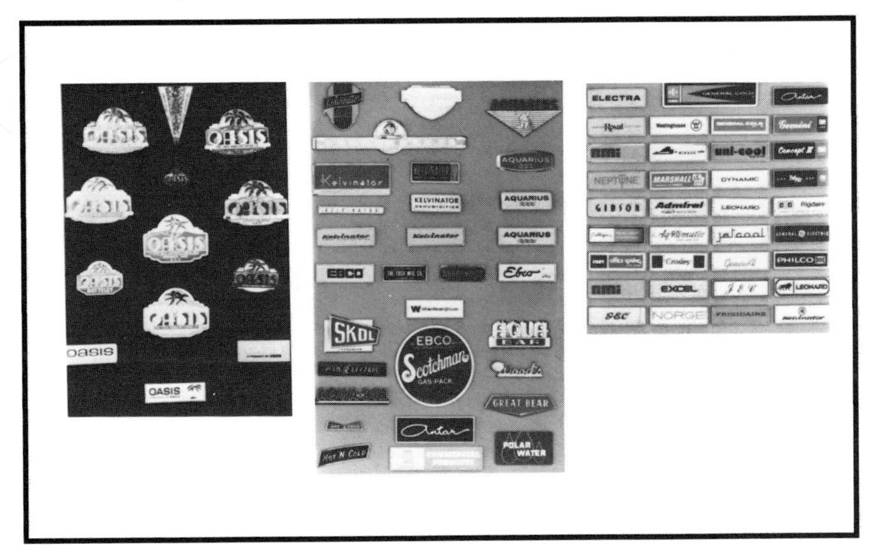

Left: These water cooler name plates are displayed in Ebco's museum.

By 1949 the company had begun production of dehumidifiers. (Humidifiers were tried in the early 1960s, but the line was short lived.) And development of new models, such as the Hot 'N Cold unit, continued, too. What with two different product lines growing steadily, Ebco quickly outgrew its plant at 401 West Town Street.

A new, award-winning plant at its present site, 265 North Hamilton Road, was opened in 1955. The $3-million, air-conditioned facility, which was named Plant of the Year by *Factory* magazine, has been enlarged three times since to its present size of more than 550,000 square feet.

More honors followed for Ebco. Twice it has been recognized by the U.S. Department of Commerce for export sales that now reach some 50 other countries. The firm received the President's "E" Award in 1963 and the "E Star" Award eight years later.

The company also has received recognition for its wheelchair cooler design. It not only allows the wheelchair to fit under the splash basin, but a light touch on any of four touch pads will start the cold water running. The water runs automatically for seven seconds, then shuts off.

Louis Benua died in 1987 and was succeeded as president by his nephew, Thomas R. Benua, Jr. At the time of Louis' death, Ebco Manufacturing Company had grown to more than 300 employees who were producing more than 88 models of water coolers and dehumidifiers available with a wide variety of options.

T. MARZETTI COMPANY

"We will start a new place and serve good food. At a profit if we can, at a loss if we must—but we will serve good food."

With this short notation on a scrap of paper, Teresa Marzetti set the tone for the company that bears her name—and which was to become America's third-largest salad dressing manufacturer.

It all started in 1896, when 13-year-old Teresa Marzetti left her home near Florence, Italy. She sailed from Genoa, was processed through Ellis Island, and continued on to her destination—Columbus, Ohio.

By 1901 Teresa and her new husband, Joseph, were operating a modest restaurant to serve the students and surrounding community near The Ohio State University campus.

When Joseph Marzetti died in 1911, his 28-year-old widow carried on alone.

Above: The famous Marzetti Restaurant at Broad and High streets in Columbus—the crossroads of Ohio—was noted for its fine food and, especially, its superb salad dressings. Courtesy, **The Columbus Dispatch**

Left: Today the T. Marzetti Company has grown to be the nation's third-largest salad dressing manufacturer, with its fleet of trucks delivering throughout the United States.

The restaurant thrived, becoming a favorite among the OSU students, and in 1919 she, along with her second husband, Carl Schaufele, opened a second restaurant at 59 East Gay Street, creating what many considered "the best dining experience in Columbus."

The new Marzetti restaurant was especially known for the salad dressings Teresa Marzetti created. Customers particularly enjoyed her creamy coleslaw and French dressings, and soon many were seen leaving the Marzetti Restaurant with small buckets of their favorites.

By 1940 the Marzetti Family had consolidated the restaurant business at 16 East Broad Street, where the upstairs kitchen became a small-scale factory to fill the many orders for the increasingly famous dressings. In 1955 Marzetti's opened a processing and bottling plant on Indianola Avenue, and started selling their dressings through grocery stores to all those Ohioans who had spread their fame by word of mouth.

The Marzetti Family sold the growing business to Columbus-based Lancaster Colony Company in 1969, but the family continued to influence new dressing recipes until Teresa's death in 1972. Perhaps for sentimental reasons, the restaurant at Broad and High was closed that same year.

But the Marzetti family legacy was secure. The T. Marzetti Company has since grown to produce more than 25 different salad dressing flavors under both the Marzetti and Pfeiffer brand names. Marzetti Slaw Dressing has been America's number-one seller for two decades. And, in 1982, Marzetti introduced its refrigerated, produce-department dressings with 14 new flavors under the "T. Marzetti" signature.

With both retail and food-service divisions, Marzetti is now America's third-largest salad dressing manufacturer. Marzetti plant locations in Atlanta, Buffalo, and Columbus supply fine restaurants as well as grocery stores throughout the nation—a fitting tribute to Teresa Marzetti's pioneering Columbus restaurant.

The addition of Mountain Top frozen pies, New York frozen breads, and Inn Maid egg noodles—all part of the Lancaster Colony Specialty Foods Division—have significantly expanded the Marzetti family of quality foods. And each product reflects Teresa Marzetti's original, handwritten pledge to excellence and "good food."

THE OAK RUBBER COMPANY

Resilient. A word that describes not only the products manufactured by The Oak Rubber Company of Ravenna but also the very nature of the firm itself.

Oak Rubber, which operates two plants in Ravenna and another in the Columbus suburb of Reynoldsburg, began in Akron in 1916. It manufactured toy balloons by a new dipping method developed by Orville Pike of Akron. Founders Paul Collette and John Shira had hardly been in business a year, however, when the plant was flooded, prompting a move.

Shortly after moving to South Prospect Street in Ravenna, disaster struck again. An explosion ripped through a curing room, causing $5,000 damage.

***Above:** The main plant in Ravenna, as seen in 1944 soon after The Oak Rubber Company received the Navy "E" Award for producing raincoats during World War II. This building rose out of the ashes of a previous plant destroyed by fire in 1920 and currently houses offices.*

***Left:** Co-founders John Shira (left) and Paul Collette in the 1930s.*

In 1919 the company moved to the old Farmer's Store at the corner of West Spruce and South Sycamore. But on March 15, 1920, a raging inferno fueled by barrels of naphtha and gasoline broke out at the plant. Firemen from as far away as Alliance and Akron fought shooting flames that were visible for miles. The entire building was destroyed—but soon rebuilt and, in fact, is still used today.

By 1922 Oak Rubber had nearly 140 employees. By 1928 its balloons were sold in more than 100 countries. Yet hard times would soon return. During the Great Depression Oak Rubber struggled to keep most of its employees working at least part time. During World War II a rubber shortage caused a switch in production to neoprene ponchos and raincoats for the Army and weather balloons.

After the war Oak Rubber began to change. Paul Collette died in 1950. John Shira retired as chief executive officer four years later and was succeeded by Collette's son, W.R. "Bob," who still holds this position.

The 1950s saw Oak Rubber acquire its Redfern plant on South Chestnut Street. Vinyl balls and a few vinyl gloves were made at the 125,000-square-foot facility dedicated to plastics manufacturing.

During the 1960s the firm continued to diversify, becoming the world's first manufacturer of vinyl disposable gloves for the medical trade. Soon a wholly owned subsidiary, Oak Medical Supply Company, was formed.

Oak Rubber expanded its glove line in the 1970s and became a major supplier to the emerging microelectronics industry. Its efforts were so successful that Oak Medical Supply Company was renamed Oak Technical Incorporated. Gradually almost all production capacity was diverted to the microelectronics market.

Meanwhile the parent company continued to expand its rubber product line, selling industrial dipped products to customers such as Carrier Air Conditioning, Cessna Aircraft, and Kenner Products. It also supplied most of the bags used by anesthesiologists to mix oxygen and anesthetic gases in the 1960s and 1970s.

Also active in developing new manufacturing methods, Oak Rubber introduced new ways to make different types of products from new synthetic rubbers and exotic plastics. It also devised new decorating and printing methods for balloons, and designed specialized equipment that improved the messages imprinted on balloons.

In the mid-1980s grandson Murray Collette assumed greater responsibilities, particularly in sales and marketing. He currently is executive vice-president of the parent company and president of Oak Technical.

The Oak Rubber Company—a firm rooted in 70 years of tradition yet eager to pursue new opportunities in mature or emerging markets, and that continues to demonstrate its resilience.

THE M.A. HANNA COMPANY

For more than a century this giant supplied some of the basic resources—iron ore, coal, nickel, and more—used to build America's heartland. More recently it has become a leader in the polymers industry. Forged through the hard work of its employees, past and present, famous and not-so-famous, the M.A. Hanna Company boasts a colorful past and a reputation for corporate responsibility, fiscal responsibility, and entrepreneurial spirit.

The firm's true beginnings date back to 1845, when Daniel Rhodes started a coal mining venture near Youngstown. Benefiting from the growing demand for coal by Great Lakes vessels, he made a fortune and then expanded it in the 1860s by operating blast furnaces and constructing rail lines.

Left: Marcus Alonzo Hanna gained control of Rhodes & Company, predecessor to The M.A. Hanna Company, in 1875.

Right: George M. Humphrey, as a talented young lawyer, was brought in to restructure the company, which weathered the Depression without any money loss. Humphrey went on to serve as secretary of the treasury under President Dwight D. Eisenhower.

Meanwhile, Marcus Alonzo Hanna, the company's namesake, moved to Cleveland. Thrown out of college for a juvenile prank, he joined the grocery business co-owned by his father, Leonard, and his uncle Robert. Hanna worked as a dockhand, warehouse clerk, and purser, taking his father's place in business after the man's death in 1862.

Hanna also began courting Daniel Rhodes' daughter, Charlotte, in 1862. However, Hanna, a staunch Republican, did not see eye to eye with Daniel Rhodes, a strict Democrat and devoted cousin of Senator Stephen Douglas, who is best remembered for his debates with Abraham Lincoln. But over time mutual respect grew, and in 1864 Marcus and Charlotte were married.

That same year Hanna's company went bankrupt when its new ship sank soon after launching. Determined to make a new start, Hanna built a small oil refinery. However, it burned soon after its construction, and in 1867 Rhodes brought Hanna into Rhodes & Company. Hanna made full use of his experience in transportation to build a vessel fleet for the firm, which was now also involved in iron ore mining. When Rhodes died in 1875, Hanna gained management control of the business, changing its name to M.A. Hanna & Company in 1885.

With time Hanna grew increasingly interested in politics. Soon he left the business in his brother's hands to pursue politics full time. He was a staunch ally of Ohio Governor William McKinley, whom he had met years earlier when McKinley defended workers accused of violence in a strike involving Hanna's coal interest. In fact, the lessons Hanna learned through the strike led him to become an outspoken advocate of labor/management cooperation in his later years. In 1894 Hanna began the process of making McKinley president of the United States, serving as key campaign strategist and crisscrossing the country on McKinley's behalf.

After being elected president in 1896, McKinley chose Senator John Sherman of Ohio to be his secretary of state. McKinley persuaded the newly elected governor to appoint Hanna to the vacated senate seat. A year later Hanna won reelection by one vote in one of the most bitter senate elections in Ohio history.

After President McKinley was shot, Hanna's power waned. When Hanna died three years later, he had made his mark as the only nationwide political boss in U.S. history.

Meanwhile, the company grew and looked after its employees by being among the first industrial firms to offer life insurance. Later it was a pioneer in providing a pension plan (1946) and major medical coverage for employees.

In 1922 its partners decided to incorporate as The M.A. Hanna Company. In the reorganization, many key assets were pulled out, leaving a collection of marginal properties. By 1924 the firm was falling into hard times.

Fortunately, a talented young lawyer named George M. Humphrey stepped in to restructure the company. Humphrey shed marginal assets and entered the iron ore business on a large scale, acquiring mining properties in Michigan and Minnesota. The firm returned to profitability by 1926 and lost no money during the Great Depression despite losing half its sales.

The corporation's first president, Howard Melville Hanna, promoted Humphrey, who became an architect of National Steel Corporation, one of the major steel busi-

northern reaches of Labrador and Quebec. The project involved building a 360-mile railroad, organizing one of the largest civilian airlifts in history, and constructing the largest deep-water shipping port in North America. The project stimulated the construction of the St. Lawrence Seaway to help move iron ore economically to Midwest steel mills.

Known for his acumen and conservative financial management, George Humphrey went on to become secretary of the treasury under President Dwight Eisenhower. And a former president of the Iron Ore Company of Canada and Hanna director, Brian Mulroney, currently serves as prime minister of Canada.

In the late 1950s The M.A. Hanna Company separated its operating units from its investments and renamed itself The Hanna Mining Company. But during

Above: In 1924 this 60-ton electric locomotive gave Hanna's Wabigon Mine in Buhl, Minnesota, the distinction of being the first completely electric open-pit iron ore mine.

Right: The largest civilian airlift in history was used to build the Labrador and Quebec projects of the Iron Ore Company of Canada, the largest iron ore producer on the North American continent.

nesses in the country. He orchestrated its formation from some Hanna businesses and partnerships with Great Lakes Steel in Detroit and Weirton Steel in West Virginia, creating a streamlined operation that owned its own mines, coking ovens, steel plants, shipping vessels, and finishing mills.

The birth of National Steel set a pattern for a host of new projects, such as Consolidated Coal in the mid-1940s. Time and again The M.A. Hanna Company would create a new business through deals, take the organization to partners or to the public markets to raise capital, and keep a share of the new firm's stock interests.

After World War II and through the 1970s The M.A. Hanna Company's activities became national and international in scope. The firm developed the nation's only nickel production project at the request of the U.S. government and assisted in successful mining ventures in Brazil, Canada, and Australia. Back home, the company constructed some of the largest bulk cargo vessels ever to sail the Great Lakes.

The most dramatic of its projects was the Iron Ore Company of Canada, the continent's largest iron ore producer. Humphrey spearheaded exploration, then got various corporate partners to join this huge enterprise to develop the

the 1980s, when hard times hit natural resources markets, Hanna restructured and resurrected the name the M.A. Hanna Company to reflect its diversified business base.

The restructuring involved the downsizing of the company's iron ore business to a single remaining interest in Canada, the withdrawal from the nickel business, and a downsizing of its energy businesses. In turn, the firm embarked on a major acquisition program that involved expenditures of more than $500 million to buy five companies in the polymers industry, including Burton Rubber Processing, headquartered in Burton, Ohio, and Day International, a *Fortune* 500 company formerly headquartered in Dayton, Ohio.

As a result, the firm has leadership positions in a number of formulated polymers businesses, from which it derives most of its revenues and earnings. It also maintains small but profitable positions in its historic natural resources businesses.

Well into its second century, the M.A. Hanna Company remains a strong competitor in international business and a leading corporate citizen.

MIAMI VALLEY HOSPITAL

Like the biblical mustard seed, Miami Valley Hospital has grown from a staff of two to more than 3,000 since it opened its doors nearly a century ago.

German Lutheran minister Carl Mueller recruited two deaconesses from Cincinnati to serve the needs of German families of St. John's German Lutheran Church in 1890. His parishioners and other Daytonians were plagued by malaria, diphtheria, typhoid, pneumonia, and "the fevers." Only one hospital was caring for Dayton's rapidly expanding population. Looking down from his pulpit each Sunday, Mueller could see the toll illness and disease were taking on his parishioners and, as a result, he enlisted the help of the first two deaconesses.

However, after only a few months, Mueller realized that two women going from house to house caring for the sick would not even begin to solve the enormous problems among his parishioners and others in the city. So, from that same pulpit, he sought 803 Daytonians who subscribed one dollar each to form the Protestant Deaconess Society, the predecessor of today's Miami Valley Hospital.

On October 18, 1891, seven physicians, the deaconesses from the motherhouse in Germany, and volunteers opened the hospital's doors in a converted house on Fourth Street in Dayton. The nurses worked 12- to 14-hour days, scrubbing floors on their hands and knees, boiling laundry, preparing meals, and sleeping next to the beds of critically ill patients. Volunteers, active then as now, raised money for the new laundry; sewed nightgowns, sheets, and tablecloths; and decorated the hospital for the holidays.

In Otto Moosbrugger's original pharmacy, herbs, roots, barks, and vegetables filled pharmacy shelves. Ground dandelions were boiled in alcohol and tincture to treat bronchitis, lung diseases, and pneumonia. Pills were made by hand until 1892, when tar products and aspirin became available.

The simple house-turned-hospital quickly became too small. Land was donated atop Charity Hill, and a new facility was dedicated in 1894. The hospital's location was especially appreciated a few years later in 1913, when the worst flood in Dayton's history sent thousands to the hospital unscathed by the roaring waters below.

With the increase in patients, the need for trained nurses became acute. The Miami Valley School of Nursing opened its doors in 1899 in an effort to curb that shortage.

By 1916 "The Valley" had grown to five buildings, and the use of laboratory tests, X-rays, and other modern treatment techniques began to increase. Critical overcrowding created pressure to grow during the 1920s, but the Depression stopped any talk of physical expansion. Using the facilities already available, the hospital set up clinics for heart

Though primitive by today's standards, this was "state-of-the-art" surgery in the early days of Miami Valley Hospital.

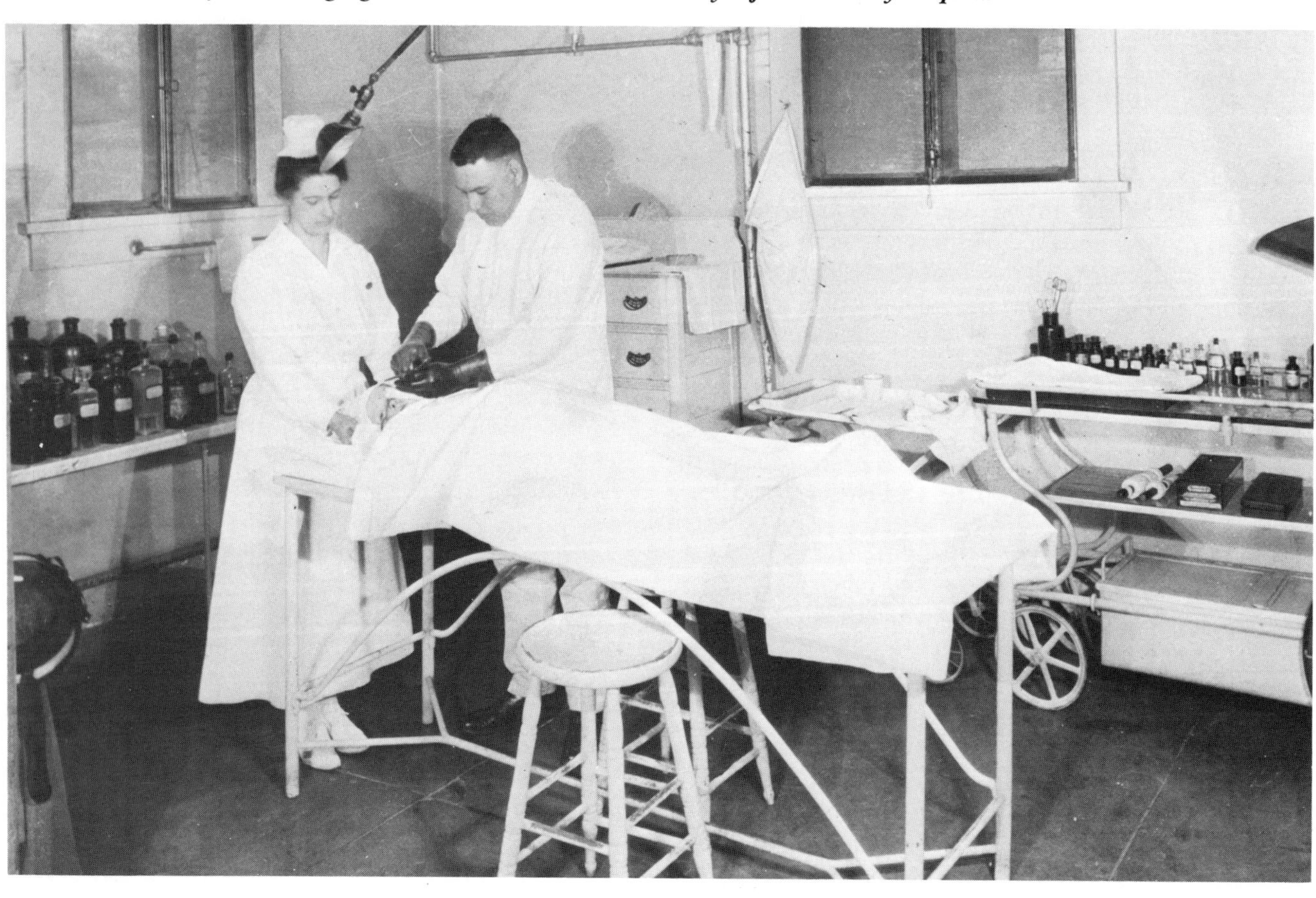

disease, diabetes control, and tuberculosis diagnosis.

Lured by Charles F. Kettering's Hypertherm for treating arthritis and vascular diseases, technicians from around the nation came to Miami Valley. While the institution's technology continued to grow, its old facilities were still in use throughout the war years and for several years following. The hospital's new, main structure was not started until the early 1950s on Wyoming Street. During the 1950s Miami Valley became the regional center for polio treatment.

While its physical plant grew and changed, so did the methods and technology used by its physicians and professional medical staff. The city's first cardiac catheterization was done at the hospital as well as the city's first kidney transplant and the establishment of the first intensive care unit—procedures and facilities that are now routine.

In the 1980s, almost 100 years after its founding, Miami Valley Hospital continues to serve the community and has been selected as a regional center for high-risk pregnancy, cancer therapy, kidney dialysis, physical medicine and rehabilitation, chronic pain management, alcoholism recovery, adult burn treatment, and cardiac care. Its Emergency Center was verified as a regional trauma center by the U.S. Department of Health and Human Services and the American College of Surgeons.

In 1983 a $65-million modernization and development program was completed, consolidating ambulatory services and providing facilities for additional education programs, as well as expanding the cardiology and critical care area and adding physicians' offices and a parking garage.

Again, as its physical plant continues to grow, Miami Valley Hospital's medical services continue to be recognized by the community. In a 1986 survey the hospital was picked as Dayton-area residents' preferred hospital, and its physicians and nurses were cited as the "best around."

From a renovated house to a multimillion-dollar medical center, Miami Valley Hospital has grown with Dayton for the past 90-plus years for one reason—its dedication to quality patient care. Its governing board and staff plan to continue that dedication and growth into its second century.

Nearly 100 years since its predecessor opened its doors, Miami Valley Hospital continues in its role as one of the major health-care providers in the Dayton area.

CLARK CONSOLIDATED INDUSTRIES INC.

A publicly owned holding company, Clark Consolidated Industries Inc. owns and oversees a collection of operating companies, mainly based in Ohio. These businesses distribute electrical supplies or manufacture paper tubes, steel pulleys, and other products.

Clark Consolidated Industries, which is headquartered in the Cleveland suburb of Rocky River, provides capital and financial resources, directs planning, and guides and directs policy for its operating companies. It focuses on established industrial firms making or distributing traditional products.

The corporation traces its past back to the Ohio Aircraft Hardware Company, a firm set up during World War II to support the war effort. Ohio Aircraft manufactured specialty screw fasteners for aircraft and ammunition parts on prime and subcontracts to Army ordnance. It also brought together three very different men with complementary talents who would later become partners in a new enterprise.

Above: Inspection and pressure welding of terminals and cables at Clark Cable's Berea Road plant in the late 1940s.

Left: Packing telephone cables to be shipped to the Navy in the late 1960s. The cables had floats to allow them to be laid without damage on the ocean floor.

Below: Manufacturing wire harness assemblies for Department of Defense vehicles at the plant on West 32nd Street in the early 1950s.

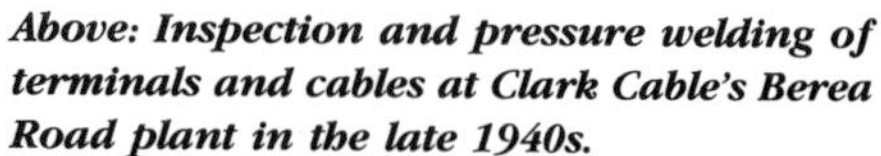

The three men were William S. Beckenbach, a gentleman and a technical specialist possessing a keen sense of humor; William Clark, a gregarious man's man who excelled in marketing and promotion; and J. Edward Sanford, a reserved and hard-working, self-taught financial wizard. In 1945 the trio acquired Proof Machine & Brass Foundry, Inc., which produced brass battery terminals.

Seeing more opportunity in making battery cables and cable assemblies for vehicles on contract, the partners sold the foundry to Essex Wire. But they retained the technical staff and incorporated Clark Cable Corporation in January 1946. Clark Cable made battery cables, ignition sets, ground straps, and related items for automotive parts jobbers, wholesale distributors, tire and oil companies, and the automotive industry.

Two years later the firm focused its efforts on military procurement for replacement parts. The partners had the expertise to interpret and process government paperwork, farm out the machining and assembly work to area subcontractors, and then inspect, pack, and ship the completed products. They attributed their success in this venture to

Founders William S. Beckenbach (above), William S. Clark (center), and J. Edward Sanford (right).

Cleveland's excellent base of tool and die makers and machinists. The partners were able to subcontract for just about all the parts needed within the area, doing business with about 500 area vendors.

With the start of the Korean War, however, totally new equipment rather than replacement parts was the order of the day. As a specialist in replacement parts, Clark experienced a drop in business in 1954 and began diversifying. The first move was to create Test Institute Corporation, a firm that made sophisticated hydraulic components for the military, followed by Benmar Heater, a manufacturer of engine heaters for military vehicles used in cold climates.

In August 1960 Clark Cable purchased all the outstanding capital stock of Proof Industries and Test Institute. Then, for the first time, Clark Cable offered its stock to the public; in March 1961 company stock began to be listed on the American Stock Exchange.

That November the firm acquired Duellman Electric Company, a Dayton distributor of electrical components. Later certain business assets of Mitchell Electric Supply, a Cleveland wholesale distributor of electrical components, were added to this business.

In 1963 Sanford retired as chairman, and Clark resigned as vice-president. William S. Beckenbach was joined by his son William C. in the business.

In the years since, Clark Consolidated Industries has been involved in the manufacture of solid and semipneumatic business via Swift Wheels, a Detroit firm purchased in 1964. The company also has marketed V-belt pulleys as owner of the Salem Stamping and Manufacturing Company, a Salem, Ohio, firm purchased in 1965 and later renamed Clark Pulley.

Other activities included handling a proprietary line of heavy-duty industrial mixing equipment through the acquisition of Cleveland Mixer, and manufacturing tire-mounting machines and tube-bending machines through Mize-O-Matic, a firm bought in 1968 and discontinued in 1973.

In 1968 another venture began with the acquisition of J.C. Baxter Company in Minerva, a manufacturer of spiral-wound paper tubes and cores. Founded by James C. Baxter in 1944, the firm makes custom paper sleeves, tubes, cores, and telescope containers in a variety of sizes, shapes, and finishes, with or without end caps, as well as corrugated cardboard pallets. In all there are more than 5,000 different products.

A year after coming on board, Baxter Tube bought Ohio Valley Products in Jefferson, Indiana. It also opened a new facility in Toledo in 1979 and one in Minerva in 1985.

Clark Cable Corporation sold its heater and government contracts, and cable inventories and equipment in the early 1970s, so its name no longer fit. In June 1973 the firm was renamed Clark Consolidated Industries to reflect its new industrial conglomerate nature.

In the 1980s the company continued to grow. It consolidated its Clark Pulley operations in Alabama and acquired the outstanding assets of Elgee Electric Company and Lighting Plus, both of Columbus. The new acquisitions strengthened the firm's mainstay electric components business, adding a Columbus link to the existing chain of branches in Cleveland, Dayton, Bedford Heights, Greenville, Huron, and Sidney.

Today Clark Consolidated Industries has 300-plus employees and does more than $65 million in business annually. Its management and stockholders expect the company to continue to grow through acquisitions of established, well-run businesses.

"Our philosophy toward the individual business units has been to let them run themselves," says William S. Beckenbach, chairman and chief executive officer. "They have their own entrepreneurial spirit, and we provide management and financial assistance. We provide incentives and a gentle shove without being critical."

Notes William C. Beckenbach, president and chief operating officer, "Our corporate headquarters consists of less than a dozen people. We operate mainly as a board of directors and bank.

"Owners of companies interested in selling find us through word of mouth," he adds. "Typically, they are founders who own small, closely held companies and have no heirs who are interested in carrying on in the business. To the founders, their employees and their company are like family members, and they want to ensure that both will be in good hands in the future."

KENDALE INDUSTRIES, INC.

Kenneth A. Honroth (left), chairman and chief executive officer, and son Dale Honroth (center), president and chief operating officer, with Paul Hollingsworth.

Those in search of excellence might check out Kendale Industries, Inc. This Cleveland company has thrived by putting new life into a mature industry through wise management and a shrewd application of technology. Kendale makes standard and special flat washers in "just about any material that can be punched without shattering" and custom stampings. It also produces semiprecision ball bearings, bearings and skate wheels for conveyors, injection-molded nylon parts, lock levers and catches for shipping drums, and curled rings for electric motor shock mounts.

In 1960 Kenneth Honroth, after a proxy fight, lost his job as president of another washer and stamping company. He immediately started a new firm, naming it "Kendale" by combining his and his son's first names. The company began operations within 60 days and expanded out of its 6,500-square-foot building on Sweeney Avenue after just 90 days. Forty former associates joined Honroth.

Honroth built his business on three premises: Supply quality products, maintain promised delivery dates, and keep abreast of new technology.

To achieve quality, Kendale people receive training in statistical process control (S.P.C.). Today the firm boasts a General Motors Spear 2 and Ford Q1 rating, and the distinction of being a certified supplier for many key customers.

To make promises that can be kept, Kendale people from sales through shipping use computers to track the status of every order. Their system also facilitates just-in-time delivery so customers need not carry or store excess inventory.

Regarding new technology, if the need is there, management never says, "Do it some other time."

Kendale's people policies have proven their worth in practice as well. When a manager is about to retire, a successor is recruited early to learn the ropes for a smooth transition. The Safety Committee is controlled by the employees on the floor and stays ahead of OSHA. A key management technique is walking through the plants and talking with people face to face. And anyone can go to the top with problems or concerns.

These policies have resulted in growth and profitability. In 1964 Kendale built the first all-electric plant in Cuyahoga County and bought Capco, a screw machine company. Three years later the firm expanded that plant and also purchased Argosy Products to make parts for ball-bearing assemblies. A 90,000-square-foot plant and offices in Valley View were built in 1973.

Kendale's newest expansion was the purchase in 1986 of Tri-Tech, a plastic injection-molding company. "We plan to expand the plastic end very quickly," says Honroth. "We're about to make patented spray gun parts that will revolutionize the industry."

Today Kendale Industries, Inc., can produce more than 20 million pieces of product per shift, within specs and on time. From the very start its management and employees have been dedicated to the idea of doing things right the first time.

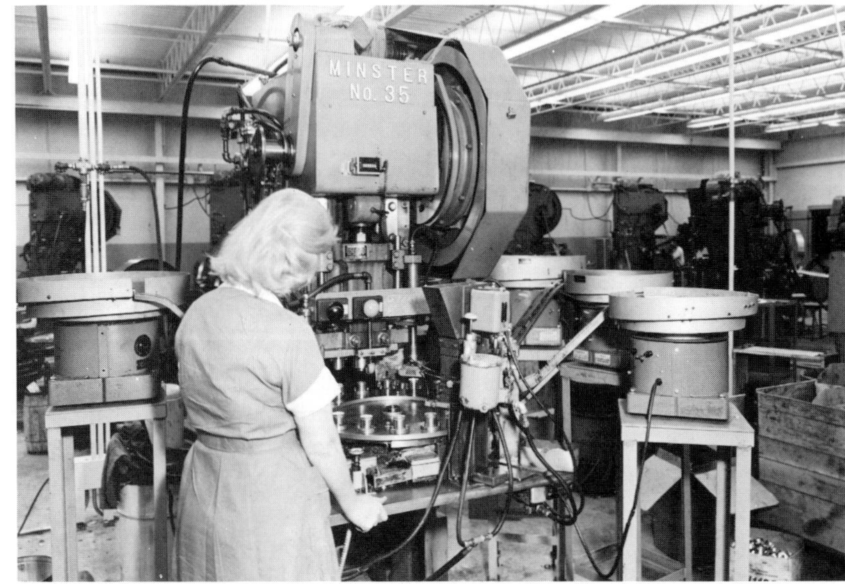

Kendale employee Dorothy Rockwell uses statistical process control (S.P.C.), the most efficient manufacturing equipment, to scout out potential deadline problems well in advance.

CRESCENT METAL PRODUCTS

Visit the kitchens of major restaurants and cafeterias, and chances are you will see a variety of tall mobile cabinets made of aluminum. It was Clevelander George T. Baggott who developed the prototypes for these products. In fact, he and his company, Crescent Metal Products, put the food-service industry on wheels.

Baggott started Crescent Metal Products in 1936 in his barn with a $60 loan from his sister. Through the 1940s his metalworking company made machine guards, industrial ovens, and fluorescent lighting fixtures, and filled government war orders.

In the early 1940s the firm began fashioning aluminum mobile food-handling and cooking equipment. From building one unit to meet a customer's special requirements, business blossomed into serving the needs of a rapidly growing industry.

***Above:** The Crescent Metal Products exhibit at a 1962 trade show with (left to right) George E. Baggott; Colonel Harland Sanders, of Kentucky Fried Chicken fame; a colleague; and George T. Baggott, with a Cres-Cor heated holding cabinet.*

***Left:** CNC (computer-numeric-controlled) machinery used in fabricating stainless steel and aluminum components. In the left foreground is a shearing cell and in the right background is a turret punch press.*

A breakthrough occurred in the late 1940s, when Baggott pioneered the use of corrugated walls for his mobile cabinets. The slots in the corrugated metal allowed trays and pans to be inserted at any level and to be secure during transport. The corrugations also served to strengthen the cabinet's sidewalls. Baggott's cabinets became the cornerstone of his Cres-Cor line. Because of the line's quality and efficiency, the late Colonel Harland Sanders came to Baggott to develop special holding cabinets as he was launching his Kentucky Fried Chicken restaurant chain.

Over the years Crescent Metal Products has expanded from one building to a cluster of structures on Taft Avenue in Cleveland. It has grown to more than 200 employees serving an international market. Baggott's sons—Clifford, chief operating officer, and George E., president—now share in the management of the company.

In 1986 the firm celebrated its 50th anniversary with a surprise party in honor of the founder. It attracted nearly 400 guests, including representatives of the National Association of Food Service Equipment Manufacturers, the Food Service Consultants Society International, the Culinary Institute of America, and several national trade publications.

Today Crescent Metal Products manufactures about 800 different products for food preparation, storage, transport, serving, and cleanup. They include the Crown-X line of convection ovens and Cres-Cor line of hot and cold cabinets, dish dollies, serving counters, food warmers, and mobile racks. Both lines are now designed on computers and manufactured with the help of computer-controlled metalworking machinery.

However, some things have not changed in a half-century at Crescent Metal Products. The company maintains a family atmosphere with a sense of involvement and caring. Crescent Metal people still have the pride in workmanship needed to turn out products that are often referred to as the "Cadillac" of their industry. Their concern for helping customers cope with an ever-changing industry inspires them to design even more new products. And George T. Baggott still shows that tireless drive that guided the company through its difficult early years and later propelled it to the forefront of its industry.

OHIO BELL TELEPHONE COMPANY

The first telephone line in Ohio connected the wholesale office and retail yard of Rhodes and Company, a Cleveland coal supplier. The year was 1877, just two years after Alexander Graham Bell had patented his telephone. Today phone lines crisscross every corner of the state—more than 85 percent of them owned and operated by the Ohio Bell Telephone Company.

Ohio Bell's early roots go back to 1879, the year Western Union Telegraph set up Ohio's first exchange. Served by a switchboard in the Board of Trade Building on Water Street (now West Ninth Street), its 76 subscribers paid $72 per year. The following year local investors bought the exchange and incorporated under a Bell license as The Cleveland Telephone Company.

In 1883 the first long-distance line in Ohio linked Cleveland and Youngstown. Within a decade the lines of the American Telephone and Telegraph Company (AT&T) reached Cleveland from the East Coast.

The Cleveland Telephone Company thrived and grew until 1914, the year the Bell patents expired. A year later the firm was absorbed by the Columbus-based Ohio State Telephone Company. After yet another merger, Ohio Bell Telephone Company emerged in 1921 as a subsidiary of AT&T of New York.

Ohio Bell pursued new technologies aggressively. By 1922, 14 percent of the company's half-million phones had dials, which meant faster service and lower service charges.

During the Great Depression the firm lost one-quarter of its subscribers. Despite rate cuts ordered by the Public Utilities Commission of Ohio, this business was not recovered until 1940.

When World War II began, access to telephone buildings became restricted, and employees were issued photographic identification cards. In addition, government regulations controlled the installation of new service, giving priority to military users.

Above: A line crew repairs phone lines in Steubenville following a severe hailstorm in the 1920s.

Above, right: Outside plant technicians pulling fiber-optic cable in Toledo. Fiber networks represent a marked improvement in transmission and capacity over copper wire at dramatically lower costs.

After the war Ohio Bell undertook huge construction programs that averaged $50 million per year to satisfy the backlog in demand. By 1954 the company served 2 million telephones, 93 percent of them dial, accounting for 85 percent of users in Ohio. By 1971, the firm's 50th anniversary, 4 million Ohio Bell telephones were in service.

Ohio Bell became a member of the Ameritech family of companies in 1984, when AT&T was required by law to spin off its system operating companies.

Today Ohio Bell Telephone Company, headquartered in Cleveland, employs more than 13,500 people statewide. Continuing in a long tradition, the corporation and its people promptly apply new communication technologies, such as fiber optics, to improve service and lower costs.

OHIO UNIVERSITY

The campus gate at Ohio University is the main entrance to the College Green. Photo by Harry Snavely, University Publications Photography

Ohio University is proud of its rich academic and cultural traditions as "Ohio's First University." The institution traces its origins to the Northwest Ordinance of 1787 and was the first institution of higher learning in the old Northwest Territory.

On March 1, 1786, the university's founders, Reverend Manasseh Cutler and General Rufus Putnam, gathered with Revolutionary War officers in the Bunch of Grapes Tavern in Boston. The group sought recompense for their war service, and hoped to establish homes in the "western country." At that meeting, they formed the Ohio Company, and adopted a plan for the creation of a university.

The next year, with a territorial government established by the Northwest Ordinance of 1787, Cutler lobbied Congress to accept the Ohio Company of Associates' contract for the purchase of Ohio River land. As part of the purchase agreement, Congress reserved two townships of land to be used for a university. Manasseh Cutler wrote the new institution's charter, and in 1802 the Second Territorial Legislature created the American Western University.

On February 18, 1804, the Ohio General Assembly rechartered and renamed the institution, calling it Ohio University. Within one year after joining the Union, Ohio had established its first state university.

Today Ohio University is a comprehensive, state-assisted institution serving more than 15,000 undergraduate, graduate, and professional students on its main campus in Athens, and another 7,000 students on regional campuses in Belmont County, Chillicothe, Lancaster, Ironton, and Zanesville, and at a resident credit center in Portsmouth.

The Athens campus consists of more than 500 acres and 85 major buildings. The main campus area, known as the College Green, is the location of most classroom and administrative buildings, and is listed on the National Register of Historic Places. The main administration building, Cutler Hall, was built in 1816 and is registered as a National Historic Landmark.

Ohio University offers more than 250 major academic programs through nine undergraduate colleges: Arts and Sciences, Business Administration, Communication, Education, Engineering and Technology, Fine Arts, Health and Human Services, University College, and the Honors Tutorial College. Master's degrees are available in nearly every major division, a variety of Ph.D. programs are offered, and the College of Osteopathic Medicine grants the D.O. degree.

The university has a history of international involvement, and is proud of the diversity of its student body. Students come not only from each of Ohio's 88 counties and from every state in the nation, but also from 90 different countries worldwide.

Among Ohio University's well-known alumni are Columbus real estate developer John Galbreath, retired Nationwide chairman Dean Jeffers, Cleveland Mayor George Voinovich, Congressman Donald Pease, and Lieutenant Governor Paul Leonard.

Cutler Hall, on the College Green, built in 1816, is registered as a National Historic Landmark. Photo by Fred Nelson, University Publications Photography

PORTER, WRIGHT, MORRIS & ARTHUR

English-born Richard A. Harrison, fresh out of Cincinnati Law School in 1846 at age 22, could not have imagined that his first law partnership with Judge William A. Rogers in London, Ohio, would be the first root of a family tree that today represents the largest law firm in Columbus: Porter, Wright, Morris & Arthur.

Since the 1840s there have been nearly 30 mergers or partnership successions involving dozens of distinguished lawyers. In addition to Rogers and Harrison, there were three other founding firms: Hamilton & Henderson, in 1877; Watson & Burr, in the late 1870s; and Arnold & Morton, in 1891.

The three oldest partnerships led to the Porter, Stanley, Platt & Arthur branch of the family tree. In 1977 that firm merged with the Arnold & Morton founding branch that had grown to become Wright, Harlor, Morris & Arnold. These two main branches thus formed Porter, Wright, Morris & Arthur.

Among all the founding fathers, perhaps Harrison had the most interesting career. He was elected to the Ohio House in 1857, the Ohio Senate two years later, and the U.S. House of Representatives in 1861. At the height of the Civil War, however, he retired to private practice, first in London, then moving to Columbus in 1873. Sixteen years later Harrison merged with the Hamilton & Henderson branch, which became Harrison, Olds & Henderson.

William O. Henderson, who had played on the first intercollegiate football team at Yale University, had established a law office on East State Street with George O. Hamilton of Marysville, Ohio. Joseph Olds of Circleville, Ohio, had been Harrison's partner after serving as a judge of the district's common pleas court.

Another of the founding firms was established in the 1870s by Colonel James Watson and Charles E. Burr. That practice became part of the family tree through a 1903 merger, and it was Burr's son, Karl, who was a driving force in the development of the Porter branch during the first half of the twentieth century.

An Ohio State University graduate, Karl E. Burr was admitted to the bar in 1901 and joined his father's firm, then Henderson, Livesay & Burr, four years later. He was a brilliant attorney and a community leader. He served as general counsel for the Central Union Telephone Company, now Ohio Bell, and was district solicitor for the Pennsylvania Railroad Company. Burr died in 1945 but not before attracting to the firm many of its top clients from among manufacturers, the railroads, and the utilities.

The youngest founding branch of the family tree began in 1891, when Harry B. Arnold and Elbert C. Morton organized the firm of Arnold & Morton. Arnold was an 1836 Yale Law School graduate who went on to be a founder and president of the Midland Mutual Life Insurance Company in Columbus.

Today Porter, Wright, Morris & Arthur has some 170 attorneys at its Columbus headquarters in the Huntington Center and another 100 in Cleveland, Dayton, Cincinnati, Washington, D.C., and Naples, Florida. The firm's practice is wide ranging, meeting the demands of business and industry in a rapidly changing world. And yet the old values remain, as evidenced by the number of clients who have been with Porter, Wright, Morris & Arthur since the turn of the century.

Left: William E. Arthur (left) and Frank R. Morris, partners, in the atrium of the Columbus law firm's headquarters in the Huntington Center. Jeff Rycus, Rycus Associates Photography

Below: Samuel H. Porter, a partner in the law firm and chairman of the executive committee. Jeff Rycus, Rycus Associates Photography

THE HOOVER COMPANY

The story of how The Hoover Company of North Canton became a household name begins in 1907 with J. Murray Spangler, a local inventor who got asthmatic attacks from dust. Driven by the need to work as a night janitor, he invented an electric sweeper to stay on the job. Spangler later showed his sweeper to W.H. "Boss" Hoover, the forward-thinking owner of a leather goods factory, who immediately saw its promise. In August 1908 Hoover, Spangler, and their partners formally formed the Hoover Electric Suction Sweeper Company.

Hoover and his partners took their vacuum cleaners on the road to show prospective dealers their marvelous cleaning abilities. They also ran advertisements in the *Saturday Evening Post,* offering consumers a free 10-day home trial of a vacuum cleaner shipped through a dealer. Next Hoover introduced the door-to-door concept of marketing, training a nationwide network of salespeople in the art. Since then door-to-door sales have been discontinued in favor of retail outlets.

Meanwhile, the company made tremendous strides in cleaning quality and design. Its engineers were the first to recognize the importance of carpet vibration in loosening embedded dirt. They patented the agitator bar in 1919, inspiring the motto: "It beats, as it sweeps, as it cleans."

A tireless strategic planner, Boss Hoover established a Canadian plant in 1911, launched an English subsidiary eight years later, and soon did business in all four corners of the world. In 1922, the year the name was shortened to The Hoover Company, Boss Hoover turned the business over to his son H.W., telling him simply, "Make of it what you can."

H.W. Hoover made the best of it, continuing the tradition of being a good corporate citizen and motivating the salespeople with yearly international sales meetings at Hoover Camp—now Hoover Park, a recreational park open to employees and community groups. During the Great Depression he kept his people busy by supplying die castings to other manufacturers and spreading the notion that a vacuum cleaner was indeed a "must."

During World War II the company switched its production lines over to helmet liners, bomb fuses, and other components. It received 19 citations for its efforts. With the return of peace, Hoover again built vacuum cleaners, making up for lost time.

Hoover built on its reputation for quality and innovation with a new series of firsts: ultraflex double stretch hose (1950), walk-on-air canister (1954), floor washer that scrubbed floors and also picked up the wash water (1959), shampoo-polisher (1959), self-propelled cleaner (1969), and edge cleaner (1973).

In 1985 a thriving Hoover Company was acquired by Chicago Pacific Corporation, an international home products firm headquartered in Chicago. The new arrangement has proven complementary and mutually beneficial.

Today Hoover maintains immaculate world headquarters in North Canton. It has 5,300 U.S. employees, 3,300 of them in Stark County. Another 9,700 people work in Australia, Canada, Colombia, England, France, Mexico, Portugal, Scotland, and Wales.

Long ago The Hoover Company left its competitors behind in the dust; the firm remains the world's number-one manufacturer of floor care equipment and its leading brand name.

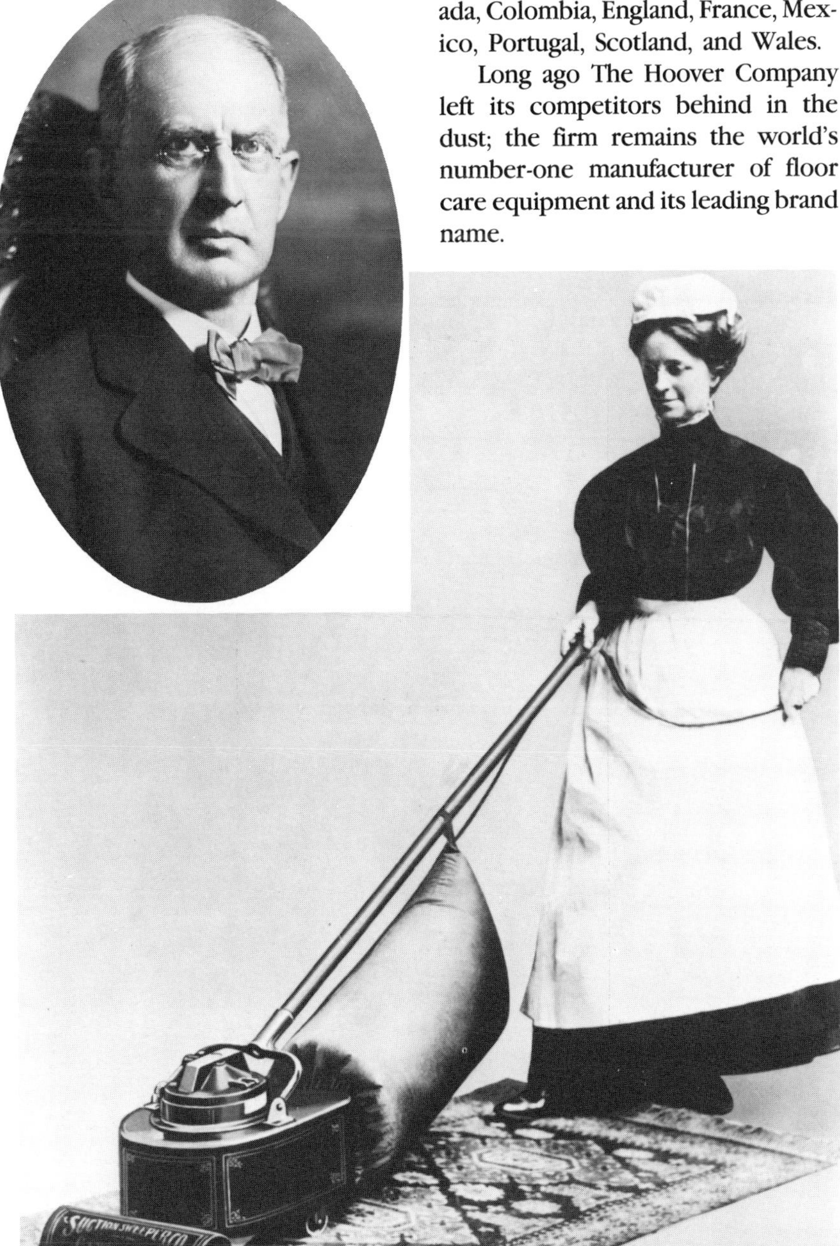

Center: W.H. "Boss" Hoover, founder of The Hoover Company, had a reputation for benevolence, as well as a commanding presence.

The company's first suction sweeper, the Model "O," manufactured in 1908.

THE DAVEY TREE EXPERT COMPANY

As enduring as the white oak logo on its stationery, The Davey Tree Expert Company is rooted in a tradition of hard work and self-determination. Its industry was nurtured by a remarkable family for more than 70 years. Ownership of what became the largest residential and commercial tree care business in North America was acquired in 1979 by its employees, who secured their own future through a heroic effort.

Founder John Davey, the son of a poor English farmer, was 21 years old when his family no longer required his wages for survival. He then learned to read and set out to study horticulture and landscaping.

After completing his training, Davey came to America. He started a family and became caretaker of Standing Rock Cemetery in Kent. In his spare time he studied science and wrote *The Tree Doctor,* a landmark work in the science of tree preservation.

In 1901, at age 55, Davey borrowed $7,000 to publish his book. Soon he received so much tree preservation work that he started a business. But it was his son Martin who would establish a school of tree surgery and provide business leadership for the future of the company.

Martin Davey incorporated the business in 1909, selling stock to raise capital. He set up territories and assigned each a capable salesman to solicit work and a skilled foreman to supervise the crew. He also advertised nationally and secured work from the White House and other prestige accounts to win a national reputation.

Martin Davey's abilities led to politics and his election as governor of Ohio in 1935 and again in 1939. However, a heart attack cut short both his political and business careers. He was succeeded by his son, Martin "Brub" Davey, Jr., who returned from Army service in 1946. Surrounding himself with a "brain trust" of Davey veterans, Brub Davey took steps to increase sales, introduce new services, improve training and benefits, and update equipment. He, too, was later sidelined by heart problems.

The 1960s and 1970s brought new technology, rapid expansion through acquisitions, and a new appreciation of the environment by customers. It also brought management shifts, an industrywide recession, and an exhausting reorganization.

In 1977 the Davey family announced its intention to sell. Employees worried that a conglomerate or competitor might gain control and sought to acquire the company themselves. In August 1978 the family accepted the final of four employee purchase offers. The plan featured an Employee Stock Ownership Plan (ESOP) that would buy shares for subsequent distribution to employees plus shares that employees had to purchase directly.

On March 15, 1979, ownership passed to Davey Tree employees. At the time they owed the banks 70 percent of the company's value, and many employees had taken second mortgages to buy stock directly.

Between 1979 and 1983 Davey employees, led by president J. W. "Jack" Joy, put forth a monumental effort to improve earnings. They achieved an annual growth rate of 14 percent and quadrupled earnings.

Today Davey Tree's 4,000 employees in the United States and Canada own 95 percent of the firm. But the momentum and euphoria generated during their long struggle are still evident at The Davey Tree Expert Company.

Right: ***John Davey, father of tree surgery and founder of The Davey Tree Expert Company. His motto: Do it Right or Not at All.***

Below: The company's headquarters in Kent, known as Tree City. Completed in 1985, the complex features a training center and a research laboratory for testing new products for safety and effectiveness.

BUCKEYE RUBBER & PACKING COMPANY

Founded in 1937, Buckeye Rubber & Packing Company is headquartered at 23940 Mercantile Road, Cleveland.

The Buckeye Rubber & Packing Company—more than 50 years in the rubber seals business and headquartered in Cleveland—is best known for its contribution to the development of the rubber O-ring. This simple doughnut-shape sealing device is universally used in just about everything mechanical, from hypodermic needles to space shuttles.

Engineers have found that when an O-ring is properly designed into the mating metal parts, it can positively seal a variety of fluids and gases over a wide range of temperatures and pressures. Manufacturers have found nothing to surpass its low-cost, trouble-free performance.

Don Barner, who started on the ground floor in the seals distribution business after completing a night school education in engineering, founded Buckeye Rubber & Packing Company in 1937. In the late 1930s he worked closely with the inventor of the O-ring, Niels Christensen, furnishing many samples of O-rings manufactured from different compounds.

Christensen, a noted Cleveland inventor and counsel for the Norwegian government, developed power brake systems for automobiles, buses, trucks, and off-the-road equipment. He also worked on wheels and brakes for aircraft and fluid power devices for machine tools and concluded that a circular ring of circular cross section contained in a groove of slightly greater area than the ring cross section was the solution. In 1939, after 50 years of sealing experiments, Christensen received U.S. Patent No. 2,180,795, covering the use of O-ring seals.

By far the most demanding applications for the O-ring was in aircraft landing gear. At the start of World War II Buckeye furnished Cleveland Pneumatic Tool Company with many O-ring samples and participated in various phases of Cleveland Pneumatic Tool's landing gear drop-testing program.

Early on Buckeye had little to offer customers in oil-resistant compounds, Du Pont's Neoprene being the only synthetic rubber commercially available. However, chemists at Du Pont, Goodrich, Dow Corning, and elsewhere have introduced many new materials in recent years, creating many applications for O-ring seals. Buckeye, by now firmly entrenched as a seals specialist, has added to its staff of sales engineers and found many new uses for the product. The company also has had extensive experience in the custom design and manufacture of other types of rubber seals, as well as die-cut gaskets, and Teflon and molded rubber parts.

The late Albert Catlin, sales manager, and Buckeye Rubber & Packing Company's sales team, namely Edward Klemm, James Golden, Richard Phillips, Robert Hill, Mark Janasek, and James Sampson, would be quick to credit the quality assurance department for much of the firm's success. There is much evidence that a simple O-ring, the least expensive component of many a mechanical device, is worthless and dangerous unless careful attention is given to ensure that it is free of defects and meets all necessary physical specifications.

The company's products are scrupulously examined in the compound verification and certification area to ensure they are free of defects.

R.W. BECKETT CORPORATION

Forty years ago, in the home heating industry, about 200 manufacturers supplied oil burners to furnace and boiler-makers and oil replacement burners to distributors. Today just a few independent U.S. oil burner makers survive, and the leader is R.W. Beckett Corporation of North Ridgeville.

Founder Reg Beckett was just 17 years old when he finagled his way into the Canadian Field Artillery to serve in World War I. Of the 67 men in his regiment, only he and one other survived.

After the war Beckett earned a degree in electrical engineering from the University of Toronto. In 1925 he became chief engineer of the Silent Automatic Corporation of Detroit—maker of the Noiseless Oil Burner—which fell victim to the Great Depression. In 1932 he found work as chief engineer for the Toridheet Division of Cleveland Steel Products, and a year later married Jean Patterson, his sweetheart of five years.

The original Commodore oil burner (above) and the recent Model AF oil burner (left). In a furnace or boiler, the burner is the unit responsible for producing heat.

In 1937 Beckett decided to launch his own company. He began development work on his oil burner in the basement of his home in Elyria. Jean kept the books, and Stanton Fitzgerald became his partner, contributing sales and finance expertise.

The oil heating industry was just emerging then, as owners of bothersome, hand-stoked coal furnaces converted to oil heat. Sensing opportunity, hundreds of firms of all stripes started making oil heating equipment. But Beckett's highly engineered burner stood out. In a 1938 trade show at the Commodore Hotel in New York City, the company got its first order for 50 burners, inspiring Beckett to call his burner the Commodore.

Business thrived, but World War II put a halt to production. Beckett had to enter the insulation business to keep his employees working and help the nation conserve fuel. But the firm was ready to capitalize on the postwar boom and, to staff the resurging company, Beckett recruited Russ Sage, Howard Rathwell, George Waller, George Merle, Betty Baracskai, and others, many of whom stayed until retirement.

An emphasis on quality and engineering, supported by 20 patents, fueled sales. In 1952 business hit an all-time high of 24,000 units, and the company moved to a new plant in North Ridgeville.

The mid- and late 1950s, however, brought a measure of frustration. The Ohio Turnpike Commission cut the firm's land in half; a competitor infringed on several patents, prompting an exhausting legal response; and natural gas began to encroach upon the oil burner markets. In addition, the company's share of the market had begun to slip after competitors introduced new compact models that used less costly components. Beckett, when finally persuaded to design a new compact model, did so with characteristic intensity and success.

In 1963 Fitzgerald retired and sold Beckett his share of the partnership. As sole owner, Beckett felt at liberty to ask his son John to join him in business. Reg involved John, a 1960 graduate of the Massachusetts Institute of Technology, in every facet of the burner business. But in February 1965 Reg Beckett suffered a massive heart attack and died at age 67.

John Beckett, after much soul-searching, decided to carry on the family business. One of his first actions was to ask for his employees' help. Out of necessity and natural inclination, he related to his staff as a team and drew on their experience and wisdom. He also filled the company's management gaps, hiring Robert Cook in marketing and Paul Deuble in sales. Within the year the new team had affirmed its position with key customers, and production

Above: Reginald W. Beckett, founder.

Right: The Beckett management staff today. Seated, left to right: Donald Faulhaber, general sales manager; John Beckett, president; Robert S. Cook, executive vice-president; and Frank Andolsek, plant superintendent. Standing, left to right: Edward Seabold, director of community services; Daniel R. Mobert, controller; Jack Eschweiler, production manager; and Shekhar Chakrawarti, director of engineering services.

was running smoothly.

Then one night John was awakened by a call from the North Ridgeville Fire Department. The plant was on fire. Upon arriving at the company's headquarters, he found the storage area engulfed in flames. Together Beckett and the fire fighters plunged into the acrid blackness, finding key doorways and areas where volatile materials were stored. They brought the fire under control hours later. Though the entire burner inventory had been destroyed, the main plant narrowly escaped the flames. That fall a monumental effort by every employee, plus the cooperation of suppliers, enabled Beckett to fill every order on schedule.

In 1965 Myron Cooperrider joined engineering, where he was pivotal in developing a new generation of high-performance burners such as the Model A and Model AF with flame retention.

During the early 1970s sales to furnace manufacturers and major oil companies expanded, and R.W. Beckett Corporation entered the distributor/dealer market, with Don Faulhaber joining the sales force.

The firm had just doubled its plant space in 1973 when the Arab oil embargo began. During that difficult period mergers and plant closings shrank the industry. Beckett, though set back temporarily, forged ahead with sales to the strong replacement market. The company brought on board Shekhar Chakrawarti to enhance quality, Jack Eschweiler to oversee manufacturing, and Frank Andolsek to head production control.

Sales and the number of employees reached another all-time high in 1978 with the help of exports. A year later Beckett started Advent Industries, a community-service business that hires and trains unemployable youth in the area.

In 1979 another international oil crisis hit at the same time interest rates skyrocketed and the economy slumped. U.S. residential burner production suddenly shrank by half, and every effort was made at Beckett to cut costs short of layoffs.

Rather than wait out the slump, Beckett employees created a program of dealer/installer communications, addressed trade gatherings, aggressively sold the benefits of fuel-saving burners, and pushed burner performance to new limits. As a result, Beckett did much better than the industry as a whole. What's more, consultants conducting an attitude survey among employees in 1984 and a marketing survey among customers in 1986 reported that they had never seen such positive results.

In 1987 John Beckett received industry awards on behalf of R.W. Beckett Corporation and its 150 employees from the Metropolitan Energy Council in New York and the National Association of Oil Heat Service Managers, recognizing 50 years of achievement that brought the company to a position of prominence.

R.W. Beckett Corporation's basic formula for success is straightforward: a devotion to excellence, innovation, and quality, not only in its products but also in the relationships among all who make up the family of Beckett employees. It's a formula Beckett people really live by, not just repeat, as exemplified by the way John Beckett and Bob Cook have shared overall management responsibility in mutual respect and cooperation for 22 years. Above all, serving the customer's needs is the first priority throughout the entire Beckett organization.

ROSS LABORATORIES

The modern industrial complex that is Ross Laboratories today can, like most large American companies, be traced to very modest beginnings where enterprise and business sense combined to make a success out of ideas and hard work.

These elements in Ross Laboratories' history came together in 1903, when Harry C. Moores and Stanley M. Ross founded the Moores and Ross Milk Company in the rented storeroom of a small frame building at 429 East Long Street near downtown Columbus. With financing supplied by Ross and dairy know-how supplied by Moores, the two began the business of bringing milk to the growing capital of a growing state.

Their idea of bottled milk for home delivery was new. It was this extra service that set apart the young business from the beginning. The convenience it offered could not be matched by most milk companies, whose carts carried milk only in large cans from which each customer order was ladled into a pail.

Within four years of its founding the company's rented facilities gave way to larger quarters on Ninth Street, just a few blocks away. Innovations in milk handling, processing, and delivery continued to emanate from the solid partnership of the two founders; the stand-and-drive milk truck was developed and introduced by Moores.

Another contribution typifying the firm's inventiveness was a better way of heating and cooling milk to minimize changes in taste during pasteurization—a somewhat controversial process. The wire-bottom milk case also came from Moores and Ross.

In 1924 the firm was using portions of the old Franklin Brewery buildings at 525 Cleveland Avenue for milk storage and production of cheese and sundry dairy items. The following year it undertook the manufacture of a product prepared from milk for use specifically as an infant formula.

Ross was investigating cow milk for infant feeding when he met Alfred Bosworth, a renowned milk chemist from Boston who had successfully developed such a formula. The two men, sharing a common goal of better infant nutrition, soon reached an agreement to produce and market the formula, and a new Columbus industry was born. Bosworth later settled in Circleville.

Initially the new product was known as Franklin Infant Food because it was manufactured by the Franklin branch. Subsequently the name of the product was changed to Similac, a name that is now known worldwide.

As the formula part of the business became increasingly successful, the partners sold the dairy, ice cream, and milk-processing operations to Borden, Inc., in 1928, and the former Franklin branch was incorporated as M&R Dietetic Laboratories.

The new company embarked on a unique selling program, bringing the merits of Similac as a food for babies directly to the attention of doctors. While acknowledging that human milk was best for infants, Similac's benefits in the absence of breast milk were pointed out to the medical world.

The firm's physical properties grew with the business. In 1936 an icehouse behind the main structure was obtained, followed by a former stable in which Ford Motor Company truck bodies were made. A combination bottling

Below: Uniformed milkmen and their milk wagons lined up outside the Moores and Ross Milk Company in downtown Columbus about 1910. The firm, which delivered milk to the home, was the predecessor to Ross Laboratories.

Right: The infant pictured on the first cans of baby formula was founder Stanley Ross' son, Richard, who became president of the company. The product later became known as Similac.

plant and office building was acquired in 1949.

Sales had reached nearly $2 million when World War II broke out. M&R was active in the war effort; it was the only company in the milk-processing industry to win the Army/Navy "E" Award.

In the atmosphere of technology and intense scientific advancement that characterized the postwar years, Similac gained its present position of preeminence in infant feeding. During the baby boom of the late 1940s and early 1950s, Similac was adopted almost as the standard for bottle feeding. To meet the higher demand for Similac—sales had jumped to more than $12 million in 1950—a modern plant was opened in Sturgis, Michigan.

The following year a new age of ease in home preparation of formula was ushered in with Similac Concentrated Liquid. It was a success from the beginning, mixing easily with water and making formula preparation less involved and more accurate.

A two-story office building at 625 Cleveland Avenue was completed in 1950 and then expanded twice again to accommodate the firm's administrative departments. A sizable addition to manufacturing and warehousing facilities was completed in 1956, the year a new division—Ross Laboratories—was created.

The product lines and revenues continued to grow. Among the new products introduced in the 1950s were Pream, the first powdered coffee creamer, and Similac with Iron, which provided the iron supply necessary for babies to avoid iron deficiency anemia. Due to the success of these and other products, sales reached nearly $32 million by 1960. Overseas expansion occurred in 1961, when Similac formulas began coming off the production line at a new plant in Zwolle, The Netherlands. The first prebottled, presterilized system for feeding babies in hospitals, known as the Similac 20 Hospital Feeding Procedure, was introduced in 1963, just one year before a major change in the company.

In 1964 the firm merged with Abbott Laboratories, one of the world's largest health care companies. Ross Laboratories became a division of Chicago-based Abbott.

Other developments in the 1960s included prebottled and presterilized Similac formula for the consumer market; a soybean-based formula, called Similac Isomil, for babies unable to take cow's milk; Pediamycin, an oral antibiotic for children; Vi-Daylin, a group of vitamin preparations in dosage forms and flavored for children; and Pediaflor, an oral fluoride solution.

Testing product samples is a part of quality control at Ross Laboratories.

Ross Laboratories also has been expanding its personal health product lines, which include Selsun Blue and Murine, and its adult nutritional market with such products as Enrich, Ensure, and Osmolite.

To keep up with the growth in sales, which in 1986 topped one billion dollars for the first time, Ross Laboratories built a $20-million, state-of-the-art, fully automated warehouse and shipping facility between Fourth and Fifth streets just north of downtown. In addition, the company improved its service to West Coast markets by opening a new plant in Casa Grande, Arizona, in 1984.

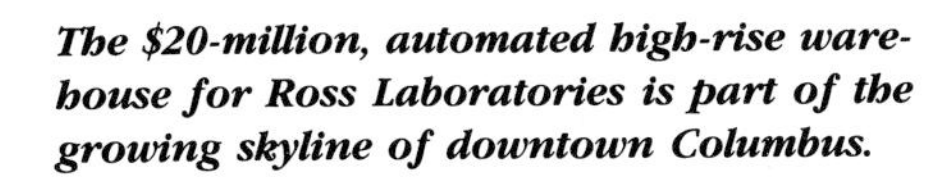

The $20-million, automated high-rise warehouse for Ross Laboratories is part of the growing skyline of downtown Columbus.

HONDA OF AMERICA MANUFACTURING, INC.

From the introduction of Honda motorcycles to the United States in 1959 to the continued expansion of its Ohio manufacturing facilities in 1988, Honda has successfully met challenge after challenge to become a major participant in the American motor vehicle industry.

Honda is the fourth-largest automaker in the United States, a position attained in 1985, only three years after producing its first car in America. Honda remains the largest manufacturer and seller of motorcycles in the United States and the world, and is a major producer of power equipment such as lawn mowers, generators, and general-purpose engines. In fact, Honda is the only motor vehicle manufacturer to produce both auto and motorcycle engines in the United States.

In 1954, when Honda was only six years old, the firm adopted an international viewpoint. Honda dedicated itself to supplying products of the highest efficiency at a reasonable price for worldwide customer satisfaction. This international viewpoint remains the cornerstone of Honda today.

Honda's corporate philosophy is an integral part of its approach to business. Part of this philosophy has always been that Honda products be manufactured in the markets in which they are sold. When the decision was made to begin construction of a production facility in Ohio, it was the Honda philosophy that was responsible.

That philosophy is in evidence today near Marysville and Anna, Ohio, where Honda of America Manufacturing (HAM) has constructed motorcycle, auto, and engine plants, representing a total manufacturing investment and commitment of $1.7 billion and employing more than 5,100 associates.

In 1974 Honda began to study the possibility of locating a production facility in the United States. The new era of Honda of America Manufacturing began on October 11, 1977, when Ohio Governor James Rhodes and Honda Motor Co. president Kiyoshi Kawashima announced plans to construct the Motorcycle Plant near Marysville, about 40 miles from Columbus.

The Motorcycle Plant began production on September 10, 1979. The 260,000-square-foot facility was Honda's first motor vehicle manufacturing plant in the United States, producing 60,000 motorcycles a year for customers in America and other nations worldwide. HAM became the exclusive manufacturer of the Gold Wing motorcycle, Honda's top-of-the-line luxury touring model, which is exported to 15 countries worldwide, including Japan. A $10-million renovation of the Motorcycle Plant was completed in 1987, making the facility the most efficient and flexible in the world.

No sooner had the first motorcycle rolled off the assembly line than Honda of America made the historic announcement in January 1980 that it would construct an automobile plant on a site adjacent to the motorcycle facility. The Honda decision was years in the making, initiated long before international economics and talk of trade restraints suggested such action to others.

Ground was broken for the $250-million, one-million-square-foot facility in December 1980. The Auto Plant is the most integrated auto manufacturing plant in North America because it houses stamping, welding, painting, plastic injection-molding, assembly, quality assurance, and related operations under one roof. Production of the Accord four-door sedan began at the facility on November 1, 1982.

But HAM's commitment to the United States—already sizable—was not yet complete. In January 1984 Honda announced plans to proceed with a $240-million expansion of the Automobile Plant that would add a second production line and more than 1.2 million square feet. The decision was regarded as a sign of HAM's success in building an automobile of quality equal to that produced in Japan.

With the completion of the expansion in April 1986, HAM began producing the three-door Accord on the new second line, and in July 1986 added the four-door Civic sedan to production. By the end of 1986 HAM was producing Accords and Civics at the rate of 1,330 per day. In 1988 the Auto Plant will produce 360,000 Honda Accord and four-door Civic models.

Both auto and motorcycle engines are cast, machined, and assembled at the Honda of America Manufacturing Engine Plant near Anna.

Honda of America unveiled plans in March 1984 to construct a $30-million Engine Plant in Anna, Ohio, about 40 miles from the Motorcycle and Auto plants. The facility was originally designed to manufacture large displacement motorcycle engines for Honda's most popular American models, including the GL1200 Gold Wing. But no sooner was the facility completed when HAM announced plans on June 12, 1985, to expand the Engine Plant for production of 1.5-liter engines for the Honda Civic automobile, making HAM the first company to produce both motorcycle and auto engines in the United States.

The first GL1200 motorcycle engine was produced at the Engine Plant on July 22, 1985, with Civic engine production following on September 23, 1986. The Engine Plant began the casting and machining of aluminum alloy wheels for the Honda Accord in January 1987.

Honda announced plans in January 1987 for a second expansion of the Engine Plant to begin full-scale production of Accord and Civic engines, drive trains, suspension, and brake parts. The $450-million, 650,000-square-foot expansion of the Engine Plant is Honda's largest single investment in the United States. When the plant reaches full production of 500,000 engines a year in 1991, all of the high-value major components for the Honda Accord and Civic four-door sedan will be made in the United States.

In September 1987 Honda announced a five-part strategy for the future of Honda's operations in the United States, including the export of Ohio-built Hondas, the construction of a second $380-million auto plant near the site of the first auto plant, the expansion of U.S. research and development activities, an increase in domestic content in Ohio-built Honda autos to 75 percent by 1991, and an additional $150-million expansion of the Engine Plant.

As a result of this strategy, Honda will establish in the United States a self-reliant motor vehicle company, which will be an important part of Honda's international operation, with the resources to compete in the world market.

By establishing manufacturing facilities in the markets where the demand for Honda products exists, Honda gives people who buy Honda products the chance to build Honda products. No matter whether the Honda Accord is manufactured in Japan, Ohio, India, or Canada, it is made to the same exacting standards—Honda standards.

The Honda approach to quality is based upon respect for what the individual associate can achieve. Honda teaches quality as a satisfying way of life and asks each associate to take individual responsibility for the quality of Honda products.

Honda's success in Ohio is not a Japanese success or the success of a Japanese company. It is an American success—the success of the American operation of an international company.

In the final analysis Honda cannot be explained by mere words or numbers. The essence of Honda is a feeling—it is a philosophy—that can be understood by standing on the factory floor and by talking with Honda associates.

What Honda of America Manufacturing, Inc., has found in Ohio is that the Honda philosophy can exist, and indeed flourish, halfway around the world from where it was conceived. By continuing to apply that philosophy, the achievements of the past decade will prove to have been just a beginning.

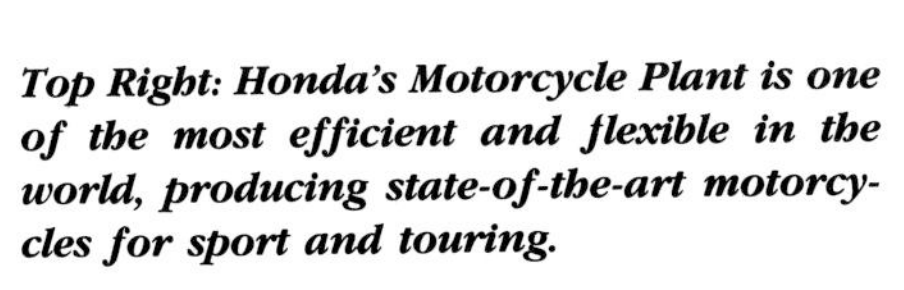

Top Right: Honda's Motorcycle Plant is one of the most efficient and flexible in the world, producing state-of-the-art motorcycles for sport and touring.

Right: Honda Accord models and Civic four-door sedans are produced at the Honda of America Manufacturing Auto Plant near Marysville.

DURAMAX-JOHNSON

A world-class rubber products supplier today, Duramax-Johnson grew up from being a wooden pail manufacturer. It did so by adhering since 1895 to a philosophy of making quality products a tradition and making service a commitment.

That year a traveling salesman by the name of Joe Johnson talked brothers Howard and Walter Shellito into centralizing all their pail manufacturing in Middlefield, a town 30 miles east of Cleveland. He had explained how they could make pails locally from start to finish more profitably than making the wooden staves and shipping them out of state for assembly.

Johnson soon joined the brothers' business, the name of which was changed in 1914 from Udall-Shellito Company to Ohio Pail Company. Around 1920 the demand for wooden pails gave way to steel pails, so the firm added a steel pail and container facility. Johnson, by then president, devised a flat rubber tube to help seal the lid of paint, oil, and ink pails, and later set up the Johnson Rubber Division to keep up with the demand for gaskets. Soon other rubber products were produced, including refrigerator seals, floor mats, and garters.

Above: Nearly a century after its founding Duramax-Johnson has grown into an international supplier of products engineered to meet the needs and challenges of a variety of industries. By skillfully applying new technologies and maximizing processes, the firm plans on a second century of success.

Left: Evolving from a manufacturer of wooden pails with roots dating back to 1895, the Johnson Rubber Company is still located in the same general area. It now occupies more than 450,000 square feet of facilities and is considered Geauga County's largest employer. Also included in the Duramax, Inc., family of companies are (clockwise, from top right): Johnson Rubber Company (Canada) Limited, Waterloo, Ontario, Canada; Yarbrough Elastomer Products, Inc., Conroe, Texas; Norbalt Rubber Company, North Baltimore; Welter Rubber Company, Chardon; and Johnson Plastic Company, Chagrin Falls.

In 1936 the organization sold its pail operations and changed its name to the Johnson Rubber Company. It focused on molded and extruded rubber products. But despite expansion and diversification, the firm faced increasing competition and declining profits. Fortunately, a dynamic young attorney from Toledo named William F. Miller, Sr., appeared on the scene. Miller provided legal counsel for businesses buying rubber products from the Johnson Rubber Company. His reputation for keen business advice to those launching new enterprises soon reached the management of the Johnson Rubber Company. They retained Miller to pull the firm out of its monumental difficulties.

Miller was so confident that he could revive Johnson Rubber that he loaned a large sum of his own money to the company when he became its president in 1946. Eventually he bought the business. Miller organized the collection of corporate departments into a single compatible unit. Slowly but surely, the Johnson Rubber Company became an efficient, profitable supplier of custom rubber products.

By the 1950s the firm had grown into a major producer of rubber products for a variety of original equipment manufacturers. New proprietary products emerged, and markets were both expanded and diversified. A Flooring

Products Division was established to produce vinyl and rubber cove base, stair treads, rubber tile, and related items under the Johnsonite trade name. According to a recent survey of industry heads by the flooring trade press, Johnsonite products are the leaders in their industry.

In the early 1960s the company became a marine industry supplier after developing a water-lubricated rubber bearing used on marine vessel propeller shafts. Today several styles of these bearings are being produced for marine craft ranging from ocean tankers, ships, and tug boats to fishing vessels, dredges, and pleasure craft. The Marine Division also manufactures protective rubber ship and dock bumpers, as well as keel coolers used to cool ships' engines and related equipment.

These products, sold under the Duramax trade name, are marketed and serviced throughout the free world through a network of agents and distributors. In addition, a line of industrial bearings that use water for lubrication are finding application in centrifugal pumps, stator pumps, and other submersed horizontal and vertical pumps.

In 1981 the parent company of Duramax, Inc., was formed to provide a broader base for the firm's continued expansion and diversification. By 1958 William F. Miller, Sr., had put the future of the corporation in the hands of son Paul C. Miller, Sr., who is currently chairman of the board; his grandson, P.C. Miller, Jr., became president and chief executive officer in 1981.

Under the parent company, Duramax, Inc., programs to stimulate growth and product quality have been strong priorities. New processing equipment is replacing the old. New plant layouts and overall facilities are being modernized to accommodate new technologies, systems, and quality-assurance techniques. In 1987 Duramax expanded into rubber products for the oil patch industries by acquiring Yarbrough Elastomer Products, Inc., in Conroe, Texas.

Today more than 1,200 people are employed throughout the Duramax family of companies. Corporate headquarters for Duramax, Inc., as well as those of the Johnson Rubber Company and its Flooring Products, Marine, and Custom Rubber Products divisions, are located in semirural Middlefield. Other Duramax, Inc., organizations are the Norbalt Rubber Company in North Baltimore, Welter Rubber Company in Chardon, Johnson Plastic Company in Chagrin Falls, Johnson Rubber Company (Canada) Limited of Waterloo, Ontario, Canada, and Yarbrough Elastomer Products, Inc., in Conroe, Texas.

The Ohio-based company has succeeded in branching out from making rubber pail gaskets into one of the nation's leading producers of custom-molded and extruded rubber products. Though an internationally recognized supplier as well, the firm still proudly produces rubber gaskets for several types of pails. Indeed, Duramax people can look back, because they look ahead.

The many succeeding generations at Duramax-Johnson have somehow passed down their mission of supplying the highest levels of product quality and service to customers, sustaining nearly a century of commitment.

Center: William F. Miller, Sr. (1888-1986), became president of the Johnson Rubber Company in 1946. An attorney specializing in corporate law, he engineered the firm's various phases of expansion and progress. In 1969 he became its chairman and retained an active role as chairman until the early 1980s, when he took time for more leisure activities.

Below: The early 1900s factory site in Middlefield is where the Johnson Rubber Company now occupies more than 450,000 square feet of modern facilities.

VORYS, SATER, SEYMOUR AND PEASE

Vorys, Sater, Seymour and Pease is one of the largest law firms in Ohio, with offices in Columbus, Cleveland, Cincinnati, and Washington, D.C. The firm, guided by strong traditions, has earned an enviable reputation throughout Ohio and the nation.

The beginnings of the firm go back to 1884, when John E. Sater opened a law office on North High Street in downtown Columbus. He was later joined by Lowry F. Sater, a nephew; Edward L. Pease; and Augustus T. Seymour. The firm became known as Sater, Seymour & Sater. When John Sater left the firm in 1907 to become a federal district judge, the firm's name was changed to Sater & Seymour. The firm dates its founding to 1909, when Arthur I. Vorys joined Sater & Seymour. At that time the name of the firm was changed to Vorys, Sater, Seymour and Pease, the name it still retains.

***Above:** A 1909 photograph of the four founding partners of Vorys, Sater, Seymour and Pease (from left): Augustus T. Seymour, Edward L. Pease, Arthur I. Vorys (seated), and Lowry F. Sater.*

***Left:** Webb I. Vorys, who contributed singularly to the modern-day growth of the firm.*

In 1912, to keep pace with a growing practice, the partners purchased a lot at 52 East Gay Street and constructed a three-story building. In addition to expanded office space, the partners planned a large library, much larger than was normal for a firm of its size. The large library evidences the scholarly emphasis the early partners placed on the practice of law, which continues to be a hallmark of the firm. Today the library contains more than 20,000 volumes and is used in conjunction with the latest in computerized research technology.

As the firm continued to grow, three adjoining buildings were purchased on East Gay. The four buildings, with a total of 17 floors, serve as an office complex for the firm's Columbus-based attorneys. There are more than 200 attorneys and a support staff of more than 300 in Columbus and the three regional offices.

The modern era for Vorys, Sater, Seymour and Pease began in 1935, when Webb I. Vorys, the son of Arthur I. Vorys, became the senior partner when the last of the four founders died. At the age of 43, Webb Vorys assumed the firm's leadership and began to establish the traditions that have guided the firm's practice of law.

Today these traditions are carried on under the leadership of John C. Elam, presiding partner, and Webb's son, Arthur I. Vorys, senior partner. Both joined the firm in 1949. These traditions have become an unwritten "common law" of the firm, embodying the heritage and philosophy of more than 75 years of history.

One unique tradition is that Vorys, Sater, Seymour and Pease never has had written partnership agreements. Webb Vorys believed that the basis for working together was mutual trust and respect. If these were not present, a written agreement was of little value. The validity of this conviction is supported by the fact that the firm has never lost a partner to private practice or to another law firm.

Another tradition is community service. A wide range of civic, religious, and political organizations has benefited from services contributed by the firm's attorneys. The firm's founder, the first Arthur I. Vorys, directed the successful presidential campaign of William Howard Taft. A token of appreciation for his efforts is a life-size bust of President Taft that occupies a prominent position in the firm's lobby.

Elam and Vorys set the example for the firm today by their involvement in numerous community projects. Vorys has had an ongoing involvement with the board of Children's Hospital, the third-largest specialty children's hospital in the nation. He now serves as board chairman of The Ohio State University Hospitals. Elam has served as chairman of the Columbus Area Chamber of Commerce. He has received the prestigious Columbus Award, presented each year in recognition of outstanding service to the city.

The partners also have served the public sector on national and statewide levels. Vorys is a former Ohio Superintendent of Insurance, and Elam has been president of the American College of Trial Lawyers.

A number of the firm's lawyers have had terms of service as president of the local and state bar associations. Herbert R. Brown, who joined the firm in 1956, was elected to the Ohio Supreme Court in 1986. Another former partner, Peter McPherson, now serves as Deputy Secretary of the Treasury of the United States.

One of the second-generation partners, James O. Seymour, believed that the firm's lawyers should broaden their perspective by foreign travel. He created a trust to make it possible for the firm to pay the travel expenses for its lawyers and their spouses to any destination in Europe. Six lawyers are selected each year to participate in this program, which has been expanded to include paralegals and staff.

In the late 1960s Vorys, Sater, Seymour and Pease grew rapidly as many large corporations in Ohio became the targets of takeover attempts. The firm became heavily engaged in this area of the law, and was instrumental in drafting Ohio's first takeover law, which was later adopted by 32 states. During the late 1960s the firm was involved in 25 of the 29 major takeover attempts in Ohio. One case that received wide national attention was *Mobil* v. *Marathon and U.S. Steel.*

An interesting aspect of Vorys, Sater, Seymour and Pease is that it has never merged with any other firm. Its growth can be attributed solely to the diversity of its legal services and to the excellence of its attorneys.

The firm maintains its high level of professional competence by an aggressive and thorough recruitment program. Each fall the firm interviews second-year law students from about 25 of the nation's top law schools. Those who meet the high standards set by the firm are invited to participate in a summer associates program. At the end of the summer the firm hires those who meet its standard of excellence. About 75 percent of the firm's new associates enter the firm through this program.

While Vorys, Sater, Seymour and Pease has historically been strong in corporate and business law and litigation, it has gained national recognition for a variety of legal services embracing virtually every area of the law, including corporate, health care, real estate, labor, tax, insurance, environmental, energy, commercial, and banking. Its more than 13,000 clients represent a wide spectrum of multinational and national corporations as well as a large number of Ohio companies. In addition, the firm has a growing international practice, reflected in the many Japanese, European, and Australian companies it represents.

Among its clients are the Ohio Manufacturers' Association, Wendy's International, Honda of America Manufacturing, Inc., Owens-Illinois, Worthington Industries, General Motors, National City Bank, The Ohio State University, John W. Galbreath & Company, Bethesda Hospital, and John Hancock Insurance Company.

Above: John C. Elam (left), presiding partner, and Arthur I. Vorys, senior partner, manage the firm's continuing growth.

Left: The building in the center is the original building constructed in 1912 for the law firm. The three adjoining structures were purchased as the firm expanded. This complex is the Columbus office of the firm.

HARRISON PAINT CORP.

Harrison Paint Corp. today serves 27 states, plus the Bahamas and Virgin Islands. Its popular consumer paint lines are Dutch Standard and Kilrust, and its industrial lines are known as Harrison Chemical Coatings. But to understand why the company and its coatings are in such widespread use and high regard requires a look beneath the surface at its history, facilities, capabilities, and people.

In 1911, when paint and varnish making was a secretive operation and manufacturers zealously guarded their formulations, a Cadiz native named Clarence Harrison started a varnish-making venture in Cleveland. In those days Cleveland was the Silicon Valley of the paint industry, a magnet for people with new coating formulations and ideas.

Gordon Walters, chairman (left), purchased the company in 1929.

R.A. Walters, president and chief executive officer (right), is well known to everyone in the Canton plant.

Harrison had learned the secrets of varnish making from his father. His family's secret formulas proved to be excellent, and his C.E. Harrison Company saw success.

In the fall of 1929 Harrison sold his operation to Gordon Walters, a young Cleveland salesman. Of course, the Depression years followed, but Walters tenaciously held onto the business, having faith in its eventual success.

Walters' faith proved justified. Production gradually expanded, and immediately after the deepest part of the Depression, sales to paint dealers increased rapidly.

Soon the firm—renamed The Harrison Paint and Varnish Company in 1933—needed larger facilities, more equipment, and a railroad siding, since raw material could then be purchased by the box and tank car. Of the locations considered, The Arlington Paint and Varnish Company, by coincidence located on Harrison Avenue in Canton, offered the best facilities. Its plant had been designed expressly for the manufacture of paint, though it needed a complete renovation, a new varnish stack, and new machinery, as well as a transfer of equipment from Cleveland. The company began full-scale operation in Canton in April 1934.

During World War II the output of The Harrison Paint and Varnish Company was devoted almost exclusively to the defense industries. To further increase the production of war-essential materials, the government granted a priority in 1944 for the erection of a plant to manufacture alkyd resin finishes. This capacity was also put to full use during the postwar boom.

In 1959 The Harrison Paint and Varnish Company purchased the Midland Varnish Company of Cleveland and moved all its machinery and equipment to the Canton plant. Midland, a highly successful firm in business for 40 years, specialized in industrial finishes, product finishes, and transportation enamels. These products are now being manufactured and sold by the ever-expanding Chemical Coatings Division. In 1964 the company changed its name to Harrison Paint Corp.

In 1980 the firm bought the Trade Sales and Kilrust Division of Hanna Chemical Coatings of Columbus. Seven years later it completed the purchase of Worth Paint & Chemical, a regional paint manufacturer located at Lake Worth, Florida. This gave the company a southern manufacturing base for supplying paints formulated for a southern climate. After a major renovation project, Harrison Paint Corp. will have a new southern distribution point as well as a plant for manufacturing both Dutch Standard and some Worth finishes. The firm also warehouses its products in Columbus; Tampa, Florida; Wilmington, North Carolina; and Birmingham, Alabama.

In Canton, Harrison Paint's steady growth over 77 years has been reflected by its many physical expansions. It started with 35,000 square feet of Arlington manufacturing space, then added the wartime alkyd plant. Other additions included a new three-story office, laboratories, and store built in 1957; a two-story warehouse in 1966; a warehouse addition in 1973; and an office addition in 1977. Today the offices, plant, laboratories, garages, and warehouses in Canton occupy a total of 173,250 square feet of floor space.

Now recognized as having one of the most modern paint-manufacturing plants in the country, the Harrison Paint Corporation offers customers a full line of products and a spectrum of services. The company manufactures alkyd, polyester, and acrylic enamels for air-dry and bake applications; EPA-compliance high solids and waterborne topcoats and primers; and alkyd, acrylic, two-part epoxy, vinyl,

Above : An aerial view of the Canton operation today.

Right: Dutch Standard paint in the 1950s (right) and today (right, top).

and polyurethane enamels for maintenance.

The firm's advanced facilities allow careful testing and storage of all incoming raw materials and precise control of manufacturing tolerances. Its fully automated production lines use an automated batch-making process, and its computer controls provide excellent color matches. Turnaround time from order processing to delivery is one to 7 days.

Sales grew because the company's products withstood the test of time. In addition, industry liked the convenience of being able to order special production and maintenance finishes, and having bulk deliveries made by Harrison's two tank wagon trucks, purchased in 1968. Dealers liked the personalized service and having materials supplied directly to them via the firm's fleet on a regional basis.

Both industry and dealers also benefit from Harrison Paint's sophisticated paint development laboratories, regarded as one of the most modern and fully equipped in the industry. Its paint chemists' constant research, testing, and development work assure the trade of paint and varnish finishes designed to give surfaces state-of-the-art beauty, protection, and durability under various application conditions.

Harrison Paint Corp.'s technical achievements include thermoset films that bend without cracking, air-dry coatings that cure in cold temperatures, and special baking enamels that can be applied by either dipping or spraying with no color change. An area of notable progress is the formulation of Enviro-coat®, its newest paint line of compliance coatings designed to meet EPA emission regulations.

Creating and maintaining the reputation for growth, service, innovation, and quality are the Harrison Paint Corporation's 165 dedicated employees. Setting the pace is Gordon Walters, the original buyer and still active chairman of the board. Walters still traverses the Canton factory daily to talk with employees on solving problems and improving processes. Son R.A. Walters, now president, also enjoys a participatory role in promoting growth and quality. Says R.A. Walters, "I've had countless opportunities to make junk paint, and I've turned every one of them down."

SUN REFINING AND MARKETING COMPANY

The Toledo refinery reportedly just after its purchase by the Diamond Oil Company in 1894. Diamond was owned by the Sun Oil Line Company and by Merriam & Morgan Paraffin Company of Cleveland.

It was the oil discoveries of 1885 near Lima in northwest Ohio that led to the founding of the Sun Company by two pioneers in the natural gas business in Pennsylvania.

Joseph N. Pew, a Pennsylvania farm boy who became a land and oil speculator, formed a partnership with Titusville, Pennsylvania, banker Edward O. Emerson in the late 1870s. Together they explored the commercial uses of natural gas primarily around Pittsburgh.

When oil began to flow in neighboring Ohio, Robert C. Pew, Joseph's nephew, was dispatched to try to secure some leases, which he did in Findlay Township. The acquisition of the first two leases on March 27, 1886, at a cost of $4,500, marked the beginning of what would become the Sun Company.

As the boom continued, the partners' Ohio operations soon overshadowed those in Pennsylvania. Consequently they incorporated in 1889 as the Sun Oil Line Company, which rapidly expanded.

A major step in that expansion was the merger with the Merriam & Morgan Paraffin Company of Cleveland to form the Diamond Oil Company, followed by the purchase of the Crystal Oil Refinery in Toledo, both in 1894. Merriam & Morgan sold out to Sun a year later, and Diamond Oil was dissolved.

The Toledo refinery, on 14 acres in the countryside, spewed forth a host of products, including kerosene, gas oil, fuel oil, paraffin, illuminating oils, naphtha, and grease. With just five workers the first year, the refinery processed some 58,000 barrels of Ohio crude, and distributed products as far west as Wisconsin.

There have been numerous milestones for the company. Emerson was bought out in 1899 as the Pew family took the business over. One of the world's great oil fields, Spindletop, near Beaumont, Texas, came in two years later, and a Pew was there to form the Sun Company (New Jersey) and to refine Texas crude at a new refinery at Marcus Hook, Pennsylvania. On December 12, 1925, Sun was listed on the New York Stock Exchange.

Many innovations have been Sun's through the years. The firm's research into thermal cracking in the late 1920s made possible the upgrading of gasoline, such as the unleaded high-octane Blue Sunoco—The High-Powered Knockless Fuel. In 1937 the company unveiled the first commercial catalytic cracker at the Marcus Hook refinery. During World War II Sun research helped develop the catalyst process for making butadiene, the principal ingredient in synthetic rubber.

Today the Toledo refinery is one of four operated by Sun Refining and Marketing Company, a division of Sun Company of Radnor, Pennsylvania. It has the capacity to process up to 120,000 barrels of crude daily. Major products include gasoline, home heating oil, jet fuel, kerosene, liquid petroleum gas, petrochemicals, mineral spirits, residual fuels, and asphalts.

The Toledo refinery has some 500 employees, although there are twice that many at work for the Sun Refining and Marketing Company throughout Ohio. Two of Sun's convenience store operations—Stop-N-Go and King Kwik—are based in Dayton. Sales terminals are in Akron, Cleveland, Dayton, Columbus, Youngstown, and Toledo, and The Sun Pipe Line Division has employees and pumping stations in both Kent and Oregon, Ohio.

The Toledo refinery's fluid catalytic cracking unit breaks up heavy gas oil into lighter components such as gas, gasoline, and furnace oil. A dustlike catalyst moves along with the oil in this process at a rate of 50 tons per minute.

ANHEUSER-BUSCH, INC.

With more than 1,000 employees and an annual capacity of 6 million barrels of beer, the Columbus brewery has helped make Anheuser-Busch the world's leading brewer. The Columbus plant marked its 20th anniversary in 1988.

Since its opening in 1968, the Columbus brewery has played a key role in helping to maintain the position of Anheuser-Busch, Inc., as the world's leading brewer.

Construction began on the plant in the spring of 1966 on a 252-acre site on the north side of Columbus. Upon completion it became the sixth brewery in the Anheuser-Busch family, and today it is part of the company's nationwide network of 12 breweries.

To keep pace with the firm's rapid sales growth, the Columbus brewery has undergone a number of expansions and modernizations over the past 20 years. Today the facility has a shipping capacity of 6.7 million barrels, nearly six times its original capacity.

Product lines also have been expanded. Originally only Budweiser and Michelob were brewed at the plant. Now the Columbus plant brews Bud Light, Michelob Light, Busch, Natural Light, and King Cobra, in addition to Budweiser and Michelob. These products are shipped throughout Ohio, as well as to Michigan, Indiana, Kentucky, Pennsylvania, and West Virginia.

Growth in production has meant growth in the brewery's most important resource—its work force. More than 1,000 people from Columbus and the surrounding communities are employed at the brewery, making it one of the largest private employers in the area.

The brewery and its employees support a broad range of local human service, educational, and cultural activities, ranging from Operation Brightside—a summer employment and education program for predominantly minority teenagers—to leadership development programs with the local Boy and Girl Scout councils.

In 1986 the Columbus brewery was awarded Anheuser-Busch's Gold Eagle Award, the corporation's highest award for excellence. To be selected for the award, the brewery had to meet stringent criteria in a number of areas, including operating efficiency, safety, sanitation, employee productivity, and community involvement. "Quite simply," says William E. Hickman, plant manager, "this means Columbus was the best of the best."

Anheuser-Busch's presence in Ohio is not limited to the brewery. The corporation also operates three other facilities: the Metal Container Corporation and Busch Properties Inc. in Columbus and the Container Recovery Corporation in Marion.

With an annual capacity of 1.5 billion cans, Metal Container's Columbus plant provides nearly all the requirements of the Columbus brewery. Container Recovery receives and recycles metal beverage containers from both voluntary recycling programs and mandatory deposit states. Busch Properties has developed an award-winning industrial park, known as the Busch Corporate Center, in Columbus. The development includes leased buildings, offices, warehouses, and light industry on 155 acres of land adjacent to the brewery.

Taken together Anheuser-Busch's Columbus operations have a sizable economic impact on the region. Annually wages and benefits for more than 1,400 employees top $69 million, state and local tax payments total $16.8 million, and $56 million is paid in federal excise taxes. In addition, the Columbus brewery and its employees purchase millions of dollars in goods and services from local suppliers each year.

Only the finest natural ingredients are used for Anheuser-Busch beers in a time-honored, Old World brewing process. Here an employee checks a stainless-steel brew kettle at the Columbus brewery.

THE REYNOLDS AND REYNOLDS COMPANY

Reynolds and Reynolds' Dayton plant in the mid-1930s. The firm was founded more than 111 years ago for the manufacture of standard business forms of the day.

From a patent for a simple sales book cover to the latest in data base computer systems, Reynolds and Reynolds has spanned more than 111 years and experienced amazing changes in technology from its home in Dayton, Ohio.

The predecessor of the current company, Gardner & Reynolds, was founded in Dayton by Lucius D. Reynolds, a former Bellefontaine, Ohio, newspaper editor and his brother-in-law, James R. Gardner. The firm provided mass production of standard business forms of the day to be sold to the blossoming retail establishment in Dayton and beyond. More important, unlike other form printers, Gardner & Reynolds would sell its forms in small quantities to small businesses. More than a century later the company still produces more than 4,000 standard forms adapted to the needs of business and industry. Today paper forms account for nearly 60 percent of Reynolds' yearly sales of more than $630 million.

Only a year after the company was formed, Gardner sold out to Ira Reynolds, Lucius' father and a central Ohio businessman. Since 1867 the firm has been known as The Reynolds and Reynolds Company.

More than just a forms manufacturer, Reynolds has been an innovator in the industry—from sales forms to computer software and hardware systems for business management. The company's first patent came in 1869 on a removable, reusable hard cover for duplicating sales books, the successors of which are still used in some smaller retail operations. Three years later the elder Reynolds patented a method for binding ledgers that allowed the books to lie flatter when opened for bookkeeping entries—an important advancement.

By 1889 the firm incorporated and was recording phenomenal growth as the Midwest's economy expanded. Between the time it opened and 1885, the organization had moved four times to meet expanding printing and office needs. Finally, in 1885, the company settled into a new 56,000-square-foot building at 800 Germantown Street, which now houses the Computer Systems Division. In June 1987 the Business Forms Division moved to its newly renovated 60,000-square-foot headquarters building at 3555 South Kettering Boulevard. Corporate headquarters have been established at 129 South Ludlow Street in downtown Dayton.

By the late 1920s the firm's growth had leveled. Founder Lucius Reynolds died and was replaced by his son, Edwin Stanton Reynolds. In an effort to cut its losses, the corporation sold its Western Tablet and Stationery Company in Dayton. The sale provided the means to stay with the business the company knew best—producing standard business forms. To go with the forms, a paper-based accounting system for General Motor's Chevrolet division was developed and marked the beginning of a relationship with the nation's auto industry that continues to be the backbone of the company today.

In 1935 the third generation of the Reynolds family, Edwin Stanton Reynolds, Jr., replaced his father as president. Just two years later he resigned, and former sales manager L.H. Forster was elected president. In 1939, for the first time since the firm opened its doors, there were no members of the Reynolds family among the owners. The family of Richard Hallum Grant acquired controlling interest of the company. R.H. Grant, Sr., Reynolds' new chairman of the board and president, had played a leading role in General Motors' rise to domination of the auto industry. He would do the same for Reynolds. By the end of the year, under the senior Grant, Reynolds had increased its sales offices to 19 nationwide. To further its automotive division, Reynolds opened a special office in Detroit to act as liaison between the company and Detroit's top auto manufacturers.

The late 1940s and early 1950s saw the addition of a number of new facilities and products. While the nation developed a new love for space and technology, Reynolds and Reynolds took its first steps into electronic data processing by purchasing Controlmat, a Boston firm that specialized in computer accounting for auto dealerships. After two years of development and testing, Reynolds became the first to offer computer services to auto dealers throughout the nation. At the same time it saw a new customer developing in the hospital industry and established a special division to market standard forms and systems for the nation's hospitals.

In 1961 the company made its first public stock offering and was able to finance the purchase of the Edward I. Barry Division of the Security Lithographing Co. in California and open a Canadian division with the purchase of the automotive division of Windsor Office Supply in Windsor, Ontario. This company provided the base for Reynolds & Reynolds (Canada) Ltd., a supplier of automotive forms

In 1939 R.H. Grant, Sr., became chairman of the board and served until 1957.

New Reynolds and Reynolds ERA™ Computer Systems work in tandem with integrated ERA software for streamlined information management in every automobile dealership department. The innovative modular-designed ERA™ 96,000 features the Motorola 68020 processor and is powerful enough to meet the needs of even the largest dealership.

and systems to Canadian auto dealers.

On its 100th anniversary in 1966 the company could count 6 production plants, 8 data-processing centers, 1,600 employees, and 91 sales offices in the United States and Canada. In 1964 Electronic Accounting data-processing centers were opened in Newark, New Jersey, and Dallas, Texas, and a year later in Burlingame, California; Atlanta, Georgia; and Chicago, Illinois.

The year 1969 was a pivotal one for Reynolds—a year that opened the door to successes of the 1970s, 1980s, and beyond. During that amazing year the company purchased the auto dealer form business of its largest Canadian competitor, Alger Press Ltd. of Oshawa, Ontario, Canada, and released three new, sophisticated, electronic data-processing programs to the firm's customers.

For the next five years, despite an economic slump, Reynolds continued to grow. By 1974 it was ready to invest more than $20.5 million for facilities and equipment to manufacture computer hardware and software for the auto industry. It took only four years to dramatically measure the success of the VIM III computer system and subsequent computer packages. In 1978 computer-related sales rose to 50.6 percent of the company's total sales of $140.2 million, surpassing form sales for the first time.

In recent years Reynolds has balanced its forms and computer businesses. The company acquired The Arnold Corporation, a company with no automotive forms business and a large general forms printing business. The Computer Systems Divison also diversified into other areas. Reyna Financial Corporation was formed to assist customers in purchasing computers, hardware, and software. In 1979 Reynolds acquired a computerized tax-preparation service called ACCUTAX. The company began marketing computer systems for office-based physicians, and in 1986 acquired National Medical Computer Services, a leading vendor of billing systems to hospital-based physicians, making Reynolds the sixth-largest vendor of medical computer systems.

Reynolds expanded internationally as well. In addition to its Canadian operations, the company established both a forms and a data-processing subsidiary in Australia. Reynolds opened a French operation in 1983, which has become the largest vendor of in-house computer systems to autmobile dealers in France with the acquisition of Beri, S.A., in 1987. Reynolds also has operations in the United Kingdom and New Zealand.

Today The Reynolds and Reynolds Company continues to expand through purchasing existing firms and developing new and innovative products. Its latest innovation, ERA, is the latest generation of data-base software for the auto industry. Products like these will keep the company moving forward to its 125th year and beyond.

THE TOLEDO HOSPITAL

Toledo as a municipal corporation was just 38 years old with a population of 40,000 when, in 1874, a group of church women sensed a need to minister to the sick and aged among the immigrants, newcomers, and indigents who had no homes, families, or financial means. Led by Mrs. Thomas Daniels, the Women's Christian Association purchased property at 171 Union Street and opened The City Hospital of Toledo.

The white-frame house on Union Street had room for just eight patients at a time. The cost for those able to pay was seven dollars per week. It was a struggle for the founders to keep the facility open. The two physicians who constituted the first medical staff—S.S. Lungren and Symmes H. Bergen—donated their time as did the women of the association. Only the warden and a matron received a salary until 1876, when the first nurse was hired.

That year the founders' association with the institution was dissolved as The Toledo Homeopathic Medical Society formed a new board to govern what then became the Protestant Hospital of Toledo. Later allopathic physicians were included. As Toledo and the hospital grew, the name was changed twice again, to the Toledo Hospital Association and, finally, to The Toledo Hospital in 1901.

***Above:** From 1888 until 1893 The Toledo Hospital was housed in the former Valentine B. Ketcham home. Later the building was used for The Toledo Hospital School of Nursing.*

***Left:** The Toledo Hospital today.*

A school of nursing opened its doors to five students in 1893. In subsequent years it awarded more than 2,700 diplomas before closing in June 1988.

A "new" four-story brick building, erected in 1893 for 100 patients, received an annex eight years later for the hospital's first X-ray machine and for 50 private rooms. A second annex was built in 1914. Under its first professionally trained superintendent, P.W. Behrens, the institution won recognition in 1921 as a standard hospital from the American College of Surgeons, and three years later as a training facility for interns from the American Medical Association.

In the late 1920s, when the hospital had again outgrown its facilities, two Toledo businessmen, William W. Knight, president of the board of trustees, and Frank Collins, chairman of the building committee, raised funds for a 250-bed facility. The site was 22.5 acres on North Cove Boulevard between Oatis and Midwood avenues, the location of the present hospital. Although hit by the Depression with $500,000 still owing on the new building, the work of the hospital and its outstanding research programs never faltered.

The discovery of colibactragen for the prevention of peritonitis in surgical cases led to the construction of an Institute of Medical Research on the grounds in 1943. In later years, under Dr. Bernhard Steinberg, the institute was recognized for its leukemia research.

Patient capacity went up to 500, then to 700, and finally to more than 800 today. The institution is currently Toledo's second-largest employer, with a staff of more than 4,500 and a medical staff of 800. More than 31,000 patients are admitted each year.

Today The Toledo Hospital serves as the regional center for pediatric and perinatal care, the only Level III perinatal center in Northwest Ohio. It also is known for its family practice center, cancer treatment, kidney dialysis, and open-heart surgery, first performed at the hospital in 1957.

HOLZER-WOLLAM REALTORS

Having been one of the top three real estate companies in Columbus for the past 10 years, Holzer-Wollam Realtors was founded in 1912 by Henry C. Wollam. A widely respected leader and innovator, Wollam often rented a horse and buggy to show clients homes in the new city suburbs near Fifth Avenue and High Street.

After a thriving first quarter-century, his son Emerson joined the company. Emerson, a graduate of Ohio State and Western Reserve universities, expanded the firm's services and oversaw its steady growth.

To ensure continued success, Emerson C. Wollam negotiated a merger in 1969 with Max W. Holzer, the founder of a new and dynamic residential brokerage firm. Both men wanted to create a highly professional organization that could compete effectively with national brokerage companies appearing on the horizon.

Under Holzer's leadership, the firm of 14 people grew into a family of companies with more than 300 employees, generating annual sales in excess of $325 million and providing a full range of "shelter services." Holzer, an Ohio State University graduate trained in both engineering and accounting, sees his profession as solving residential, investment, commercial, and industrial real estate needs.

Holzer founded Lincoln Construction, Inc., in 1970 to facilitate the construction of commercial projects, and established a development company to build premium office buildings known for their highly landscaped presentation. Next came the Apartment Locator Service in 1971 and the Temporary Corporate Housing Division in 1972. Now managed by Holzer's daughter, Lynda, her husband, and his daughter-in-law, Beth, Temporary Corporate Housing rents more than 250 fully furnished apartments in both Columbus and Cleveland.

Other diversification was driven by a need to become less sensitive to the interest market fluctuations. The Commercial Division was founded in 1976, is headed by Holzer's son Stephen, and exceeds $50 million in annual sales. Property Management and Mortgage Banking Services were established in the early 1980s to finance and manage office buildings, shopping centers, apartments, and condominiums.

In order to serve the national corporate relocation business, the Residential Division expanded through mergers and acquisitions to better serve the entire city. The Relocation Division has and is serving the largest national relocation company in the United States, "Homequity," headquartered in Chicago.

The company headquarters on Bethel Road in Columbus consists of three architecturally strong office buildings in a landscaped office park built in 1972 by Holzer-Wollam's construction arm, Lincoln Construction.

Holzer also believes in making his community a better place in which to live by spending endless hours in "nonself-serving" volunteer work to further his profession, his alma mater, and his city. Like both Wollams before him, he has served as president of the Columbus Board of Realtors. He spearheaded the drive to make low-interest mortgages available to first-time home buyers via "Issue #1" in 1982. For these and many other services, his fellow realtors named him 1985 Realtor of the Year. His latest challenge, as chairman of the Columbus and Franklin County Housing Commission, is to provide housing for the homeless and the working poor in central Ohio.

Co-owners Dick Strait, Emerson Wollam, Max Holzer, and Jerry White (from left) celebrate the firm's 75th anniversary.

THE PLAIN DEALER

The Plain Dealer, Ohio's largest newspaper, keeps a half-million daily subscribers abreast of national and international, as well as local and state, events. It got its name because its founders wanted to tell the public that the newspaper "would be a fearless advocate of truth, of liberty in faith, liberty in government, and liberty in trade . . ." The name remains, and a tradition begun in 1841 continues.

The Plain Dealer was purchased for the princely sum of $1,050 in late 1841 by Joseph Gray, a teacher, and his brother, Admiral Gray, a contractor. When the publication hit the streets on January 7, 1842, only 50 years had passed since Moses Cleaveland founded the town. On the dusty streets around Public Square pedestrians mingled with livestock, and competition was keen. The fledgling *Plain Dealer,* then a weekly, was battling six other papers for readers among a Cleveland population of 6,000 and an Ohio City citizenship of 1,677. The newspaper became an afternoon daily in 1845 and added a Sunday edition the following year. Later it became a morning paper.

One of *The Plain Dealer*'s most famous subscribers was President Abraham Lincoln, whose laughter echoed through the White House while reading the rawboned humor of columnist Charles Brown, also known as Artemus Ward. Archer Shaw, an early biographer of *Plain Dealer* history, said that Lincoln would read aloud Brown's *Plain Dealer* column to his cabinet members, and after one such reading pronounced the Emancipation Proclamation.

Though Lincoln liked reading Gray's newspaper, Gray did not like Lincoln and especially the abolition of slavery. In time Gray's shrill, unpopular politics lost him readers and revenue. He had to suspend publication on March 7, 1865, missing two of the biggest stories of the times—the surrender of General Robert E. Lee and the assassination of President Lincoln.

When the newspaper resumed publication under new owners, *The Plain Dealer* caught up with events. Upon ratification of the Thirteenth Amendment to the Constitution, its editorial stated: "We accept the edict as part of the great mystery of this eventful period."

Left: Liberty E. Holden, self-made millionaire mining investor, became publisher in 1885 and founded the present era.

Below: The copy editing desk in the 1940s.

The present era of the newspaper began in 1885, when Liberty E. Holden, a New Englander, educator, and self-made millionaire mining investor, bought *The Plain Dealer* from William Armstrong, to whom J.W. Gray's widow had sold it 20 years before.

Holden brought in two brilliant newspapermen, Charles Kennedy, editorial manager, and Elbert Baker, business manager, to run the enterprise. After much work the newspaper began to prosper.

The keys to success were Baker's rules of political impartiality and objective reporting that became the nucleus of *The Plain Dealer* philosophy. In Baker's day it was an innovative philosophy.

Many great editors have upheld the Baker tradition. Erie Hopwood became editor and founded the American Society of Newspaper Editors. Paul Bellamy followed in 1928. These two men forged a reputation of journalistic excellence that was recognized across the nation.

Wright Bryan, former editor of the *Atlanta Journal*, was editor from 1954 through 1963. When Bryan retired, the Holden legacy passed on to Tom Vail, Liberty Holden's great-grandson, who became publisher and editor. Only two years later *Newsweek* magazine reported that Vail had turned the newspaper into an exciting, crusading publication, exposing political and social corruption.

In 1967 *The Plain Dealer* was sold to Newhouse Newspapers, which is in turn held by Advance Publications Inc., owner of national magazines, cable television systems, and book publishing concerns.

Today nearly 1,800 employees produce and deliver *The Plain Dealer*. News bureaus are maintained in Washington, D.C., Columbus, Warren, and Cincinnati. Vail says the emphasis at *The Plain Dealer* is to provide "original material that keeps our society honest, is useful, interesting, and important to people—the kind of materials you can't find anywhere else."

The Plain Dealer has made a difference in the lives of many Ohioans. For example, its ongoing series, "Our Hospitals: Private Power, Public Money," led to the introduction of state legislation cracking down on substandard open-heart-surgery units at hospitals in Ohio, and to an investigation by the state attorney general into the business affairs of a local hospital examined in the series.

Stories by a real estate reporter detailing overcharges on home mortgages prompted more than $1.4 million in refunds to home owners in Ohio and in 27 other states.

A series of reports by a *Plain Dealer* investigative reporter regarding inadequate safety precautions and inspection of amusement park rides led to the enactment of one of the nation's toughest state laws regulating such uses. That same year state officials made sweeping changes in Ohio's surplus equipment donation program following the reporter's evidence of prevalent abuse and mismanagement.

The Plain Dealer has been on the cutting edge of reporting on child sexual abuse, day-care problems, the state's savings and loan scandal, and the mysteries of Acquired Immune Deficiency Syndrome (AIDS).

At *The Plain Dealer* the incisive reporting goes on, always meeting the challenges of the times. It's a journalistic tradition that continues to grow and meet the needs of new generations.

***Center:* The current publisher and editor Tom Vail, Liberty Holden's great-grandson.**

***Below:* Today reporters use word-processing equipment to submit their stories.**

BLUE CROSS & BLUE SHIELD MUTUAL OF OHIO

***Left:** A new member solicitation at East Ninth and Euclid in downtown Cleveland in the late 1940s.*

***Above:** John R. Mannix, pioneer of prepayment health care and one of the founders of Cleveland Hospital Service Association, predecessor of Blue Cross & Blue Shield Mutual of Ohio.*

America was mired in the Great Depression, but Clevelander John R. Mannix, a pioneer of prepayment health care, was optimistic in 1934, when the Cleveland Hospital Service Association first opened its doors. Mannix was so optimistic, in fact, that he bet a colleague a straw hat that the new hospital insurance plan would have 10,000 subscribers by 1939. Mannix, however, was wrong: It took the association just one year to win 10,000 subscribers.

Today Blue Cross & Blue Shield Mutual of Ohio, the descendant of the Cleveland Hospital Service Association, has well over one million policyholders and pays out hundreds of millions of dollars each year. Moreover, it is at the forefront of helping to keep the region's health care costs down.

But cost containment has always been an integral part of Blue Cross' historic fabric. It was in the 1920s that Mannix, a Cleveland area hospital administrator who would eventually head Blue Cross in Cleveland, came to a simple but important realization: If the annual hospital costs of an area were to be divided by the population and applied to individuals, residents would only have to pay a miniscule amount for hospital needs.

With similar efforts sprouting up nationwide, Mannix' dream of prepaid hospitalization became reality on March 30, 1934. It was then that the nonprofit Cleveland Hospital Service Association, with the support of everyone from local hospital presidents to labor leaders, was incorporated. Giving it teeth, the association wielded the Cleveland Inter-Hospital Agency Contract, which, in essence, was a guarantee that local hospitals would go along with the plan.

Indeed, prepaid hospital care was an idea whose time had come. At first, only individual subscribers were covered, and then even they had to be part of a private company's group plan. But as the subscriber rolls in Cleveland grew ever larger, plan improvements came one after another, from including entire families to adding maternity care coverage. By September 1941 enrollment reached 500,000.

While Cleveland Hospital Service Association grew, a related move was afoot that would take health care insurance in Cleveland one step further—payment of doctor's fees. And while the short-lived Cleveland Medical Service Association sought to fill that role in 1941, it was not until Medical Mutual of Cleveland, Inc., was created in 1945 that the public had the benefits of prepaid doctor's fees.

Although separate entities, the Cleveland Hospital Service Association and Medical Mutual had strong ties, including numerous shared subscribers. Over the years, of course, both organizations burgeoned and, because of their respective high standards, were approved as affiliates of the nationally known Blue Cross and Blue Shield plans.

The years would bring other changes, too. In 1947, for example, the Cleveland Hospital Service Association left its original headquarters in the 1900 Building on Euclid Avenue and settled into the Rose Building at East Ninth Street and Prospect Avenue. A decade later that site became headquarters of Blue Cross of Northeast Ohio, the resulting corporation of the merger between the hospital association and its nearby counterpart, the Akron Hospital Service. And in June 1984, when the merger of Blue Cross of Northeast

Above: John Burry, Jr., current president.

Right: In 1947 the Rose Building at East Ninth Street and Prospect Avenue became the headquarters for Blue Cross & Blue Shield of Ohio.

Ohio and Medical Mutual of Cleveland was approved by the state, the Rose Building became home to Blue Cross & Blue Shield Mutual of Northern Ohio.

To enhance the efficiency of the companies, the Cleveland-based plan and the Toledo-based plan merged on April 8, 1986. The resulting corporation, Blue Cross & Blue Shield Mutual of Ohio, is the 13th-largest health insurance company out of 700-plus carriers in the country.

Formed as a "hospital service organization," the plan's Blue Cross component (that part that covers hospital bills) was required, under state law, to contract with all hospitals within its service area. As a part of its effort to contain the increase in health care costs, Blue Cross & Blue Shield of Ohio sought and, in 1987, the legislature passed, the Health Insurance Reform Act.

The "selective contracting" legislation, which went into effect October 1, 1987, allows Blue Cross & Blue Shield plans in Ohio to contract with those hospitals judged to provide quality health care at reasonable prices.

The names and faces of the leaders would change also as men such as Arthur D. Baldwin, the Cleveland Hospital Service Association's first president, and Eugene L. Martin, Medical Mutual's first director, passed the mantle on to others. But through it all—changes in leadership, good economic times and bad—serving the policyholders remained paramount.

Still these remain challenging times for Blue Cross & Blue Shield Mutual of Ohio; the battle against high medical costs no doubt will continue into the 1990s and beyond. But people like president John Burry, Jr., remain optimistic. "I look forward to the next 10 to 15 years," Burry said on the occasion of Blue Cross' 50th anniversary. "No one knows the health care business better than we do. And we have the best health care system in the world, much of it right here in Ohio. The Blue Cross and Blue Shield Plan has played an important part in making all this possible, and I don't see our role going away."

Similar sentiments, no doubt, are what won John Mannix a straw hat a half-century earlier.

EAST OHIO GAS COMPANY

Ninety years ago the Standard Oil Company, under the tutelage of John D. Rockefeller, filled the West Virginia countryside with the oil derricks that would provide the foundation for the energy industry.

As workers drew the oil from the ground they were faced with a difficult and potentially troublesome problem: The production of oil usually meant the unwanted production of natural gas, a hydrocarbon that is closely related to oil. It was considered a by-product of no value that had to be "flared" or lighted at the wellhead and burned off.

Standard Oil executives, however, believed a market for natural gas was waiting for whoever could deliver the fuel. It is a clean-burning fuel that has none of the negative qualities associated with oil or coal—namely soot, storage problems, and variable quality. The executives proved to be right on target; industrial, commercial, and residential applications for natural gas were present or on the horizon. A new firm, the East Ohio Gas Company, was formed to provide natural gas service.

The dog days of the summer of 1898 were marked by heavy rains, making the brutal work of laying a pipeline even more difficult. Oxen hauled supplies through mud up to their bellies; strong men were overcome by heat and humidity. But they pushed on, from the oil fields and Pipe Creek Station on the Ohio River to the burgeoning city of Akron.

By the end of the summer a six-inch branch line was laid from the 10-inch transmission pipeline, or TPL 1, to the railroad center in Dennison, Ohio. T. Emmet Van Lehn, whose house still stands on North Fifth Street, was the first traditional residential customer of the new East Ohio Gas Company.

Before the end of the following year 3,984 new customers in Canton, Massillon, Akron, Dover, and New Philadelphia were served by gas. Growth was phenomenal: By the end of 1910 the Standard Oil subsidiary served 161,997 customers in Northeast Ohio.

From Akron the pipeline was extended to Cleveland, and two more pipelines were added to carry natural gas from the Ohio River to the ever-growing city on Lake Erie. Warren and Youngstown, which would make their marks as broad-shouldered industrial cities, joined the system.

The first three decades of the twentieth century saw East Ohio's customers increase to 331,991 in 1920 and to 472,904 in 1930. The Depression slowed the growth of East Ohio, but by World War II, 521,510 homes and businesses relied on natural gas for heat, hot water, cooking, and processing industrial products.

In 1943 East Ohio became part of the Consolidated Natural Gas Company, which has corporate headquarters in Pittsburgh, Pennsylvania. Of the Consolidated System's 11 subsidiary companies, East Ohio is the largest.

The history of East Ohio includes the tragic fire of October 1944, in which liquefied natural gas, stored in spherical containers near Cleveland's East 62nd Street, leaked and ignited. The death toll was 130 people, including 50 East Ohio employees. Eighty-two homes and businesses were destroyed.

Today a similar incident is extremely unlikely. East Ohio stores natural gas thousands of feet underground in storage fields that once held native Ohio gas. It is, in fact, this storage capability that permits the firm to buy gas supplies throughout the year. On a peak winter day as much as 70 percent of the gas used by residents and businesses comes from

Pipe laying in downtown Akron, circa 1920.

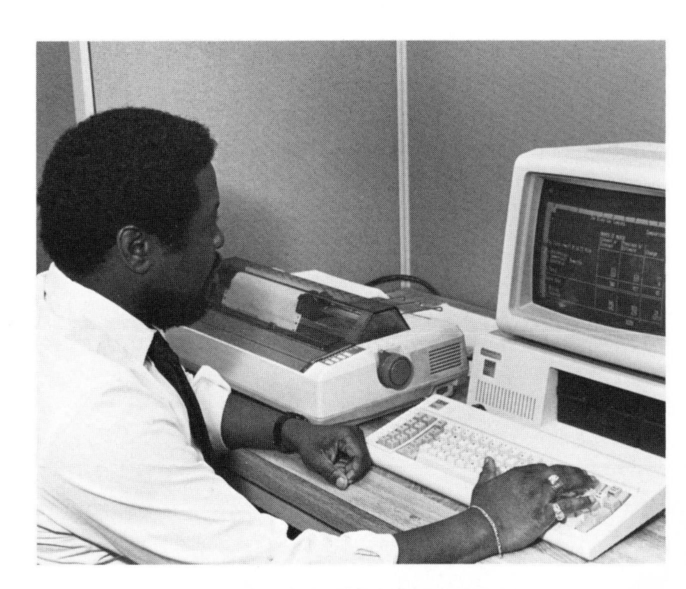

Today business at the East Ohio Gas Company is expedited through the use of computers in everything from computer-aided radio dispatching operations (above) to finance (top, right) to customer service (right).

storage fields.

By 1943 East Ohio began to contract for gas supplies from the rich fields of the Southwest. By 1950 some 590,000 customers were using natural gas supplied by East Ohio. Twenty years later that number had risen to 925,000.

The 1970s, a decade of legislative confusion and international energy crises, slowed all energy companies. Price controls issued by the federal government provided no incentive for producers to drill deeper for natural gas, and thousands of producers went bankrupt. The record-setting winter of 1976-1977 only made matters more difficult. Congress acted and passed the Natural Gas Policy Act of 1978, which would provide incentive for drillers and deregulate the natural gas industry over a period of years.

With new supplies on the market and stable prices, the East Ohio Gas Company looked to its one-millionth customer. In February 1987 East Ohio installed its one-millionth meter in the home of Troy Black in nearby Hudson Township. In his remarks at the ceremony, East Ohio president Dick Kelso said the firm remains committed to its original mission of providing dependable service to customers while making significant contributions to the communities served.

Today East Ohio is by any measure a large company, with more than 2,500 employees, 30 shops or buildings, 1,000 vehicles, 16,000 miles of underground pipeline, and sales in excess of one billion dollars annually. Corporate headquarters are in Cleveland, and offices are located in Akron, Ashtabula, Canton, Youngstown, Warren, Wooster, and New Philadelphia. The 3,000-square-mile service area includes the major industrial centers of Northeast Ohio and the south shore of Lake Erie from the western suburbs of Cleveland to the Pennsylvania border. In all, 269 communities are served within the 20-county service area.

In addition to being a major employer and taxpayer in Northeast Ohio, the East Ohio Gas Company is a corporation marked by a commitment to the quality of life in communities it serves. The firm and its employees are enthusiastic contributors to a wide variety of civic and charitable organizations, including the United Way, the United Negro College Fund, the Hispanic Community Forum, and the Salvation Army. Natural gas, the fossil fuel millions of years old, is remarkably adaptable to new and emerging technologies. In the experienced hands of the East Ohio Gas Company, natural gas remains the energy for this century and beyond.

BP AMERICA, INC.

BP America headquarters tower (left) stands near Terminal Tower on Public Square in downtown Cleveland. The building features an eight-story atrium containing shops, trees, and fountains.

Best known in Ohio for its Sohio® service stations, Cleveland-based BP America, Inc., also counts among its businesses oil and natural gas exploration and production, chemicals, copper, gold, coal, high-tech composite materials used in aerospace—even animal feeds.

But for Ohioans, the firm's heritage is represented by the names The Standard Oil Company and "Sohio," and by John D. Rockefeller. In 1870 the ambitious young Clevelander joined with partners to incorporate their young refining business. The result: the original Standard Oil Company, whose assets and operations comprise much of BP America.

Few companies have seen their fortunes rise, fall, and rise again as dramatically as Rockefeller's Standard Oil Company.

Soon after Edwin Drake's 1859 discovery of oil in Titusville, Pennsylvania, Rockefeller saw oil's potential as a source of light and heat. He joined with partners to build his first refinery in Cleveland in 1863. Then the meticulous, 23-year-old bookkeeper focused on raising volume as a way to trim unit costs and hike profits. Incorporation opened the door to growth. By 1872 Standard Oil controlled 21 of 26 refineries then in Cleveland, plus refineries in New York, Philadelphia, and Pittsburgh.

Spectacular growth continued until 1879, when problems of managing a collection of owned and semi-independent companies led to the formation of a trust, which included the original Standard Oil. In 1882 a new trust replaced it, creating a series of Standard Oil companies to administer different markets nationwide. That same year the trust's headquarters was moved from Cleveland to New York, leaving the original Cleveland-based company as a small outpost.

By 1889 the trust, under legal attack, was replaced by a holding company, the Standard Oil Company of New Jersey. Legal efforts led the United States Supreme Court

Below: BP America's Lima chemicals plant produces chemicals including acrylonitrile, widely used to make plastics and fibers. Some 95 percent of the world's "acrylo" is made via the company's exclusive process.

Right: John D. Rockefeller, founder of The Standard Oil Company. Courtesy, Western Reserve Historical Society, Cleveland

Left: A modern Sohio self-serve station in the Cleveland area.

Below: A typical Standard Oil service station of the early 1930s on Detroit and West Clifton in Cleveland.

to dissolve the holding company into 34 independent firms in 1911.

The original Standard Oil Company, still headquartered in Cleveland, emerged with one refinery, a fleet of horse-drawn tankwagons, and a few retail outlets confined to the state. Fortunately for this orphaned firm, the automobile had begun its reign in America. Standard Oil grew with the demand for gasoline, though it struggled through most of the 1920s as its market share dwindled.

But starting in 1928 Standard Oil took steps to turn its situation around. The firm introduced the Sohio brand name, increased advertising, bought a refinery in Kentucky, built a pipeline to it with crude oil, and initiated research.

Over the next two decades Standard Oil developed an Ohio marketing operation—supplied by pipelines from refineries to key distribution points—that captured one-third of its Ohio gasoline market and much higher percentages of bulk petroleum product sales. This business provided the base for later expansion into crude oil transportation, exploration, and production. Success in research led to its move into the chemicals business in 1954.

Beginning in the late 1950s the company began a period of diversification through development of oil production and entry into other energy fields—coal, oil shale, and uranium.

As it entered the 1970s Standard Oil embarked on a multibillion-dollar venture that would transform the corporation from a regional oil refiner and marketer into one of the nation's largest energy companies. On January 1, 1970, in exchange for portions of its stock, Standard Oil acquired from The British Petroleum Company p.l.c. (BP) rights to about half of the 10 billion barrels of oil at Prudhoe Bay in Alaska. Standard Oil also acquired other properties, including service stations on the East Coast.

A seven-year struggle followed to develop Prudhoe Bay oil and construct the 800-mile trans-Alaska pipeline and a fleet of oil tankers to carry the oil to markets in the "lower 48" states. By the time the oil started to flow, the total cost for this investment reached $15 billion. The pipeline start-up in 1977 signalled a new period of growth and expansion financed by earnings from this enormous investment.

Standard Oil rapidly expanded its interests in oil and gas exploration and coal, and entered the metals and industrial products businesses. By 1984 it was one of the 25 largest companies in the nation.

In 1987, holding 55 percent of Standard Oil stock, British Petroleum (BP) made an offer to buy the remaining publicly held shares. The offer went through. BP merged newly acquired Standard Oil companies with its other U.S. businesses. The result: BP America, BP's U.S. holding company and in terms of assets, the largest of BP's subsidiaries, which operate in more than 70 countries.

Today, in Ohio, BP America markets gasoline and other petroleum products through more than 1,300 Sohio service stations—including car washes and ProCare® full-service auto centers—plus Sohio and Truckstops of America® truck stops. It operates retail marketing offices and pipeline terminals in several cities, Chase Brass & Copper Company facilities in Solon and Montpelier, refineries in Toledo and Lima, and a chemical plant in Lima.

Nationwide, the company markets gasoline and other petroleum products through nearly 8,000 service stations and 45 truck stops. It owns 51 percent of the oil in the Prudhoe Bay, Alaska, field. And with almost 3 billion barrels of crude oil and liquid gas reserves, the firm is one of the nation's largest holders of domestic petroleum and is exploring for added reserves. It manufactures petrochemicals and advanced ceramics and composite materials for aerospace and electronics; mines coal, copper, gold, and other metals; and conducts research in energy and other technologies. Its Purina Mills Company, based in St. Louis, is the nation's leading supplier of branded animal feed.

MOUNT CARMEL HEALTH

The philosophy of the Sisters of the Holy Cross, expresses a deep and lasting commitment to the quality of patient care.

That commitment was born on a limestone peak on the coast of Israel before the birth of Christ. Known as Mount Carmel, the mountainside was a refuge, a sanctuary, a place of spiritual and physical healing.

Mount Carmel Health in Columbus is such a place, too, thanks to Dr. W.B. Hawkes and Dr. John Hamilton. Hawkes, a prominent Columbus physician and president of the board of trustees of the Columbus Medical College, believed the growing community needed another hospital. He provided the initial funds, donated the 150-square-foot lot of what is now 793 West State Street, and en-listed fellow trustee Hamilton to help him bring his vision to life.

Before construction could begin, Hawkes died, but Hamilton saw to it that the project continue. He also sought the help of the Sisters of the Holy Cross in Notre Dame, Indiana, an order well known for its hospital management services. Today Mount Carmel Health is a member of the Holy Cross Health System and is still under the auspices of the Sisters of the Holy Cross.

On July 5, 1886, Mother M. Angela and Sister M. Rufina Dunn arrived in Columbus to bring a hospital to life. Eleven days later the four-story Hawkes Hospital of Mount Carmel opened its doors. It had 18 private rooms, an operating room, an amphitheater, and two wards.

Above: Stained-glass windows, originally part of a chapel built in 1908, adorn the modern Medical Staff Building Auditorium.

Left: The Hawkes Hospital of Mount Carmel in 1886.

Although she lived only a short time after the hospital opened, Mother M. Angela started a tradition of strong leadership that has been carried forward for more than 100 years.

Sister M. Lydia, in charge when the hospital was incorporated in September 1886, received permission a year later to acquire another plot of land. Sister M. Therese directed the hospital in 1891 when the cornerstone was laid for the addition and when six more lots were purchased in 1895. That same year the hospital first received permission to admit obstetrical cases.

Sister M. Brendan, known as "the builder," ushered in the twentieth century. Although the institution was still in debt from previous additions and purchases, she forged ahead with new plans. A nursing school was begun in 1903, a six-story hospital wing was added in 1908, and a new chapel was opened that same year.

On the Tuesday after Easter in 1913, the Sisters again found themselves reaching out in charity. The Olentangy and Scioto rivers overflowed their banks and Mount Carmel was an island in a muddy sea, providing food, clothing, and shelter for the homeless. For a time Mount Carmel was nicknamed "The Ark."

Sister Brendan recalled the time thusly: "The roar of raging water, the ominous, weird voices of the elements at war, the cries of the distressed filled me with thoughts of . . . the omnipotent power of God, flooding my soul with thanksgiving for His goodness in sending us so many homeless ones to be cared for in His name . . ."

After the flood and after her new nurses' home was com-

Right: A young couple looks on in obvious joy at the beginning of a new life. At Mount Carmel Medical Center, the whole family is encouraged to participate in the birthing experience.

Lower Right: A Mount Carmel nurse takes time for a private moment with a patient. The "high touch" approach is integral to the philosophy of Mount Carmel Health and the Sisters of the Holy Cross.

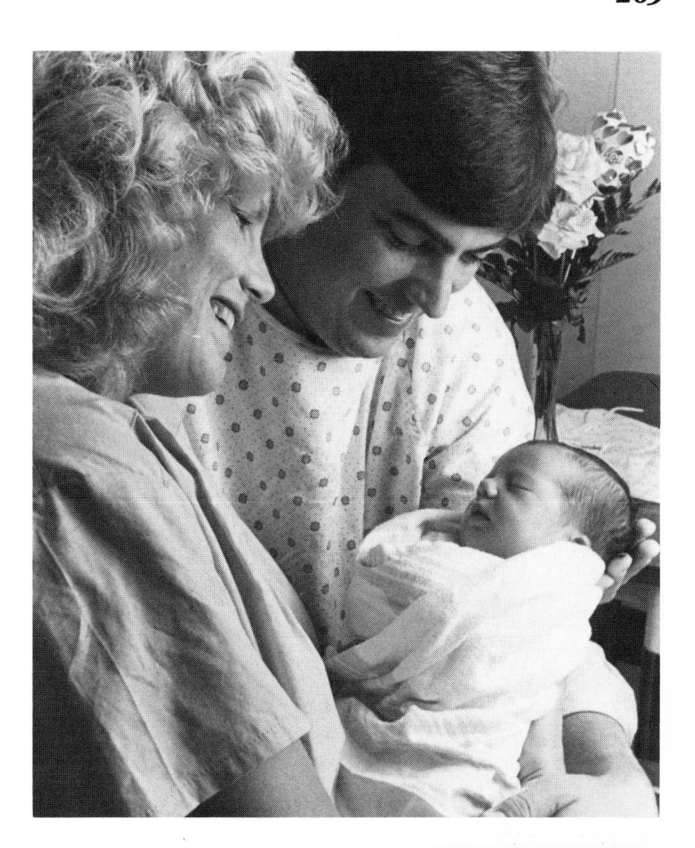

pleted, Sister Brendan died. But Mount Carmel continued to build on its solid foundation. A new 39-room convent became a reality in the late 1920s to accommodate the growing number of Sisters. The patient load had grown, too, and by the late 1930s the 250-bed Mount Carmel Hospital and its staff of 77 physicians was serving nearly 7,000 patients annually.

The 1940s had more milestones for Mount Carmel. Following World War II the hospital's first set of triplets was born. And once again it was time for expansion. Work was begun on a nine-story addition to the East and South wings.

The School of Nursing's first male student was graduated in 1951, the year the new Physical Medicine Department was opened. Two years later the addition was dedicated as the hospital swelled to 415 beds and 64 bassinets, just in time for the Baby Boom.

With moon walks, computers, lasers, and the discovery of DNA, the pace of technological sophistication accelerated. "Full hospital care must now be made available on a scale never before known, and this takes more equipment, more technicians, more medical specialists, and more floor space," said Sister M. Lolita, administrator.

Columbus' first outpatient alcoholism clinic, a day care center, the first catheterization lab and coronary care unit in the area, and the first dialysis unit in central Ohio were all but a part of Mount Carmel's growth in the 1960s. The total number of beds reached 500, and work began on a second hospital, Mount Carmel East.

The Sisters welcomed their first patient to the 233-bed facility—since expanded to 292 beds—in 1972. By the end of the decade the two hospitals were admitting more than 18,000 patients annually, responding to 34,000 emergency cases, and performing nearly 9,000 surgeries a year.

By the time Mount Carmel reached 100 years of service in 1986, it encompassed 523 beds in its teaching hospital (the Mount Carmel Medical Center), 292 beds at Mount Carmel East Hospital, four primary care centers, the Mount Carmel School of Nursing, the Ohio Heart and Vascular Institute at Mount Carmel, and Mount Carmel Graduate Medical Education. Emergency services had expanded as well, in line with the institution's status as a tertiary care center for central Ohio and beyond.

Additional special programs include the Cancer Institute at Mount Carmel, the Alzheimer's Center, family-centered maternity care, and outpatient clinic and surgery

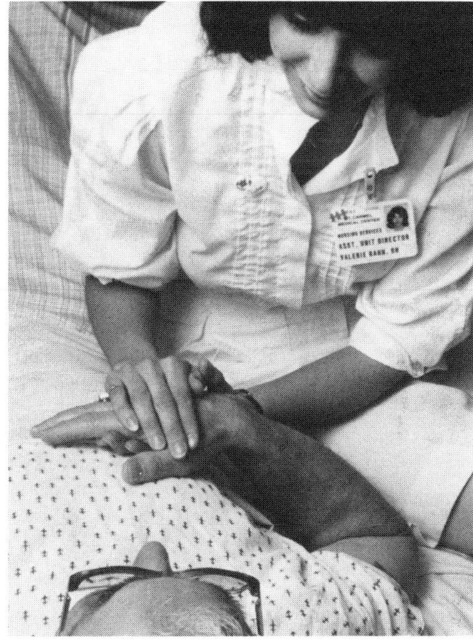

centers at each hospital.

Mount Carmel has gone far beyond serving the needs of the sick and injured. The legacy of the 1980s includes an emphasis on wellness, helping people to choose and lead the life-styles that will keep them out of acute care units.

As Mount Carmel Health headed into its second century, Sister Gladys Marie, president, reflected on the occasion. "It is through the vision of those who have come before us that we have become who we are and who we will be," she said. "They were clear-sighted people who saw the world as it was, imagined it as it should be, and courageously created what they envisioned.

"We are proud to continue to live in their spirit . . . the spirit of vision, the spirit of imagination, the spirit of life."

ARTHUR ANDERSEN & CO.

Around Ohio, the United States, and the world, Arthur Andersen & Co. is well known and highly respected for its wide range of services in accounting and auditing, tax consultation, and management information consultation. With more than 800 Ohio employees in Cleveland, Columbus, Cincinnati, Toledo, and Dayton, the firm's success can be attributed to a time-tested recipe that combines fairness, hard work, and honesty in client relationships.

The phrases that were important to Arthur Andersen when he began the company 75 years ago, in fact, are still important today—concepts such as Think Straight, Talk Straight, Quality Without Compromise, Growth From Within, The Client Comes First, and The One-Firm Philosophy.

Throughout its history a large part of Arthur Andersen's corporate philosophy has also been its keen respect and constant encouragement of creativity and innovation, from taking part in the installation of the first business computer in 1952 to creating the first and most wide-ranging internal training program for its employees. Excellence, meanwhile, is always important and is evident in such practices as the company's uniform standards of operation worldwide.

Founded in 1913 in Chicago and built on such a straightforward philosophic foundation, Arthur Andersen currently has some 200 offices in more than 50 countries. The firm employs approximately 40,000 people and serves more than 100,000 clients worldwide.

The company came to Ohio when the Cleveland office opened in 1946 with just 17 employees. With 325 employees today, the Cleveland office is the firm's largest in the state and is located in the heart of the city's financial district from where it serves both *Fortune* 500 companies and small, closely held businesses throughout northeastern Ohio.

Arthur Andersen is well represented in other major Ohio cities as well. The Cincinnati office, which opened in 1957, has 250 employees. The Columbus office, which started 10 years later, has 210. Meanwhile, the Dayton office, which opened in 1976, and the Toledo facility, which followed in 1977, both have 30 employees.

From northern to southern Ohio, Arthur Andersen serves many of the state's major corporations and successful closely held businesses as well as major banks, department stores, law firms, and hospitals, not to mention local government.

It is much the same around the country and the world. After all, Arthur Andersen & Co.'s reputation was built on a proud foundation, a base that makes the firm strong today and speaks well for tomorrow.

Though the skylines may change, Arthur Andersen's service remains the same.

Columbus Office: 41 South High Street

Cincinnati Office: 425 Walnut Street, Suite 1500

Dayton Office: Court House Plaza, Suite 1900

Cleveland Office: 1717 East Ninth Street

Toledo Office: 300 Madison Avenue

SEA WORLD OF OHIO

An animal behaviorist greets Shamu, the 6,800-pound killer whale who eats 150 pounds of restaurant-quality fish daily. Sea World trainers and marine mammals share a close, friendly relationship based on trust.

Since 1970 Sea World of Ohio has entertained and enlightened more than 22 million visitors. Most come away from these close encounters with marine mammalkind with wonder and respect.

The story begins in 1964, when three fraternity brothers from the University of California started an oceanarium on a salt marsh in San Diego. It thrived, and the firm soon looked to Ohio for expansion.

Sea World found an ideal spot by Geauga Lake (formerly Picnic Lake) in Aurora, a town 500 miles from the sea but within 100 miles of 8 million people. A fun spot since the 1840s, the area once featured the elegant Kent House hotel, as well as a dance pavilion, roller rink, roller coaster, and boat launch.

Sea World of Ohio opened in May 1970 with a whale and dolphin show, sea lion show, Hawaiian Village, dolphin and sea lion feeder pools, and a few food and gift shops. It soon saw a new water ski stadium featuring some of the world's best skiers and dancing water fountains synchronized to music (1971), a new aquarium (1972), Sunja, the 650-pound water-skiing elephant (1973), and Cap'n Kids' World (1975).

Sea World's success in California, Ohio, and Orlando, Florida (which opened in 1974), attracted the interest of investment-oriented companies. In 1976 Harcourt Brace Jovanovich, the nation's largest textbook publisher, purchased Sea World for $50 million. Under new management, Sea World bought Florida's Cypress Gardens, and built Boardwalk and Baseball in Baseball City, Florida. Its fourth and largest marine life park opened in San Antonio, Texas, in the spring of 1988.

Investments in the Ohio park have continued. It added the Nautilus Theatre to feature Canadian lumberjacks and other top-name acts (1977), introduced walrus to the seal and otter show (1979), hosted Boomer the dog of NBC-TV fame (1980-1982), witnessed the birth of its first harbor seal and sea lion pup litters, and unveiled a one-million-gallon Shamu facility (1982).

In recent years the park has kept crowds lingering at night with an evening show package that includes a permanent full-color laser light show synchronized with music and fireworks. In 1985 it opened Penguin Encounter, a $3.5-million home to 110 penguins of six species. In 1986 it began hosting Winter Festival between Thanksgiving and the weekend after New Year's Day, offering skating, tobogganing for children, seal and otter shows, snow flier skiers, holiday shopping, and a winter wonderland.

The Ohio park employs 125 people year round and about 1,200 more during the summer. The summer employees earn money for tuitions, fatten teaching salaries, or boost retirement incomes or household allowances.

Sea World takes its education mission seriously, offering year-round classes and workshops at "hands-on" educational exhibits. It also sponsors outreach programs that bring instructors equipped with life-size inflatable whales and other props to landlocked midwestern schools.

Years ago Sea World, Inc., initiated a beached animal program to care for injured or stranded marine animals worldwide. Animals able to survive in the wild are released; the rest find a "nursing home" in one of the parks. Sea World research teams also cooperate with various private and government institutions in scientific studies. They are finding out about how long penguins live and how one might breed endangered sea cows.

Daring young men on flying water skis, one of seven shows making waves at Sea World.

MK-FERGUSON COMPANY

***Left:** Busy at work on the National Cash Register Company's assembly line in Dayton, Ohio. This was the first contract awarded to The H.K. Ferguson Company shortly after its founding in 1918 by Harold Kingsley Ferguson.*

***Above:** The Defense Nuclear Waste Processing Facility shown here is yet another MK-Ferguson project in the firm's long history of working with nuclear energy.*

Cleveland-based MK-Ferguson Company is a major subsidiary of the Morrison Knudsen Corporation, one of the world's largest engineering and construction firms. Founded in Cleveland on August 5, 1918, by Harold Kingsley Ferguson under the name The H.K. Ferguson Company, it became a wholly owned subsidiary of Morrison Knudsen Corporation in 1950. The firm then became MK-Ferguson Company in 1985 to emphasize its expanding role as a major Morrison Knudsen subsidiary, supplying engineering and construction services to both the industrial and power markets. Since 1918, the firm has completed thousands of projects for many of the world's largest concerns in all 50 states and more than 55 foreign countries.

In the early decades of this century, construction involved a long and tedious process. After a period with General Electric's electric motor plant in Schenectady, New York, Harold Kingsley Ferguson helped streamline that construction process by offering design, engineering, and construction services by one company. His namesake business was begun with limited capital but unlimited ambition and vision, and became one of America's first total responsibility builders. Soon some of America's sharpest manufacturers beat a path to the company's doors.

Work order number one went to National Cash Register (now NCR Corporation) in Dayton. Later that year Procter & Gamble awarded the first of more than 150 contracts to The H.K. Ferguson Company. In 1919 General Electric signed the first of more than 70 contracts with the firm, and two years later H.K. Ferguson carried out its first project for the chemical process industry.

H.K. Ferguson continued to refine and advance its technology. The firm earned repeat business through its interest in improving a client's productivity, as well as by staying on schedule and within budget. Its rapid growth paralleled the growth of the companies—and industries—it served.

During World War II the firm geared up for a vast wartime effort to construct numerous defense plants and depots. At one point, as many as 25,000 employees were on the payroll. The organization vastly diversified; it became the first to build synthetic rubber plants in the United States and was also the designer and constructor of the first full-scale thermal diffusion plant for the Manhattan Project in Oak Ridge, Tennessee.

The Manhattan Project was completed in 1944 and marked the firm's beginning of a long history of working with nuclear energy. Over the past five decades the company has covered all aspects of the nuclear cycle, from uranium ore processing and commercial nuclear plant construction to operating plant retrofit and nuclear waste disposal.

In 1950 The H.K. Ferguson Company was purchased by Morrison Knudsen Corporation of Boise, Idaho. Founded in 1912, Morrison Knudsen had made its name early in water-reclamation projects and had been prominent in the construction of the Hoover, Bonneville, Imperial, and Grand Coulee dams. Today it ranks as one of the world's largest engineering and construction organizations with Ferguson contributing significantly to that reputation.

The H.K. Ferguson Company continued to be headquartered in Cleveland and to build on its reputation with a client list that reads like a Who's Who in power and industry.

The mid-1950s also marked the firm's entry into the steel industry. The construction of Dominion Foundries & Steel in Hamilton, Ontario, led to the company's participation in the design and/or construction of more than one-quarter of the United States' basic oxygen furnace steel-

This 507 MW, two-unit coal-fired power plant, constructed by MK-Ferguson, is one in a wide range of power generation projects in the fossil energy area.

making capacity. It built one of the first steel mills in the nation to combine three major processes under one roof: basic oxygen steel-making, vacuum degassing, and continuous casting.

Today MK-Ferguson Company successfully tackles the construction and engineering of manufacturing, process, power, and research and development facilities for an increasingly wide variety of industries and government. These markets include aerospace, cement, chemicals, metals, food and beverage, electronics, general manufacturing, paint and resins, pharmaceuticals, plastics and rubber, steam and power generation, cogeneration, and energy from waste.

For thriving Anheuser-Busch, Inc., America's largest beer maker, the company has engineered and built six grass roots breweries in addition to major expansion, renovation, and modernization projects.

And, as American industry has increasingly focused on high technology, MK-Ferguson has paved the way with increasingly sophisticated capabilities. The firm has erected clean rooms for manufacturing and testing solid-state electronics, installed state-of-the-art instrumentation and control systems, supplied planning in environmental control and energy conservation, and developed automated systems approaches in computer-integrated manufacturing, robotics, materials handling, logistics, and communications and monitoring.

MK-Ferguson's involvement in energy is broad based and covers nuclear, fossil, and alternate energy activities. During its long history of involvement in the nuclear energy field, MK-Ferguson has constructed nuclear power generation plants and today serves as a major contractor for the modification, retrofit, and maintenance of operating facilities. As a major contractor for the Department of Energy, the company is in the forefront of activities in the area of high- and low-level nuclear waste storage, disposal, and remedial action.

In the fossil energy area, MK-Ferguson has participated in a wide variety of power generation projects that have included central stations, institutional heating plants, industrial steam plants, and cogeneration plants, as well as services to operational facilities including retrofit, upgrade, and maintenance.

Since the early 1970s MK-Ferguson has been a leader in the development of alternative energy facilities. In addition to cogeneration facilities, the firm has been involved in geothermal facilities, municipal solid waste facilities, and research and pilot plant projects.

Even before wartime efforts, MK-Ferguson has been and continues to be a provider of services for government agencies on the local, state, and national level. The company today performs work for the Department of Energy, the Department of Defense, the Department of State, the National Aeronautics and Space Administration (NASA), and numerous other state and local governments and agencies.

Today, with headquarters in downtown Cleveland, offices in San Francisco, and operations throughout the country, MK-Ferguson Company looks forward to completing its seventh decade of achievement and to building new worlds in the decades ahead.

MK-Ferguson has designed and built six grass roots breweries for Anheuser-Busch, including this Columbus, Ohio, facility.

UNIVERSITY HOSPITALS OF CLEVELAND

University Hospitals of Cleveland, one of the largest and best known teaching hospitals in the country, cosponsors Ohio's largest biomedical research complex with Case Western Reserve University schools of medicine, nursing, and dentistry. UHC unites five specialty hospitals under one management: Lakeside and Hanna House hospitals for adult medical-surgical cases, MacDonald Hospital for Women, Rainbow Babies and Childrens Hospital, and Hanna Pavilion for psychiatric care.

UHC's 125-year history lists many impressive firsts, such as the first infant formula, the forerunner of Similac (Dr. Henry Gerstenberger and Dr. Chauncey Wyckoff, 1915), first gas anesthesia used in surgery (Dr. George Crile, Sr., 1916), the first formula to eliminate goiter (Dr. David Marine, the Father of Iodized Salt, 1924), and the first cornea transplant (Dr. Charles Thomas, 1939). It was the first U.S. hospital to house a whole body MRI scanner, a revolutionary device that makes detailed pictures of the body's interior using safe radio waves and a magnetic field—saving patients from exposure to X rays (1982).

Its staff has included pioneers, such as Dr. Claude Beck, who performed the first mitral valve heart surgery (1924), the first surgical operation for the treatment of coronary artery disease (1935), and the first successful defibrillation of a human heart (1947). It has pioneered lifesaving techniques, such as cardiopulmonary resuscitation (Dr. Claude Beck and Robert Hosler, 1950).

UHC's member hospitals began as charities. The roots of Lakeside Hospital date to 1863, when a group of citizens meeting in the Old Stone (now First Presbyterian) Church established a "Home for the Friendless" for Civil War refugees. Later its sponsors began to provide medical care for the poor and created the Cleveland City Hospital. Severe overcrowding led to a move to the Marine Hospital on Lake Street in the mid-1870s, with a name change to Lakeside Hospital.

In the mid-1890s Lakeside Hospital erected a modern 11-building complex on Lake Avenue and formally affiliated with Western Reserve University. By 1906 the dispensary cared for 24,000 patients a year.

In 1910 the Flexner national study on medical schools cited the close, mutually beneficial relationship between Lakeside Hospital and Western Reserve University. Motivated by the report and the need for more space, Lakeside Hospital decided to build next door to the university's future medical school in the University Circle area. Its plans were interrupted by war, which saw Lakeside's medical unit become the first Army unit active overseas during World War I.

Following the war construction of the new medical center finally began. The medical school was completed first, followed by Maternity Hospital and Babies and Childrens Hospital in 1925, and Lakeside Hospital in 1930.

Maternity Hospital began in an old house at 58 Huron Street in 1882. At first largely a charitable institution, it grew as hospital delivery became more widely accepted. Eventually its trustees decided to build larger quarters at University Circle. (Maternity Hospital was renamed MacDonald House in 1936 in tribute to its first superintendent, Calvina MacDonald.)

Though Lakeside Hospital had a children's ward, members of Cleveland's medical community desired a hospital devoted to children. Its forerunner, the Infant's

Below: A Lakeside Hospital operating room circa 1905.

Right: The pediatric clinic, circa 1930, which later became part of Rainbow Babies and Childrens Hospital.

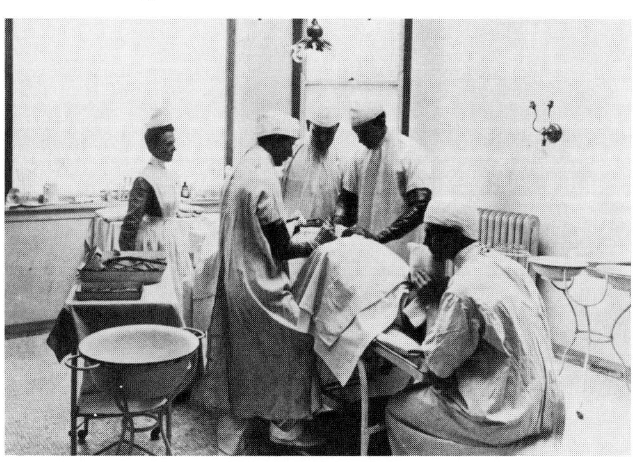

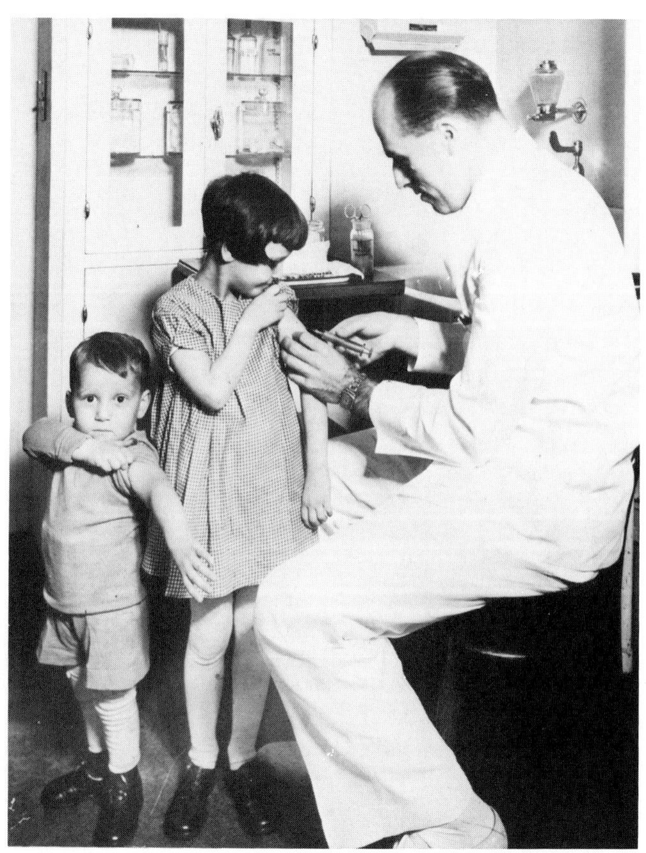

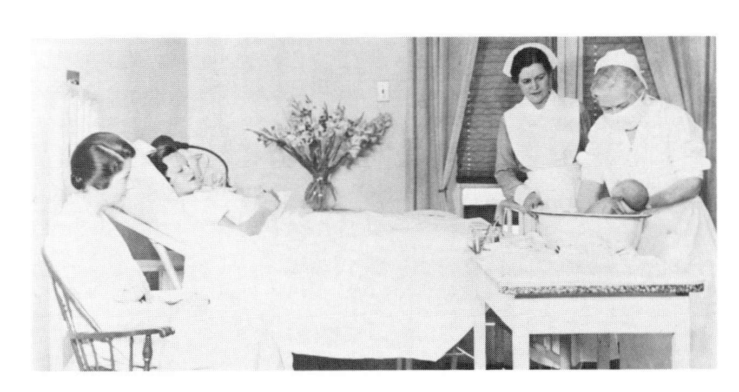

A new mother receives infant care instruction from nurses in the 1930s at Maternity Hospital, forerunner of MacDonald Hospital for Women.

Part of the research facilities of Ireland Cancer Center, headed by Dr. Nathan Berger. The center brings together a team of experts in treating cancer patients and has been designated by the National Cancer Institute as part of a comprehensive clinical cancer center, one of only 20 nationwide.

Clinic of the Milk Fund Association (1906), set up dispensaries where mothers could bring their infants for physician exams and to get milk bottled under sanitary conditions.

In 1923 the founders of the dispensary conducted a successful fund-raising campaign to build a babies' and children's hospital. Both it and Maternity Hospital joined Lakeside Hospital to form University Hospitals of Cleveland in 1925. To improve efficiency, the administration of all individual hospitals was consolidated in 1940.

Another forerunner, Rainbow Hospital for Crippled and Convalescent Children, began in 1887 when a group of young women began looking after the needs of poor children. They established Rainbow Cottage in 1891, and for many years the cottage provided care to children with bone infections, rheumatic fever, polio, and other crippling illnesses. In 1969 Rainbow moved to University Circle and two years later united with Babies and Childrens Hospital, the first Cystic Fibrosis Center in the country (established by Drs. LeRoy Matthews and Carl Doershuk, 1956).

In 1972 the Rainbow Babies and Childrens Hospital staff (Drs. John Kennell and Marshall Klaus) first observed the importance of close physical contact between mother and child during the first hours of life. Today it boasts one of the nation's most successful pediatric intensive care units, as 94 percent of its infants go home.

Meanwhile, MacDonald Hospital has become the only women's hospital in Ohio. It now goes beyond traditional obstetrics and gynecology into areas such as breast care. It also has a nationally recognized program in menopause founded by Dr. Leon Speroff, who developed the first combination menopause pills.

Benjamin Rose Hospital, a pioneer in the field of geriatric care and rehabilitation, merged into UHC in 1957. UHC assumed full responsibility for the operation in 1969, when it became Abington House. Today the elderly receive help at the Geriatric Care Center (1984), a joint effort between UHC and Veterans Administration Medical Center. The center addresses psychiatric, social, and environmental factors for complete care.

Its new Alzheimer Center, headed by Dr. Peter Whitehouse, offers the latest diagnostic techniques, clinical research, drug therapies, and rehabilitation for patients. To assist diagnosis, UHC has installed the first positron emission tomography (PET) scanner in Ohio, an imaging device useful in diagnosing this and other disorders.

The emotionally disturbed and the mentally ill receive treatment at the Hanna Pavilion, an 80-bed psychiatric hospital founded in 1956. A leader in psychobiology and the treatment of schizophrenia, Dr. Herbert Meltzer helped shape its current program.

Over the years the original Lakeside Hospital continued to grow in specialization and size, necessitating a major expansion of its campus in 1967. In recent years the 280-bed hospital has enhanced care through primary nursing, where each patient's care is coordinated by one nurse.

Since 1984 UHC has been one of five Ohio medical centers to participate in a statewide organ transplant consortium. The hospital and its physicians contribute about 25 percent of gifts and professional fees to a fund to defray patients' transplant costs.

Because cancer recognizes no hospital boundaries, UHC organized the R. Livingston Ireland Cancer Center in 1986. The center builds on UHC's expertise in radiology, chemotherapy, and bone marrow transplantation. It pursues improved care through research into monoclonal antibodies, high-dose chemotherapy, and clinical trials of new therapies and treatments. Some of this and other research is conducted at the Wearn Laboratory for Medical Research, a joint effort between UHC and its university affiliate.

University Hospitals of Cleveland today has more than 1,000 physicians and 1,200 nurses. They follow a strong tradition of quality, their work sharpened by the challenge of research and training some 550 residents. The level of care keeps UHC's 874 beds more than 83 percent occupied and attracts more than 171,000 outpatient visits and 58,000 emergency room/trauma center visits yearly.

CHEMICAL ABSTRACTS SERVICE

There are no chemicals at Chemical Abstracts Service. No laboratories, no Bunsen burners, no glass vials, no beakers, no maze of tubes.

But among the more than 1,400 employees of the Columbus-based service, many are chemists, as well as biologists, physicists, engineers, computer specialists, and a host of other professionals working to make the latest in chemical research accessible to users throughout the world.

The task of reviewing and refining some 12,000 scientific and technical journals from 150 nations as well as thousands of public and private papers is given to the CAS document analysts. They are specialists in both a subject and a language—everything from Afrikaans or Azerbaijani to Macedonian and Vietnamese. Their product is a concise English summary of the research for publication by CAS.

About 9,000 of these summaries are published each week, or more than 450,000 annually. Each has been carefully and completely indexed so that a medical researcher wondering if a particular chemical has proven to be effective against tumors, or an industrial chemist interested in a new process for manufacturing a particular chemical compound, can be led to the pertinent journal articles and patents.

Each weekly issue of the publication, *Chemical Abstracts,* contains more than 9,000 condensations. Nearly 4,000 pages of abstracts are published every month, and every five years CAS compiles the semiannual indexes into a massive collective index of its chemical publications. Most recently this gargantuan undertaking encompassed 163,000 pages in 93 volumes.

In recent years the computer has come to the aid of recording and storing much of this information, ready for CAS on-line access. This makes it possible for scientists almost anywhere in the world to go to terminals in their laboratories or offices, dial up the computer in Columbus, and have displayed almost immediately the titles of everything published on a particular chemical topic in the past 20 years.

That's a long way from the genesis of CAS more than 80 years ago. American chemists, dissatisfied with the coverage of American chemical literature in European abstract journals, advocated a national journal that would recognize their accomplishments. They got their wish in January 1907, when the American Chemical Society first published *Chemical Abstracts* as a nonprofit editorial enterprise.

The first editor was William A. Noyes, Sr., chief chemist for the Bureau of Standards in Washington, D.C. He was succeeded by Austin M. Patterson, which was fortunate for Columbus. Because the former chemical editor of *Webster's Dictionary* lived in Xenia, the society agreed in 1909 to move the editorial office to the campus of The Ohio State University, which had invited the move.

Top left: The entire* Chemical Abstracts *editorial staff in 1928 was housed in a single room of The Ohio State University's McPherson Chemistry Laboratory.

Above: More than 1,400 people work in Chemical Abstracts Service's building complex adjacent to The Ohio State University campus in Columbus.

There were four members of the staff at that time, working in one 15- by 30-foot room. Together they published 15,459 abstracts that year.

In 1914 Patterson resigned due to poor health and was succeeded briefly by John J. Miller, who also resigned that same year. Evan J. Crane, who had been on the staff since 1911, was named editor in 1915. He remained at the helm for the next 43 years and became the first director of

Scientists worldwide can access and search the massive store of chemical information in Chemical Abstracts Service's Columbus computers through terminals in their offices and laboratories.

Chemical Abstracts Service document analysts create English language summaries of and precise index entries for new chemical information published in many languages.

Chemical Abstracts Service when the growing editorial organization was renamed and elevated to the status of a division of the American Chemical Society in 1956.

The years Crane served were both critical and formative years for CAS as it strived for "complete coverage" of the world's chemical literature. Two world wars made the collecting of data particularly difficult.

During World War II, for instance, European papers were sent through Italy and Siberia. Many documents on microfilm were smuggled into Switzerland and routed through Moscow to Columbus, including all-important German patents.

Following the war chemical literature from throughout the world began to pour into Columbus. By the mid-1950s about three-quarters of the publications abstracted for *Chemical Abstracts* came from outside the United States.

As the volume grew so did expenses, and CAS found itself in financial difficulty. The American Chemical Society determined that if CAS was to continue to be self-supporting, subscription policies must be changed drastically. Today CAS pays its own way, including a share of the society's general and administrative expenses, and contributes toward maintaining CAS's general reserve fund.

When Crane, a Columbus native, retired in 1958, he was followed as director by Dale B. Baker, a chemical engineer who had come to CAS from Du Pont in 1946. He, in turn, was succeeded in 1986 by Ronald L. Wigington, an electrical engineer who had been deputy executive director for Washington operations of the American Chemical Society.

During the 1960s and 1970s CAS advanced into the modern era, introducing the world's first computer-produced periodical, *Chemical Titles,* a weekly that lists newly published articles relating to chemistry. Other periodicals that have been added include *CA Selects, CA Section Groupings, Chemical Industry Notes, CAS BioTech Updates,* and *BIOSIS/CAS Selects.*

In 1965 CAS moved into its own large building just north of the OSU campus. A second structure of almost equal size was added in 1973.

In the last half of the 1960s, with financial support from the National Science Foundation, CAS set out to build a highly automated processing system that would produce printed abstracts and indexes more efficiently and economically, and at the same time create a machine-readable data base that could provide the basis for new forms of information services.

That was largely achieved by the mid-1970s. Automated processing opened new doors for publishing, locating, and retrieving chemical information. Major emphasis was placed on expanding the direct delivery of information through on-line computer services and providing answers in seconds that can take hours or even days of page turning to discover through printed abstracts and indexes.

While Chemical Abstracts Service began as an American information service, it is global today in the primary sources it covers, the database it creates, the audience it serves, and the reach of its printed and electronic services. But what has not changed is the total commitment to providing the most comprehensive and accurate secondary information on chemical science and technology in the most useful and convenient form to support the continuing progress of scientific research and development.

NATIONAL CITY CORPORATION

Left: BancOhio's headquarters in Columbus.

Above: National City Center in Cleveland is the headquarters of National City Corporation and National City Bank.

National City Corporation ranks among the nation's top 40 bank holding companies, with 10,000 employees, more than $14 billion in assets, and a network of 335 banking offices. Its banks have about 600,000 personal checking accounts and a portfolio of roughly 40,000 commercial borrowers and 1.5 million retail loans.

The corporation, headquartered in Cleveland, gives its banks much autonomy, including primary responsibility for marketing products. This streamlines decision making, results in faster customer-related decisions, and encourages operating excellence.

The largest of the organization's banks is National City Bank. Its forerunner, City Bank of Cleveland, was, in 1845, the first bank to receive a charter under the Ohio Bank Act. City Bank experienced rapid growth coinciding with the finding of iron ore in Michigan, the construction of area railroads, and the discovery of oil in Pennsylvania.

City Bank became National City Bank in 1865, when the National Bank Act ended the state banking system. National City grew steadily and prospered, maintaining a conservative policy and avoiding speculative loans. It was the only bank in Cleveland that never restricted payments to depositors during the Great Depression of the 1930s.

Its assets grew from $15.5 million in 1919 to $35 million in 1932, $200 million in 1939, and $475 million in 1945. For decades it played a major role in the growth of the local economy through close ties to the corporations that were the foundation of Cleveland's industrial strength.

To meet the challenges of increased competition in the financial services field, NCB directors in 1973 formed a bank holding company, National City Corporation. The corporation has added nine affiliate banks since then. Together they have financed more Ohio businesses than any other financial institution.

National City Corporation took a dramatic step forward in 1984, when it acquired BancOhio Corporation of Columbus, a bank holding company with $6 billion in assets and branches throughout Ohio. BancOhio, incorporated in 1929 by brothers Robert and Harry Wolfe of Columbus, was Ohio's first bank holding company. Its name was spelled "Banc" because under Ohio law only true banks could use "bank" in their names.

The Wolfe brothers, prosperous owners of a shoe factory, entered banking during an economic recession in 1907. An anxious public began lining up at Ohio Trust (later part of First Citizens Trust Company), one of the city's largest banks. The brothers restored confidence by personally depositing $100,000 of their own money. They eventually gained controlling interest in First Citizens Trust and Ohio National Bank.

The Wolfes saw the idea of a bank holding company as a means to simplify the management of two separate institutions. The structure also proved efficient because of economies of scale, service, and technical advice.

BancOhio's creation just before the Great Depression vigorously tested its mettle. Yet its presence helped stabilize the central Ohio economy. Banks in Chillicothe, Delaware, Newark, Zanesville, Washington Court House, Cadiz, and New Lexington joined BancOhio during those trying years. By 1954 there were 21 affiliated banks with deposits in excess of $150 million.

During the 1960s and 1970s BancOhio experienced rapid growth in services and technology, and continued growth in holdings. Then, in 1978, the Ohio Legislature passed a law allowing banks to branch into contiguous counties. After careful consideration, BancOhio decided to merge 40 of its banks, operate the Ohio State Bank of Columbus as a separate institution, and continue the multibank holding company's franchise with both state and national charters. With this move in 1979, the successor, BancOhio National Bank, became the 31st-largest bank in the United States and the largest in Ohio with assets of more than $4.2 billion.

National City Bank, Akron (1984), is an $890-million

Above: National City Bank, Akron.

Center: First National Bank, Dayton.

Right: Ohio Citizens Bank, Toledo.

institution with 30 offices serving Summit, Stark, and Portage counties. It grew out of a merger between two strong institutions, The Goodyear Bank and the Akron area BancOhio National Bank. The Goodyear Bank (1933), founded by The Goodyear Tire and Rubber Company as a convenience to employees, was likely Ohio's only company-owned bank. BancOhio National Bank descended from Dime Savings Bank (1900s), which began by serving small depositors disdained by the large commercial banks, and Akron Morris Plan Bank (1918), also an institution catering to consumers from its earliest days.

First National Bank, Dayton, was originally called The National Bank of Dayton. Its earliest roots show a link to First National Bank of Dayton. It was created in 1961 through the merger of Merchants National Bank and Peoples Bank and Trust Company. Merchants National Bank (1871) began when First National Bank of Dayton (1863) was dissolved, and its directors organized a new national bank to take its place. Peoples Bank and Trust Company grew out of The Morris Plan Bank (1926), which evolved into Peoples Bank of Dayton (1941) and was given the Peoples Bank and Trust Company name (1957). With assets of more than $800 million, First National has 29 offices serving four counties.

In Toledo, Ohio, Citizens Bank opened for business as The Ohio Citizens Trust Company in 1932. A true community effort, the bank's initial $350,000 in assets were supplied by more than 1,000 individuals, including many prominent Toledoans. At the end of 1987 assets exceeded one billion dollars. The bank operated out of its Ohio Building quarters exclusively until it added a West Toledo office (1949), a Colony office (1952), and an Oregon office (1960), and others. Mergers with Spitzer-Rorick Trust and Savings (1959), The Whitehouse State Savings Bank (1966), and The Peoples State Bank of Wauseon (1979) further strengthened the institution and expanded its service area. Over the years the bank has pioneered many new services in the Toledo area. In 1982 its holding company, Ohio Citizens Bancorp, Inc., completed a merger with National City Corporation—an arrangement beneficial to Ohio Citizens' expansion in Northwest Ohio.

The smaller member banks have also had long, rich histories. First National Bank of Ashland traces its heritage in an unbroken line back to 1851, when area merchants formed a bank called Luther, Crall, and Company to extend credit to farmers and cash checks paid to farmers for grain or cattle. Its earliest furniture consisted of a few stools and a counter, while security consisted of a pistol and a small safe. The bank was renamed First National Bank of Ashland in 1874, and has served its community ever since.

National City Bank, Norwalk, is one of the oldest continuing businesses in Norwalk. It was founded in 1881 by former Probate Judge Daniel Fox as a consolation to Norwalk for having lost the railroad route.

National City Bank, Northeast, grew out of the merger between National Union Bank, an institution with roots dating before 1909, and five BancOhio offices in Trumbull County, whose histories date back to the opening of Niles Trust Company in 1909.

Third National Bank of Sandusky (1872) is the oldest national bank in Sandusky and Erie County, an institution that has remained sound through panics, wars, depressions, booms, deflation, and inflation. It became a member of National City Corporation in 1975.

UNITED TELEPHONE COMPANY OF OHIO

Things have changed dramatically from the "good old days" of telephone service. This United Telephone Company of Ohio line crew from shortly after the turn of the century worked day and night to keep basic phone service working.

In the beginning there were many telephone companies in Ohio. They had names like Lemoyne, Frazeysburg Home, Damascus, and Crooksville. Ottawa Farmers Mutual, Oil Belt, and West Cairo were there, too, and all of them, plus nearly 150 more, had the words "telephone company" behind them.

These were all independent companies, independent of the American Telephone and Telegraph Corporation and its Bell System. As the nation turned into the twentieth century, the competition for customers was vigorous, to say the least, and for a time the independents had the upper hand. In 1903, for instance, AT&T had 1,514 main exchanges nationwide and 1.278 million subscribers; the independents combined had four times as many main exchanges and more than 2 million customers.

These independents, most of them in rural areas rather than the cities, were particularly strong in the Midwest. In the "hot" urban markets, it was not unusual for businesses and homes to have telephones of an independent and from Bell to be sure to reach everyone in the city.

A year before the death of telephone inventor Alexander Graham Bell in 1922, the Graham Act exempted telephony from the Sherman Antitrust Act and effectively put an end to the two-telephone-company towns. The act stated that telephone companies constitute a "natural monopoly" and should be allowed to operate as such.

By 1939 the Bell System controlled 83 percent of all the telephones in the United States. But in Ohio a number of small independents continued on that way until 1966. It was on June 30 of that year that what is today known as "the phone company" in 52 communities of Ohio's 88 counties—United Telephone Company of Ohio—was formed.

At the time of incorporation, the new organization served about 87,000 telephones in 26 exchanges located in five Ohio counties. Twenty years later United of Ohio offered service to more than 425,000 access lines in 164 exchange areas.

United of Ohio is a wholly owned subsidiary of United Telecommunications Inc. of Kansas City, Missouri, and a part of United Telephone System, which, in 1966, already was serving customers in 17 states. Mansfield is the headquarters for United of Ohio and is one of three regional offices. The others are in Lima and Warren.

The hallmarks of United of Ohio are innovation and customer satisfaction. In 1981 the company was the first in the state to install fiber optics, hair-thin glass fibers that replace the traditional, and more cumbersome, copper cable.

This pacesetting tradition was evident once again in 1987 with the installation of 112 miles of fiber-optic cable to connect seven central offices from Mansfield to Sidney.

United of Ohio also has made a major commitment to digital technology. In 1978 there were no digital lines; today more than 50 percent of the firm's customers have the benefits of digital switching, such as better connections and voice clarity, and the ability to subscribe to advanced telecom services such as call waiting and call forwarding.

A third innovation was the formation of United Telephone Long Distance Inc. in 1986, the United Telephone Company of Ohio's own long-distance company. The wholly owned subsidiary today competes for customers in equal access areas for customers who prefer one local source for their local and long-distance service and one bill for those services.

In 1981 United Telephone Company of Ohio became the first phone company in the state to install fiber optics. The hair-thin optical fibers must be fused together under a microscope so that the connection is perfect for clear transmission.

THE JUDSON-BROOKS COMPANY

Above, left to right: The original Brooks Company pressroom, 1934; wooden type blocks, 1930s; one of the first documents conforming to the new Securities and Exchange Commission Act of 1933 was a prospectus for the new Republic Steel Corporation, printed by the Judson Company in 1935; and a steel line gauge used for typespacing and page layout, 1930s.

Left: The Judson-Brooks Company operates out of the renovated 73,000-square-foot Brooks Company printing house, founded in 1888 and located near the heart of Cleveland's legal and financial district.

Cleveland had for years the nation's third-largest concentration of corporate headquarters. This meant a steady market for quality legal and financial services—and legal and financial printing. The Judson-Brooks Company of Cleveland, now Ohio's largest legal and financial printer, is geared to its clients' special needs.

Judson-Brooks employees are on call 24 hours a day, six days a week. They provide strict confidentiality and immediate turnaround on printing jobs. The firm supplies conference rooms where lawyers and financial officers can revise drafts around the clock. Then, after the documents are cleared and printed, the company delivers them locally using its own personnel, and nationally using couriers. Service has always been and will always be Judson-Brooks' key to success.

The Judson Company began in Cleveland in 1875 as Wynn and Judson, a general printing firm for many years.

In 1933 the Securities and Exchange Act gave birth to the Securities and Exchange Commission and to a set of regulations governing how securities should be issued. The Judson Company was chosen to print one of the first documents conforming to the new SEC Act—a prospectus for the new Republic Steel Corporation (now part of LTV Steel). Judson's performance in printing the mountain of materials needed led to many other filings, such as those for Thompson Products (now TRW), Cleveland Graphite Bronze (Clevite), and Timken Roller Bearing.

A second chapter started January 1, 1950, when Joe Fogg and Walter Pryor bought The Judson Company. The two young men had as their goal to provide exceptional service, and their efforts paid off. By 1960 they were able to purchase the Brooks Company, a printing business founded in 1888, and its 73,000-square-foot building near the heart of Cleveland's legal and financial district.

The partners now had the location, capacity, quality offset printing presses, and people with specific printing skills to specialize in legal, financial, and ballot printing. They also understood SEC regulations and filing requirements.

Their newly merged organization, The Judson-Brooks Company, benefited from the dramatic increase in securities offerings and new federal regulations requiring more detailed disclosures to investors. It also benefited from computer equipment, which has helped its typesetters keep up with a quadrupling of sales in the past decade.

Typical printing jobs include prospectuses, registration statements, municipal bond offerings, and general corporate housekeeping documents. Three project orders that stand out in size and scope are the financing of the pipeline for Standard Oil (now BP America) and the creation of Centerior Energy and the recent sale and leaseback of some of Centerior's properties.

In 1985 the most recent chapter began when The Judson-Brooks Company was purchased by Bowne & Company, a nationwide financial printer headquartered in New York. Today Judson-Brooks has more than 100 employees between its Cleveland, Cincinnati, and Columbus offices, and serves a market that covers Ohio, western New York, and northern Kentucky.

Recent mergers and takeovers have brought a flood of business, but this shrinks the pool of customers. Fortunately, The Judson-Brooks Company is witness to Ohio's ability to generate many new businesses year after year.

SCOTT KRAUSS NEWS AGENCY

The Scott Krauss News Agency sprang from an 11-year-old boy's opportunity to sell newspapers. The opportunity came February 15, 1898, the day the news reached Columbus that the battleship *Maine* had been sunk in Havana harbor.

"Extra! Extra! Extra!" Scott Adkins Krauss shouted on the streets near his home on the city's near north side. Front doors flew open at the shout. From parlor to barbershop, cash customers clamored for a copy of the newspaper. Everyone, it seemed to the youngster, was eager for his service.

The pennies he pocketed that day, along with a willingness to work and a grim determination to succeed, led to the creation four years later of a Columbus business that is still going strong.

Krauss made it through the eighth grade before opportunity knocked again, this time in the unlikely guise of smallpox. Newsboy Krauss was buying his papers from a branch agent of the *Ohio State Journal* and the *Columbus Evening Dispatch.* Unfortunately for the agent, John Neiderlander, smallpox broke out in the apartment above his store.

Bad news travels fast. Soon no one would touch the papers handled through the Neiderlander store. The agent was forced out of business.

Above: Scott Krauss (left) at age 15 in the doorway of his first place of business in Columbus.

Left: The headquarters for the Scott Krauss News Agency is located at 777 East Goodale Boulevard, Columbus.

Although only 15, Krauss became the new agent, and with \$15—\$5 of it borrowed from a friendly merchant—he put down the first month's rent on a vacant storeroom at 654 North High Street. In 1903, four years to the day after carrying the news of the *Maine,* Krauss opened his own business.

"I had a stock of candy, tobacco, pipes, gas mantles, paperback thrillers, and novels," he recalled 50 years later. "Of course I had to watch the penny profits." But he did "chisel a 15-cent collar out of the business in order to put up a front, and to it was added a prefabricated cravat."

He remembered he had an assistant that first year, "one Hank Gowdy, and he was paid \$2.50 per week. This is the same Hank Gowdy who became the Hall of Fame catcher of major league baseball . . . If you think Hank was underpaid, it can be recorded here that he had candy privileges while I went home to supper."

The news distribution business expanded rapidly. In 1906 the young entrepreneur acquired the distribution of the *Cincinnati Enquirer,* a real coup, and Krauss moved into the high-rent district downtown, right across from the capitol. Shortly thereafter Krauss picked up the Curtis Publishing Company franchise, too, giving him distribution rights to the *Saturday Evening Post* and its sister publication, the *Ladies Home Journal.*

That was but the beginning of an ever-expanding enterprise. By the time the Scott Krauss News Agency reached its Golden Jubilee year, it was distributing more than 5 million magazines annually, nearly as many comics, 1.5 million newspapers, and the same number of pocket-size books to central Ohio customers in nearly 100 communities. More recently the territory and the number of publications handled has increased again, producing sales of \$23 million in 1986.

Nine years before he died in 1976 at age 89, Krauss sold the agency to Roger L. Scherer, who had similar distributorships in Michigan. Today the periodical division of the Scherer Companies, based in Columbus, is the nation's eighth-largest distributor of magazines and books.

PREFORMED LINE PRODUCTS COMPANY

Hidden in the Cleveland suburb of Mayfield Village is the world's leading cable dynamics and vibration laboratory. In this lab Preformed Line Products engineers simulate wind storms and ice conditions to test products designed to protect power and telecommunication cables from damage. Their research helps utilities and telecommunications companies worldwide ensure the steady transmission of energy and communication—the lifelines of modern civilization.

Since 1947 Preformed Line Products has been the recognized leader in the industry it built, overhead line vibration-control products.

Its story begins in the early 1940s, when a customer complained to Thomas Peterson, an electrical engineer with U.S. Steel & Wire Company, about conductors strung between high-voltage transmission towers breaking at the point of support. To protect such lines, electric companies commonly wrapped them with several feet of soft aluminum wires and then clamped the wire ends. But these wires were prone to loosening, and the conductors still snapped or badly abraded.

Peterson came up with the idea of preforming armor rods—strong aluminum alloy rods manufactured in a helical (tubular spiral) shape. In tests he found that the correct diameter preformed rod wrapped around a power line required no clamps and gave better protection.

In 1947 Peterson set up Preformed Line Products Company. His Armor Rods reached the market just as the entire electrical utility industry started booming with the growth of suburbia.

A series of new products followed, including WRAP-LOCK® Ties used to attach conductor cables to insulators on poles and buildings, ARMOR-GRIP® Suspension fittings used to support cables and control damaging vibration and stress, spacers that prevent cables from slapping together, dampers to quell vibration, and a variety of "dead ends" for anchoring cables.

To create and test effective products, the company set up a vibration laboratory. Jon Ruhlman, an aeronautical engineer experienced in aircraft vibrations, conducted fruitful research and advanced to director of research and engineering. When Peterson died in 1962, Ruhlman was elected president.

The product line found ready markets around the world, and Preformed Line Products now has 17 plants in 11 countries and 1,800 employees worldwide. In the United States there are some 550 employees and three plants—the original Cleveland manufacturing plant being phased out and modern facilities in Rogers, Arkansas, and Albemarle, North Carolina. The company's world headquarters and research center remain in the Cleveland area.

While competitors have entered the market, especially as patents have expired, Preformed Line Products has stayed a step ahead. It created a new vibration-measurement business and developed lines of underground products, largely for the telephone industry.

In recent years the telecommunications industry has been making the transition from copper and aluminum wire to fiber-optics. Preformed Line Products responded by investing in its own fiber-optics company and pursued a rapid expansion in fiber-optics technology. Telecommunications now makes up nearly half its sales, with the main product being stainless-steel splice cases to protect spliced copper or fiber-optic cables from water, dirt, and other contamination.

The firm's PREFORMED products solve a range of cable and line problems. But now and again Preformed Line Products Company people will be called on location to solve a particularly knotty line construction problem—high mountain passes in South America, high winds over long river spans such as the Massena Crossing of the St. Lawrence River, and underwater systems threatened by strong currents.

Above right: Jon Ruhlman, president of Preformed Line Products Company, oversaw its expansion overseas and into the fiber-optics market.

Right: Linemen install ARMOR-GRIP® Suspension units to protect 345-kilovolt, high-tension lines spanning the Hudson River at Indian Point, New York—a distance of 4,273 feet between two 475-foot towers.

CYCLOPS CORPORATION

At Mansfield, Ohio, Empire-Detroit Steel melts and processes a variety of carbon and electrical steels and first operation blanks. Here workers are cold rolling steel to impart the correct physical and mechanical properties.

Cyclops Corporation is an industrial holding company based in Pittsburgh, Pennsylvania, that can trace its ancestry to 1884 and Titusville, Pennsylvania. Today, however, some of the company's strongest ties are to operations across the Ohio River in the Buckeye State.

The Cyclops chronology begins with the founding in 1908 of the Universal Rolling Mill Company in Bridgeville, Pennsylvania. It became the Universal Steel Company before merging 18 years later with the Cyclops Steel Company, founded in 1884 by an English immigrant, Charles Burgess.

When the two companies merged, a new name—Universal-Cyclops Steel Corporation—was adopted. It stuck until 1965, when the present name was chosen for the parent corporation and divisions were created.

Today the corporation operates in two major business segments through a dozen companies, one-third of which are either based in Ohio or have a major operation in the state.

The first segment of the organization is the production of steel products, which includes flat rolled carbon; galvanized, silicon, and stainless steels; and fabricated tubular products.

Through the nonresidential construction segment, the company engages in the fabrication, engineering, and erection of metal and foam panel wall systems; the fabrication and sale of roof, floor, and bridge deck; and prepainted metal coils.

In 1958 Universal-Cyclops acquired its first Ohio property: Empire Steel Corporation. Empire, based in Mansfield, was 46 years old at the time, although it had operated under a number of different names. Today it is the Empire-Detroit Steel Division, but its acquisition was a first Ohio step for Cyclops.

The Coshocton Stainless Division is an outgrowth of Universal Cyclops Specialty Steel Division, which was established in 1965. The Coshocton plant was opened in 1959, however, and is known for its high-quality stainless steels, which are used in automotive and appliance trim, cutlery, cookware, kitchen utensils, and tubing.

E.G. Smith Construction Products, founded in 1932, has operations in Pittsburgh, Pennsylvania; Los Angeles, California; and Cambridge, Ohio. The latter plant opened in 1966, seven years before the Smith organization was acquired by Cyclops.

The most recent acquisition came in 1987, when Cyclops brought into its fold Miami Industries from Allegheny Corp. Miami Industries has been a part of the Miami community since 1952.

Coshocton Stainless, located in Coshocton, Ohio, produces premium-quality stainless sheet and strip for use in automobiles, appliances, cutlery, and other consumer and industrial goods.

Empire-Detroit has grown from a small producer of carbon flat rolled steels to a major producer of galvanized and stainless steels, silicon steels, first operation blanks and carbon steels.

The Mansfield plant, with a work force of about 1,400, is one of the area's largest employers. The plant area now totals nearly 780 acres, a far cry from the hand-operated rolling mill three-quarters of a century ago. Then the mill was known as National Rolling Mills Company, formed by a group of Cleveland area iron and steel makers. The entire work force numbered less than 100 people.

Two years later William H. Davey of Massillon and other members of his family bought controlling interest in the mill and changed the name to the Mansfield Sheet and Tin Plate Company. New open-hearth furnaces were installed, and the mill operations grew with the community.

In 1928 the company became Empire Sheet and Tin Plate, and five years later the Empire Steel Company emerged. When the Reeves Steel and Manufacturing Company, founded in 1900 in Dover, was acquired in 1958, the name was changed to Empire-Reeves Steel Corporation.

With the acquisition of the Detroit Steel Corporation by Cyclops and a realignment of plants within the division, the company finally reached its current identification, Empire-Detroit Steel Division.

Elwin G. Smith founded his company in Emsworth, Pennsylvania, in 1932, in a plant known to locals as "the old tin factory." Six hourly employees fabricated metal for a variety of industries, and at the end of the first year—it was the height of the Depression—sales totaled $750.

It was not until 1965 that the Ohio plant opened in Cambridge, producing standard Foamwall and painted metal products. The continuous coil coating paint line built shortly thereafter helped the firm win additional contracts for sophisticated building projects. By the late 1980s the Cambridge facility was employing some 170 workers.

Coshocton Stainless, one of the nation's leading suppliers of stainless flat rolled strip and sheet, had its first office in a farmhouse on the potato farm the company acquired for its plant. Local lore has it that the red brick house, which was torn down in the mid-1980s, served as an Underground Railroad way station 120 years earlier.

The original size of the Greenfield plant was but 140,000 square feet when the first shipment went out the door in June 1959. Today the state-of-the-art plant is four times as big, covering 10 acres of the 650-acre site.

In 1985 Coshocton Stainless launched a three-year, $30-million expansion to increase capacity and enhance quality. A major part of the expansion was a new 52-inch reversing Z mill, the most powerful of its kind in North America. The custom-designed mill went into service in December 1986, enabling the division to produce coils up to 48 inches wide.

The nonunion plant, the only one in the Cyclops Corporation, has more than 450 employees. In recent years it has been running three shifts and up to seven days a week on some units.

From its inception in 1952 Miami Industries has been a front-runner in the production of mechanical welded, mechanical annealed, and mandrel drawn steel tubing. The versatile tubing is found in furniture, store fixtures, recreational equipment, and automobiles.

The 450,000-square-foot Piqua plant, which has more than 300 hourly workers, has 16 tubing mills, making it the largest such facility in the nation.

Miami Industries was able to expand its product line in 1985 with the addition of the Roll Formed Shapes Division, a fully integrated cold formed metal shapes manufacturing operation based in Warren. It found customers among manufacturers of material handling equipment, commercial and residential doors and windows, and escalators and elevators.

The 250,000-square-foot Warren plant, which employs about 70 hourly workers, has six electric-welded tubing mills.

Empire-Detroit Steel's Dover, Ohio, plant produces galvanized strip and sheet. Here a worker inspects sheets prior to shipping.

Coil coating is just one of the operations performed at the Cambridge, Ohio, plant of E.G. Smith Construction Products.

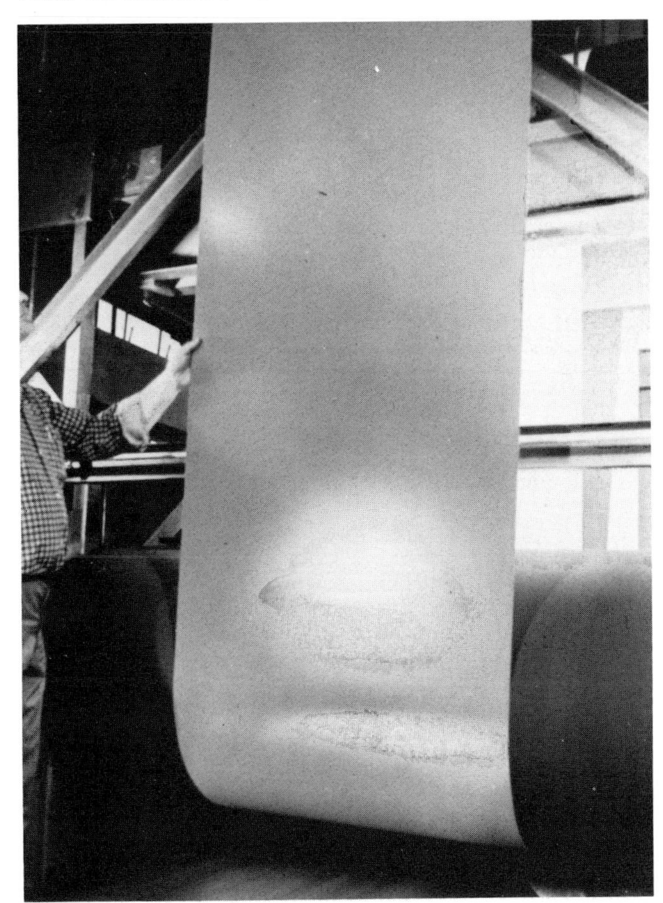

ELECTROLOCK INCORPORATED

The story of Electrolock Incorporated reads like a textbook case on why nice guys finish first.

Electrolock sells high-performance electrical and thermal insulation materials. Its main customers are motor and transformer manufacturers who use these products to insulate electrical windings, as well as manufacturers of automobiles, appliances, wire, and cables. Over the years it has evolved from a distributor and sales representative into a technical problem solver that adds greater value to what it sells. It offers precision slitting and shearing, die cutting, laminating, coating, spiral tube winding, and rewinding.

Two salesmen founded the electrical insulations distributor in August 1957. Joseph A. Williams, Jr., came in as half-owner of Electrolock in June 1959 and gained full ownership within a year.

Williams had earlier moved from the East Coast to Ohio

in search of a better business climate. He had found Midwestern businesspeople to be more receptive to new ideas and more appreciative of technical salespeople than their eastern counterparts. In addition, Cleveland was the center of the electrical equipment industry with 80 percent of all operations located within a 200-mile radius.

Although a success in sales, Williams dreamed of building a company that offered tangible benefits to both materials manufacturers and end users. He felt uncomfortable that many in his industry functioned purely as middlemen, without really contributing much value.

Williams began to emphasize service. In addition to providing cold storage for temperature-sensitive materials, Electrolock added machinery to die cut parts, spiral wrap tubing, and slit master rolls into the sizes and the tolerances needed by customers. In fact, an industry journal in 1982 cited Electrolock's skill in pushing the capabilities of Duesenberry rewind slitters to their maximum limits and achieve tolerances within five thousandths of an inch.

Electrolock also branched into high-performance thermal materials in order to offer customers wider problem-solving capabilities.

Starting in the 1970s and continuing in the 1980s, the U.S. electrical power industry faced mounting foreign competition. Manufacturers, forced to cut costs and gain efficiency, applied cost-reduction pressures on their suppliers. Many who mainly bought and resold material were squeezed out. Electrolock, as a high value added manufacturers representative and converter, continued to grow—and to expand its service.

In 1981 Electrolock set up an analytical laboratory to speed response time to questions. The laboratory also helps Electrolock evaluate the potential of new materials and helps customers find a selection of materials that might satisfy their needs. It also improves the technical competence of Electrolock's salespeople, who get hands-on experience on laboratory test equipment.

The laboratory is equipped to test electrical insulation properties, thermal conductivity, chemical composition, melting point, decomposition, and mechanical characteristics such as puncture resistance.

Left:* *Joseph Williams built Electrolock into a technical sales specialist that adds value to what it sells.

Below:* *An experienced Electrolock machine operator slits a master roll of insulation to smaller rolls that meet the size and tolerance requirements of customers.

Electrolock employees and their families at a recent company picnic.

Electrolock's technical people use computers to plot a material's characteristics and speed the setup of wrapping of wire. Its extensive experience in wrapping wire with insulation has enabled Electrolock to master the process of making insulated paper tubing using different adhesives and wrapping systems.

As Electrolock expanded its technical expertise and knowledge of its markets, businesses began to ask the company to represent their products nationwide. Electrolock now handles glass paper for Crane & Company, magnet wire for Canada Wire & Cable, Nomex papers for Du Pont, and flexible components, mica tapes, and coated fabrics for Insulating Materials. The firm is a major sales representative for Markel Corporation, Sterling Group, and many other of the industries insulating materials suppliers.

Electrolock's assistance to end users has also increased. Today the firm often works with customers in the design stage, helping them define their needs and solve problems. One result of this process has been the paper-thin thermal and electrical insulating tubes installed between the rubber and aluminum components of spark plug boots in many American-made automobiles.

Over the years Electrolock people have come up with a wealth of new product ideas. Williams wanted to satisfy customers yet keep his company sales oriented, responsive, and family size. Whenever new ideas have pulled the firm in the direction of manufacturing, Electrolock has eventually passed them on to existing manufacturers, created wholly owned subsidiaries, or spun off new companies.

In 1960 Electrolock came up with the idea for thermosetting surge ring cable—a fiberglass rope-like material impregnated with epoxy resin used to secure electrical windings. It is still made today—by an outside company.

Another idea, developed in 1962, has generated a line of epoxy-coated aramid papers used by the electrical industry to insulate motors and transformers.

In 1975 Electrolock introduced a labor-saving epoxy kit for coating electrical windings. Pull the tab to mix the premeasured resin and reactor, and apply. Electrolock's South Carolina facility is currently making thousands of kits to supply many large manufacturers.

Williams has succeeded in keeping his company a close team. "I consider it a privilege to work alongside all our people," says Williams. "They are dedicated and hard working, We are very fortunate in that we not only have been very successful over these past 30 years, but have enjoyed building that success. We have tried to create a nice working environment for our employees." Electrolock offers $850 in bonuses to employees and spouses who quit smoking.

A sales specialist examines a customer's - insulation material requirement.

Electrolock is located in one of Ohio's prettiest areas, southeast of Cleveland in Chagrin Falls. The area is known for its storybook setting, streams, and waterfalls. The firm also maintains a sales office in Cincinnati.

Electrolock currently does about $20 million in annual sales and has 25 people employed at its headquarters in Chagrin Falls.

Electrolock Incorporated sees its role expanding in the future. More and more of its customers need just-in-time delivery to hold down inventory costs. In addition, it expects to work even more closely with materials manufacturers to satisfy the needs of increasingly sophisticated end users. These two trends offer more challenges to add value—a challenge Electrolock people thrive on.

DOCTORS HOSPITAL

Doctors Hospital in Columbus has a heritage as rich as any hospital in the state. Although the osteopathic institution was organized in 1938, the property on which its first facility sat can be traced to 136 years earlier, back to the days when Thomas Jefferson was president and James Monroe was his secretary of state.

As a matter of fact, it was the signatures of those two distinguished American statesmen that were put to a land grant for Joseph Ruess Starr. That was in 1802, a year before Ohio became the 17th state to join the Union and 14 years before Columbus became the state capital.

In the mid-1800s the Starrs built a stately, three-story mansion at 1087 Dennison Avenue, the present site of Doctors Hospital. But after the Starrs sold the property in 1873, the mansion had a succession of owners.

One of them was a Dr. Clarence Maris, who professed to be a pyrologist, one who studies the properties of minerals when exposed to flame. After two years in the Starr Mansion, his flame apparently died out, and the property was sold in 1893 to the Protestant Hospital Association.

Above: Doctors Hospital, in Columbus, shortly after it opened in August 1940.

Left: Founders and board members hold ground-breaking ceremony in 1945 for the first of scores of additions, new wings, and improvement projects.

Under the Methodist organization, the mansion became the Protestant Hospital. When the association built the larger White Cross Hospital at the turn of the century, what was now known as the Dennison Mansion changed hands again.

In 1903 it became the Keeley Institute, one of a number throughout the nation that offered The Keeley Cure for alcoholism and drug addiction. The Irish-born founder believed he could cure his patients with injections of double chloride of gold. The hoax died shortly thereafter, and the old mansion had a string of new owners.

The penultimate landlords arrived on the scene in 1921, establishing the Columbus Radium Hospital for the treatment of malignancies through radium and radiation therapy. The hospital flourished into the 1930s, but the Depression took its toll. A new group of trustees was established and the name changed to Columbus Doctors Hospital.

Led by Dr. Harold E. Clybourne, Dr. Ralph S. Licklider, and Dr. James O. Watson, the group of osteopathic physicians purchased the shares of stock that had been issued by the Columbus Radium Hospital founders. On May 1, 1940, the new group acquired control. Dr. Watson, who recorded much of the hospital's early history, recalled that at the time the 24-bed facility took about $100 a day to operate.

After investing several thousands of dollars into remodeling and the purchase of new equipment, Doctors Hospital reopened for business on August 1, 1940. In addition to the small number of beds there were a few bassinets, a modest laboratory, an X-ray facility, a surgery suite, a staff of about 15 physicians, and as many nurses. Dr. L.C. Scatterday was the first chief of staff, and the first residencies were established in radiology and surgery.

By 1950 the bed capacity had increased to 150 through a series of additions to the Dennison Mansion. The facility also included six operating rooms, 24 bassinets, and a staff of 247. The expansion continued throughout the decade, reflecting the increasing demand for health care and hospital service in a rapidly growing community. The decade also saw Doctors Hospital become the first in the area to be air conditioned throughout.

Doctors Hospital was on the move again in the early 1960s as one landmark was erased and another erected.

Doctors West, opened in October 1963, was the nation's first truly complete satellite hospital. Courtesy, George E. Konold, Jr.

The need for a hospital on Columbus' rapidly growing west side resulted in the construction of the 112-bed Doctors West, the first truly complete statellite hospital in the United States. More than 2,000 visitors attended dedication ceremonies October 1, 1963. In less than five years three more floors were added to the original three, and the total number of beds jumped to more than 200.

The landmark that disappeared in 1968 was the Dennison Mansion and its four familiar white pillars. It had served physicians and patients for more than 75 years, but it had to make room for a modern—and more practical—entrance, lobby, and administrative offices at what was now known as Doctors North.

Also in the same period the Doctors Hospital Foundation was created. The controlling shares that had been acquired in the Columbus Radium Hospital transaction were turned over to the nonprofit foundation, and the voting trusts were abolished July 1, 1964.

More patient rooms and coronary care, intensive care, and emergency units, as well as a host of new or expanded services have been added since at both Doctors North and Doctors West. Of particular significance were the new ambulatory Care Teaching Facility and the family-centered New Horizons Maternity Unit at Doctors North, and X-ray, emergency room, and surgery additions to Doctors West.

Shortly after Doctors entered its 40th year it acquired Mount St. Mary Hospital in Nelsonville, an 83-bed facility built in 1950. Renamed Doctors Hospital of Nelsonville, it, too, has been extensively modernized and expanded to provide improved health care to Southeast Ohio.

Today the numbers add up to a great deal more than the 24 beds the founders acquired in 1940. The bed count has topped 600 to serve the 20,000 inpatients each year. In addition, 1,700 newborns annually receive their first hours of loving care at one of the institution's three facilities.

Doctors is known throughout the nation as an outstanding osteopathic teaching hospital, and it is the largest institution of its kind in Ohio. Each year more than one-fifth of the country's entire graduating class of osteopathic physicians apply to Doctors for internship, even though the American Osteopathic Association recognizes some 159 hospitals for internships. Doctors is also affiliated with the Ohio University College of Osteopathic Medicine for the clinical training of medical students.

The three Doctors hospitals follow a philosophy that was formulated in Kirksville, Missouri, by Dr. Andrew Taylor Still. That was in 1874 when America was a rustic, young nation, when life was dangerous, and when patients died, "cause unknown."

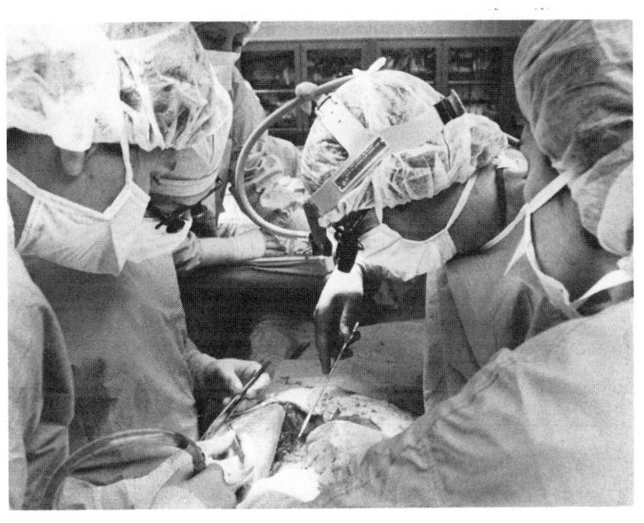

Dr. Gary Saltus, with headlamp, gives residents and interns hands-on training in open-heart surgery.

Still defined health in terms of body unity. Find health, he said, not disease. Administer treatment to the whole patient. Make a commitment to examine the patient in terms of his experience, not the physician's. Doctors Hospital has practiced this approach to health since the day its doors were opened.

The rapid and successful growth of Doctors Hospital has been an echo of the city of Columbus. In one generation it has been transformed from a small Midwest capital to a sophisticated metropolitan community that expects a level of health care consistent with new knowledge, new technology, and new methods of treatment.

The facilities and staff of Doctors Hospital are responding to today's revolutionary and evolutionary developments in the health care delivery system so that patients may have the benefit of these changes and advances in medicine.

WHIRLPOOL CORPORATION

Whirlpool Corporation is a manufacturer and marketer of a full line of major home appliances that are sold domestically and internationally under the Whirlpool and KitchenAid brand names. The company is also the principal supplier of major appliances for Sears, Roebuck and Co., which markets its appliances under the Sears and Kenmore brands.

Whirlpool owns and operates manufacturing facilities in Ohio, Michigan, Indiana, Kentucky, Tennessee, Arkansas, Mississippi, and South Carolina. National and international operations are administered from corporate headquarters in Benton Harbor, Michigan. Located in Ohio are four Whirlpool plants and the administrative offices for the Specialty Products Division.

The 3,000 employees at the plant in Clyde manufacture Whirlpool, Kenmore, and KitchenAid automatic washers. Purchased in 1952, the plant is one of the largest in the United States dedicated solely to the production of automatic washers.

For nearly 30 years the automatic washer has been essentially unchanged. However, the division recently introduced a newly engineered unit that has 30 percent fewer parts and is designed for ease of service and repair.

A totally new approach has been employed by Whirlpool in making the washer. The key is the "bottoms-up" assembly technique, which permits full operational testing on the assembly line before the washer is installed. The new manufacturing system and improved design also allow for the use of state-of-the-art automation throughout the process.

The people at Whirlpool's Marion Division have produced more than 30 million clothes dryers in the plant's 32-year history. More than 400 different Whirlpool, Sears (Kenmore), and KitchenAid dryer models are produced at the plant, each consisting of more than 300 parts. The Marion plant also manufactures both Whirlpool and KitchenAid microwave ovens and assembles the Thin Twin (washer/dryer) stack unit.

More than 14 miles of overhead conveyor are used to transport parts to and from the paint and assembly areas, and for parts storage. Building expansions have increased the plant's size from 250,000 square feet in 1955 to more than 884,000 square feet today. There are an additional 581,000 square feet at the Marion Distribution Center adjacent to the manufacturing site.

The Findlay Division of Whirlpool was the first facility built by the company solely for the purpose of producing major home appliances. Constructed in 1967, the division manufactures Whirlpool and KitchenAid built-in and portable dishwashers. In addition, Whirlpool built-in and freestanding ranges, surface units, and 30-inch built-in ovens also are manufactured at Findlay.

Left: The Findlay Division of Whirlpool was constructed in 1967 and today is Hancock County's largest employer with more than 2,000 employees. The plant and the Distribution Center cover 1.3 million square feet.

Below: Assemblers on the clothes dryer line at the Marion Division plant are wiring the controls on the top console.

The division has grown from 560 employees in 1970 to more than 2,200 today, making this facility the largest employer in Hancock County. Together the manufacturing plant and neighboring Distribution Center comprise a 1.3-million-square-foot facility.

Two Ohio cities are home for the Whirlpool Specialty Products Division: Dayton and Greenville. KitchenAid mixers and food processors, and both Whirlpool and KitchenAid hot water dispensers are produced by 200 people at three separate manufacturing facilities in Greenville.

Another 110 administrative, engineering, procurement, information service, and KitchenAid salespeople are located in the division's offices in Dayton.

THE SMITH & OBY COMPANY

Over its spectacular 90-year history The Smith & Oby Company has built mansions and major buildings for a clientele that reads like a who's who of Cleveland institutions and corporations. It specializes in mechanical contracting—the installation and service of complex heating, cooling, and piping systems.

Colonel James Smith started the business in Canton in 1867. In 1898 Smith and his partner George Oby headed for Cleveland in separate wagons. For unknown reasons, Oby never arrived, though his name is still on the door.

Because of Smith's ability, the firm built mansions for patrons named Mather, Prentiss, Blossom, Hanna, Ireland, and Severance in the early 1900s.

From Severance Hall (left), home of the Cleveland Orchestra (with the Art Museum in the left background), to the low-rise/high-rise combination of today's Justice Center Complex (above), The Smith & Oby Company has completed more than 5,000 projects for over 350 clients.

When Smith died, Walter Klie and W.J. Wetzell maintained the tradition of quality. The firm won contracts to build St. Luke's Hospital, Rainbow Babies & Childrens Hospital, Western Reserve Medical School, University School, Federal Reserve Bank, Cleveland Public Auditorium, and the Cleveland Clinic. In 1922 H.E. Wetzell, son of W.J. Wetzell, came on board. Four years later the firm completed the nation's first welded piping job for Ohio Bell Telephone Company.

The Depression of the 1930s hit Cleveland hard. Smith & Oby hired William P. Miller to handle projects in Toledo, Detroit, and Baltimore. In addition, the company began specializing in mechanical contracting, installing Cleveland's first air conditioning systems.

With the start of World War II Smith & Oby helped build many plants for war production. In the mid-1940s A.M. Brunton, Jr., and Hamilton Klie, a lawyer and son of Walter Klie, were hired to provide leadership.

Peacetime brought two decades of hectic growth. Smith & Oby participated in innumerable projects, including the Ford Motor Company plant in Brookpark, General Electric Lamp Laboratory, AmeriTrust Tower, and the Society National Bank reconstruction. During this period Gary Klie and H.E. Wetzell, Jr., joined the company their grandfathers had helped establish.

The 1960s brought technical innovations and sophistication. Smith & Oby adopted the Critical Path method of construction planning and expanded its engineering department to create large-scale coordination drawings to better manage complex systems.

Recent decades have seen intense competition because of the drop in new construction. In response, the firm has maximized efficiency through widespread use of computers that are used for job cost control, project scheduling, and labor control. "We won't cut corners to win bids," says Gary Klie, president. "Our policy is to get repeat business by providing a quality installation at a competitive price."

Recent projects include Standard Oil Research Laboratories, Kaiser Permanente, Ohio Bell Telephone Company, Blue Cross of Ohio, the Cleveland Clinic, and Society Corporation—all repeat customers. Currently Smith & Oby is working on its largest project ever—the $16-million East Filter Building renovation of the City of Cleveland Division Avenue Water Treatment Plant, installing all general trades work and electrical work in addition to the mechanical systems on this project.

Through active participation in its trade associations, involvement in its community, innovative and client-oriented ideas, and keeping abreast of new technologies, The Smith & Oby Company is committed to perpetuation well into the twenty-first century.

BEN VENUE LABORATORIES, INC. (FOUNDED in 1938)

Ben Venue Laboratories, Inc., Bedford, Ohio.

The oldest, largest, and most experienced custom manufacturer of freeze-dried and vacuum-dried drug products in the United States is Ben Venue Laboratories, Inc. Headquartered in Bedford, a suburb southeast of Cleveland, the firm uses these processes to extend the shelf life of various drugs and biological materials.

Ben Venue Laboratories was founded in 1938 by R. Templeton Smith, a Pittsburgh native who at age 50 quit his job as executive vice-president of the mammoth Pittsburgh Coal Company (now part of Consolidation Coal Company). He named his new venture after a mountain in Scotland near his ancestral home.

Smith had gotten the idea for the business from Dr. Roy McCullagh, head of research at Cleveland Clinic Foundation. McCullagh had mentioned that the doctors there had ideas that could and should be exploited for commercial use.

Ben Venue's first laboratory was one room over a laundry on Carnegie Avenue in midtown Cleveland. Its first major product was estrogen, a hormone extracted from the blood and urine of pregnant mares and used to treat menopause.

The next major product was freeze-dried human blood plasma. It was used to save lives by preventing shock and replenishing blood volume during World War II. Ben Venue processed more than a half-million units of plasma and became the first company to receive the Army-Navy "E" Award for effort.

In 1944 Ben Venue became the 13th firm to make penicillin on a commercial scale. Later it converted its penicillin factory to produce the first commercial batches of bacitracin, a new antibiotic used to treat eye infections and skin lesions. Smith first read about the drug in a *Life* magazine story about a girl named Margaret Tracy. Her leg lesion had healed, despite a mold growing on it, and that mold produced bacitracin.

Another first was a portable ethylene oxide sterilizer developed in 1957. Ben Venue still makes and sells a larger version of this portable model today.

The National Cancer Institute awarded Ben Venue a contract to process human dosages of experimental anti-cancer chemotherapy drugs in 1966. Ever since the firm has been mainly a custom manufacturer of injectable pharmaceuticals for other drug companies.

In 1985 Ben Venue began a joint venture with Cetus Corporation, the nation's oldest and second-largest genetic engineering company, to produce generic drugs with an emphasis on cancer chemotherapy. The number of employees has grown steadily from 16 in 1956 to 260 today. In addition, major laboratory expansions were built in 1982 and 1985.

Ben Venue Laboratories is one of few drug companies in northern Ohio. "But there's no reason to be anywhere else," says Kennedy Smith, president since 1967, "because customers come here."

Customers keep arriving because Ben Venue people set high standards for themselves. In fact, they have achieved perfect marks in FDA factory inspections in 1986 and 1987. They process delicate chemicals, keep them absolutely sterile, package the right dosage, and keep tight controls throughout a highly complex and demanding process.

SSP FITTINGS CORPORATION

The new SSP Fittings Corporation plant and offices built in 1986 in the Cleveland suburb of Twinsburg.

Whatever kind of stainless-steel fittings customers might require, SSP Fittings Corporation can supply them. The Twinsburg firm manufactures flared, flareless, socket-weld, and other tube fittings, as well as pipe and hose fittings, to government specifications, SSP standards, or customer designs. SSP Fittings' products are found in hydraulic equipment in steel mills, ground support controls for missiles, turbine control systems for power plants, and nuclear submarines.

Originally called The Special Screw Products Company, the firm was founded in 1926 by Orrin Douglas, an attorney and former secretary of National Acme. Douglas bought used, reconditioned automatic screw machines and filled special orders for screw products made from brass, carbon steel, and aluminum bar stocks. Other National Acme officials made investments in the company, which soon built a plant at 5445 Dunham Road in the Cleveland suburb of Maple Heights. Later Orrin Douglas' brother J.L. "Lawrence" Douglas and his son J.N. "Nick" Douglas joined the company, and the Douglas family bought out other investors.

The start of World War II boosted the demand for all types of screw machine products. Special Screw Products updated its machinery and expanded to about 75 employees. The firm also developed an expertise in making tube fittings, gradually phasing out screw products. Notably, the company designed, patented, and marketed the Koncentrik line of stainless steel tube fittings.

After the war the firm fell on hard times. In 1956 Raymond King, who had been sales manager, bought controlling interest in the business. King identified the most promising market—stainless steel tube fittings—and reorganized the business to pursue it. While stainless steel is difficult to fabricate, the firm developed a special expertise. King also had a gentlemanly approach that won the respect of suppliers, customers, and employees alike. The reorganized business slowly grew from 6 to 15 employees. It moved from a rented building to the newly purchased McMyler Interstate Office Building at 100 Northfield Road in Bedford. About that time the company became SSP Fittings Corporation to reflect its new emphasis.

In 1966 King's son Raymond King, Jr., joined the firm after graduating from college. He was particularly fascinated with the manufacturing process and spent his first years in the shop. With valuable input and cooperation from his employees, he developed specialized tooling and layouts for efficient production of the many different fittings. As a result, the firm responds quickly to demands for new products, constantly expands its product line, and experiences very low turnover. After becoming president and sole stockholder in 1972, young King oversaw continued growth that compelled a move to much larger facilities.

In 1986 the company built a 100,000-square-foot plant and headquarters in the Twinsburg Industrial Park with added manufacturing and forging equipment specifically adapted for stainless-steel fitting production. This capability enables SSP Fittings to improve product quality, gain flexibility, and supply specially made fittings in a matter of days.

Today the company fills orders from around the country. Emphasizing service, it ships off-the-shelf items the same day. In addition, the firm keeps personnel and machines ready for emergency orders.

Looking to the future, SSP Fittings Corporation will continue to expand the range and variety of its stainless connectors and investigate the exotic new alloys now available.

A battery of multiple-spindle, automatic screw machines used for high-volume.

THE DOW CHEMICAL COMPANY

The Dow Chemical Company—one of the largest chemical firms in the world and the second-largest in the United States—can trace its earliest roots to Ohio. The company's Ohio operations employ about 3,000 people and by themselves would earn a place on the *Fortune* 500.

Dow's founder, Herbert Dow, spent much of his boyhood in Cleveland. After completing study on a Case School of Applied Science scholarship in 1888, 23-year-old Dow began to look for ways of using a process he had invented to extract bromine from the salt brines that underlie Michigan and Ohio. Bromine was the main constituent of most of the popular medicines of that day and was in demand for new uses such as photographic films.

With funds borrowed from classmates and faculty friends at Case, Dow founded three companies during the next eight years—first in Ohio (The Canton Chemical Company) and then two in Michigan—with disappointing results. On his fourth try, in 1897, Dow made it pay, establishing The Dow Chemical Company. The firm's world headquarters is still in Midland, Michigan, where the original plant is the largest employer in its area.

Dow started with bromine, but was also researching the possibilities of other chemical components of the Michigan brines—chlorine, calcium, iodine, magnesium—and soon began to use them as chemical building blocks for a widening stream of products. Today the company manufactures some 2,300 items, most of them still chemically related to the components of brine.

During the World War I era, although the firm was barely 20 years old, it was thrust into national prominence. Dow Chemical was the nation's largest supplier of phenol, one of its newer products, which quickly became vital for manufacturing armaments. The government sent soldiers to protect Dow's phenol plant.

Since then, the company has experienced a number of spectacular periods of growth. Its distinguished corps of chemists, engineers, and executives has continued to develop new products. Dow Chemical has invented new families of plastics, everything from STYROFOAM* to SARAN WRAP**, modern farm chemicals, metals, textiles, and new products of all kinds that provide the chemical undergirding of modern living.

Dow's plants and offices have branched throughout the globe with manufacturing plants in more than 30 countries and sales offices covering the world. In Ohio, Dow locations include the Eastern Division headquarters in Strongsville (a suburb of Cleveland), which oversees eight manufacturing plants in five states. Ohio manufacturing sites that report to the Eastern Division include the Hanging Rock Plant in Ironton, the Licking River Film Center in Hebron, Columbus Operations in Columbus, and the Findlay Plant in Findlay. In addition, the Granville Research Center near Columbus provides technical support for Dow's films and foams businesses worldwide.

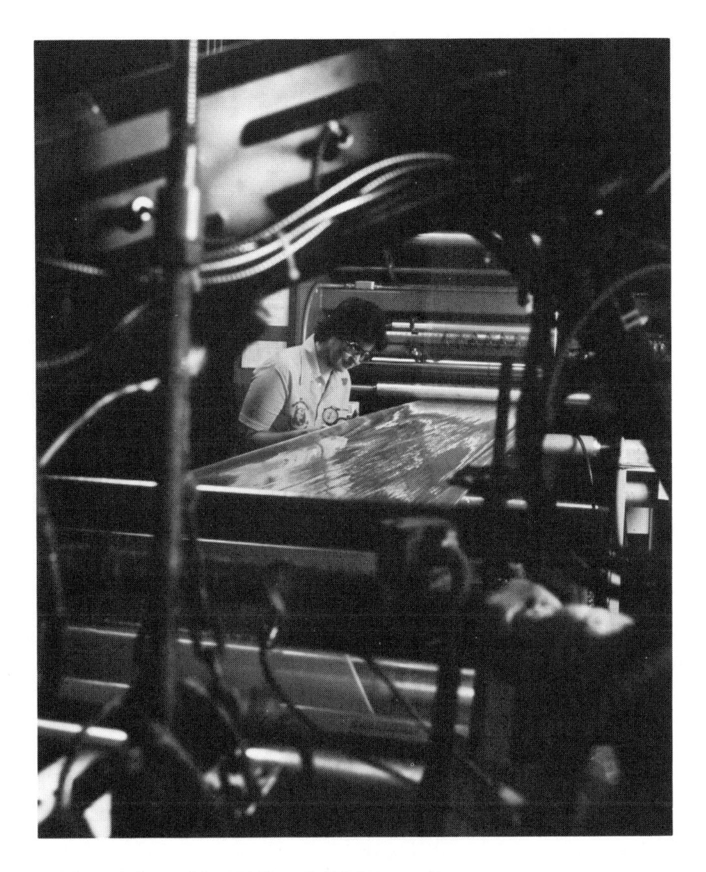

Although based in Midland, Michigan, Dow Chemical traces its origins to Cleveland. Today Ohio is home to 6 of 10 manufacturing, research, and administrative facilities for the Eastern Division of Dow Chemical U.S.A. Dow's Ohio sites primarily research and manufacture plastic film and foam products.

Dow also maintains sales offices in Cleveland, Columbus, and Cincinnati and operates Admiral Equipment in Akron (which manufactures equipment to process urethane for steering wheels and other applications).

Products manufactured in Ohio include STYROFOAM brand plastic foam used as insulation by the building industry, ETHAFOAM* plastic foam, plastic clad metal, adhesive film, polyethylene film, other plastic films, polystyrene resins, ABS resins, and polyurethanes.

During the late 1970s Dow Chemical began to shift half of its business from commodity chemicals to industrial and consumer specialty products. As part of this process in 1981, Dow purchased the entire domestic and international pharmaceutical operations of Richardson Merrell, Inc., another firm with roots deep in Ohio history. That purchase created Merrell Dow Pharmaceuticals, Inc.—a wholly owned subsidiary of Dow—which maintains global research, manufacturing, and marketing headquarters in Cincinnati.

The original pharmaceutical company was founded by William S. Merrell, an energetic altruist who had attended Medical College of Ohio with ambitions of being a doctor. But family business brought Merrell to Cincinnati, where he found a demand for medications. In June 1828 he opened a retail drug store at Sixth Street and Western Row (Central Avenue).

Four years later he started manufacturing—shipping green elm and setting up a still to make chloride from lime. He actively pursued research into "green pharmaceuticals"—drugs made from plants picked and immediately preserved in alcohol. Merrell made big sales in podophyllin (a mandrake root extract) and in leptandrin (a resinous laxative).

By 1858 William S. Merrell Company had the nation's largest selection of botanic medicines. In 1876 the company became the first to make salicylic acid, the forerunner of aspirin. During the years that followed, Merrell added products such as gelatin-coated pills to its line and expanded its administrative, research, and production facilities to East Galbraith Road, where its major research and manufacturing operations remain today.

In 1938 Vick Chemical Company purchased William S. Merrell Company. Merrell later acquired Loeser Laboratory of New York City, the National Drug Company, and Walker Laboratories. In 1940, the firm introduced CEPACOL*** mouthwash containing its new antibacterial agent. Merrell was also hailed for being the first to synthesize (1956) and introduce (1966) CLOMID***, a drug used to treat infertility in women by triggering ovulation.

Today important Merrell Dow research continues through the Merrell Dow Research Institute with centers in Cincinnati, Indianapolis, France (Strasbourg), Italy (Gerenzano-Milano), England (Egham), and Japan (Hirakata). Major research emphasis is currently in the areas of cardiovascular disease, central nervous system disease, respiratory and infectious diseases, and cancer.

Major prescription products include SELDANE*** (terfenadine), the nonsedating antihistamine that became the largest-selling prescription drug used for the treatment of allergy symptoms within four weeks of its introduction in 1985; LORELCO***, the largest-selling drug in the world for use in lowering cholesterol levels; and NICORETTE***, a chewing gum designed to aid smokers who want to quit smoking.

Through the growth of Merrell Dow, Ohio manufacturing and research facilities, and other operations, The Dow Chemical Company achieved its goal of having half its business in specialty products by 1986. The result is a sense of renewal and some of the best quarters yet seen in Dow Chemical's long, proud history.

* Trademark of The Dow Chemical Company
** Trademark of Dow Consumer Products, Inc.
*** Trademark of Merrell Dow Pharmaceuticals Inc.

Merrell Dow Pharmaceuticals, Inc., is an international leader in pharmaceutical research, manufacturing, and marketing. It maintains worldwide research, development, and commercial headquarters in Cincinnati.

ALLTEL CORPORATION

ALLTEL Corporation is one of the country's leading telecommunications companies, with telephone companies serving nearly one million customers in 19 midwestern, eastern, and southern states, and a number of communications-related subsidiaries or investments. In fact, *Forbes* magazine recently named the Hudson-based firm the top performing company in the industry.

Its roots go back to 1910, when a telegraph operator named Weldon Wood answered philanthropist James Ellsworth's challenge to make Hudson, a town southeast of Cleveland, one of the first in the nation to have underground telephone lines. In the process, Wood became owner of a 100-party telephone company, later known as the Western Reserve Telephone Company.

In the mid-1950s Weldon W. Case was named president and general manager of Western Reserve and the nearby Elyria Telephone Company. Noticing that the management techniques that were used at the two firms could be successfully applied to other telephone companies, Case consolidated the administrative functions into a holding company and named it Mid-Continent Telephone Corporation.

In its first decade alone, Mid-Continent's customer base grew—primarily through acquisitions—from 50,000 telephones in Ohio to 10 times that number, and the company became a leader in digital switching and other technologies that automate labor-intensive functions.

In 1983 Mid-Continent grew again by merging with Allied Telephone Company of Little Rock, Arkansas, a firm with similar operating philosophies and a young management team. The new organization was named ALLTEL, signifying all things in telecommunications. Following the merger, Case was named chairman, and Allied's president, Joe Ford, became president. Living up to its new name, ALLTEL has since created a number of subsidiaries that complement its core business and help promote continued growth.

Fulton's original toll board, circa 1940. Chief operator Bertha Eckard (foreground) keeps a close eye on her crew. In the early days of the industry, the small-town operator wielded considerable authority. The company's institution of rotary-dial service in 1948 decreased customers' dependence on operators.

ALLTEL Supply, with warehouses nationwide, sells a full line of telecommunications equipment and supplies to businesses, colleges, and other telephone companies.

ALLTEL Mobile Communications provides cellular telephone service and wide-area paging in a number of major markets across the country.

And ALLTEL Publishing Corporation produces more than 100 different directories for ALLTEL's service areas.

ALLTEL also has investments in Microtel, a fiber-optic-based long-distance company serving the heavy toll areas of Florida and Georgia, as well as interests in a number of communications-related companies.

In an age when business and residential customers alike regard quality telephone service both as a right and a necessity, ALLTEL Corporation continues to meet its commitment to provide a full range of Information Age telecommunications services.

Cellular telephones have proved useful in a variety of businesses including the construction industry. ALLTEL Mobile Communications—ALLTEL's cellular subsidiary—provides cellular service in Cleveland and offers virtually statewide paging in Ohio.

JACO MANUFACTURING COMPANY

Jaco Manufacturing Company custom molds small plastic parts and manufactures and sells the injection-molding machines that make them. Through mastering the art and science of injection molding, and continual injections of care and ingenuity, the firm has built a national reputation for precision work.

Jaco serves industries ranging from electronics to earth-moving equipment. Chrysler, Du Pont, Rockwell International, and General Electric number among its customers.

The company was founded in 1949 as the Berea Plastics Company. Art Jacobs, a talented inventor and self-taught engineer, started the firm in the basement of his home, making plastic salt and pepper shakers. As business increased, he moved his plastic injection-molding machine to a factory on First Street in Berea, a western suburb of Cleveland.

A local pioneer in injection-molding nylon, Jacobs picked up his first orders in an ingenious way. He would visit a company, pick out the right metal part, make a mold, and make a nylon version. Then he brought the nylon part back to the company for inspection.

In 1952 NASA asked Jacobs to make a nylon manifold (multioutlet pipe) with compression nuts. In doing so, he discovered that the sleeve and nut could be combined into one piece—eliminating a step in assembly. Jacobs patented his breakthrough, and began molding Vibra-Pruf plastic fittings in 1954. He incorporated Jaco Manufacturing to make the fitting, and also started Jaco Sales to handle sales and distribution.

Jaco Manufacturing Company, on Geiger Street in Berea, is nationally renowned for its custom molding of plastic parts and the manufacture of the injection-molding machines that produce them.

The Vibra-Pruf line was first developed for use with copper tubing but has since been adapted for plastic, aluminum, and glass tubing, too. Customers in the chemical, water softener, and refrigeration industries use the fittings to transport water, oil, and chemicals.

Orders flowed in, but filling them was frustrating at times. Early molding machines were difficult to maintain, their parts scarce, and service slow. Finally, in the late 1950s, Jacobs designed and built his own machines.

After customers and other manufacturers heard about these machines, they wanted them as well, so in 1960 the Machinery Division was organized. Over the years the machines have been refined, and vertical and horizontal models offered with a clamping force of up to 50 tons. But some of the early machines are still in use today.

In time a larger plant became necessary, and the company built a new plant and offices nearby at its present Geiger Street location. In 1969 Jacobs reorganized the firm under the name Jaco Manufacturing Company to reflect its wider scope.

When Jacobs retired in 1978, he sold Jaco Manufacturing Company to Irving Davies, a top salesman at Jaco Sales with extensive industry background. Davies became president, and L.C. Campbell, Jaco's production manager, became vice-president and partner.

Over its 38-year history Jaco Manufacturing has grown to more than 100 people today. In 1986 its plant expanded by one-fourth to 50,000 square feet.

Jaco thrives because its people win a daily fight to control temperature, pressure, and cycle timing and achieve close tolerances. Jaco people sustain quality by monitoring settings and applying optical contour, computer, and statistical quality-control techniques. Jaco Manufacturing Company leaves little to mere chance.

GREAT LAKES CHEESE CO., INC.

Great Lakes Cheese of Newbury packages and sells about 1.5 million pounds of cheese per week, mostly to retailers in the northeastern quarter of the United States. In 24 years it has grown from a one-wagon wholesaler into Ohio's largest packager and marketer of cheese. Its story shows how a recent immigrant to America can find success by staying alert to opportunities and having the fortitude to keep plugging despite both setbacks and early successes.

Hans Epprecht, a Swiss cheese maker, came to Ohio in 1948 after an apprenticeship in his native Switzerland. He found work making Swiss cheese and later delivering milk products, but soon dreamed of owning his own business. By 1958 he had saved enough money to purchase with a partner Great Lakes Cheese, a small distributing firm operating out of the Northern Ohio Food Terminal in Cleveland. The partners bought different kinds of cheese and sold it out of their truck to local grocery chains and delicatessens.

Business grew, and in 1963 the partners built a 6,000-square-foot plant in Newbury complete with packaging equipment. There they repackaged cheese for local supermarkets in hermetically sealed packages under store-brand labels.

In the early years, recalls Epprecht, a banker had faith in his ability to succeed. And certain customers gave Great Lakes a break by taking on its product line, even though it was still a very small company. Fisher Foods (Heritage House brand), Pick-n-Pay (Finast brand, formerly Edwards), and many others numbered among the early customers and remain customers decades later.

As business continued to expand Great Lakes constructed additions to its Newbury plant in 1973, 1979, and 1982. But the focus then and now is Ohio Swiss cheese. Considered a premium cheese on the East Coast, Ohio Swiss today makes up a large part of Great Lakes' sales and is the only domestic Swiss cheese sold by the company.

Great Lakes Cheese buys its Ohio Swiss from cooperatives and proprietary manufacturers. It buys about two-thirds of the output of Middlefield Cheese. The fact that Middlefield Cheese is 17 miles down Route 87 is a prime reason why Great Lakes is headquartered in Geauga County. Middlefield Cheese, in turn, buys much of its milk from farmers in Geauga, Portage, Ashtabula, and Trumbull counties.

Great Lakes increased its product variety and volume in 1982 by purchasing a packaging plant in Plymouth, Wisconsin. Like the plant in Newbury, it repackages bulk cheese into consumer sizes, but it emphasizes Wisconsin-style cheeses. Because Wisconsin produces close to 40 percent of the nation's cheese, the availability of the raw material attracted the growing company to Wisconsin.

In 1984 the firm acquired its Adams, New York, cheese plant from Dairylea, a New York State farmers' cooperative. After completely remodeling the plant and installing the most modern whey- and cheese-processing equipment, Great Lakes began manufacturing a specialty cheddar cheese for aging. Only three other companies produce this type of sharp cheddar in any volume in New York State.

The Adams plant processes one million pounds of milk daily during a four-day week. It makes cheddar in 680-pound blocks for aging and also four flavors of curds, a popular form of cheese in Upstate New York. Some of the blocks are transported to Newbury for packaging and distribution.

Today Great Lakes Cheese maintains and schedules a fleet of 15 tractors and 22 trailers to ship cheese from its Ohio plant. Most of their business is east of the Mississippi, though some of its products reach the West Coast, Alaska, and Hawaii.

Between all its plants, Great Lakes Cheese handles about 25 major varieties of domestic cheese. It repacks 80 percent of this cheese into small chunks or shreds for consumers' convenience. The company also imports and repackages foreign cheeses. Unfortunately, trade restrictions keep the firm from exporting its own Adams plant or Ohio Swiss cheeses to Canada and Europe.

Great Lakes sells only natural cheese. It does not process any cheese, which involves cooking natural cheese and

This was the Great Lakes Cheese plant in 1967.

adding ingredients. The company has no immediate plans to do any processing. Still, it watches with interest the research on modifying milk to reduce its milk sugar (lactose), which may allow those consumers unable to digest milk sugar to eat more cheese.

During the firm's short history, cheese consumption nationwide has grown from six pounds per capita to more than 24 pounds per capita. Most of the growth has been in natural cheese. The difference has to do with changing life-style and dining habits. "People are moving away from three daily sit-down meals to more snack-type meals," says Epprecht. "And cheese really fits that style of eating." He notes that cheese marketers nationally have done an excellent job providing consumers with a tremendous variety of cheese and satisfying regional preferences. Aside from the quality of Ohio cheese and the growth in the natural cheese business, the main factors in the growth of Great Lakes Cheese are its people.

Epprecht modestly describes challenges as a manager over the years as "making more good decisions than bad." Among his many good decisions over the years was to reinvest profits back into the business to stay low cost and efficient. He buys state-of-the-art equipment, such as two slicing machines each able to slice 12,000 to 20,000 pounds of cheese per eight-hour shift.

Most of all, he credits a team of dedicated people for making the organization as competitive and efficient as it has been. In fact, the firm has motivated and rewarded its employees with a profit-sharing plan, which now owns roughly 9 percent of the company.

Says Epprecht, "I'm a firm believer that it takes the dedication of every employee, that if it's not total teamwork, the job of being competitive just does not get done. You don't need an MBA, but you have to be a good manager."

Today Epprecht is responsible for about 370 employees. About 190 people work at the Newbury plant, and the balance is split between New York and Wisconsin. Two of his employees are his children. He takes pleasure in noting that a son and a daughter are active in the business, and a third is considering it.

He also takes obvious pleasure in his work overall. "I don't look at it as hard work. That's what I want to do, and I get a great deal of enjoyment in providing jobs for people," he says.

A self-made immigrant who has done well by and for his customers, employees, family, and products, Epprecht might just subscribe to the idea that in America the streets are paved with gold—not with cold metal but with wholesome chunks of cheddar and Ohio Swiss cheese.

As business grew, a 6,000-square-foot facility was built in Newbury. Several additions were constructed through the years, and this is the Great Lakes Cheese plant in 1987.

MIAMI UNIVERSITY

Left: An early photograph of Elliott Hall (left) and Stoddard Hall, two of the 38 residence halls on campus.

Below: A pair of Miami University students are framed in the arches of Richard Hall as they walk along the Central Quad of the residential campus.

"Miami is All-American, wrapped up in academic gowns." That assessment of Miami University was made by Richard Moll, former dean of admissions at the University of California at Santa Cruz, in his book, *The Public Ivys.*

It is easy to make the connection between Miami and the Ivy League schools of the East. There are the stately historic buildings on a mature, tree-lined campus of considerable beauty, and there is academic excellence, the measure by which every educational institution is judged.

The 1,179-acre Oxford campus of Miami takes its character from the country of southwestern Ohio with its rolling hills dotted with woodlands and prosperous farms. Almost serene in its setting, the university lies between two of Ohio's most dynamic cities—Cincinnati and Dayton each less than an hour away.

Established by legislative action February 17, 1809, Miami is the nation's seventh-oldest state institution of higher learning and the second oldest west of the Alleghenies. Students were admitted to collegiate instruction in 1824; today there are more than 19,000 on four campuses, including one in Luxembourg at Miami's European Center.

Since its founding certain concepts have been nurtured, representing an attempt on the part of those guiding the university's activities to search for the best.

First is the dedication to the liberal arts, with a focus on the humanities, the social sciences, and the natural sciences required of each student. Second is the commitment to a strong undergraduate program. A major portion of faculty time is devoted to undergraduate instruction, and senior faculty members regularly teach freshman- and sophomore-level courses.

Third is the dedication to the concept of a residential university. There are 38 residence halls on the Oxford campus, housing nearly 8,000 students. And finally is the commitment to high standards for the undergraduates and faculty alike.

For instance, 83 percent of the freshman class in 1986 ranked in the top 20 percent of their high school class. In addition 92 percent of Miami's faculty hold the highest degree in their respective fields.

The university is organized under one college—the College of Arts and Science—and six schools: the School of Education and Allied Professions (1902), the School of Business Administration (1927), the School of Fine Arts (1929), the Graduate School (1947), the School of Applied Science (1959), and the School of Interdisciplinary Studies (Western College Program) (1974).

Miami's program in paper science in the School of Applied Science is one of only seven in the nation. At the School of Business Administration undergraduates receive hands-on experience at area firms in addition to classroom training.

Field experience also is important for students in the

Patterson Place is in the heavily wooded Western campus of Miami's School of Interdisciplinary Studies.

School of Education and Allied Professions, which offers programs in home economics, health, physical education, and sports studies in addition to the teaching profession.

Departments of art, music, and architecture are included in the School of Fine Arts, and each leads to a bachelor's degree. A Bachelor of Philosophy degree is awarded graduates of the School of Interdisciplinary Studies where an individualized major is created based on the student's interests and career goals.

It is not only academic excellence for which Miami is known. Its list of alumni is a distinguished one, and many of the university's buildings bear the names of its graduates.

Benjamin Harrison, 23rd president of the United States, graduated from Miami in 1852. His running mate in 1892, Miami graduate Whitelaw Reid, distinguished himself as publisher of the *New York Tribune*, as an ambassador to France, and as special ambassador to Great Britain. Not before or since have running mates been graduates of the same institution.

Other graduates whose names adorn the campus are David Swing, 1852, and his wife, Elizabeth Porter; Samuel Spahr Laws, 1848, inventor of the stock market ticker and president of the University of Missouri; and John Shaw Billings, 1857, organizer and first director of the New York Public Library.

Probably no published work of a professor at Miami was more widely read that that of William Holmes McGuffey. In the early 1830s McGuffey prepared and tested with neighbors' children some of the readers in a series that was to play such an important part in the education and moral training of young Americans for the next 100 years.

The home McGuffey built and occupied near the edge of the campus still stands, surrounded by other buildings of more recent vintage. The cottage is maintained by the university as the William Holmes McGuffey Museum, which includes the world's largest collection of *McGuffey Readers*.

The McGuffey home is a National Historic Landmark, as is the Langstroth Cottage on the Western College campus. It was the home of Lorenzo Langstroth, the father of modern beekeeping. Miami also is known as the Mother of Fraternities and was the founding site of the famous Miami Triad of Beta Theta Pi, Phi Delta Theta, and Sigma Chi. The first two have national headquarters on campus, as do Phi Kappa Tau, the professioal business fraternity; Delta Sigma Pi; and one sorority, Delta Zeta, also founded at the university.

To those who follow sports, Miami is recognized as the Cradle of Coaches. Its graduates have filled coaching and athletic administrative ranks at all levels. Among the notables who made their mark at the university: Earl "Red" Blaik, Woody Hayes, Walter Alston, Paul Brown, Weeb Ewbank, Ara Parseghian, Carmen Cozza, Dick Crum, Paul Dietzel, Wayne Embry, John Pont, and Bo Schembechler.

The university's system of libraries include five on the Oxford campus and one each on the Hamilton and Middletown campuses. They house more than one million cataloged volumes, 1.7 million microform materials, thousands of recordings and other nonprint materials, and 80,000 maps.

Of special note is the E.W. King Juvenile Collection in the King Library. It includes approximately 8,000 English and American books dating from the early seventeenth century through the 1930s. There are numerous first editions of children's books, providing a most valuable source for the study of the development of literature and publishing for children.

TRUSTCORP, INC.

The revitalization of the city of Toledo in the 1980s has demonstrated that a comprehensive approach to urban problems can yield remarkable results. Toledo's accomplishments have drawn international acclaim, in part, because of the dynamic role taken by Trustcorp, Inc.

Through its nonbanking affiliate, SeaGate Community Development Corporation, Trustcorp has been instrumental in coordinating the efforts of government, the private sector, and concerned citizens in the revitalization of Toledo and other cities in northwest and central Ohio.

At Trustcorp, community involvement is as high a priority as financial service. The corporation believes that a major financial institution must provide leadership and promote the development and growth of the community in which it operates.

That community commitment began May 6, 1868, when Toledo Savings Institution was founded on Summit Street. Richard Mott was the president of Toledo's first financial institution, which was capitalized with $100,000.

Toledo Savings consolidated with Toledo Savings and Bank Trust in 1875, but it wasn't until December 31, 1923, that The Toledo Trust Company was created in the merger with the Summit Trust Company.

The strength of the growing institution soon became evident. Toledo Trust was the only bank headquartered in Toledo to survive the Depression. At the time it had assets of $53 million and capital of $8 million. Since then Toledo Trust has added milestones of growth. It passed the $500-million asset mark in 1972, one billion dollars in 1979, $2 billion in 1984, $3 billion in 1985, $4 billion a year later, and $5 billion in 1987.

The city's first skyscraper, the Second National Bank Building, was home to Toledo Trust beginning in 1934. In 1978, however, the company announced it would build a new headquarters on the riverfront in a development partnership with Owens-Illinois, Inc. The $13-million triangular Toledo Trust Building was completed in 1981 and, with Owen-Illinois' new headquarters, served as a catalyst for more than $300 million worth of riverfront redevelopment known as SeaGate.

The new headquarters building of Trustcorp, Inc., opened in 1981 at Three SeaGate, Toledo.

Northwest Ohio Bancshares, Inc., the bank holding company created in 1971, was renamed Toledo Trustcorp, Inc., in 1979. On April 10, 1986, the name of the holding company was changed to Trustcorp, Inc., to reflect its growing regional expansion.

Today Trustcorp includes one Ohio bank subsidiary, Trustcorp Bank, Ohio, formed in 1988 by consolidating three former banks: The Toledo Trust Company, Toledo; Trustcorp Company, N.A., Columbus; and Trustcorp Company, Dayton.

The corporation expanded across state boundaries in 1986 with acquisitions in Indiana and Michigan. By yearend 1987 in Indiana, the corporation had two bank holding companies: St. Joseph Bancorporation, Inc., South Bend, and First Bancshares of Huntington, Inc., Huntington, with nine banks and 89 locations. Trustcorp has two pending acquisitions in Indiana: Summcorp, Fort Wayne, and Citizens Bank, Indianapolis.

Another corporate bank subsidiary is Trustcorp of Michigan, Inc., based in Ann Arbor. The affiliates include Citizens Trust, Ann Arbor; Commercial Savings Bank, Adrian; The Jipson-Carter State Bank, Blissfield; and Ypsilanti Savings Bank, Ypsilanti.

Trustcorp's nine nonbanking affiliates include Atlas Tours & Travel Service, Inc., SeaGate Community Development Corporation, SeaGate Appraisal Services, Inc., SeaGate Capital Management Company, SeaGate Venture Management, Inc., SeaGate Corporation, Trustcorp of Florida, N.A., Trustcorp Mortgage Company, and Trustcorp Insurance Company.

The corporation has continued to strategically advance into regions that complement the industrial, commercial, and agricultural mix of the Ohio, Michigan, and Indiana communities it both knows and serves well. Trustcorp, Inc., also has continued its leadership role, accepting the responsibilities of corporate citizenship that this entails.

The main office corridor of the Second National Bank in 1913.

The Second National Bank on Summit Street following the grand opening in 1913. This served as the headquarters for the bank and its corporation until 1981.

FULLER & HENRY

Fuller & Henry's principal office is located on the 17th and 18th floors of One SeaGate, the cornerstone building of the Seagate complex. From its founding the firm's offices have been located downtown. For over 16 years Fuller & Henry's office was in Edison Plaza, constructed in 1971 on the site of the long-demolished office building in which Harry King and T.H. Tracy started the firm in 1892.

In the spring of 1892 Toledo was already a thriving industrial, commercial, and transportation center. Its location at the mouth of the Maumee River at the western end of Lake Erie gave it the natural advantages necessary to prosper as a business community.

On April 1 of that year two Toledo attorneys, Harry E. King and Thomas H. Tracy, formed a partnership for the practice of law. King & Tracy soon established itself as a leading business law firm, a heritage that continues today under the name of Fuller & Henry.

In 1914 King retired to pursue business and investment interests, and the firm assumed the name it would retain for the next 31 years: Tracy, Chapman & Welles. It was during that period that a national practice and reputation for the firm emerged. At the time of his death in 1933, the *Toledo Blade* observed that "for more than a half-century Mr. Tracy had been one of the leading figures at the bar of Ohio, and his fame as a corporation lawyer extended far beyond the borders of the state."

As Toledo matured as a city in the first third of this century, the law firm played a prominent role as representative of numerous utility and transportation clients, largely under the leadership of Tracy and, in later years, Edward W. Kelsey, who joined the firm in 1912 and remained in active practice until his death in 1949.

The firm's reputation as preeminent trial and appellate practitioners also was established in the early years. George D. Welles, who began practice in 1903 and became a partner of the firm in 1908, and Kelsey were the leaders of the firm's litigation practice in the formative years. In 1926 Fred E. Fuller became associated with the practice and was to make his mark not only as a litigator but also as a leading business and corporate lawyer in years to come.

Representation of its private clients was not the firm's only interest, however. Its members were active in the growth and development of the city. For instance, George Welles was a principal draftsman of Toledo's first city charter in 1914. Twenty years later Welles again was called on to write the charter amendments to give Toledo one of the earliest city manager systems of local government in the nation.

The firm's steady growth continued so that by 1935, when a reorganization of the firm took place, there were 10 partners and six associates. By the mid-1950s the practice had increased in size to more than 20 lawyers, and by the end of 1981, when the present name of Fuller & Henry was assumed, there were 50 attorneys on board.

The years of greatest growth began following World War II and coincided with the leadership of Fuller. As a young trial and business lawyer, he had been trained by Tracy, Welles, and Kelsey. In 1946 he became general counsel of the Owens-Illinois Glass Company and senior partner of the law firm three years later.

In later years Fuller would also become general counsel of Toledo Edison Company and of the Glass Container Manufacturers' Institute. In addition, he was a founder of the Antitrust Law Section of the American Bar Association and a nationally recognized antitrust practitioner throughout the 1950s and 1960s.

The leadership of Fuller & Henry's utility and corporate law practice had passed to Leslie Henry and Wilson W. Snyder by the end of the 1960s. Henry enjoyed a reputation as a preeminent corporate and securities practitioner and at the time of his death in 1976 was widely regarded as the dean of legal counsel within the electric utility industry in the United States.

Snyder, who died in 1977, was chiefly responsible during the 1960s and 1970s for developing a new area of administrative and regulatory practice: environmental law. Since then, the law relating to air and water pollution and the regulation of hazardous materials has become one of the firm's most important practice areas on a local, statewide, multistate, and national basis.

Throughout the 1970s and 1980s, Fuller & Henry played a key role in the redevelopment of downtown Toledo. As legal advisors to developers, architects, landowners, and anchor tenants, the firm was involved in the development of the entire SeaGate complex, which includes corporate headquarters buildings, general office and commercial facilities, a festival marketplace, two new luxury hotels, and a convention center. In early 1988 the firm's own principal office was relocated from Edison Plaza to the 17th and 18th floors of One SeaGate, on the Maumee River shoreline.

As Fuller & Henry anticipates its centennial anniversary in 1992, it continues to grow and to pursue its founders' goals—to provide clients with legal counsel and representation characterized by competence, integrity, timeliness, and efficiency.

PRESCOTT, BALL & TURBEN, INC.

Prescott, Ball & Turben, Inc., engineered a dramatic growth spurt over the past decade to become one of the country's largest regional investment banking and brokerage firms.

The organization's predecessors date back to 1907. From the 1930s to the 1960s Merrill, Turben & Company and Prescott & Company were among Cleveland's most prominent investment firms. Pooling their resources in 1968, they laid a strong foundation for growth.

Prescott entered the New York market in 1969 through a merger with Vanden Broeck & Company that also yielded a securities clearing capability. Mergers with four other New York firms reinforced Prescott's presence in metropolitan New York. In 1973 Prescott joined forces with another major Cleveland firm, Ball, Burge & Kraus. This union strengthened the firm's position in the fixed-income (bonds) market.

By the mid-1970s Prescott had grown to well over 400 employees, but found itself narrowly focused on retail business. Its management saw diversification as the key to building a secure profit base and raising capital. The company began to develop its corporate finance and investment banking capabilities, increase its fixed-income operation, expand its over-the-counter trading, build an asset management/investment advisory department, and enter the travel business.

While Prescott, Ball & Turben prides itself on being a strong regional firm—its roots firmly grounded in the Midwest—it is also involved in the bond business nationally. Through its subsidiary, Selected Financial Services Co., Prescott, Ball & Turben currently manages more than one billion dollars in pensions and mutual funds. Prescott Travel has become Ohio's largest travel agency.

Furthermore, in the first nine months of 1987, Prescott, Ball & Turben has managed more municipal offerings in both Ohio and Michigan than any other banking institution.

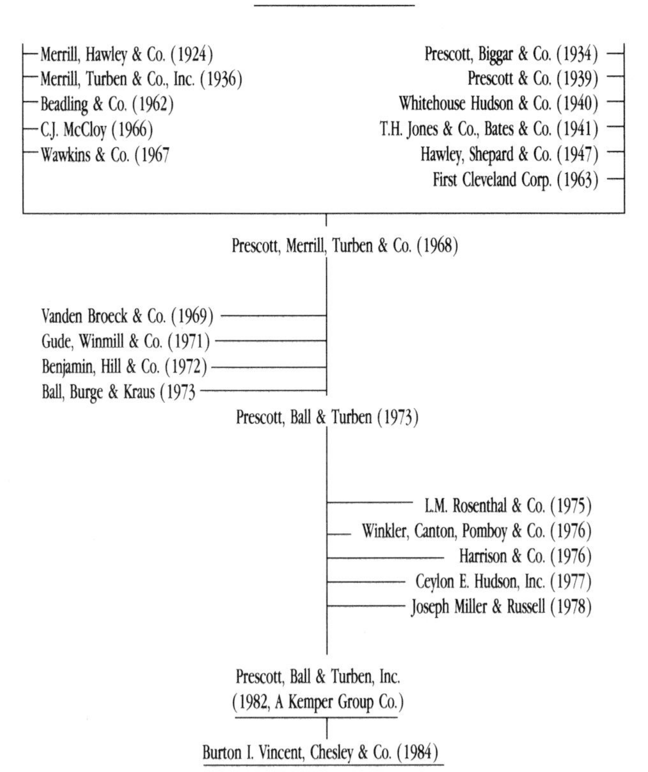

Above: Prescott, Ball & Turben's genealogy includes more than 20 firms.

Left: Prescott, Ball & Turben's headquarters in the historic Linder Building on Cleveland's Playhouse Square. The company bought and restored the building to its original 1913 look, a move that was a catalyst to the area's development.

In 1982 Kemper Corporation, a Chicago-based insurance company, became Prescott's majority shareholder. This development assured stability and access to capital for future growth.

Today Prescott boasts of approximately 20 offices in Ohio, 5 in New York, 5 in Michigan, as well as one each in Chicago; Boston; San Francisco; Atlanta; Sarasota; Florida; Erie, Pennsylvania; and Louisville, Kentucky.

But despite its size—1,300 employees and $175 million in annual sales—its people have the entrepreneurial drive of a much smaller company. In fact, Prescott's profit margins are among the highest in the industry.

Prescott management has made a deliberate decision to remain flexible and loosely structured, the firm is managed by its operating department heads. The result has been a creative, efficient operation that responds to customers' needs and the rapid changes in the industry.

The genealogy of Prescott, Ball & Turben, Inc., embraces numerous distinguished firms and many talented individuals. Their names have been absorbed, but their professionalism, integrity, and skill are recognized by Prescott customers, and their contributions are evident on the bottom line.

PETER J. SCHMITT COMPANY, INC.

Success in the wholesale and retail foods business hinges on efficiency, variety, consistency, and competitive products. The Peter J. Schmitt Company's performance has made the multidivision company a billion-dollar industry leader.

The Peter J. Schmitt Company's success story began in 1976, when Weston, the Canadian parent firm, merged its two Upstate New York subsidiaries—Loblaws Supermarkets and Peter J. Schmitt—in hopes of increasing efficiency. The following spring Weston appointed Charles Barcelona as chief executive officer to avert an economic crisis at the newly consolidated Peter J. Schmitt Company.

Barcelona halted the flow of red ink by slimming down management. His strong, forthright leadership quickly infused an entrepreneurial spirit throughout the organization. Later he and his team of turnaround specialists worked the same magic with other acquisitions around Buffalo, New York (1979), Sharon, Pennsylvania (1982), Rochester, New York (1982), and again in Buffalo (1985).

In 1985 Peter J. Schmitt moved one of its headquarter offices to Akron after purchasing Santisi Produce Company, Inc., of Youngstown and Betsy Ross of Akron. The Youngstown operation began in 1940, when John Santisi traded his horse and wagon for a 1923 Ford truck to deliver produce. The family enterprise thrived, adding a retail store, partnerships, and a wholesale distribution business that eventually served 55 Sparkle Market retail stores.

The Akron operation began when a group of independent Akron-area grocers formed the Sparkle Market Association in the early 1950s and created Betsy Ross Foods, Inc., to service the association in 1954. Ten years later Betsy Ross outgrew its original Akron Coffee facilities and built a new warehouse and offices on Gilchrist Road. That warehouse site became the present divisional headquarters.

Peter J. Schmitt's growth has created one of the largest completely voluntary food distribution systems in the tristate region, serving nearly 1,000 retail and institutional customers. To better handle this growth, four divisions were created and placed under their own senior vice-presidents.

The Tri-State Division, headed by Francis Henn, serves nearly 400 retail stores in Ohio, southern and western Pennsylvania, and West Virginia. Customers include Sparkle Markets, Apple's Markets, Bi-Rite Markets, Kuhn's, and about 65 independents that operate under their own name.

The Northeast Division, led by Timothy Foley, oversees operations in Upstate New York and northern Pennsylvania. Like the Tri-State Division, it supplies supermarkets with national brands in grocery, frozen, dairy, tobacco, meat, produce, and supplies. Peter J. Schmitt also handles no-name products, a large variety of bulk foods, and private labels such as Bells, National, Valuplus, and Shurfine.

The General Merchandise Division, under William Petrocco, provides the Tri-State and Northeastern divisions with a full line of health and beauty aids and general merchandise. Finally, the Institutional Service Division, led by Tom Gemkowski, supplies hotels, restaurants, and chains such as Wendy's and Howard Johnson Restaurants from Ohio to New England.

Today the 14,000 employees of Peter J. Schmitt, Inc.,

***Top:** Peter J. Schmitt Company, Inc., supplies more than 400 retail stores such as Apple's Markets with national brands in grocery, frozen, dairy, tobacco, meat, and produce items.*

***Above:** The company fleet of trucks is constantly on the move throughout Ohio, southern and western Pennsylvania, and West Virginia.*

THE CLEVELAND CLINIC FOUNDATION

King Khaled of Saudia Arabia, President Joao Figueiredo of Brazil, and King Hussein of Jordan have come to The Cleveland Clinic Foundation for care. They and thousands of other patients from around the world consider it an international health resource.

In addition, more than 110,000 patients yearly arrive from throughout Ohio and the United States, referred by their doctors or coming independently when facing complex or stubborn health problems. And they find an institution with the vitality, complexity, and resources that inspire awe and confidence.

The Cleveland Clinic's founders provided the spark. Their energy and fortitude, their insight into the needs of patients, and their shared values, experiences, and goals charted the path to growth and greatness.

A close association between Cleveland surgeons Frank Bunts, George Crile, and William Lower began in the late 1880s and early 1890s and continued for the rest of their lives. They shared offices first on Church Street and then in the Osborn Building from 1897 to 1921. Their mutual trust and regard were reflected in Dr. Crile's journal entry: "We have been rivals in everything, yet through all the vicissitudes of personal, financial, and professional relations, we have been able to think and act as a unit."

The idea of the Cleveland Clinic took root in a military hospital in Rouen, France, during World War I. The trio, all volunteers in the Lakeside Unit, had been impressed by the efficiency of a team including every branch of medicine and surgery.

Dr. John Phillips joined the trio after their return home. The four founders honed their plan for the Cleveland Clinic and summed up their intentions: "better care of the sick, investigation of their problems, and further education of those who serve."

The doors of The Cleveland Clinic Foundation opened on February 26, 1921. A group practice, it drew criticism from colleagues in private practice who felt it unfair competition. But the founders, who all had national reputations and medical professorships, agreed that medicine had become too complex for one person to comprehend. For the sake of patients they were specializing, pooling resources, and reinvesting part of their fees in education and research.

The clinic prospered and built its own hospital by 1924. This provided convenient access to patients and encouraged close cooperation among doctors on difficult cases, a tradition that continues to this day.

Disaster struck in May 1929. Fumes from smoldering nitrocellulose X-ray films caused the deaths of 123 employees and patients, including Dr. Phillips, and injuries to 50 more people. There were $3 million in lawsuits, and that October the stock market collapsed. Nonetheless, the surviving founders persuaded the board of trustees to continue to expand.

Since the start of The Cleveland Clinic Foundation, its professional staff (now 430) has grown by about 5 percent annually, and specialties and subspecialties have proliferated. Today there are five clinical divisions—medicine, surgery, radiology, anesthesiology, and laboratory medicine—research, and education, plus operations and public affairs. Each division is subdivided into departments, with medicine and surgery jointly containing 28 departments equipped to provide state-of-the-art care for the range of medical problems.

The founders (clockwise, from top left): Frank Bunts, the dignified and reserved senior surgeon; George Crile, Sr., the innovative surgeon and dynamo who had a special interest in research and is credited with performing the world's first blood transfusion; William Lower, the consummate technician in surgery, notable pioneer in urology, and prudent treasurer; and John Phillips, the confident and imperturbable organizer of a very successful medical division.

At different times different diseases have received prominent attention. In the early years, until the discovery of an iodine treatment for goiter, thyroid surgery was a huge part of the clinic's activity. In the 1940s demand for operations for cancer of the colon and rectum increased, due to the skill and success rate of Dr. Thomas Jones. Other clinic surgeons have since built up the clinic's reputation for pioneer-

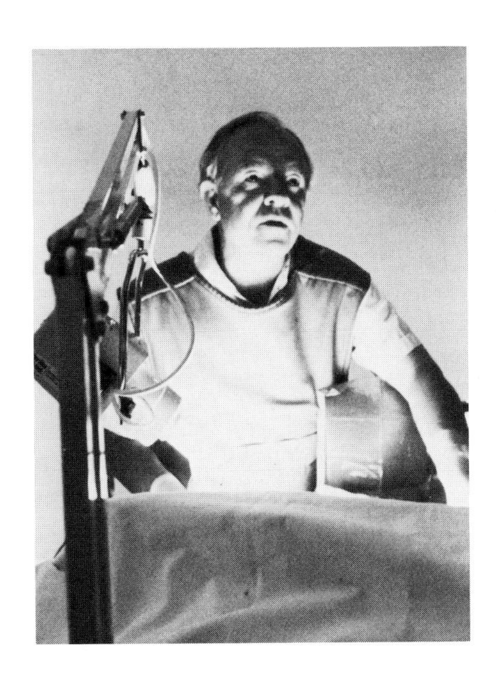

A view, facing northwest, of the Cleveland Clinic campus today.

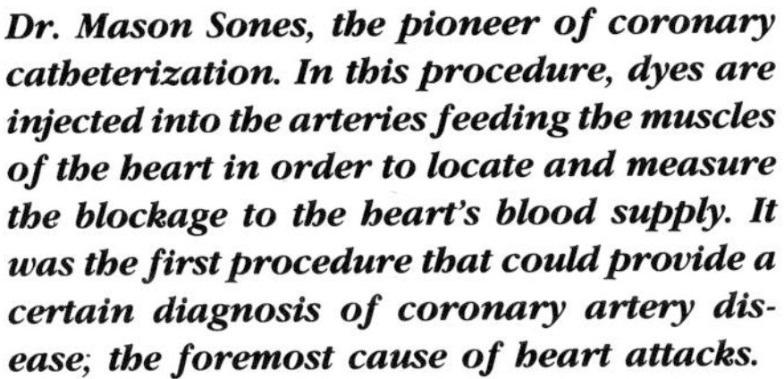

Dr. Mason Sones, the pioneer of coronary catheterization. In this procedure, dyes are injected into the arteries feeding the muscles of the heart in order to locate and measure the blockage to the heart's blood supply. It was the first procedure that could provide a certain diagnosis of coronary artery disease; the foremost cause of heart attacks.

ing less radical surgical treatment of cancers of the breast, thyroid, rectum, and intestines.

Similarly, Cleveland Clinic researchers have long focused on the health problems of the day rather than conducting research for its own sake. In the 1940s the clinic began to concentrate its efforts on the foremost modern health problem—heart disease. In 1945 Dr. Irvine Page arrived to direct research into the causes of blood pressure and the link between diet and heart disease.

Major contributions from this thrust include the role of cholesterol in cardiovascular disease and the discovery and synthesis of serotonin and angiotensin, two hormones that influence blood pressure.

Clinical breakthroughs gave the world the first catheterization to capture visual images of the arteries feeding the heart (Dr. Mason Sones, 1958), and first saphenous (leg) vein bypass surgery to restore the heart's blood supply and prevent heart attack (Dr. Rene Favoloro, 1967). In recent years the clinic has performed more than 3,000 heart operations annually with pacesetting success rates.

Another important line of pioneering work dealt with artificial organs and assist devices, particularly the kidney and the heart (an effort begun by Dr. Willem Kolff). Other advances have come from work designing artificial joints, improving the methods of kidney repair and transplantation, investigating less invasive radiologic techniques, understanding brain and nervous system disorders, and restoring blood flow through vascular surgery. Currently about 450 research projects are being funded, many of them supported by the clinic's own resources.

The Cleveland Clinic Foundation also backs a strong education program. It operates the nation's largest freestanding postgraduate medical education program. There are more than 630 physicians in 33 separately approved residency programs, 430 medical students in clerkship studies, and 400 students in 21 different allied health programs. In addition, more than 6,800 participants attend clinic-sponsored continuing medical education courses.

Steady growth of its care, research, and educational roles has led to continual expansion of the campus, including the addition of buildings to house education (1964), research (1974), laboratory medicine (1980), medical magnetic resonance diagnostics—the first center of its kind in the world—(1982), a new outpatient clinic facility (1985), and hospital wing (1986). National and international demand for care has led to the construction of offices in Fort Lauderdale, Florida, and an affiliation in Istanbul, Turkey.

In recent years the Cleveland Clinic has become one of Ohio's largest institutions and employers. As such, it has become increasingly involved with its community and state, as well as providing continued national leadership in health issues and acting as an international ambassador of good will.

The nation's concern with health care costs, the health care needs of an increasingly older population, and the ever rising hopes and expectations of patients will challenge The Cleveland Clinic Foundation in the future. Patients' problems will change and the cast of care providers will shift, but the founders' values and shared commitments to patient care, research, and education will continue to sustain The Cleveland Clinic Foundation for decades to come.

GENCORP INC.

GenCorp Inc. is a technology-based company with strong positions in aerospace, automotive, and related polymer products. Over its 72-year history, it has shaped its own success in a wide range of industries, starting with tires.

In 1915 founder William O'Neill incorporated The General Tire & Rubber Company of Akron. He nurtured the tire-manufacturing business into a strong force in the replacement tire market.

In 1936 the firm began its first overseas operation in Poznam, Poland. It enlisted a group of foreign investors and supplied the manufacturing and operating know-how, retaining minority interest. The pattern of partnership was a success, and later led to the creation of about 30 such companies worldwide.

Other tire business milestones included the start of sales to truck manufacturers (1937), selling tires for off-the-road vehicles starting in the late 1950s, construction of a giant tire facility in Bryan (1967), and building the first all-radial-tire production plant in America in Mt. Vernon, Illinois (1973). Though firmly committed to tire manufacturing, the company also sought entry into other less seasonal and more profitable markets.

One major area of diversification was manufacturing industrial rubber products. The effort spurred the start-up of a major plant in Wabash, Indiana (1936), that made car and refrigerator gaskets, and parts to smooth vehicle rides.

The company entered the entertainment scene by acquiring Boston's Yankee Radio network (1942). That led to a wide range of activities under RKO General, including television (1946), movies (1955), cable television (1960), and soft-drink bottling (1965).

The thrust into aerospace began with the purchase of Aerojet Engineering (1944) and its merger with Cincinnati's Crosley Motor to create Aerojet-General (1953). A specialist in developing propulsion systems, Aerojet numbered among its many achievements the rocket engines that landed the first men on the moon and returned them to earth.

The chemical operation began as a support for the rubber plants but grew into a significant business of its own. The first plastics facility was started to manufacture film and sheeting (1950). The Chemical Division (1951) was organized with headquarters in Akron and is the first plant (1952) in an Akron suburb. The company, spotting the promising future of vinyl-coated fabric, acquired Textileather of Toledo and Bolta Company (1953), makers of vinyl chloride resins.

GenCorp is among the leading suppliers of automotive weatherstripping and vibration isolation components for cars and trucks. GenCorp weatherstripping is being applied here to a late-model passenger car. The company first began supplying weatherstripping to the automotive industries in the 1930s.

In 1984 the firm was renamed GenCorp in recognition of its diversity. Three years later it sold its tire and entertainment divisions to survive a takeover bid. GenCorp now consists of Aerojet General, which is active in jet propulsion, ordnance, and defense electronics; GenCorp Automotive, which supplies automotive components; and GenCorp Polymer Products, a diversified subsidiary with businesses related to each other by polymer technology.

GenCorp-Automotive's operations make reinforced plastic panels for Corvettes and other vehicles, sealing systems, vibration-control products, and soft trim material for vehicle interiors.

GenCorp Polymer Products supplies rigid and flexible films, roofing materials, and latex used for fine-coated printing papers and for bonding materials.

GenCorp Polymer Products includes the world's largest manufacturer of wall covering for commercial applications and Penn Athletic Products, the world's most innovative tennis and racquetball maker.

Today GenCorp Inc. moves ahead on many fronts, riding on wheels of new technologies.

Aerojet General, GenCorp's defense and aerospace subsidiary, has been producing propulsion components for more than four decades. Early in its history Aerojet produced the jet assist takeoff (JATO) rockets used to launch fighter planes from the decks of aircraft carriers during World War II.

CASE WESTERN RESERVE UNIVERSITY

Cleveland's Case Western Reserve University traces its history to a small pioneer-era college, the first in Northeast Ohio. Today, as a major research university, it helps to sustain its region and nation through pioneering work in areas including health care, engineering, social services, and management.

The university boasts two major progenitors—Western Reserve College, founded in 1826 in Hudson, Ohio, 26 miles from today's campus, and the Case School of Applied Science, founded in Cleveland in 1880.

The college took its name from its region, the Western Reserve of Connecticut—3.5 million Ohio acres retained by the eastern state when it ceded the rest of its western claims to the federal government after the Revolution. Founded by the area's earliest white settlers, Western Reserve College passed more than a half-century in Hudson before a gift from Cleveland entrepreneur and railroad builder Amasa Stone made possible a move in 1882 to the bustling port of Cleveland, where it joined its medical department, founded in 1843.

Cleveland leaders, envisioning even then the benefits of a joint enterprise, provided an adjacent campus for the two-year-old Case School of Applied Science, named for its benefactor, Cleveland philanthropist Leonard Case, Jr. The move placed as neighbors a typical liberal arts college of the time and a new kind of school established by its founder to teach "mathematics, physics, engineering mechanical and civil, chemistry, economic geology, mining and metallurgy, natural history, drawing, and modern languages."

The two friendly rivals waited until 1967—by then bearing the names Western Reserve University and Case Institute of Technology—to join forces formally as Case Western Reserve University. But they collaborated from the beginning. Among the most productive joint efforts was that of Case physicist Albert Michelson and Western Reserve chemist Edward Morley. The Michelson-Morley Experiment disproved the existence of "the ether," thought to be the medium for light's travel through space, and opened the way for the theory of relativity.

***Left:** Adelbert Hall, the first building at Western Reserve College when the institution moved to Cleveland from Hudson, Ohio, now houses Case Western Reserve University's central administration.*

***Below:** Case Western Reserve students, in fields from engineering to English, are right at home with computers. Here students are at work in one of the university's computer centers.*

A century after the famous experiment, Case Western Reserve carries on education, research, and service through undergraduate and graduate programs in the arts, humanities, engineering, sciences, and social sciences, and through professional schools in the fields of medicine, nursing, dentistry, law, management, and applied social sciences.

Committed to a major role in regional and national economic development, the university has organized centers for applied research in such areas as polymers; automation and advanced manufacturing; animal biotechnology; adhesives, sealants, and coatings; advanced ceramics; entrepreneurial development; biomedical technology; and sensor technology. An innovative subsidiary, University Technology, Inc., has been set up to speed the commercial development of university research.

Case Western Reserve University centers such as the Mandel Center for Non-Profit Organizations, the Center for Professional Ethics, and the Center on Aging and Health reflect a wide-ranging effort to enhance regional, national, and even worldwide well-being.

OHIO'S INVESTOR-OWNED ELECTRIC COMPANIES

Ohio's investor-owned electric companies today produce more than 90 percent of the electricity used in the state. They serve more than 30,000 industries, almost 400,000 businesses, and a total of more than 4 million customers.

The eight companies are Cincinnati Gas & Electric, Cleveland Electric Illuminating, Columbus Southern Power, Dayton Power and Light, Monongahela Power, Ohio Edison, Ohio Power, and Toledo Edison.

Thomas Alva Edison was not even born when, in 1837, the Ohio Legislature granted a charter to a new enterprise, the Cincinnati Gas-Light and Coke Company. Electric illumination came to the city in the early 1880s and, despite heavy competition, it was the gas company that became the city's sole purveyor in 1901 under its new name, Cincinnati Gas & Electric. Today CG&E serves approximately 645,000 electric and 379,000 gas customers in an area covering 3,000 square miles. It has approximately 4,500 employees.

In Cleveland it was Charles Francis Brush who illuminated Public Square with arc lights one evening in 1879. Two years later his Brush Electric Light and Power Company crews strung the first service lines for the city's 88 electric street lamps. That company was a forerunner of Cleveland Electric Illuminating Co., which reached a milestone in 1955 with the installation of its 500,000th electric meter.

Electric street lamps came to Dayton in 1883, about the time the ancestry of Dayton Power and Light also began. However, that name was not adopted until 1911 as a result of a series of mergers.

Today Ohio's eight investor-owned electric companies provide a safe, reliable supply of electricity to more than 4-million customers statewide.

This Dayton Lighting Company crew, circa 1911, is typical of what a customer might have expected to see in the early days of electrification in Ohio.

Columbus Southern Power has a number of branches in its family tree as 60 predecessors emerged and merged over the years. Two primary companies came together in the final consolidation in 1937. They were the Columbus Railway, Power & Light Company, serving the Columbus area, and the Southern Ohio Electric Company, which served communities and rural areas of southern Ohio.

An interesting note is that the Columbus company began in 1863 not as a utility but as a horse-drawn streetcar company that later became electrified.

Ohio Edison is the result of a five-company consolidation in 1930. Those firms served the areas of Youngstown, Akron, and Springfield. Today Ohio Edison is one of the largest electric companies in the state, serving more than 873,000 customers in its 7,500-square-mile territory.

Tradition has it that Ohio Power Company was "born" on Christmas Eve 1883. That's when the lights went on in Tiffin, thanks to the first central power station west of the Allegheny Mountains that was owned by one of Ohio Power's ancestors, the Tiffin Edison Electric Illuminating Company. In 1884 the same firm provided power to St. Paul's Methodist Church, the first public building in the world to be wired while being built. Today the Canton-based Ohio Power Company serves some 630,000 customers in 53 of Ohio's 88 counties.

Like the others, Toledo Edison Company came out of a series of mergers and consolidations over a period of more than 60 years. But the first company was the Toledo Gas-Light and Coke Company, formed in 1853. One hundred and twenty-five years later Toledo Edison opened the state's first nuclear power plant.

In 1951 these eight companies formed The Ohio Electric Utility Institute, a trade association based in Columbus. OEUI represents the investor-owned electric companies as an information clearinghouse and as a point of contact for the media, public, and government representatives in search of data on the state's electric industry.

GREATER CLEVELAND GROWTH ASSOCIATION

The Greater Cleveland Growth Association is the largest metropolitan chamber of commerce in the United States in terms of members and operating dollars. It is a nonprofit, voluntary organization of business, professional, and institutional leaders who work closely with government and community leaders to enhance economic opportunity and quality of life in the Greater Cleveland area. Since its inception the Association has undergone many changes, but its basic mission remains intact: to attract, expand, and retain area business investment.

In 1848 a group of 36 merchants formed the Board of Trade of the City of Cleveland. It was the first body organized to promote Cleveland commerce and civic welfare, and attracted widespread participation. By 1893 membership had increased to 1,000, and the name had changed to the Cleveland Chamber of Commerce.

In 1926 the chamber and the Cleveland Advertising Club—the second-oldest regional advertising club in the country—introduced a three-year campaign to sell Cleveland to the world. In 1937 the chamber's industrialists launched the Cleveland Plan to pull the city out of the Great Depression. During World War II they developed the Jobs for All After Victory program to prepare for a vigorous peacetime economy.

In 1964 a separate board targeted directly at economic development was formed called the Greater Cleveland Growth Board.

Within four years the group merged with the Cleveland Chamber of Commerce to create the Greater Cleveland Growth Association. The name "chamber of commerce" suggests a meeting place where people discuss trade, but "growth association" suggests a group actively promoting growth. Indeed, the Association offers services to encourage and support the growth of its members and the community, and promotions to attract new investments from outside the region.

Summer days attract Cleveland residents to a festival along the riverfront.

Offering a wealth of services to members, the Greater Cleveland Growth Association compiles and distributes business, economic, and marketing data on the area; newsletters and business events calendars; and directories of members, leaders, and legislators. It also organizes and sponsors roundtables, conferences, and seminars; courses on planning and strategy; and a variety of councils and forums.

As part of its services, the Association lends assistance in business start-up, location and site selection, loan development, finance and credit issues, retail research, downtown development, exporting, recruitment, employee relations, management, and long-range planning. It also communicates the business point of view to the community; local, state, and national government; the U.S. Small Business Administration; and other organizations.

In addition, the organization builds area resources and sponsors volunteer involvement opportunities, such as the Leadership Cleveland Program, Downtown Business Council, Council of Smaller Enterprises (COSE), and Cleveland World Trade Conference. It also offers low-cost insurance and disability programs to its members.

Demonstrating steady growth over the past five decades, the Greater Cleveland Growth Association now includes 7,874 corporate members and 12,000 individual members, operating within a $4-million annual budget. As it grows it continues to lengthen its list of accomplishments. Recent successes include helping to bring the Rock and Roll Hall of Fame and Museum to Cleveland, ensuring the continued eminence of the NASA Lewis Research Center, and helping establish plans for the $285-million redevelopment of Cleveland's lakefront.

***The Greater Cleveland Growth Association is dedicated to the enhancement of economic development and quality of life in the Greater Cleveland area. Courtesy,* The Plain Dealer**

WHITE CASTLE SYSTEM, INC.

White Castle buildings and the unique and distinctive White Castle hamburger have been a part of Ohio since the first White Castle restaurants were opened in Cincinnati in 1927 and Columbus two years later.

The company was founded in 1921 in Wichita, Kansas, by former carnival cook Walter Anderson and E.W. "Billy" Ingram, Sr. Their brief partnership was formed when Anderson, who had a trio of hamburger stands, wanted to open a fourth on property owned by a dentist. He refused to grant Anderson a lease unless Ingram, then in real estate and insurance, was a backer.

Thus, the White Castle System of Eating Houses Corp. was founded on $700 in borrowed capital that was paid back in 90 days. The transaction established for the firm the principle of little or no debt that served it well during the Depression years. "He who owes no money," said Ingram, "cannot go broke."

The name White Castle was selected because it signified purity and cleanliness as well as strength, stability, and permanence. The name has served well what is today the nation's oldest privately owned and operated hamburger chain.

The first White Castle in Wichita under the Anderson-Ingram partnership was a funny looking cement block building with but five stools where customers could get a hamburger for five cents. But already the building featured the now-famous tower and battlements, an architectural style inspired by Chicago's equally famous Water Tower.

***Above:** This white cement block building, which had five stools and offered hamburgers for five cents, opened in March 1921 in Wichita, Kansas. It was the first in the White Castle System.*

***Left:** Walter Anderson (left) and E.W. "Billy" Ingram, Sr., were the founders of the White Castle System in Wichita, Kansas.*

From the beginning White Castle designed and erected its own buildings and most of the fixtures. In 1928 the modular, all-metal structure was introduced, employing for the first time porcelain enamel as an architectural material. Six years later the Porcelain Steel Buildings Company was established in Columbus to manufacture all the buildings and fixtures for the restaurant chain.

With restaurants in several states, Ingram had been looking to move his office to a more centralized location. After Anderson left in 1933 to try his hand at the aviation industry, what with the new manufacturing operation in Columbus, Ingram moved his headquarters to Ohio's capital city, too.

As the business grew, so did the fame of the little square hamburger with five evenly spaced holes. Unlike ordinary hamburgers, White Castle's are steam cooked on a cushion of onions, without cooking oils or grease. The meat and onions are placed between a soft bun, made at one of three bakeries—in Ohio, New Jersey, and Indiana—owned and operated by the firm. At the Evendale facility just outside Cincinnati, more than 224 million buns are baked annually for White Castles in Ohio and to as far west as Kansas City.

The company has been responsible for many innovations, not the least of which are the griddles on which the hamburgers are cooked. After some 60 years of development, the griddles are now made of cast aluminum, designed so they can be removed and cleaned easily.

This White Castle restaurant in Milford, Ohio, is the new look for the 1980s.

Another innovation, which dates back to the early 1930s, is the idea of selling hamburgers by the sack. In order to keep the hamburgers intact for the customer as well as retain as much of the heat as possible, White Castle developed individual heat-resistant cartons for its hamburgers, an idea that only much more recently has caught on at other fast-food hamburger chains.

The PSB Company, today's name for the Porcelain Steel Buildings Company, also has been an innovative leader in products other than those for its parent corporation. During World War II, for instance, it manufactured parts for amphibious trucks and radio antennas.

In more recent years PSB has been manufacturing its own Prizelawn line of lawn spreaders as well as private-label spreaders for a number of companies. The firm also fabricates and paints parts for other businesses in widely diverse industries such as automotive, appliance, air conditioning, construction, and communications.

It is the hamburger, however, that has captured the lion's share of attention, earning a cultish following that borders on the fanatical. The company has recorded some of the "incredibles" it has received from its customers, and a few stories have been developed into television commercials.

One story involved a White Castle-starved fan that had waited for years for a unit to open near him. When one finally did, he waited for 12 hours outside the door just so he could be the first customer. He bought 1,500 hamburgers for himself and his co-workers.

Another true story that was made into a television commercial concerned the brother of a woman who had moved to a distant city without a White Castle location. To satisfy her craving for the hamburgers, he periodically flew his private plane over her house and dropped a shipment of the hamburgers.

While it still may be some time until White Castle restaurants span the continent—there are more than 225 now—the company is looking to make frozen White Castle hamburgers available in grocery stores nationwide.

Founder Ingram was succeeded by his son, E.W. Ingram, Jr., in 1966 and by his grandson, E.W. Ingram III, in 1979. The younger Ingram prefers "a deliberately moderate but steady expansion . . . rather than leaping the continent in a single bound." However, White Castle is in Japan where the licensee plans to have more than 200 units open before the end of the century.

White Castle offers employees a benefits plan described by president Ingram as among the most comprehensive in the industry. In 1986, for example, the firm invested more than $36 million in the benefits program that served more than 9,000. For all employees, full time and part time, there is an annual cash bonus program based on sales rather than profit. The employees also enjoy a benefit expense plan, life and health insurance, a profit-sharing plan, and retirement benefits.

The White Castle hamburger is "the taste some people won't live without."

The founder's philosophy that "we have no right to expect loyalty except from those to whom we are loyal" has been practiced by his successors.

The philanthropic activities of White Castle System, Inc., and the Ingram family are channeled through three conduits: the corporate contributions fund; the Edgar W. Ingram-White Castle Fund, which is an advised fund of The Columbus Foundation; and the Ingram-White Castle Foundation. The latter offers support for agencies and institutions concerned with the quality of life, especially education.

PATRONS

The following individuals, companies, and organizations have made a valuable commitment to the quality of this publication. Windsor Publications and the Ohio Chamber of Commerce gratefully acknowledge their participation in *The Buckeye Empire: An Illustrated History of Ohio Enterprise.*

ALLTEL Corporation*
Arthur Andersen & Co.*
Anheuser-Busch, Inc.*
Bardes Corporation*
Battelle Memorial Institute*
R.W. Beckett Corporation*
Ben Venue Laboratories, Inc. (Founded in 1938)*
Blue Cross & Blue Shield Mutual of Ohio*
BP America, Inc.*
Buckeye Rubber & Packing Company*
Canton Castings Inc.
Case Western Reserve University*
Chemical Abstracts Service*
Clark Consolidated Industries Inc.*
The Cleveland Clinic Foundation*
Columbia Gas of Ohio*
Copper and Brass Sales, Inc.
Crescent Metal Products*
Cyclops Corporation*
The Davey Tree Expert Company*
Dills Supply Company
Doctors Hospital*
The Dow Chemical Company*
Duramax-Johnson*
East Ohio Gas Company*
Ebco Manufacturing Company*
Electrolock Incorporated*
Ernst & Whinney*
Stanley C. Ewing
Fuller & Henry*
Gencorp Inc.*
Greater Cleveland Growth Association*
Great Lakes Cheese Co., Inc.*
The M.A. Hanna Company*
Harper Supply, Inc.
Harrison Paint Corp.*
Holzer-Wollam Realtors*
Honda of America Manufacturing, Inc.*
The Hoover Company*
Jaco Manufacturing Company*
The Judson-Brooks Company*
Kastle Electrical Contractors*
Kendale Industries, Inc.*
Scott Krauss News Agency*
Don Kremer Lincoln Mercury
The Lima News
The Logan Clay Products Company
T. Marzetti Company*
Miami University*
Miami Valley Hospital*
MK-Ferguson Company*
Mount Carmel Health*
National City Corporation*
The Oak Rubber Company*
Ohio Association of Realtors
Ohio Bell Telephone Company*
The Ohio Electric Utility Institute
Ohio Packing Co.-Harvest Brand Meats
Ohio's Investor-Owned Electric Companies*
Ohio University*
Pizza Huts of Cincinnati, Inc.*
The Plain Dealer*
Polymer Valley Search-Akron
Porter, Wright, Morris & Arthur*
Preformed Line Products Company*
Prescott, Ball & Turben, Inc.*
The Reynolds and Reynolds Company*
Ross Laboratories*
Saint Luke's Hospital*
Peter J. Schmitt Company, Inc.*
Sea World of Ohio*
The Smith & Oby Company*
SSP Fittings Corporation*
The Stationery Shop, Inc.
The Stouffer Corporation*
Sun Refining and Marketing Company*
The Toledo Hospital*
Trustcorp, Inc.*
United Telephone Company of Ohio*
University Hospitals of Cleveland*
Van Waters & Rogers Inc.
Vorys Brothers Inc.
Vorys, Sater, Seymour and Pease*
Vulcan Tool Company*
Whirlpool Corporation*
White Castle System, Inc.*
W-H-M Equipment Co.
Worthington Foods, Inc.®*

*Partners in Progress of *The Buckeye Empire: An Illustrated History of Ohio Enterprise*. The histories of these companies and organizations appear in Chapter 9, beginning on page 207.

Bibliography

American Greetings Corporation. "The First 75 Years." "American Greetings News."

Andreano, Ralph, ed. *The Economic Impact of the Civil War.* Cambridge, Massachusetts: Schenkman, 1962.

"Autobiography of Thomas Ewing, The." Clement L. Martzloff, ed. *Ohio Archaeological and Historical Society Publications,* 22 (1913): 126-204.

Baughman, James L. "Classes and Company Towns: Legends of the 1937 Little Steel Strike." *Ohio History,* 87 (1978): 175-192.

Beachley, Charles E. *History of the Consolidation Coal Company, 1864-1934.* New York: Consolidation Coal Company, 1934.

Beaver, R. Pierce. "Joseph Hough; An Early Miami Merchant." *Ohio Archaeological and Historical Society Quarterly,* 45 (1936): 37-45.

Becker, Carl M. "A Most Complete Factory: The Barney Car Works 1850-1926." *Cincinnati Historical Society Bulletin,* 31 (1973): 48-69.

------. "Entrepreneurial Invention and Innovation in the Miami Valley During the Civil War." *Cincinnati Historical Society Bulletin,* 22 (1964): 5-28.

------. "James Leffel: Double Turbine Water Wheel Inventor." *Ohio History,* 75 (1966): 200-211, 269-270.

Benedict, C. Harry. *Red Metal; The Calumet and Hecla Story.* Ann Arbor: University of Michigan Press, 1952.

Bilstein, Roger E. "Putting Aircraft to Work: The First Air Freight." *Ohio History,* 76 (1967): 247-258.

Blackford, Mansel G. "Scientific Management and Welfare Work in Early Twentieth Century American Business: The Buckeye Steel Castings Company." *Ohio History,* 90 (1981): 238-258.

Blocker, Jack S. "Market Integration, Urban Growth and Economic Change in an Ohio County, 1850-1880." *Ohio History,* 90 (1981): 298-316.

Bob Evans Farms. "The Bob Evans Story."

Bond, Beverley W., Jr. *The Foundations of Ohio.* Columbus: Ohio State Archaeological and Historical Society, 1941.

------. *The Civilization of the Old Northwest.* New York: Macmillan, 1934.

Boryczka, Raymond, and Lorin Lee Cary. *No Strength Without Union; An Illustrated History of Ohio Workers, 1803-1980.* Columbus: Ohio Historical Society, 1982.

Buley, R. Carlyle. *The Old Northwest.* 2 vls. Bloomington: Indiana University Press, 1951.

Butler, Joseph G. *Fifty Years of Iron and Steel.* Cleveland: Penton, 1920.

Canton Hardware Company, The. Canton: Canton Hardware Company, 1934.

Carnegie, Andrew. *Autobiography.* Boston: Houghton Mifflin, 1924.

Carruth, Eleanore. "Federated Department Stores: Growing Pains at Forty." *Fortune* (June 1969): 142-147, 200-202.

Chamberlain, John. *The Enterprising Americans.* New York: Harper and Row, 1963.

Chase, Stuart. *Prosperity; Fact or Myth?* New York: Charles Boni, 1929.

Christiansen, Harry. *Northern Ohio's Interurbans and Rapid Transit Railways.* Cleveland: Transit Data, 1965.

Cincinnati Milacron. "Cincinnati Milacron, 1884-1984: Finding Better Ways."

Clark, Victor S. *History of Manufacturers in the United States.* 3 vls. New York: McGraw-Hill, 1929.

Cleveland *Plain Dealer,* October 10, 1986.

Cotkin, George B. "Strikebreakers, Evictions and Violence: Industrial Conflict in the Hocking Valley, 1884-1885." *Ohio History,* 87 (1978): 138-150.

Crout, George C. and Wilfred D. Vorhis. "John Butler Tytus: Inventor of the Continuous Rolling Mill." *Ohio History,* 76 (1967): 132-145, 176-177.

Dana Corporation. "Toward the Year 2000." "Product and Service Guide."

Davis, Harold E. "Economic Basis of Ohio Politics, 1820-1840." *Ohio State Archaeological and Historical Quarterly,* 47 (1938): 288-318.

DeWitt, Catherine C. "Bog Iron in Lake County." *Lake County Historical Society Quarterly,* 13 (August 1971).

Diebold Incorporated. "Diebold Incorporated, Established in Canton 100 Years Ago." Supplement to *Wooster Record,* August 21, 1972.

Downard, William L. *The Cincinnati Brewing Industry: A Social and Economic History.* Athens: Ohio University Press, 1973.

Duggan, Edward P. "Machines, Markets, and Labor: The Carriage and Wagon Industry in Late-Nineteenth-Century Cincinnati." *Business History Review,* 51 (1977): 308-325.

Farrell, Richard T. "Cincinnati, 1800-1830: Economic Development Through Trade and Industry." *Ohio History,* 77 (1968): 111-129, 171.

50 Years in Steel: The Youngstown Sheet and Tube Company: 1900-1949. Youngstown: Youngstown Sheet and Tube Company, 1950.

Fine, Sidney. "The Toledo Chevrolet Strike of 1935." *Ohio Historical Quarterly,* 67 (1958): 326-356.

"Five Hundred, The." *Fortune* (April 29, 1985): 266-285.

Fisher, Douglas A. *Steel Serves the Nation: The Fifty Year Story of United States Steel, 1901-1951.* New York: United States Steel Corporation, 1951.

"Four Hundred Richest People in America, The." *Forbes* (October 27, 1986): 106-312.

Garber, D.W. *Waterwheels and Millstones: A History of Ohio's Gristmills and Milling.* Columbus: Ohio Historical Society, 1970.

Gates, William C., Jr. and Dana E. Omerod. *The East Liverpool, Ohio, Pottery District.* California, Pennsylvania: The Society for Historical Archaeology, 1982.

Greater Cleveland Growth Association. "Headquarters Cleveland."

Greif, Martin. *The New Industrial Landscape: The Story of the Austin Company.* Clinton, New Jersey: Main Street Press, 1978.

Drismer, Karl H. *Akron and Summit County.* Akron: Summit County Historical Society, n.d.

Gutman, Herbert G. "An Iron Workers' Strike in the Ohio Valley, 1873-1874." *Ohio Historical Quarterly,* 68 (1959): 353-370.

Hampton, Taylor. "Cleveland's Fabulous Vans." *Cleveland News,* August 1955.

Hartwell, Dickson. "The Mighty Jeep." *American Heritage,* 12(1) (1960): 38-41.

Hatcher, Harlan. *The Buckeye Country: A Pageant of Ohio.* New York: H.C. Kinsey, 1940.

------. "Commerce and Culture, The Pattern in Ohio: An Address." *Ohio Historical Quarterly,* 66 (1957): 270-277.

------. *The Western Reserve: The Story of New Connecticut in Ohio.* Indianapolis: Bobbs-Merrill, 1949.

Havighurst, Walter. *Ohio: A Bicentennial History.* New York: Norton, 1976.

------. *Vein of Iron: The Pickands Mather Story.* Cleveland: World, 1958.

Herryman, Maurice. *In Quiet Ways: George H. Mead, the Man and the Company.* Dayton: The Mead Corporation, 1970.

History of Geauga and Lake Counties, Ohio. Philadelphia: Williams Brothers, 1878.

Holmes, Robert E. "Ohio's Industrial Growth, 1900-1957, and Some Possibilities for Study." *Ohio Historical Quarterly,* 66 (1957): 290-299.

Hook, Charles R. *Romance of Iron and Steel: Contribution to the Central Ohio Valley.* New York: Newcomen Society, 1950.

Hoover Company. "How the Vacuum Cleaner Began." "Hoover Historical Center." "Celebrating Seventy-Five Years." "Our Proud Past . . . And Exciting Future."

Hulbert, Archer B. *The Cumberland Road.* Cleveland: Arthur Clark, 1904.

Hunter, W.H. "The Pathfinders of Jefferson County." *Ohio Archaeological and Historical Society Publications,* 6 (1898): 95-406.

Hurt, R. Douglas. "Dairying in Nineteenth Century Ohio." *The Old Northwest,* 5 (Winter 1979-1980): 387-399.

------. "Pork and Porkopolis." *Cincinnati Historical Society Bulletin,* 40 (1982).

Hutslar, Donald A. "Ohio Waterpowered Sawmills." *Ohio History,* 84 (1975): 5-56.

Jefferson Furnace. "Celebration of the Ninety-second Anniversary of the Founding of Jefferson Furnace."

Jones, Robert L. "Ohio Agriculture in History." *Ohio Historical Quarterly,* 65 (1956): 229-258.

Jordan, Philip D. *Ohio Comes of Age, 1873-1900.* Columbus: Ohio Archaeological and Historical Society, 1943.

Keir, Malcolm. *The Epic of Industry.* New Haven: Yale University Press, 1926.

Knepper, George. "A Survey of Ohio's Economy." *The Akron Beacon Journal,* December 1985.

Lindley, Harlow, compiler. *Ohio in the Twentieth Century, 1900-1938.* Columbus: Ohio State Archaeological and Historical Society, 1942.

Lippincott, Isaac. *A History of Manufactures in the Ohio Valley to the Year 1860.* New York: Arno, 1973.

Lundberg, Ferdinand. *The Rockefeller Syndrome.* New York: Kensington, 1976.

Lupold, Harry F. *The Latch String is Out.* Mentor: Lakeland Community College, 1974.

Mabry, William A. "Industrial Beginnings in Ohio." *Ohio State Archaeological and Historical Quarterly.* 55 (1946): 242-253.

M.A. Hanna Company. "M.A. Hanna Company, A Corporate History: The First Hundred Years."

Mak, James. "Interregional Trade in the Antebellum West: Ohio, A Case Study." *Agricultural History,* 46 (1972): 489-497.

Marathon Oil Company. "Five Eventful Decades: A History of the Ohio Oil Company, 1887-1937." "The Ohio Oil Company, 60th Anniversary: 1887-1947."

Marion Power Shovel. "A History of Marion Power Shovel's First 100 Years."

Martin, Linda Grant. "What Happened at NCR After the Boss Declared Martial Law." *Fortune* (September 1975): 100-105, 178-182.

Martzloff, Clement L. "Zane's Trace." *Ohio Archaeological and Historical Society Publications,* 13 (1908): 297-331.

Maurer, Maurer. "McCook Field, 1917-1929." *Ohio Historical Quarterly,* 67 (1958): 21-34.

McGannon, Harold E., ed. *The Making, Shaping, and Treating of Steel.* 8th edition. Pittsburgh: United States Steel Corporation, 1964.

McGrath, Edward J. "Reuben Springer, Cincinnatian: Business Man, Philanthropist." *Bulletin, Historical and Philosophical Society of Ohio,* 13 (1955): 271-285

Mead Corporation. "Mead Corporation History."

Millis, John S. "The Impact of Science Upon the History of Ohio." *Ohio Archaeological and Historical Quarterly,* 61 (1952): 227-234.

Mills, William C. "Archaeological Remains of Jackson County." *Ohio Archaeological and Historical Society Publications,* 21 (1912): 175-214.

Moley, Raymond. *The American Century of John C. Lincoln.* New York: Duell, Sloan and Pearce, 1962.

Moore, Opha. *History of Franklin County, Ohio.* 3 vls. Indianapolis: Historical Publishing Company, 1930.

Morner, Aimee L. "For Sohio, It Was Alaskan Oil—Or Bust." *Fortune* (August 1977): 172-184.

Murdock, Eugene E. *Life of Tom L. Johnson.* Ph.D. Dissertation, Columbia University, 1951.

"National Road in Song and Story, The." Columbus: Ohio Archaeological and Historical Society, 1940.

NCR. "Celebrating the Future."

Nevins, Allan. *The Emergence of Modern America, 1865-1878.* New York: Macmillan, 1927.

------. *Study in Power: John D. Rockefeller, Industrialist and Philanthropist.* 2 vls. New York: Scribners, 1953.

Ohio: An Empire Within an Empire. 2nd edition. Columbus: Heer, 1950.

Ohio Cultivator, June 15, July 15, 1848; June 1, 1849.

Ohio Guide, The. Harlan Hatcher, director. New York: Oxford University Press, 1940.

Ohio Roster, The 86. Cleveland: Edward Howard, 1986.

O'Reilly, Maurice. *The Goodyear Story.* Elmsford, New York: Benjamin, 1983.

Overman, William D. "The Rubber Industry in Ohio." *Ohio Historical Quarterly,* 66 (1957): 278-289.

Parker Hannifin Corporation. "Parker Corporation."

Pearson, Ralph L., ed. *Ohio in Century Three: Quality of Life.* Columbus: Ohio Historical Society, 1977.

Reichert, William O., and Steven O. Ludd, eds. *Outlook on Ohio: Prospects and Priorities in Public Policy.* Palisades, New Jersey: Commonwealth Books, 1983.

Roadway Services, Incorporated. "A Look at Roadway."

Robertson, Ross M. *History of the American Economy.* 3rd edition. New York: Harcourt Brace Jovanovich, 1973.

Rose, William G. *Cleveland: The Making of a City.* Cleveland: World, 1950.

Roseboom, Eugene H. *The Civil War Era, 1850-1873.* Columbus: The Ohio Archaeological and Historical Society, 1944.

------ and Francis P. Weisenburger. *A History of Ohio.* Columbus: The Ohio Historical Society, 1969.

Rosenberg, Norman L., and Emily S. Rosenberg. *In Our Times.* 2nd edition. Englewood Cliffs, New Jersey: Prentice-Hall, 1982.

Rubbermaid Incorporated. "1985 Annual Report." "Housewares Catalog."

Sass, Jon A. *The Versatile Millstone, Workhorse of Many Industries.* Knoxville, Tennessee: The Society for the Preservation of Old Mills, 1984.

Scheiber, Harry N. *Ohio Canal Era: A Case Study of Government and the Economy, 1820-1861.* Athens: Ohio University Press, 1969.

Schneider, Norris F. *Blennerhasset Island and the Burr Conspiracy.* Columbus: Ohio Archaeological and Historical Society, 1950.

------. "The National Road: Main Street of America." *Ohio History,* 83 (1974): 114-146.

"Service 500, The." *Fortune* (June 9, 1986): 113-152.

Sherwin-Williams. "Company History." "Sherwin-Williams History."

Smith, Thomas H. *An Ohio Reader.* 2 vls. Grand Rapids, Michigan: Eerdmans, 1975.

Speer, Michael. "The Little Steel Strike: Conflict for Control." *Ohio History,* 78 (1969): 273-287.

Spence, Hartzell. *Portrait in Oil.* New York: McGraw-Hill, 1962.

Stephenson, Bert S. "Iron and Steel Making in Ohio." *Ohio Magazine,* 2 (January 1907): 64-72.

Stevens, Harry R. "Samuel Watt Davies and the Industrial Revolution in Cincinnati." *Ohio Historical Quarterly,* 70 (1961): 95-127.

Stout, Wilber. "Charcoal Iron Industry of the Hanging Rock District." *Ohio State Archaeological and Historical Quarterly,* 42 (1933): 72-104.

------. "Early Forges in Ohio." *Ohio State Archaeological and Historical Quarterly,* 46 (1937): 25-41.

------. *History of Clay Industry in Ohio.* Columbus: Ohio Geological Survey, 4th Series, Number 26, 1923.

Take a Look at Ohio. Columbus: Office of the Governor, n.d.

TIME, September 8, 1986.

Timken Company. "A Brief History."

TRW. "The Little Brown Hut That Could. . . ." "A Company Called TRW: Putting High Technology to Work."

Tucker, Leonard L. "Cincinnati, Athens of the West." *Ohio History,* 75 (1966): 11-25, 67-68.

United States Shoe Corporation. "History of U.S. Shoe Corporation From Board Minutes, 1931-1981."

Utter, William T. *The Frontier State, 1803-1825.* Columbus: The Ohio Archaeological and Historical Society, 1942.

Van Tassel, Charles S. *Story of the Maumee Valley, Toledo and the Sandusky Region.* 3 vls. Chicago: S.J. Clarke, 1929.

Weisenburger, Francis P. *The Passing of the Frontier, 1825-1850.* Columbus: The Ohio State Archaeological and Historical Society, 1941.

Wendy's International, Inc. "Historical Highlights of Wendy's International, Inc." "R. David Thomas." "History of Wendy's Advertising, 1973-1984."

Wheeler, Robert. "Water to Steam." *Western Reserve Magazine,* September-October 1978.

Wiley, Richard T. "Ship and Brig Building on the Ohio and its Tributaries." *Ohio Archaeological and Historical Publications,* 23 (1913): 54-64.

Wish, Harvey. *Society and Thought in Modern America.* 2 vls. New York: Longmans, Green, 1950, 1952.

Wood, Marie. *None Called Him Neighbor.* Parkersburg, West Virginia: Marie Wood, 1951.

Wunder, John, ed. *Toward an Urban Ohio.* Columbus: Ohio Historical Society, 1977.

Zeisberger, David. *History of the Northern American Indians.* Archer B. Hulbert and William N. Schwarze, eds. In *Ohio Archaeological and Historical Society Publications,* 19 (1910): 1-173.

INDEX

Partners in Progress Index

ALLTEL Corporation, 296
Andersen & Co., Arthur, 270
Anheuser-Busch, Inc., 255
Bardes Corporation, 220-221
Battelle Memorial Institute, 219
Beckett Corporation, R.W., 242-243
Ben Venue Laboratories, Inc. (Founded in 1938), 292
Blue Cross & Blue Shield Mutual of Ohio, 262-263
BP America, Inc., 266-267
Buckeye Rubber & Packing Company, 241
Case Western Reserve University, 309
Chemical Abstracts Service, 276-277
Clark Consolidated Industries Inc., 232-233
Cleveland Clinic Foundation, The, 306-307
Columbia Gas of Ohio, 218
Crescent Metal Products, 235
Cyclops Corporation, 284-285
Davey Tree Expert Company, The, 240
Doctors Hospital, 288-289
Dow Chemical USA, 294-295
Duramax-Johnson, 248-249
East Ohio Gas Company, 264-265
Ebco Manufacturing Company, 224-225
Electrolock Incorporated, 286-287
Ernst & Whinney, 223
Fuller & Henry, 303
Gencorp Inc., 308
Greater Cleveland Growth Association, 311
Great Lakes Cheese Co., Inc., 298-299
Hanna Company, M.A., The, 228-229
Harrison Paint Corp., 252-253
Holzer-Wollam Realtors, 259
Honda of America Manufacturing, Inc., 246-247
Hoover Company, The, 239
Jaco Manufacturing Company, 297
Judson-Brooks Company, The, 281
Kastle Electrical Contractors, 215
Kendale Industries, Inc., 234
Krauss News Agency, Scott, 282
Marzetti Company, T., 226
Miami University, 300-301
Miami Valley Hospital, 230-231
MK-Ferguson Company, 272-273
Mount Carmel Health, 268-269
National City Corporation, 278-279
Oak Rubber Company, The, 227
Ohio Bell Telephone Company, 236
Ohio Chamber of Commerce, 208
Ohio's Investor-Owned Electric Companies, 310
Ohio University, 237
Pizza Huts of Cincinnati, Inc., 210-211
The Plain Dealer, 260-261
Porter, Wright, Morris & Arthur, 238
Preformed Line Products Company, 283
Prescott, Ball & Turben, Inc., 304
Reynolds and Reynolds Company, The, 256-257
Ross Laboratories, 244-245
Saint Luke's Hospital, 216-217
Schmitt Company, Inc., Peter J., 305
Sea World of Ohio, 271
Smith & Oby Company, The, 291
SSP Fittings Corporation, 293
Stouffer Corporation, The, 212-214
Sun Refining and Marketing Company, 254
Toledo Hospital, The, 258
Trustcorp, Inc., 302
United Telephone Company of Ohio, 280
University Hospitals of Cleveland, 274-275
Vorys, Sater, Seymour and Pease, 250-251
Vulcan Tool Company, 209
Whirlpool Corporation, 290
White Castle System, Inc., 312
Worthington Foods, Inc., 222

General Index

Italicized pages indicate illustrations

A
Abraham and Straus, 186
Agriculture, 26, 31, 64, *73, 74,* 75; machinery, 83, 87, 118
Aircraft manufacturing, 158
Akron, 48, 49, 62, 64, 69, 80, 98, 100, 101, 119, 158, 166
Akron Board of Trade, 98
Allyn, Stanley C., 173
Aluminum Company of America, 166
American Cereal Company, 64
American Dental Association, 186
American Electric Power, 180
American Federation of Labor, 130, *130*
American Greeting Publishers, 151
American Greetings Corporation, 151
American Magazine, 118
American Rolling Mill Company (ARMCO), 140, *141,* 142, *175*
American Ship Building Company, 89, *177*
American Steel and Wire Company, *76-77, 78,* 87
American Wire Company, 91
Anderson, William R., 174
Andrews, Samuel, 75
Andrews, Stanley, 94, 95
Archbold, John D., 95
Arcole Furnace, 53
Armed forces, 164
Armstrong Mills, *31*
Ashland Iron and Mining Company, 140
Atlantic and Great Western Railroad, 62
Austin Company, 162, 163, *164,* 166, 170
Autolite, 153
Automatic Electric, 170
Automobile industry, 83, 106, 108, 110, 138, 139, 188, 189; accidents, *110*
Aviation industry, 145

B
Baker Electric Vehicles, *108*
Baker Motor Vehicle Company, 108
Baldwin, Michael, 33
Ball, Aultman, and Company, 64
Baltimore and Ohio Railroad, 66
Banknotes, *27,* 28, 40, *40, 41*
Banks, 28, 42
Barber, Ohio Columbus, 64
Barber Match Company, 64
Barbertown, 138
Barker, Joseph, 38, 39, 65
Barley, 32
Basic Vault Door, 175
Battle of Fallen Timbers, 29
Bellaire Nail Works, 87
Bellevue Brewing Company, *194-195*
Belpre, 21
Bennett, James, 55
Bessemer, Henry, 83
Bessemer converter, 83, 87
Bessemer-Kelly method, 87
Bethlehem, 154
Bicycles, 110
Big Bear Supermarkets, 184
Big Bottom, 21
Big Boy, *184*
Bissell, George H., 92
Black Hoof, *8-9, 10*
Blacksmiths, *95*
Blennerhasset, Harman, 38, 39
Blennerhasset Island, 28, 38
Bloomingdales, 186
Blue Jacket, *8-9, 10*
Bolivar, 23
Bond, Beverly, 26
Boryczka, Raymond, 46, 82, 137
Bowler Foundry, *90*
Boyd County, 53
Bread, 140
Breweries, 56, 72, 146, *194-195*
Brown, Ethan Allen, 44-45, *44*
Bruce-Mansfield, 191
Brush, Charles, 80, *81*
Buchtel, John R., 64
Buckeye Buggy Company, *107*
Buckeye Coal, *91*
Buckeye Mower and Reaper Works, 64, 65
Buckeye Steel Castings, 119-122, *121,* 136; baseball team, *135*
Buckongahelas, *8-9, 10*
Bullock's, 186
Burdine's, 186
Burger King, 180
Burgess Steel and Iron, 87
Burr, Aaron, 38
Business Week, 184, 187

C
Cadillac, 139
Caldwell, 29
Calumet Paint Company, 123
Cambridge, 43
Canals, 45, 46, *48,* 49, 66, 71, 72, 89
Canton, 49, 119, 154, 175
Capitol City Products, 120
Carlisle Chemical Company, 172
Carnegie, Andrew, 86, 87, 89, 128
Carriage industry, 70, 113
Carter County, 53
Cary, Lorin Lee, 46, 82, 137
Case Western Reserve School of Medicine, 98
Casual Corner, 187
Cat's Creek, 29
Centinel of the North-Western Territory, 27
Central Blast Furnace, 91
Central Trust Building, *192*
Century Club, 132
Champion Company, 64, *72*
Champion Paper and Fiber Company, *152*
Champion Spark Plug Company, 111
Chandlersville, 29
Charcoal, 89; furnaces, 53
Chase, Stuart, 146
Chesapeake and Ohio Railroad, 150
Chicago, 55
Chillicothe, 23, 24, 26, 28, 33, *33,* 42, 43, 52
Chisholm, Henry, *92*
Cimcool, 172
Cincinnati, *2-3,* 22, 23, 24, 26, 32, 33, 36, *38,* 42, 43, 45, 49, 52, 54, 56, *57,* 66, 67, *67,* 69, 70, 80, 82, 113, 115, 117, 137, 158, *172,* 175, 180, *196-197, 198*
Cincinnati Butcher's Supply Company, *56*
Cincinnati, Hamilton and Dayton Railroad, *37*
Cincinnati Milacron, 173
Cincinnati Milling Machine, *7,* 149, *149,* 150, 160, 161, *161,* 162, 171, 172, 173
Cincinnati Screw and Tap Company, *149*
Cincinnati Southern Railway, *66,* 67
Cincinnati Steam Mill, 52
Cincinnati Steel Works Plant, *55*
Circleville, 52
Civil War, 64
Clark, William, *8-9, 10*
Clay, 17
Cleveland, Moses, 17
Cleveland, 23, 45, 48, 49, 54, *59, 60-61, 62,* 68, 69, 70, *70,* 71, 72, 75, 80, *82-83,* 87, *88,* 89, 91, 93, 94, 98, 104, 119, 150, 154, 158, 162, 180, 191; during the Depression, 149; population, 68, 71
Cleveland and Pittsburgh Railroad, *86*
Cleveland Chamber of Commerce, 134

Cleveland-Cliffs Company, 88
Cleveland Iron Company, 87
Cleveland Iron Mining, 87, 88
Cleveland Malleable Iron Company, 91
Cleveland Medical College, 98
Cleveland Rolling Mill Company, 87, 91, *92*
Cleveland Shipbuilding Company, *88*
Cleveland Trust, 134
Cleveland-Youngstown-Pittsburgh line, 89
Clinton, DeWitt, 45, 46
Clothing industry, 70, 98, 113
Coal, 17, 53, 54, 62, 66, 78, 80, 89, 98, 106, 137, 160; strikes, 160; mines, 129
Collier's Weekly, 118
Columbiana, 17
Columbus, *4-5,* 23, 43, 44, 49, *49, 50, 51,* 52, *96-97, 98,* 119, 142, 180, *197, 204*
Columbus and Hocking Valley Railroad, 66
Columbus Buggy Company, 104, 108
Columbus Coated Fabric, 191
Comer Manufacturing, 152
Committee for Industrial Organization, 153
Computer Research Corporation, 173
Computers, 173
Confederation Congress, 19
Congress for Industrial Organization (CIO), 153, 154, 160
Connecticut Western Reserve, 32
Connellsville, 89
Consolidated-Vultee, 163
Corn, *14,* 26, 29, 70, 75, 118
Corrigan McKinney Plant, *127*
Cotton: mills, 52, 55; textiles, 62
Council of Defense, 137
Country Music Convention, 184
Crawford, Frederick C., 174
Crest toothpaste, *185,* 186
Crisco, 117
Crooksville China Company, *138*
Crosley Jr., Powell, *81*
Crouse, George W., 101
Crowell, John, 118
Crowell-Collier Company, 118, 119
Crowther, Samuel, 131
Croxton, Fred C., 137
Cumberland Road. *See* National Road
Cutler, Ephraim, 29
Cutler, Manasseh, *18,* 19, 29
Cuyahoga County, 71
Cuyahoga River, 72, 106, *162-163*
Cuyahoga Valley, 137

D
Dairies, 31, 55; products, 72
Dana, Charles A., 170
Dana Corporation, 170, 171
Data Corporation, 171
Dayton, 23, 45, 55, 69, 142, 145, 158, 173, 174, 191, *199*
Dayton Engineering Laboratories Company (DELCO), 139
Dayton Wright Airplane Company, *144*
DeBartolo Sr., Edward J., 187
Delaware Indians, 10, 19, 22
Depression, the Great, 146, *147,* 148, 149, 150, 151, 154, 174, 176; salaries, 148; unemployment, 149
Detroit National Bank, 175
Devol, Jonathan, 28, 36, 38
Diamond Match Company, 64-65, 102
Diamond Rubber Company, 102, *102,* 105
Diebold Incorporated, 175
Dillon, Moses, 52
Diseases, 46
Distilleries, 33
Dividend Day Celebration, *128*
Doan, John, 29
Doolittle, Jimmy, 142
Douglas Aircraft, 163
Drake, Edwin L., 92
Dueber-Hampden Watch Works, 119, *119, 120*
Dunlop, John B., 100
Dunlop Tires, 176

E
Eagle Iron Works, *54*
East Cleveland Railway Company, *71*
East Liverpool, 17, 54, 55, 69, *69*
East Ohio Gas Company, *167*
Eaton, Daniel, 52
Eden Park, *202*
Edison, Thomas, 80, *81*
Electric Auto Lite Company, 111, *111*
Electric Vehicle Association, 106
Ellis Adding-Typewriter Company, 140
Empire Barley Mill, 64
Empire Mower and Reaper Works, 103
Energy Crisis, 177
Enola Gay, 168
Erie and Pere Marquette Railroad, 150
Erie Canal, 44, 45, 93
Erie Railroad, 66, 93, 106
Euclid, 162
Evans, Bob, 182, *182, 183,* 184
Evans Farms Inc., Bob, 183
Evans Steak House, Bob, 183

F
Fallen Timbers, 23
Farm and Fireside, 118
Farming, 31, 46, 72, 75, 146; equipment, 69, *73*
Federal Glass Company, *112*
Federated Department Stores, 186
Filene's, 186
Findlay, 95
Firestone, Harvey, 80, 103, 104
Firestone Spark Plug Factory, *103*
Firestone Tire and Rubber Company, *99,* 104, 105, 130, 139, 166, 176
Fisher Foods, 184
Flagler, Henry, 94, 95
Flour, 28; mills, 52
Foley's, 186
Forbes, 187
Ford, Henry, 106, 113, 128
Ford Motor Company, 149
Fort Defiance, 23
Fort Greenville, 23
Fort Harmar, 19
Fort Meigs, 40
Fort Recovery, 23
Fortune, 174, 175, 180, 186
Fort Washington, 21
Fort Wayne, 22
Foundries, 56, 72
Fountain Square, *204*
Foyt, A.J., 176
Franklinton, 23
French and Indian War, 10
Furniture factories, 56, 70, 117

G
Gallia County, 53
Gallipolis, 17, 29, 183
Gamble, James, 113, 115
Garfield, James Abram, 48
Gasoline, 93; stations, *107*
Geir, Frederick A., 150
General Motors, 139, 153, 163, 190
General Telephone Corporation, 170
General Tire and Rubber, 160, 166, *166*
Georgetown, 111
Glass industry, 83
Gleem Toothpaste, 186
Globe Iron Works and Shipyard, 91
Globe-Wernicke, 117
Gogebic, 88
Golden Lamb hotel, *13*
Goldsmith, 186
Good Housekeeping, 115
Goodrich, Benjamin F., 98, 100, *100*
Goodrich Company, B.F., 101, 102, 103, 105, *131,* 139, 166
Goodrich Trouser Guards, *104*
Goodyear, Charles, 100, 103
Goodyear Aerospace Corporation, 176
Goodyear Aircraft, 165, *165,* 176
Goodyear Airdock, 165
Goodyear International Corporation, 176
Goodyear Relief Association, 136
Goodyear Technical Center-Europe, 176
Goodyear Tire and Rubber Company, 64, 103, 104, 105, *134,* 138, 139, 164, 166, 176, 177; Akron plant, *101;* assets, 177; riots, *160*
Gordon, W.J., 87
Grain, 31
Great River, 21, 26
Great Western Tea Company, 119
Green County, *14, 15*
Greenhall, Beverly, 186
Greenup County, 53
Greif, Martin, 162
Grismer, Karl, 65, 105, 106
Gristmills, 28, 29, 52
Grumman Aircraft, 163
Grumman and Curtess-Wright, 165
Gulf Consolidated, 169, 171
Guthrie, Stephen A., *30*

H
Hahn and Co., William, 187
Hamilton, Alexander, 33
Hamilton, 43, 175
Hanging Rock, 52, 53, 54, 89
Hanna, Marcus A., 80, 134
Hanna Coal Company, *163*
Hannifir Manufacturing Company, 176
Hardee's, 180
Harding, Warren G., 118
Harmar, Josiah, 22
Harper's Weekly, 115
Harrison, William Henry, *8-9, 10, 23,* 24, 39, 40
Harrison Land Law, 24
Hartwell Furniture, 118
Harvey, Lena, 132
Hatcher, Harlan, 91
Havighurst, Walter, 48
Heaton, James, 52
Hecla Furnace, 53
Henri Bendel, 187
Herring-Hall-Marvin Safe Company, 175
Hiram House, *84*
Hobby House Restaurants, 182
Hocking County, 53
Hocking River, 24
Hocking Valley, 66
Hocking Valley Coal Mine, *89*
Hocking Valley Railroad, *68*
Hogs, 32, 70
Homesteading Days, 184
Honda of America Manufacturing, *188,* 189, *189, 190*
Hook, Charles Ruffin, 140
Hoover, Herbert, 148
Hoover Company, *159,* 163, 164, *164,* 171
Hoover vacuums, 119
Horton, Valentine Dexter, 54
Hotels, 92
Hudson River Rubber Company, 98
Hull, William, 40
Hyatt Regency Hotel, *199*

I
I. Magnin, 186
Immigrants, 56, 80, 82, *82*
Indian raids, 12
Indians. *See* individual tribes
Indian Wars, 22, 24, 39
Industrial Exposition: in Cincinnati, *14;* in Cleveland, *14*
Inland Steel, 154
Interlake Steamship Company, 89
International Chicken Flying Meet, 184
Interstate Commerce Act, 67
Interstate Commerce Commission, 150
Iron, 17, 52, 53, 68, 71, 78, 82, 87, 88, 89, 91, 98, 119
Iron Age, 142
Irondale, 31

Ironton, 17, 53
ITT, 169
Ivorydale, *116-117, 200*
Ivory Soap, *114,* 115, *115,* 117

J
Jackson County, 30, 53
Jefferson County, 31
Johnson, Tom Loftin, *72,* 75, 110
Jones and Laughlin Steel Corporation, 89, *89*
Joseph and Feiss, *131, 132*
The Jungle, 129

K
Kahn's Company, *168*
Kanawha River, 30
Kelly, William, 83
Kelley's Island, *80*
Kentucky Fried Chicken, 182
Kerosene, 92, 93
Kettering, Charles, 80, *81,* 122, 139
King, George, 137
Knepper, George, 123
Knights of Labor, 132
Knowlton, Hiram, 114
Kroger Company, 180, 184
Kroger Grocery and Baking Company, 118

L
Labor, 80, 105, 154, 158, 177; child, 65; unemployment, 191; women, 65, 161
Ladies Home Journal, 115
Lake Erie, 43, 45, 48, 70
Lake Erie and Western Railroad, 150
Lancaster, 43
Land Grants, *18*
Lane, Robert H., 177
Lane Bryant, 187
Langley Field, 145
Laughlin and Junction Steel Company, 87
Lawrence, 17, 53
Lazarus, Fred, 186
Lazarus Company, 186, *187*
Lenscrafter, 187
Lerner's, 187
Lewis, John L., 153, 160
Lewis, Meriwether, *8-9, 10*
Lexington Pike, *42-43*
Libbey, Edward D., 111
Libbey Glass Company, 111-112, *113*
Libbey-Owens-Ford, 161
Licking River, 26
Lilt-Home Permanents, 186
Lima Locomotive Works, *92*
Limestone, 24
The Limited, 186
Ling Electric, 169
Ling-Temco-Vought, 169
Linnville, *143*
Litchfield, Paul W., 134, 139
Little Miami Railroad, 49
Little Miami River, 17, 19, 21, 26
Little Turtle, *8-9, 10*
Livestock, 26, 28, 31, 32, 75
Long John Silver's, 180
Lordstown, 190
Losantiville, 21

M
McCook Field, 142, 145
McCormick, Cyrus, 64
McDonald's, 180
Madison, 53
Madison Dock, 53
Mad River, 49, 70
Mahoning River, 52, 157
Mahoning Valley, 17, 53, 54
Marathon Oil Company, 95
Marietta, 19, 21, 22, 24, *24-25,* 26, 28, 29, 33, 36, 38, 39, 52, 69, 93
Marion Steam Shovel Company, 118, 137, 166; Department of Personnel Training, 140
Martin, Jack, 170
Martin Company, Glenn L., 165
Marysville, 188
Massillon, 49, 154
Match industry, 64, 65
Mather, Samuel L., 87, 88
Mauldin, Bill, 167
Maumee River, 30, 40
Maumee Valley, 23, 49
Mead, Daniel, 171
Mead Corporation, 171, *203*
Mead Data Control, 171
Meat packing industry, 70
Mecca, 92
Meigs County, 54
Men's Welfare Work League, 132
Merrill, Edwin H., 55
Mesabi, 88
Miami and Erie Canal, *46-47,* 122
Miami Canal, 45, 46, 55
Miami Exporting Company, 28
Miami Indians, 10, 22
Miami-Maumee Canal, 52
Miami Valley, 17, 21, 23, 32, 62
Michelin, 176
Mikada Steam locomotives, *191*
Miller, Lewis, 64
Miner's Supply Company, *55*
Mines, 87; housing, *91*
Mingo Indians, 10
Mingo Junction, 87
Mississippi River, 19, 38
Missouri Pacific, 150
Mitchell, Ed, 176
Model-A, 106
Model-T, 106, 108
Monarch Machine Tool Company, 122
Moore Shirt, 152
Morrow, Jeremiah, 45
Mt. Adams (incline), *84-85*
Murphy, Frank, 153
Muskingum River, 19, 21, 24, 26, 28, 29, 38, 45
Muskingum Valley, 10, 17, 30
Mutual Aid Committee, 150

N
Naphtha, 92
National Cash Register Company, 122, 164, 173, 174; Electronics Division, 173
National City Corporation, 180
National Defense Council, 137
National Industrial Recovery Act (NIRA), 152
National Labor Relations Boards, 153, 154
National Road, *42-43,* 44, *44*
Nationwide, 180
Natural gas, 80
Nevins, Allan, 128
Newburg, 87
New Orleans, 55
Newspaper publishing, 140
New York Central Railroad, 66, 93
Nickel Plate Railroad, 150, *153*
Niles, 154
Norris, Elizabeth Ann, 114
Norris, Olivia, 114
Northwest Ordinance, 19
Northwest Territory, 19, 21

O
Oatmeal, 64
Office machines, 69, 83
Ohio and Erie Canal, *45,* 46, 48, 49, 54
Ohio Casualty, 180
Ohio City, 72
Ohio Company of Associates, 19, *20,* 21, 29, 38
Ohio Furnace, *53*
Ohio Oil Company, 95
Ohio Relief Production, *151,* 152
Ohio River, 17, 19, 23, 38, 43, 45, 48, 55, 117, *172, 178-179, 180*
Ohio Roster, 192
Ohio State University, 75, *202*
Ohio Steel Works, 91
Oil, 71, 72, 82, 91, -93, 95
Oil City, 92
Oklahoma City Douglas Aircraft, 163
Olds, Ransom E., 106
Olive Green, 29
Otis Iron Steel Company, *79*
Otis Steel Company, 87
Ottawa Indians, 10
Outlook, 115
Ownes, Michael J., 112

P
Pampers, *185,* 186
Paper industry, 113, 140
Paraffin, 92, 93
Parker, Arthur, 176
Parker, Helen, 176
Parker Appliance Company, 176
Parker Hannifin Corporation, 176
Parkersburg, 38, 39
Parmalee, Philip O., 142
Patterson, John, 122, 131, 132
Peck-Williamson, 118
Peerless Motor Car Company, *108*
Peller, Clara, 183
Pennsylvania-Ohio Canals, 54
Pennsylvania Railroad, *65,* 66, 86, 93
Pennsylvania Steel Company, 86
Perfect Circle and Aluminum Industries, 170
Perkins, George T., 100
Perry, Oliver H., *34-35, 36,* 40
Petroleum, 78, 92, 140
Phosphorous necrosis, 65
Pickands, James, 88
Pickands Mather Company, 88
Pickney Treaty, 26
Pioneer of Industrial Welfare, 131
Pittsburgh, 89, 91, 93, 98
Plainfield, 21
Pomeroy, 54
Pope Motor, 111
Population, 40, 42, 52, 55, 69, 72, 80, 82, 106
Pork, 56, 78, *168*
Portage County, 54
Portsmouth, 17, 45, 52, 69
Pottery, 69
Prell Concentrate shampoo, 186
Proclamation Line of 1763, 12
Proctor, Harley T., 115
Proctor, William, 114, 115
Proctor, William Cooper, 132, 133, *133*
Proctor & Gamble Company, 56, 113, 114, *114,* 115, *116,* 117, 122, 132, 186, *201*
Prohibition, 145
Putnam, Rufus, 19

Q
Quaker Oats, 64
Quebec Act, 12

R
Railroads, 48, 49, 55, 66, 67, 70, 71, 72, 75, 80, 83, 86, *86,* 94, 111, 119; accidents, 67; *See also* individual lines
Ramo, Simon, 174
Rauch and Lang Company, 108
Refineries, 93
Republic Iron and Steel, 87
Republic Steel Company, 89, 119, 154, *154,* 169
Rhodes, Daniel, 88
Rike's, 186
Rio Grande farm, 183, *183*
River transportation, *20,* 46, 48, 53, 67
Roadway Express, 180, 184, 185, 186
Roads, 24
Robinson, John K., 64, 93, *93*
Rockefeller, John D., 71, 75, 80, *93,* 94, 95, 128
Roebling Bridge, *206*
Rogers, H.H., 95
Roos, Delmar G. "Barney," 166
Roosevelt, Franklin D., 151
Roosevelt, Theodore, 128
Roush, Galen J., 184
Rowley, Enoch, 55
Rubber industry, 83, 98, 100, 106, 112, 134, 137, 171
Rubbermaid, 184
Rye, 32

S
St. Clair, Artur, 21, *21,* 22, 23
St. Clair, 38
St. Clair, 22
Salome Silk, 142
Saloons, 92
Salt, 28, 29, 30, 31; salt springs, 29, 31
Salt Spring Company, 29
Sanders, Harland, 182
Sandusky, 49, 70
Saperstein, Jacob, 151
Saperstein Greeting Card Company, 151

Sawbrook Steel Mill, *203*
Sawmills, 28
Schumacher, Ferdinand, 64, *64*
Scioto County, 53
Scioto River, 17, 19, 24, 32, 33, 45, 52
Scioto Salt Works, 30
Scioto Valley, 33
Seaway Food Town, 184
Second United States Bank, 40
Seiberling, Charles, 138
Seiberling, Frank, 103, 136, 138
Seiberling, John F., 64, 103
Settlers, 17, 19, 21, 26
Shaker Heights, 150
Shawnee Indians, 10, 22, 30
Shepard, Alan, 176
Shepard Chemical Factory, *203*
Sherman Anti-Trust Act, 95, 126
Sherwin, Henry, 123
Sherwin-Williams Company, 123, *133,* 134, 167
Sherwin-Williams Paint, 123
Shillito's, 186
Shipbuilding, 36, 38, 52, *88,* 158
Shoe industry, 70, 119
Sidney, 122
Sidney Machine Tool Company, *122*
Silcrome valve, 174
Silliman, Benjamin, 92
Sinclair, Upton, 129
Smith and Findlay, 26
Smith's European Hotel, *123*
Soap factories, 72
Spicer Company, 170
Springfield, 44, 49, 64, 69, 70
Squatters, 17, *17,* 18, 29
Standard Oil Company of Ohio (SOHIO), 94, *94,* 95, 98, *139*
Standard Oil of New Jersey, 95
Standard Oil Trust, 94, 95
Standard Sewing Machine Company, *193*
Stanley Steamer, 106
Stark County, 49
Statler Hotel, 140
Steamboats, *138*
Steel, 71, 72, 82, 83, 86, 87, 89, 91, 98, 119, 139, 191
Steinbacher, Erhard, 64
Stephenson, Bert S., 89
Steubenville, 24, 28, 33, 49, 52, 69
Stocks, 94
Stone, Amasa, 75
Stranahan, Frank, 111
Stranahan, Robert, 111
Strikes, *124-125, 126,* 129, 130, 133, 153, 158
Suffrage, *136*
Sugar, 28
Summit County, 55, 62
Sumrill's Ferry, 19
Sun-Glo Industries, 152
Sunrise, 38
Super Food Services, 180, 184
Surveys, 19
Symmes, John Cleves, 21, *22*

T
Taco Bell, 180
Tar, 93
Taylor, Frederick W., 139
Tecumseh, 39, *39*
Tennessee Valley, 166
Tenskwatawa, *39*
Terrain, 17
Textile mills, 52
Thomas, R. David, 182
Thompson, Charles E., 174
Thompson Aircraft Products Company (TARCO), 162
Thompson Products, 162, 174
Thompson Ramo Woolridge, 174
Thomson Company, Edgar, 86
Tibbeytts, Paul, 168
Tide, *181,* 186
Timber, 78, 80, 83
Timken, Henry, 171
Timken Company, 171, *203*
Timken Roller Bearing Company, 119, 171
Tippecanoe Creek, 39
Tire industry, 100, 102, 103, 105, 164-165; bicycle tires, 102, 103, 104
Titusville, 91, 92
Tobacco, *146*
Toledo, 69, 80, 119, 160; during Depression, 149
Toledo Garment, 152
Toledo, St. Louis and Western Railroad, 150
Tollgates, 43
Tool manufacturing, 83, 140
Townships, 19
Trade, 24, *25,* 30
Transportation, *65,* 66, 70; trucking, 185
Treaty of Greenville, *8-9, 10,* 23, 24, 26, 39
Truman, Harry, 169
Trumball County, 43, 92
TRW, Inc., 174
Turnpikes, 43, 44
Tuscarawas Valley, 10, 23
Tytus, John Butler, 140, 142

U
Union Rolling Mill, 91
Union Trust Company, 175
United Mine Workers of America, 130, *130,* 153, 160
United Rubber Workers, 153, 192
United States Playing Card Company, 118, *118*
United States Shoe Corporation, 186, 187
United States Steel Corporation, 86, 140, 153, 154
University of Pennsylvania, 172
Upper Sandusky, 40
Urbana, *14, 155, 205*
Utter, William T., 32, 42

V
Van Dorn Iron Works, *87*
Vaniman's airship, Melvin, *104-105*
Van Sweringen, Mantis James, 150, 151
Van Sweringen, Oris Paxton, 150, 151
Vermilion (Minnesota), 88
Victoria's Secret, 187
Victor Manufacturing and Gasket Company, 170
Vinton County, 53
Virginia Military District, 19

W
Wagner Company, 122
Wagon industry. *See* Carriage industry
War of 1812, 40, 43
War Industries Board, 136, 137
War Labor Policies Board, 137, 158
Warren, 92, 93, 154
Watch industry, 119
Water, 98
Waterford, 21, 29
Waterpower, 53, 78
Watkins, George H., 45
Watson, Thomas, 122
Wayne, Anthony, *8-9, 10, 22,* 23
Wendy's International Inc., 182, 184
Western Company, 169
Western Reserve, 17, 19, 23, 29, 32, 43, 49, 55
Westerville Anti-Saloon League, 145
Wexner, Leslie H., 187
Wheat, 28, 75, 118
Whipple, Abraham, 38
Whiskey Rebellion, 33
Whiskey Tax, 32
White Motor Company, 108, 137
Whittlesey, Charles, 87
Williams, Andrew, 186
Williams, Edgar P., 123
Williams, Vickie, 186
Willys, John, 111
Willys-Overland, *110,* 111, 160, 166, 167, *167;* Willys Jeep, *167*
Wingfoot Clan, 136
Winton, Alexander, 102
Winton Bicycle Company, 110
Winton Carriage Company, 110
Winton Company, 102, 108, 174
Winton Motor Car Company, 110
Wolf Creek, 29
Wolf Ledge Brewery, *146*
Woman's Christian Temperance Union, 145
Woman's Home Companion, 118
Women's Art League, *145*
Woodward Company, 171
Wool, 54, 62
Woolridge, Dean, 174
Wooster Rubber Company, 184
Work force, 46
Works Progress Administration, 152
Worthington, Thomas, 33, 44, *44*
Wright, Orville, 142, *142, 143, 144*
Wright, Wilbur, 142, *142, 143, 145*
Wright Field, 145
Wyandot Indians, 10, 22

X
Xenia, 49
Xenia Machine Works, *129*

Y
Yeatman, Griffin, 26
Yeatman's Cove, *21*
Yellow Creek, 31
YMCA, 136
Youghiogheny River, 19
Youngstown, 69, 80, 89, 98, 119, 137, 154, 191, 192
Youngstown Sheet and Tube, 89, *89, 134-135,* 154, 169

Z
Zane, Ebenezer, 24
Zane's Trace, 24
Zanesville, 17, 28, 43, 44, 52, 54
Zeisberger, David, 29